Inside the Third World

Paul Harrison is a freelance writer and journalist based in London. He has travelled widely in Asia, Africa and Latin America, visiting 23 developing countries. He writes regularly for the *Guardian, New Society* and *New Scientist*, and for major development agencies such as the World Health Organization and the The International Labour Office. Harrison attended Manchester Grammar School and Cambridge, where he got a double first in European literature and languages (of which he now speaks six). After a Council of Europe scholarship in Italy, he took a master's degree in political sociology (with distinction) at the London School of Economics. His interest in the Third World began in 1968 while he was lecturing in French at the University of Ife, Nigeria. For the past ten years he has been in journalism. He is married, with two children, and is a part-time peasant on a small allotment with problematic soil.

Inside the Third World

THE ANATOMY OF POVERTY

Paul Harrison

THE HARVESTER PRESS

This edition first published in Great Britain in 1980 by
THE HARVESTER PRESS LIMITED
Publishers: John Spiers and Margaret A. Boden
16 Ship Street, Brighton, Sussex

First published in Great Britain by Penguin Books Ltd. 1979

British Library Cataloguing in Publication Data
Harrison, Paul
  Inside the Third World.
  1. Underdeveloped areas – Economic conditions
  I. Title
  330.9'172'4   HC59.7
  ISBN 0–85527–946–X

Printed in Great Britain by
REDWOOD BURN LIMITED
Trowbridge and Esher

For my mother
and my wife

Contents

Preface

This book is based on three years' research and travel in ten countries, between 1975 and 1978, which took me to Sri Lanka (April/May 1975), Upper Volta and the Ivory Coast (February/March 1976), Colombia and Peru (November/ December 1976), Brazil (May 1977), Indonesia and Singapore (September/October 1977), three times to India (July/August 1974, March 1976 and June 1978) and Bangladesh (September 1978).

In some ways it was a mad enterprise to attempt to cover so much ground. I have tried to do so for two reasons. The first is that I believe a non-academic general survey of the entire field of development problems will be useful both for general readers and for people involved, academically or practically, in one particular field, who would like a broad idea of what is happening in other fields. With this end in view I have tried to cover all the major topics. The second reason is that the under-development of countries and of human beings cannot be compartmentalized if it is to be fully grasped. It is a total situation, in which every element plays a part.

There are, of course, penalties to be paid for attacking such a broad front. The literature on every single subject in this book is immense. I have had to be extremely selective, and am only too aware of how much I have left out. My aim has been to cover the main problems and trends in each field as they affect the central questions of poverty and inequality. I have drawn on the major surveys by the United Nations family of agencies and on the relevant academic research. Wherever I have a personal experience to illustrate a point, I have used it in preference to a reference to the research. The main reason is to give a feeling of the concrete locations and people who are, after all, what it is all about.

Readers who wish for a broader survey of promising projects, programmes and reforms in the fields covered here might consult my book *The Third World Tomorrow*. In the present book, I have tried, very briefly, to sketch the kind of solutions being tried out by the development agencies and some progressive governments to solve the problems I have dealt with. The basic arrangement of the book is as follows:

Part One is an investigation of the geographical and historical roots of poverty in the developing countries. Chapter 1 examines the handicap presented by tropical climates. In Chapter 2 I attempt to explain why western countries 'developed' before the Third World, enabling them to carve out colonial empires, and discuss some of the consequences. Chapter 3 discusses the fascination of Third World leaders, continuing after independence, with western models of development, a fascination which has lead them into so many pitfalls.

Part Two is concerned with agricultural and agrarian problems. As this is one field where the situations in the three continents differ, I have devoted a chapter to each, discussing common themes under the continent where their impact is greatest: the effect of primitive technology under Africa, increasing landlessness, debt and mechanization under Asia, and agrarian conflict under Latin America. Chapter 7 reviews the common ecological processes threatening agriculture in all three continents: desertification, deforestation, silting and salinization.

Part Three looks at the exploding cities of the Third World and their economies. Chapter 8 examines the causes and dimensions of the exodus of rural poor to the cities in search of work and higher incomes. In Chapter 9 I look at the physical and social problems of Third World cities, while Chapter 10 surveys the employment problem and the failure of large-scale industry to solve it. The problems and promise of small-scale enterprise and traditional industry, which employ the majority of non-agricultural workers in the Third World, are the subject of Chapter 11. Chapter 12 briefly summarizes the major imbalances of developing countries' economies.

Part Four turns its attention to the human resources of the Third World and attempts to trace the mechanisms by which poor people become trapped in their poverty. Chapter 14 looks at the dynamics and effects of the population explosion. Chapters 15 and 16 survey the extent and impact of malnutrition and disease, and their links with each other. The state of education in the Third World, and its failure so far to alleviate poverty or to aid development, is the subject of Chapter 17.

Part Five examines the wider context of national and international politics. Chapter 18 reviews the major problems of the international economy as it affects the poor countries, including commodities, the activities of multinational companies, indebtedness and aid. In Chapter 19 I look at the political mechanisms of developing countries which keep the poor in their place and frustrate reform – corruption and the influence of wealth in politics – and at the sources of political instability and dictatorship. The increasing international and national inequalities which result from these processes are surveyed in Chapter 20. Chapter 21 shows how inequality, both within and between nations, may be exerting a braking effect on the economies of developing and developed countries alike.

The list of people and institutions who have helped to make this book possible is enormous. I should like to thank my wife Alvina for patiently tolerating the prolonged absences which the research involved.

Financial assistance for the travel came from the World Bank, Population Services International, the International Labour Office, the International Planned Parenthood Federation and UNICEF. I am indebted, too, for direct personal encouragement and liberal provision of documents to Alun Morris and Mark Cherniavsky of the World Bank, Jan Vitek and Peter David of the ILO, Tim Black of PSI, Donald Allan of UNICEF, and the information offices of the World Health Organization, the Food and Agriculture Organization and the Organization for Economic Cooperation and Development. I should point out that the views expressed in this book are my own and not necessarily shared by these organizations.

The valued comments on the draft of a number of development experts helped to improve the final version of this book: I should like to thank especially Professor Hans Singer, and also Dr David Morley, Professor Mark Blaug, Javed Ansari, Janice Jiggins, John Rowley, Penny Kane, Ann Weston, Chris Stevens and Martin Hogg.

Thanks, too, to the editors of *Human Behavior, New Scientist, New Society, People* and *World Health* for permission to incorporate material from articles of mine which they published.

I wish I could thank by name all the many people who gave up their valuable time in transporting me, often along appalling roads, guiding me round villages, cities and projects and translating for me, but I am afraid they are too numerous to mention and in some cases might prefer to remain anonymous. And last but not least gratitude is due to all the ordinary people who figure in the following pages, who were kind enough to answer my questions. Though I always explained my purpose, I am sure that many of them thought I was a spy, or a tax inspector. Others thought I might be able to help them to get a well for their village, medicines for their illnesses, justice for the injustices they suffered, and it pained me that I could not. All I can hope for is that this book contributes a little to an understanding of their predicament, and to a climate favourable to changing it.

Currencies quoted here in the context of first-hand reports are generally translated into dollars and pounds sterling at the rates prevailing at the time of my visit. In other cases, where dollar and sterling amounts are given, I have ignored the daily fluctuations in the currency market and converted at the rate of £1 to $2.

Areas are sometimes given in acres, sometimes in hectares, according to the source. For guidance, one hectare equals 2·47 acres.

The American billion, equal to one thousand million, is used throughout.

Introduction

The battered Moroccan bus heaved its bulk up the Atlas mountains, eroded by the tracks of a hundred absent streams, then
traversed the flat, stony plain of the Dades river and stopped
for water, where camels were gulping in great draughts. I got
out at Tinerhir and walked up into the hills, into the valley of
the Todra.

The river flowed down through towering gorges of pink
granite, spreading out into a valley of sandstone with strata
buckled and folded like a switchback. The dwellings were of the
same tawny colour as the rocks, tall, crenellated, punctured by
tiny rectangular windows. Each settlement was so carefully designed that it resembled a single house, the buildings linked to
each other so that one man's roof was another man's courtyard. By the great wooden doors, groups of Berber women in
flowered dresses sat and chattered in their strange, high-
pitched voices. The dusty, shaded alleys swallowed the sound.
Near by, the Todra coursed through groves of date palm and
oleander, dividing in parts down narrow channels through
fields of maize and green vegetables.

But the picturesque was only a surface quality, a skin-deep
idyll. As I walked along the dirt road, a group of children approached. One little boy of about eight, more daring than the
rest, kept blocking my way, backtracking to keep up with me.
In a well-rehearsed gesture he raised his hands in prayer,
spread them out and repeated in rote-learned French: 'Sir, give
me money for my mother.' And after that he said: 'Sir, give me
the schoolbook.' I said I had no schoolbooks, but he pointed to
the notebook I was carrying and got me to tear out some blank
pages for him. No doubt his parents could not afford writing
materials for school, and school success was the passport out
of the Todra valley, the key to family prosperity. Not yet satisfied, he went on pleading: 'Sir, give me the picture from the
book.' I had no idea what he meant. He grasped the magazine

I was holding and pointed to an advertisement of a banker getting out of a plane. I tore it out for him, wondering what he could possibly want it for. He found time for his own needs as a child with a final plea: 'Sir, give me a sweet.'

Another boy, Ahmed, made friends, hoping to practise his French and maybe pick up a gift or two. He was a bright-faced thirteen-year-old temporarily home from state boarding school. 'Do you want to see the big machine?' he asked. 'It is the only machine in the village.' He dragged me off into a low building with a chugging, clunking noise coming from inside. I went in, and after my eyes had adjusted to the dark saw a great, heavy millstone revolving slowly round a lower one, driven by a small diesel engine. Ahmed demonstrated, pouring a few grains of corn through a hole in the top. On the wall were magazine pictures of film stars, motorbikes, cities. That was why the little boy had wanted the advertisement. The villagers used them in their homes too, like paintings, and they had chosen images of what to them seemed paradise: city life, cars, cigarettes, material possessions and that aura of city dwellers, chic and blasé with a wealth that to them was beyond belief.

Ahmed showed me more of the village. A group of women were talking, and I asked if I could take pictures, but immediately they pulled veils over their faces. An old man brought a girl over to me, classically beautiful, eyes rimmed with black *kohl*, and said something in Arabic to Ahmed. 'Do you want this girl for a wife?' he translated. It was partly a joke – but only partly. For there was not a single man in the village between the ages of eighteen and fifty. Where were they all, I asked Ahmed. Away. Where? In France, Paris, working, sending money back home. Couldn't they get jobs here? There were no jobs, I only had to look around. What about the fields, didn't they need working? The women did that. I asked Ahmed if he wanted to leave too. Of course, he replied, that was why he was studying. Why else would anyone go to secondary school? He didn't want to go on herding the goats over the mountains. But he didn't want to go to France. He wanted to be a lawyer or doctor in Casablanca or Rabat.

Here was an apparent arcadia, to which Europeans were beginning to come in respectful awe – the rich staying in the plush Sahara Palace near by, the hippies on the roof of the bungalow at the entrance to the valley, or tenting it up in the gorge. Yet the inhabitants of this arcadia were leaving for what *they* imagined to be arcadia: France, or those imitation bits of France in the coastal cities, driven partly by necessity, partly by a dream of unattainable rewards.

The contradiction was profoundly disturbing. I was young and did not have time to get to know Todra properly, but much later I found that the problems under its idyllic surface were repeated with variations in practically every village of the Third World. They were, in short, the problems of underdevelopment.

The process of development, the fate of the people going through it, is a global drama. It is the story, often tragic, of billions of individual lives, their hopes and frustrations, their efforts and their failures, their sufferings and their conflicts. It is perhaps the central story of our time. One that concerns, directly, three quarters of humanity, and ought to concern the other, industrialized quarter much more than it does, if only because its inhabitants live in relative comfort on a planet in which there is so much staggering poverty.

But if self-interest is to be our only guide for concern, then we should pay very close attention to what is happening in the Third World, because it is already affecting us, and will affect us increasingly in the future. First, through jobs. Only a few Third World countries have developed industry to any extent. Yet already the West is squealing about floods of cut-price imports produced by coolie labour. Second, a slowly growing shortage of key resources will make life problematic for the West but even more so for the developing countries, who may in future want to hang on to more of the resources that up to now they have been selling off to the rich nations. Third, there will be threats to world peace. Not that the poor of the earth are likely to pile into supertankers and invade the West. The poor are also weak. But scarcity and growing social polarization in developing countries mean that – unless something is done about it – civil wars and international conflicts may become (indeed, already are becoming) more frequent, with the superpowers inevitably drawn in on opposing sides.

Day-to-day coverage of the Third World in the popular media is confined to disasters, riots, coups and corruption. This book attempts to fill in the background to those apparently chaotic events and to the strident exchanges between rich and poor countries in the north–south dialogue, especially concentrating on the central issues of poverty and inequality.

Part One
The Roots of Poverty

'Unto every one that hath shall be given, and he shall have abundance; but from him that hath not shall be taken away even that which he hath.'

Gospel according to St Matthew

1. The Cruel Sun: The Curse of the Tropics

'We live under the tyranny of the tropics, paying heavy toll every moment for the barest right of existence.'

RABINDRANATH TAGORE

For four months there had been scarcely a drop of rain on the fields of Ife in Nigeria and the hot *harmattan* wind had brought down dust clouds from the Sahara. Now the rains were here again, in great anvil-headed clouds with red and purple billows, three miles high. Inside them sheet lightning flashed on and off like a faulty neon sign. Way below, the women in their peacock headscarves and the men in their *dashikis* took on a ruddy hue in their black pores. Under the cliff of nimbus, it was like a scene from some deep abyss of hell. The breeze became a fair gale: palm trees tossed like heads of hair, leaves tore off and flew far away. The sky was covered over completely with a low roof of darkness. Then the storm broke: it rained as if sky and earth were linked with a solid net of water. Rain hammering the land and the forest, and lightning now in thick poles spearing into the ground and tearing limbs off trees. Everyone was running for cover, men with their tops pulled over their heads, baring shiny backs, children under umbrellas of broad banana leaves.

It was typical tropical weather, never moderate, always extreme. Too much rain, or too little. Too much heat. These brute physical facts of life in developing countries are not often mentioned as primary causes of poverty. For our materialistic age, it is a strange omission. Perhaps the idea conflicts with our constitutional optimism that wealth can be created solely by human endeavour.

Let us do a little map-reading. If you open any decent atlas at those nice, blotchy maps on temperature, rainfall, soils and vegetation, you begin to notice some curious things. Very roughly speaking, the problem of underdevelopment appears to be confined to the tropics, between about thirty degrees north and south of the equator.

Now look at the rainfall maps. The developing countries get more than their fair share of rainfall, and of drought. Again, to generalize crudely, they have almost all those dark blue and purple patches, the areas with more than 1,000 millimetres of rain per year, along with most of the brown patches denoting 250 millimetres or less. Most poor countries are either soaked or parched, and many of them are both at different times of the year.

The most striking correspondence of all is with temperature (see Maps 1 and 4, pages 454–5 and 460–61). All but a tiny handful of developing countries lie inside the red zones where average annual temperatures exceed 20° Centigrade. Of those that lie outside – Turkey, Argentina, Chile, South Africa, South Korea – all are relatively more developed and only Korea has an annual average income of less than $1,000 per person. To confirm the point, all the richer countries lie outside this danger zone, except for the desert areas of the United States and Australia. A schoolboy could be forgiven for taking one look at the map and proclaiming the theory that an average annual temperature of 20° or above was the cause of underdevelopment. Would he be so very far from the truth, with his little discovery? Is it merely a coincidence that these factors of heat and rainfall define so surprisingly well the area of underdevelopment?

To answer that question we have to look at the causes and effects of the world-wide pattern of climate. In effect, the astronomical order is as unfair to the Third World as the economic order they so often rail against. Briefly, the tropics are hotter because the earth is round. As the earth's surface is curved, rays pouring down from the sun strike it much more obliquely towards the poles. The same amount of energy has to pass through a thicker layer of air and spread out over a wider area than in the tropics, so the ground heats up less. As we all remember from our school globes, the earth's axis is tilted at an angle of about $23\frac{1}{2}°$ from the vertical, in relation to its orbit. So, as the earth circles the sun, first the Tropic of

Cancer, then the Tropic of Capricorn is thrust into the hot spot receiving vertical rays, thus spreading the heat problem more widely than if we were square on to the sun.

Overall, the earth has to maintain a radiation balance, that is, it must reflect back into space as much solar energy as it receives, or it would heat up to intolerable temperatures. But the *parts* of the globe do not keep such a balance. Tropical areas between latitudes 37° north and south have a large radiation surplus – they absorb more energy than they reflect. The rest of the world has a radiation deficit. By a convenient arrangement, the tropics export their surplus heat to the temperate zones. The balancing act is done by the global weather machine of winds and rains, which is powered by the relentless beating of the sun on the hot countries. It is this heat transfer that keeps the world's temperature extremes within the relatively moderate limits that make human life possible over most of its surface.

But the costs the poor countries bear from holding mankind's front line against the sun are considerable. Warmth speeds up chemical reactions and therefore also biological cycles. So the typical ecological formation of the humid tropics, the rainforest, is a vibrant explosion of life forms. Thousands of different tree species flourish, clothed in creepers, orchids, lianas, bromeliads. The home of the urn plants that grace our conservatories is on tree branches, where they catch their own water from the rain. The *monstera deliciosa* that slowly wilts and grows more spindly in my living-room corner romps in a dense wreath of two-foot leaves up forest trunks in Sri Lanka. A botanist friend of mine in Nigeria whooped with delight when he identified more tree species in one square mile of jungle than existed in the whole of Britain.

This vital exuberance might make one think the soil is very fertile. But it isn't. Heat does increase the production of vegetable matter – the tropical forest rains down three times as much weight of leaves as a temperate forest. But heat also speeds up the activities of the bacteria that break up decaying vegetation. This is where that temperature of 20° Centigrade acquires its deadly significance. Up to that temperature, humus forms at increasing rates, enriching the soil with plant nutrients, making it porous and good at retaining moisture. Above 20°, the bacteria start to work faster than the supply of dead vegetation. Above 25°, humus is broken down much more quickly than it forms. The tropical rainforest is a cunning solution to this problem. The high canopy of tree crowns shades the ground below, keeping temperatures lower than 25°. The humus is not rich and forms only a shallow layer, but the abundant shower of falling leaves from above constantly renews it. So the trees have shallow roots, feeding on this richer zone, and the bigger ones have to prop themselves up like gothic cathedrals with spectacular buttresses.

Only the most primitive hunting and gathering forms of human life can survive in the original rainforest. As soon as agriculture begins, the forest has to be cleared away, the shade is lost, temperatures rise and the supply of decaying vegetation is reduced. Humus disappears from the soil, the level of plant nutrients drops and the soil structure deteriorates, losing a lot of its ability to retain moisture. Outside the humid tropics, in the semi-arid and arid areas, these conditions prevail anyway. Anyone with a backyard vegetable plot can imagine what kind of results he would achieve in these circumstances.

The incubator effect of heat on biological activity leads to another hazard: the flourishing of life forms hostile to man. The Abbé Dubois, an eighteenth-century French traveller in India, remarked with disgust that here 'every kind of irritating, destructive and abominable insect swarms and multiplies in a manner that is both surprising and amusing'. Mosquitoes, tsetse flies, blackflies, sandflies, thrive, as do the diseases they carry, along with a million forms of parasites, microbes and fungi, attacking, debilitating and killing men, wilting and blighting their plants, eating crops alive in the fields or quietly feasting on them in granaries and storerooms. In my pantry in Nigeria there was a different kind of insect living in practically every sack or packet. Hence the Third World farmer is a good deal more likely to lose his crops, and to avoid losses he needs to use a good deal more insecticide than farmers in the more favoured temperate areas. (See Map 6, pages 464–5.)

Heat can also directly affect his productivity as a worker. Work generates heat and the body has to lose excess heat if it is to go on working efficiently. Studies in Europe and the USA have shown that the productivity of manual workers decreases by as much as half when the temperature is raised to around 35° Centigrade – quite common in the tropics. White contractors in Nigeria used to complain how hard it was to get their labourers to work at typical European rates, but on reflection it was more remarkable that they got them to work at all after noon. Only mad dogs and Englishmen go out in the midday sun.

Disease can further cut productivity by as much as a third, as can malnutrition. Hunger is chiefly a symptom of poverty, but tropical soils do not help. They are often low in nitrogen supplies and do not provide a good environment for natural protein-rich plants or fodder legumes for livestock. Hence the soil itself can contribute to protein shortage. If we take all these direct and indirect effects together, we find that the combined impact of heat, disease and hunger could cut the productivity of labour by as much as three quarters. There are, of course, many other factors involved in malnutrition and disease which we shall be looking at later, but heat plays its part.

Droughts and downpours

The wayward pattern of rainfall in the tropics – too much or too little – creates equally serious problems. Once again, the weather machine is to blame. Rain occurs when a mass of warm air laden with water vapour rises. As it does so, it expands, and its temperature falls to the point where the moisture condenses out and falls as rain. Near the equator, where the sun evaporates greater quantities of water from the oceans, the air is moister and hotter. So it rises up further and faster than at higher latitudes, moulding those towering nimbus clouds and creating downdraughts that hurl the rain at the earth below and stir up lightning through the friction of great masses of vapour brushing past one another.

The belt in which these tempestuous processes occur moves north and south of the equator as first the northern, then the southern hemisphere is inclined towards the sun. Hence most tropical areas have rainy and dry seasons. In some of them the same effect is created by the monsoon: in Asia, for example, the air over the great land mass heats up in summer and rises, sucking in moist air from the ocean which also rises and falls as rain. In winter the land cools and air is drawn away to the ocean, creating a dry season.

Too much rain is the problem of the equatorial lands in the Amazon and Congo basins and in the islands of South-East Asia. Too little rain is the headache of the arid and semi-arid belts north and south of the wet zone. The air on the equator soars upwards and cools, flowing away north and south at high altitudes, but descending again in the high-pressure belts between 20° and 30° north or south. In this zone lie the dry lands that occupy more than a third of the world's surface. The air that descends here has already shed a lot of its moisture in tropical rains. As it drops, it heats up again and so is even less likely to condense out what moisture is left over.

When it does come to humid or arid lands, water does not drop as the gentle rain from heaven of temperate lands: it comes in torrential and destructive downpours. In northern Nigeria, for example, 90 per cent of all rain falls in storms of more than twenty-five millimetres per hour (for comparison, this is half the average *monthly* rainfall of London's Kew Gardens). In Ghana cloudbursts regularly disgorge 200 millimetres per hour, four times Kew's monthly ration. In Java a quarter of the annual rainfall comes in showers of sixty millimetres an hour, more than Berlin gets in an average month. Sudden storms are the worst possible way to obtain water: most of it gets lost, carrying with it great quantities of precious topsoil. The first heavy drops in a downpour clog the pores of the soil with fine particles washed from the surface. After only a few minutes the soil cannot absorb more than a small fraction of the falling rain to store it for crop growing. More than two thirds of it may run off in sudden sheets and rivulets, which can do tremendous erosion damage. Studies in

Upper Volta found that in one year nearly 90 per cent of the entire annual erosion happened in just six hours.

Excessive rainfall leaches out valuable minerals and nutrients from the soil. This, combined with the fact that the rocks of much of the tropics are ancient and highly weathered, makes many tropical soils infertile. Often the only minerals that remain are the insoluble oxides of aluminium and iron, which give to much of the soils in developing countries that rusty red tint, the visible symbol of the ravages of rain and sun.

A few limited areas in the tropics do have fertile soils, where the nutrients lost through leaching are constantly replenished from other sources. These are the alluvial soils of great river valleys and deltas, enriched at the expense of the watersheds whose topsoil is washed downstream. Areas of alluvium support the densest concentrations of people in the Third World: in the Ganges valley in India and Bangladesh, the Yangtse and Yellow rivers of China, the Mekong delta, the valley of the Nile in Egypt. Soils of this type also formed the basis of the earliest great civilizations: Egypt, Sumer, Assyria, Harappa, the Maurya and Gupta empires of India, China. Volcanic soils, as found in Java, are also very fertile, as they are renewed from new rock material. But the benefits of both these soil types have been wiped out by the people multiplying to the carrying limits of the food supply, making them almost as poor as the more scattered inhabitants of infertile zones.

Only the narrow equatorial belt can rely on a thorough and regular soaking from most of the year. Elsewhere in the tropics, rainfall is notoriously variable and unreliable both within the year and between years.

Because of the heat, plants in tropical countries transpire more moisture than in temperate climates, so they need more water to begin with. But in many places the problem is not so much an absolute shortage of rain, as the fact that torrents pour down for a few months, interspersed with long periods when there is no rain at all. Much of the Third World suffers from an annual cycle of drought alternating with flood.

In Western Europe and the east of North America, rain does not vary very much from month to month in the typical year.

In New York the rainiest month has only one and a half times as much rain as the driest, at Kew Gardens twice as much, in Berlin two and a half times. Compare Delhi, with roughly the same total annual rainfall as Kew. In November it gets only ten millimetres of rain, but July and August bring more than 170 millimetres each. In Calcutta August has thirty-two times as much rain as December. Zungeru, in central Nigeria, gets fifty-four times as much in the wettest month as in the dryest. Soil can only absorb and hold a limited amount of water in storage for crops to use, like a bank account deposited in the wet season and drawn on in the dry. Though many tropical countries appear to get what seems to be adequate annual rainfall, they get it in a lump sum, like a huge win at the races. Most is squandered and the little that is left in the soil bank is used up within a few months. In Agra, home of the Taj Mahal, for example, rain exceeds the current needs of vegetation only in July and August. As the rains tail off in September the savings in the soil are spent in just three weeks, leaving nine months of the year of water debt or bankruptcy.

Regular variation in rain can at least be adapted to: in Asia, irrigation systems help to even out the supply of water over the growing season. In the Sahel, south of the Sahara, farmers grow fast-maturing grasses like sorghum and millet that can shoot from seed to ripened ear in three or four months.

But there is no easy way of coping with rains that come in fits and starts from year to year. In Europe and much of North America, rainfall follows an even keel, varying by less than 15 per cent a year on average. In most of the Third World, it fluctuates from 15 to 20 per cent, and in the semi-arid and arid lands anything up to 40 per cent or more. In the lean years, crop failures are common. If rains are late, the growing season is cut short and yields will be slashed. Famine and disease follow close behind. That is why, in the Indian sub-continent, the monsoon is awaited with such hope and trepidation, and delay of a week or two brings near panic.

A disastrous environment

The four horsemen of the Apocalypse ride preferentially in the skies of the Third World. The tropics have been cursed with an overwhelming share of natural (and unnatural) disasters. More than nine out of ten disaster-related deaths occur in developing countries. (See Map 1, pages 454–5.)

Droughts, floods, cyclones and earthquakes are the major destroyers. We have seen how the global weather machine makes the tropics prone to the first two. The most destructive cyclones also form here, between the latitudes of 8 and 15 degrees north or south of the equator, in the warm cores of anvil clouds. They tear with unfailing regularity across the island chains of South-East Asia, over the Bay of Bengal into southern India and Bangladesh, and through the Caribbean. The only developed areas liable to them are the south-eastern United States and the eastern coast of Australia. Earthquakes and their handmaidens, volcanoes, occur in the zones where the drifting continental plates that form the earth's crust meet, exerting enormous pressures as they slide over or under each other. By the luck of the draw, these areas are almost all in the Third World: all up the spine of Latin America, along the island chains of the Pacific and across the southern edge of the Himalayas, through to Turkey. Inhabitants of these areas seem to develop sensors in the soles of their feet to tell them if an earthquake is coming. I was sitting in a meeting hall in Bali when suddenly everyone present got up and ran out for no apparent reason: there had been a tremor so slight that I did not even feel it. Among developed nations, only the western seaboard of the United States and parts of Italy, Yugoslavia and Japan are prone.

The annual toll of disasters is like a stiff tax, in money, resources and human lives, on already poor countries. Take the roll call for a single twelve-month period, in 1975–6. In September 1975, floods in north-eastern India made 233,000 people homeless and caused damage estimated at £300 million ($600 million). In February 1976 came the Guatemalan earthquake which killed 24,000 people, injured 77,000 and destroyed the homes of 1·2 million, or more than a fifth of the population. In May typhoon Olga hit the Philippines, making 800,000 people homeless. June and July were earthquake months in Asia: twenty villages were wiped out in West Irian and 85,000 people lost their homes in Bali. And in China perhaps half a million died in the earthquake in the mining area of Tangshan. August was a month of floods. In Pakistan, the Indus overflowed its banks and killed 370 people, and the Bolan dam in Baluchistan collapsed, washing away twenty-five villages and flooding an area of five thousand square miles.

It was just another typical year of human tragedies and massive setbacks for development programmes. The costs can be enormous. Floods, cyclones and storms alone brought damage of $30 billion (£15 billion) in Asia between 1961 and 1974, cost 280,000 lives and affected those of 485 million others, flooded 139 million hectares of land and wrecked 35 million homes. Disasters in five countries of Central America between 1960 and 1974 cost an average of 2·3 per cent of their gross domestic product – if this sum could have been invested in agriculture or industry, it would have made a considerable difference to the speed of development.

Disasters, of course, are not entirely due to the injustice of nature: the injustice of man also plays its part. Poverty contributes both to the causation and impact of disaster. It is a major cause of deforestation and desertification which aggravate floods and droughts. Poverty and the pressure of population drive the poor to live in increasingly dangerous places, like slums perched on steep slopes, or the flood- and cyclone-ridden islands of the Ganges delta in Bangladesh. Poor people can afford only flimsy houses of wood, mud and straw, liable to collapse in a heavy storm. Serious disasters appear to be increasing in frequency. A study by the University of Bradford found that the average number per year rose from five between 1919 and 1971, to eleven between 1951 and 1971, and over seventeen between 1968 and 1971. It seems unlikely that nature's inclemency is growing at this rate. The increase is probably due to the increasing disaster-proneness of the poor.

But disasters of themselves accentuate poverty and make their victims more disaster-prone for the future.

All in all, the physical environment has not favoured the developing countries. The low productivity of the soil and of man has hampered growth and, along with the setbacks of variable rains and disasters, helped to prevent the emergence of a large and stable agricultural surplus. Such a surplus is the first requirement of development.

There are some potential advantages in being closer to the sun. Given enough fertilizer and water, year-round sunshine can create an extraordinary agricultural potential, allowing as much as three crops a year. But water shortage restricts the areas where this is possible. As the oil runs out and solar power becomes more economical, the Third World will have greater supplies of endlessly renewable energy than the developed temperate zone countries.

But these prospects are as yet only hypothetical. Up to the present day, the hostile environment has been one of the key restraints in holding back economic development, raising the barrier countries have to leap before they can begin to industrialize.

2. Winner Takes All: Pre-Colonial Societies and Colonialism

As dawn rises over the mud-walled royal palace at Ouaga-dougou, the emperor's horse, impatient in its heavy trappings of emerald, scarlet and gold, snorts and paws the ground. Quietly the court minstrels gather by their drums and lutes, ready for *Ouend Pous Yan* (God rises), the central daily ritual of the Mossi empire in Upper Volta. The ministers and great provincial chiefs – the *baloum naba, samande naba* and *ouedrange naba* – stride up in their flowing kaftans, take their hereditary places on ancient stone seats, and wait. The emperor himself, the Moro Naba, enters, bulky and bull-necked, in a flame-red robe symbolizing the sun, every inch of him a vision of his chosen name, Kougri, which means the rock.

His chiefs approach and prostrate themselves, noses almost rubbing the floor. Then, thumbs raised in the air, they strike the ground three times and rub the palms of their left hands with the fingers of their right. The emperor calls for his horse. A page lets off an old dane gun with a great cloud of smoke. The chiefs make pleading gestures. The Moro Naba orders his horse to be unsaddled.

The mechanical ritual is all that survives of a vanished power and splendour. It re-enacts a tale from the seventeenth century, when the reigning emperor Waraga wanted to ride off in search of his favourite wife Poko. His ministers, who knew she had died, dissuaded him, but he swore he would go on trying every morning, and his descendants after him, until the ministers finally let one of them mount up. The Moro Nabas are still trying.

The Mossi empire is the oldest surviving in West Africa. Despite the prevailing image of African society as an amorphous collection of primitive villages without any higher level of organization, many empires arose in the savannahs of West and East Africa, the grasslands between rainforest and desert. Early travellers marvelled at the riches of Mali, Benin, Ghana,

Songhay, Kanem Bornu, all states complete with ministers, bureaucrats, court scribes and musicians and a territorial organization reaching into every village.

All three continents of what is now the Third World were the home of sophisticated civilizations. Many of their cities were centres of fabulous wealth far in advance of anything their first European visitors knew back home. Mathematics, astronomy, medicine were all highly developed among the Arabs, the Indians and the Chinese. It is wrong to call these civilizations backward. In an intellectual, moral and spiritual sense, several of them were far in advance of Europe. Europe was able to bring them all to their knees for one reason only: because she was more developed in purely material respects. She had achieved breakthroughs in the technology of war and of sea travel which were the basis of her military conquests. And she had evolved industrial capitalism, along with its peculiar contempt for and exploitation of human beings and of nature. (See Map 2, pages 456–7.)

It is not to the discredit of non-western civilizations that they failed to develop these things. But it did lead to their subjection, and so requires explanation.

Why the Third World didn't develop

The question is easiest to answer for Africa. The limited riches of empires like the Mossi (always modest compared to the Asian empires) were not based on the productive wealth of agriculture or industry. These were market empires, as historian Michael Crowder has called them. They straddled the main trade routes across the Sahara from North Africa to the Guinea Coast, and their revenue came in the main from siphoning off a percentage on the commerce: gold, slaves and ivory went north; salt, horses, beads and cloth came south in exchange. These societies were so far from developing industry that it is purely academic to ask why they did not. The primary reason for their poverty, then and even today to some extent, is the absence of any significant agricultural surplus over and above the survival needs of the farmers. And that, in turn, is due to the infertility of the soil and the primitive state of agricultural technology. Long fallow periods left more than three quarters of the land unused at any time. The plough was unknown, the hoe the most advanced implement in use. Crops were not rotated, livestock and arable farming were separate. Again there is no credit or discredit in any of this. Technology did not progress any further because there was no need for it to do so. The population was sparse, there was no shortage of land, and production was adequate to meet people's felt needs.

Empires of the sun

To reach Macchu Picchu you have to catch a little train from Cuzco that shunts zig-zag fashion up the steep slopes above the city, then along and down the rocky Anta valley that joins the river Urubamba. At Ollantaytambo the road stops. Only the river and the railway go further, the train's hooter echoing from the steep valley sides under snow-capped peaks. Descending, the cool mountain air warms up and becomes mediterranean. Prickly agave and eucalyptus line the track, and further down still the air grows damp like the inside of a greenhouse, and the vegetation thickens into jungle woven with creepers and vines. The train halts at Santa Ana station and buses haul you up the steep road. Only at the very top do you catch a glimpse of what you have come to see: Macchu Picchu, the lost city of the Incas, rediscovered by Hiram Bingham in 1911.

As an architectural feat it is incredible. The stone buildings perch on a hill crest between vertical cliffs, carved into an island by the river meandering far below. The masonry colours and shapes echo those of the precipitous, jungle-clad mountains around. They are worked so finely that a penknife cannot squeeze between the cyclopean blocks. From the highest buildings stone water channels run down from level to level, and behind, steep terraces climb down the hillside. Maize was grown here to feed the garrison, for Macchu Picchu was a fortress outpost guarding the mountainous empire of the Incas against the warlike tribes from the Amazon jungle beyond.

Technically, the Incas were capable of feats of civil engineering some of which were in advance of western capabilities of the period. Their royal highway stretched 3,250 miles down the Andes from Ecuador to Chile, sometimes carved into the solid rock in flights of steps, sometimes spanning rivers with corbel arched, pontoon or suspension bridges. There were way stations every four to twelve miles for the couriers who carried royal messages in *quipu* strings, knotted in patterns more complex than most written languages.

The Incas did not neglect the productivity of agriculture. They built stone terraces on near-vertical valley sides, some of which are in use even today around Cuzco. They built stone-lined canals up to nine miles long for irrigation. They were well aware of the importance of manure, and allocated to each region a portion of the rich guano deposits of the Chincha islands. The Inca chronicler Garcilaso de la Vega records that anybody who killed one of the sea birds whose droppings made up the guano was put to death. The Incas took some of the agricultural surplus for themselves, for temples, courts and armies. But much was kept in public granaries for the relief of needy individuals and for times of famine. There were reserves enough to cover several years. In soil conservation and in concern for the welfare of its subjects, the socialist empire of the Incas, as historian Louis Baudin has called it, was probably the most advanced in the world.

But technology was primitive in several important aspects. The most advanced agricultural implement was the foot plough, a pointed pole with a foot rest with which it was pushed into the ground. There were no domesticated animals for draught or ploughing. All transport was on foot, and the wheel – though found in children's toys in the western hemisphere – was not used for economic purposes. There were some large non-agricultural enterprises, the gold and silver mines. But these were state-run monopolies, and all the precious metals in them belonged to the Inca. As the nineteenth-century historian William Prescott pointed out, the individual Peruvian who was not of the ruling elite could never advance himself by his enterprise or industry, and those Faustian motives that drove the Europeans like the furies hounding Orestes were unknown: 'Ambition, avarice, the love of change, the morbid spirit of discontent, those passions which most agitate the minds of men, found no place in the bosom of the Peruvian.'

Oriental despots

Neither in Africa nor the Americas was there any remote prospect of the emergence of industrial civilization. But Asia was another matter altogether.

China was more advanced than Europe in significant technical respects until perhaps the sixteenth century. The Chinese were printing by movable types in AD 1050, four hundred years before Gutenberg's first printed bible. As early as AD 1200 there were massive iron smelters employing up to five hundred men. By the seventeenth and eighteenth centuries many of the preconditions for industrialization existed: automatic water-driven machines, large concentrations of capital in the hands of merchants, banks with branches all over China, even some big factories concentrating large numbers of employees. Yet industry did not develop, and by the nineteenth century the Chinese found themselves dominated and dictated to by nations very much smaller than themselves.

India was not so advanced as China, but developed enough for her non-take-off to be something of an enigma too. Agricultural surplus was there in ample measure, created by the ox-drawn plough and the technology of irrigation. Artisan crafts were highly developed, and India was the world's biggest exporter of textiles before Britain destroyed her industry.

The major impediment to the emergence of full-scale industrialization in Asia was probably the institution of oriental despotism. Political scientist Karl Wittfogel has theorized that tyrannical bureaucratic empires evolve as a response to the problems of arid and semi-arid areas, where the crucial task is mustering scarce water resources for agriculture. Dams and canals have to be built to spread, conserve and control water, so there has to be a central authority with the power to conscript large armies of workers. To organize these, run the installations and defend the state, the oriental despot has to have an unusually efficient bureaucracy, large and well-equipped armies and all-embracing intelligence networks, and these absorb most of the agricultural surplus. Moreover, the despot is a jealous ruler and tries to suppress all sources of power and wealth independent of himself. He and his relatives may live in grotesque luxury – but anyone else who dares to is liable to be executed and have his fortunes confiscated, and there may be restrictions on the inheritance of wealth, so there is little motivation for private enterprise.

Scholars have challenged the idea that India's despotic empires evolved to control water supplies: most irrigation systems appear to have been village affairs. But Wittfogel maintains that the institutions of despotism can be picked up and imitated in areas where they are not ecologically necessary, simply because they appeal to straightforward power lust. The purely political aspects of Wittfogel's portrait fit India well. The agricultural surplus was taken over almost in its entirety by the ruler and used for wars, or squandered in conspicuous consumption, and nothing was left over to support a middle class of landlords or businessmen. The Moghul palaces of India would have made the contemporary court of England's Queen Elizabeth I look like a modest private house. In Delhi's Red Fort, the residential quarters are of brilliant marble inlaid with precious stones. The Peacock throne was encrusted with an estimated £12 million ($24 million) worth of gold and jewels. The Taj Mahal, it has been calculated, would cost around £35 million ($70 million) to build at today's prices.

In pre-colonial India villages were largely self-sufficient and could produce most of the manufactures they needed. There was no widespread demand for anything beyond basics, as the rulers had swallowed up the surplus with which people would otherwise have bought extras. The market demand for manufactures was largely limited to the courts' requirements for luxuries, and these would be one-off, hand-made items from skilled craftsmen. Caste was the final barrier to industrialization. What little economic specialization did exist was based

different
factors
attributed to
weakness

on caste. A man's occupation was hereditary, and the sweeper or cobbler had an unquestioned right to sweep or cobble for a given group of clients, and to be repaid with a share of agricultural produce. There was no competition that could have stimulated technical improvements.

Despotism was also present in China, though it was perhaps not so despotic as in India. Any wealth that a commoner acquired had to be enjoyed discreetly and was always subject to the depredations of tax and customs officials. Status was closely linked to winning a post in the mandarin bureaucracy, so merchants would often invest their ambitions in passing exams rather than expanding their operations. But there was another factor holding China back, according to economic historian Mark Elvin: it was the inexorable pressure of a huge population on limited land. China could not pass through the agricultural revolution of Western Europe, based on mixed arable and livestock farming, because there was not enough spare land for grazing in the fertile areas. Agricultural improvements were largely limited to more intensive use of manpower and of compost materials, including human manure. As the population grew, the agricultural surplus per person fell and with it the potential demand for manufactures.

It is possible that industrial civilization might have emerged spontaneously in China or India. But it is futile to speculate; Europe evolved first as an industrial force, and that fact alone changed the entire situation, crippling what industry existed in Asia and giving Europe an advantage that would last at least two hundred years.

Why Europe did develop: free cities and bourgeois merchants

How and why industrial capitalism emerged in Europe is an immensely complex question. All I can do is to sketch the synergism of enabling factors which was absent in the other continents. The essential elements were: a healthy agricultural surplus; a class of entrepreneurs free to pursue wealth independently of the state and motivated to do so; the accumulation by them of enough capital to finance investment; the development of a practical science based on mathematics and mechanics; and the availability of expanding markets to encourage the rapid development of machine production.

It was only in the Christian era that the heartland of western industrialism, north-west Europe, was extensively settled. There was a good reason for this: the heavy clay soils of the region were unworkable with the mediterranean scratch plough which, as its name implies, merely scratches the surface. They were opened up only after the invention of the heavy plough that slices through the sod and turns it over. But once exploited, these soils were potentially much more fertile than those in the core areas of earlier civilizations. Add to that a reliable climate with adequate, steady rainfall, and the physical endowments of the place go a long way towards explaining its subsequent development. This surplus – later increased by innovations like crop rotation and mixed farming – provided the basis on which cities and industry could grow.

Western cities were very different animals from the seats of Asiatic despots. They evolved as market centres for the exchange of agricultural surplus, and their inhabitants were granted considerable freedoms, first by feudal lords who wanted revenue from the markets, then by kings who (especially in England and France) saw in the city burghers a source of political support in their struggles to master the feudal nobles. Hence there emerged a class of people who had no hereditary claims to power or status, but who were free to pursue the status that wealth could bring, through trade or small-scale enterprise employing artisans. The free cities were the focus of almost everything that followed. Applied science, combining maths, experiment and engineering, emerged from the class of skilled artisans. It could never have developed among a nobility that regarded manual work as degrading.

Western merchants, too, had more freedom to act independently of their rulers, and it was their eye for profit that motivated the misnomered 'voyages of discovery', to lands many of which were long known to the Chinese, the Arabs and of course their own inhabitants. The Turks had blocked the land routes for the lucrative spice trade with the East, so a sea route – round southern Africa or round the world, westwards, had to be found. The technical basis for the voyages of Columbus, Vasco da Gama and others had been laid by developments in navigation and sail construction, speeded up by the competition between maritime nations. The merchants made massive profits from their trade with Asia. Their swapping of gewgaws and trinkets for more valuable goods was perhaps the first manifestation of the unfair terms of trade the Third World now complains of. It made possible the accumulation of enough capital to finance larger manufacturing enterprises.

Even at this early stage the exploitation of non-western societies played a key role in the emergence of western capitalism. Indeed, without that exploitation, one may doubt whether the West would ever have industrialized in the first place.

The tainted profits of conquest in South America, and then of slavery, added to the pile of capital. It was in part the cash of Liverpool, centre of the triangular trade in slaves, cotton and rum between West Africa, the West Indies and Britain, that financed the mills of South Lancashire, the cradle of the industrial revolution. The rapid development of British industry, in its turn, was spurred on by the existence of vast captive markets, in the colonies, for British manufactures. Without that massive area of potential demand, there would not have been the same stimulus to mechanize production so rapidly.

The final key to Europe's world hegemony was her military superiority, on land as well as at sea. Her tactics had been refined by long centuries of almost incessant warfare, with scientifically minded artisans working away at perfecting the weapons. Europe's very fragmentation – compared to the centuries-long stability of an empire like the Chinese – forged her military capabilities.

The colonial trauma

'Modern industry has established the world market.'
KARL MARX

The overseas expansion of European mercantile and industrial civilization was to work the greatest transformation the human world had ever seen. (See Map 3 pages 458–9.)

It was a vast upheaval of races, a reshuffling of genetic pieces on the chessboard of the globe. The arrival of the Iberian conquistadors depopulated large parts of Central and South America. The Indians who escaped their guns succumbed to their diseases, and only in the high Andes and the most inaccessible reaches of the jungle did they survive intact. Africans were uprooted from their native soil and shipped over to cope with the resulting shortage of labour. Asians were transported to East and South Africa and the Caribbean. Even the huge markets of the colonies were not big enough to employ Europe's expanding population in industry: her surplus spread out into North America, Australia, southern Africa and South America.

Paralleling this was a global transfer of plants, providing new staple foods and creating the basis for plantation economies. From South America maize and cassava spread worldwide. Cocoa from Mexico became the principal livelihood for millions of West Africans. Rubber from the Amazon took root in South-East Asia. In its turn, the New World received the crops of the Old: sugar, a native of Bengal, became the chief produce of the Caribbean and the north-east coast of South America. Coffee from the Middle East came to dominate farming in Columbia, Brazil and several countries in West and East Africa. Tea was transplanted from China to India and Ceylon, and onwards to East Africa.

But the principal result of European rule was the creation of the global economy. Peoples of the stone and iron ages were brought into destructive contact with western industrialism. The cash nexus cast its net to cover the whole world.

Previous empire builders, of East and West, had been driven

by dreams of power. For the Europeans, profit was usually the prime mover. Political domination was rarely the principal aim in their colonial conquests. Their empires arose almost as a by-product of the individual pursuit of wealth.

When the kings and queens of Spain and Portugal authorized the subjugation of the Americas, their own dominant motives may have been the spread of Christianity and of their own influence. But the expeditionary forces were not royal armies. They were more like commercial enterprises. Would-be conquistadors signed contracts with their kings. They put up their own cash or that of friends, expecting a return on their investment just like the merchant venturers of Britain or the Netherlands. The principal difference was that the profit was to be extracted by the violence of war rather than the deceit of trade.

Guns and horses enabled these entrepreneurs in plunder to conquer the greatest empires in the western hemisphere. Cortes subdued the Aztec capital, Tenochtitlan, with just 600 men, seventeen horses and ten cannon. Following his example, Pizarro took over the vast Inca empire with only 102 foot soldiers and sixty-two horsemen. After the temples and palaces had been stripped of gold and silver artefacts – so efficiently that today barely a handful have survived to show the artistic skill of the Incas – plunder had to be extracted in other ways. Indians were compelled to work the mines and the estates of the Iberians, and as the contemporary Jesuit observer, Bartolomé de las Casas, remarked: 'They laid so heavy and grievous a yoke of servitude on them, that the condition of beasts was much more tolerable.' The precious metals, shipped back to the old continent, financed Spain's empire in Europe and helped to fuel a general increase in demand. The Spanish and the Portuguese had no incentive to industrialize: flush with funds, they could afford to buy all the manufactures they needed from other countries.

Both the Dutch, the British and the early French empires grew as the result of the demands of commerce. Indeed, the major possessions of the Dutch and the British started out as the private domains of trading companies, the British East India Company and the Vereenigde Oostindische Compagnie.

The Dutch wanted to monopolize the profitable spice trade from the East Indies, so as to keep prices artificially high. But the natives persisted, perversely, in trying to get the best prices for their nutmeg and cloves, and traded with the British wherever possible. The VOC was compelled to foist a trade monopoly on the spice islands by force of arms and subsequent physical conquest. Their venture did not even produce a profit: the costs of defence almost always exceeded the income from the trade. The Dutch VOC collapsed in 1799 under a mountain of debt, and her possessions were taken over by the Dutch state.

In Asia and on the African coasts, the British too were reluctant conquerors. Their prime interest in these areas was trade. But warring tribes and kingdoms, and princes who insisted on a share of the profit, made orderly commerce impossible. Widening conquests became necessary to guarantee the safety of merchants, and the honouring of commercial contracts. Generally, the flag followed trade, rather than vice versa. Later, when several countries had joined the industrial club, political control over colonies also proved useful in excluding trade competitors.

In Europe's unseemly scramble for Africa in the 1880s (malaria had spared the continent so long, until quinine came into use) political motives were dominant for once, fuelled by rivalries in a tense Europe. Yet even here, commercial considerations were strong: an agreed carve-up gave everyone a share, whereas the fortunes of conquest could have lost each country its potential markets, as well as leading to war in Europe. Whether political or economic motives were uppermost in the minds of colonizing governments is an academic question: the two were usually inseparable. The economic interests of the ruling elites were considered to be synonymous with the national interest. And where political motives were uppermost, private enterprise still went to work wherever it could. In some colonies the costs of administration and repression exceeded the earnings from trade and business. But the general taxpayer back home paid for the first, while individual private interests pocketed the second. The fact that more cash was put into a particular colony than was taken out does not prove that the natives benefited from colonial rule, for both administration and trade were usually run to their detriment.

Economic advantage could sometimes be gained without the expense of outright conquest. China seemed to offer a massive potential market, big enough for everyone. Through a succession of minor incursions, the western powers forced China to accept unequal trade treaties, with very low tariffs against European manufactures. These could then be sold at prices with which native industry could not compete. China did not prove half as lucrative as was expected – the masses were too poor to buy much. But free trade still managed to undermine indigenous enterprise and manufactures. The same trick was played on Japan, but by immense effort and foresight the Japanese managed to build up national industries despite the initial lack of tariff walls to protect them.

This is not the place to review the distasteful history of colonial rule: the bloody wars of conquest, the suppression of rebellions, the murder of local rulers, the massacre and enslavement of entire populations, the expropriation of land. Conquest was often accomplished by a treachery that few non-European conquerors have stooped to. There were occasional examples of enlightened rule, but government was in the interests of the mother country, not of the inhabitants.

Traditional authority and status systems were undermined. In Latin America the pre-colonial society was totally atomized and the lost, demoralized souls that made it up were regrouped under the authority of the Iberian invaders. Kings and bureaucrats were supplanted in Asia, chiefs and headmen removed or manipulated in Africa. The French preferred the system of direct rule, putting in their own governors and district officers. The British applied indirect rule, using the Sahelian emirs or the princes of India to create a buffer between them and the native masses. Traditional rulers became either powerless and purely ceremonial figureheads, like the Moro Naba of the Mossi, or outright puppets and collaborators.

Apologists of empire – and there are some, even today – point to the benefits it often brought: education, science and technology, the rule of law, efficient administration and so on. In fact, almost all the imbalances that now cripple the economies, societies and politics of the Third World had their origins in colonialism. The details will emerge in later chapters. Here I shall only sketch the outline of the footprint left by the imperial boot. In Latin America the conquistadors replaced an egalitarian communal system of landholding with large estates and landless labourers. In Africa the seeds of private property were sown in a similar traditional set-up. In Bengal the British created a class of large landowners where none had existed before.

Colonial powers laid the foundation of the present division of the world into industrial nations on the one hand, and hewers of wood and drawers of water on the other. They wiped out indigenous industry and forced the colonies to buy their manufactures. They undermined the self-sufficiency of the Third World and transformed it into a source of raw materials for western industry. Sometimes they forced locals to grow the desired crops – as the French did with cotton in the Sahel or the Dutch with sugar in Indonesia. Sometimes they bought land or just seized it to set up plantations, drafting in cheap labour to work them. In this way the colonial powers created the world economic order that still prevails today, of industrial centre and primary producing periphery, prosperous metropolis and poverty-stricken satellites.

The imperial rulers created separate new western cities, parasitic growths whose sole function was to drain the economic surplus from the colony and siphon it back home. These leech cities became the exploding cities of today, modern citadels surrounded by low hovels, still sucking the life out of the countryside. The colonialists began the introduction of western technology and techniques. With their laws and medicines, which from one point of view were beneficial, they also sowed the seeds of the population explosion, leaving the new independent states to reap the bitter harvest. In industry they initiated the technological dependence which is as strong as ever today. To provide themselves with a class of junior administrators, they introduced western styles of education which unfitted people for a constructive role in their own rural societies – styles which persisted right into the seventies in most countries, and in many are still present.

And the states they left behind were for the most part artificial creations with arbitrary borders, condemned to futile border conflicts and secessionist troubles. The precious rule of law and democracy soon gave way to varying degrees of dictatorship. More serious than anything else, the elites they handed over power to were products of the colonial education system and were schooled in western ways. Instead of pursuing indigenous models of development, almost all of them set out to construct imitation western societies. So modern industry was put before agriculture, modern skyscrapers had to go up before the masses were housed, modern-sector employees had to be paid enough to enjoy imitation western consumer lifestyles while the majority languished in poverty. From these choices flowed much of the poverty and inequality with which the rest of this book is concerned. The Third World's persistent fixation on the West is so curious, and has been so fatal in its consequences, that I shall devote the next chapter to an attempted explanation.

onomically → politically → culturally

3. The Westernization of the World

'The bourgeoisie has, through its exploitation of the world market, given a cosmopolitan character to production and consumption in every country.'

KARL MARX

In Singapore, Peking opera still lives, in the backstreets. On Boat Quay, where great barges moor to unload rice from Thailand, raw rubber from Malaysia or timber from Sumatra, I watched a troupe of travelling actors throw up a canvas-and-wood booth stage, paint on their white faces and lozenge eyes, and don their resplendent vermilion, ultramarine and gold robes. Then, to raptured audiences of bent old women and little children with perfect circle faces, they enacted tales of feudal princes and magic birds and wars and tragic love affairs, sweeping their sleeves and singing in strange metallic voices.

The performance had been paid for by a local cultural society as part of a religious festival. A purple cloth temple had been erected on the quayside, painted papier-mâché sculptures were burning down like giant joss sticks, and middle-aged men were sharing out gifts to be distributed among members' families: red buckets, roast ducks, candies and moon cakes. The son of the organizer, a fashionable young man in Italian shirt and gold-rimmed glasses, was looking on with amused benevolence. I asked him why only old people and children were watching the show.

'Young people don't like these operas,' he said. 'They are too old-fashioned. We would prefer to see a high-quality western variety show, something like that.'

He spoke for a whole generation. Go to almost any village in the Third World and you will find youths who scorn traditional dress and sport denims and T-shirts. Go into any bank and the tellers will be dressed as would their European counterparts; at night the manager will climb into his car and go home to watch TV in a home that would not stick out on a European or North American estate. Every capital city in the world is getting to look like every other; it is Marshall McLuhan's global village, but the style is exclusively western. And not just in consumer fashions: the mimicry extends to architecture, industrial technology, approaches to health care, education and housing.

To the ethnocentric westerner or the westernized local, that may seem the most natural thing in the world. That is modern life, they might think. That is the way it will all be one day. That is what development and economic growth are all about.

Yet the dispassionate observer can only be puzzled by this growing world uniformity. Surely one should expect more diversity, more indigenous styles and models of development? Why is almost everyone following virtually the same European road? The Third World's obsession with the western way of life has perverted development and is rapidly destroying good and bad in traditional cultures, flinging the baby out with the bathwater. It is the most totally pervasive example of what historians call cultural diffusion in the history of mankind.

Its origins, of course, lie in the colonial experience. European rule was something quite different from the general run of conquests. Previous invaders more often than not settled down in their new territories, interbred and assimilated a good deal of local culture. Not so the Europeans. Some, like the Iberians or the Dutch, were not averse to cohabitation with native women: unlike the British, they seemed free of purely racial prejudice. But all the Europeans suffered from the same cultural arrogance. Perhaps it is the peculiar self-righteousness of Pauline Christianity that accounts for this trait. Whatever the cause, never a doubt entered their minds that native cultures could be in any way, materially, morally or spiritually, superior to their own, and that the supposedly benighted inhabitants of the darker continents needed enlightening.

And so there grew up, alongside political and economic imperialism, that more insidious form of control – cultural imperialism. It conquered not just the bodies, but the souls of its victims, turning them into willing accomplices.

Cultural imperialism began its conquest of the Third World with the indoctrination of an elite of local collaborators. The missionary schools sought to produce converts to Christianity who would go out and proselytize among their own people, helping to eradicate traditional culture. Later the government schools aimed to turn out a class of junior bureaucrats and lower military officers who would help to exploit and repress their own people. The British were subtle about this, since they wanted the natives, even the Anglicized among them, to keep their distance. The French, and the Portuguese in Africa, explicitly aimed at the 'assimilation' of gifted natives, by which was meant their metamorphosis into model Frenchmen and Lusitanians, distinguishable only by the tint of their skin.

The second channel of transmission was more indirect and voluntary. It worked by what sociologists call reference-group behaviour, found when someone copies the habits and life-style of a social group he wishes to belong to, or to be classed with, and abandons those of his own group. This happened in the West when the new rich of early commerce and industry aped the nobility they secretly aspired to join. Not surprisingly the social climbers in the colonies started to mimic their conquerors. The returned slaves who carried the first wave of westernization in West Africa wore black woollen suits and starched collars in the heat of the dry season. The new officer corps of India were moulded into what the Indian writer Nirad Chaudhuri has called 'imitation, polo-playing English subalterns', complete with waxed moustaches and peacock chests. The elite of Indians, adding their own caste-consciousness to the class-consciousness of their rulers, became more British than the British (and still are).

There was another psychological motive for adopting western ways, deriving from the arrogance and haughtiness of the colonialists. As the Martiniquan political philosopher, Frantz Fanon, remarked, colonial rule was an experience in racial humiliation. Practically every leader of a newly independent state could recall some experience such as being turned out of a club or manhandled on the street by whites, often of low status. The local elite were made to feel ashamed of their colour and of their culture. 'I begin to suffer from not being a white man,' Fanon wrote, 'to the degree that the white man imposes discrimination on me, makes me a colonized native, robs me of all worth, all individuality ... Then I will quite simply try to make myself white: that is, I will compel the white man to acknowledge that I am human.' To this complex Fanon attributes the colonized natives' constant preoccupation with attracting the attention of the white man, becoming powerful like the white man, proving at all costs that blacks too can be civilized. Given the racism and culturism of the whites, this could only be done by succeeding in their terms, and by adopting their ways.

This desire to prove equality surely helps to explain why Ghana's Nkrumah built the huge stadium and triumphal arch of Black Star Square in Accra. Why the tiny native village of Ivory Coast president Houphouët-Boigny has been graced with a four-lane motorway starting and ending nowhere, a five-star hotel and ultra-modern conference centre. Why Sukarno transformed Indonesia's capital, Jakarta, into an exercise in gigantism, scarred with six-lane highways and neo-fascist monuments in the most hideous taste. The aim was not only to show the old imperialists, but to impress other Third World leaders in the only way everyone would recognize: the western way.

The influence of western lifestyles spread even to those few nations who escaped the colonial yoke. By the end of the nineteenth century, the elites of the entire non-western world were taking Europe as their reference group. The progress of the virus can be followed visibly in a room of Topkapi, the Ottoman palace in Istanbul, where a sequence of showcases display the costumes worn by each successive sultan. They begin with kaftans and turbans. Slowly elements of western military uniform creep in, until the last sultans are decked out in brocade, epaulettes and cocked hats.

The root of the problem with nations that were never colonized, like Turkey, China and Japan, was probably their consciousness of western military superiority. The defeat of these three powerful nations at the hands of the West was a humiliating, traumatic experience. For China and Japan, the encounter with the advanced military technology of the industrialized nations was as terrifying as an invasion of extraterrestrials. Europe's earlier discovery of the rest of the world had delivered a mild culture shock to her ethnocentric attitudes. The Orient's contact with Europe shook nations to the foundations, calling into question the roots of their civilizations and all the assumptions and institutions on which their lives were based.

In all three nations groups of Young Turks grew up, believing that their countries could successfully take on the West only if they adopted western culture, institutions and even clothing, for all these ingredients were somehow involved in the production of western technology. As early as the 1840s, Chinese intellectuals were beginning to modify the ancient view that China was in all respects the greatest civilization in the world. The administrator Wei Yüan urged his countrymen to 'learn the superior technology of the barbarians in order to control them'. But the required changes could not be confined to the technical realm. Effectiveness in technology is the outcome of an entire social system. 'Since we were knocked out by cannon balls,' wrote M. Chiang, 'naturally we became interested in them, thinking that by learning to make them we could strike back. From studying cannon balls we came to mechanical inventions which in turn lead to political reforms, which lead us again to the political philosophies of the West.' The republican revolution of 1911 attempted to modernize China, but her subjection to the West continued until another Young Turk, Mao Tse-tung, applied that alternative brand of westernization: communism, though in a unique adaptation.

The Japanese were forced to open their borders to western goods in 1853, after a couple of centuries of total isolation. They had to rethink fast in order to survive. From 1867, the Meiji rulers westernized Japan with astonishing speed, adopting western science, technology and even manners: short haircuts became the rule, ballroom dancing caught on, and *moningku* with *haikara* (morning coats and high collars) were worn. The transformation was so successful that by the 1970s the Japanese were trouncing the West at its own game. But they had won their economic independence at the cost of losing their cultural autonomy.

Turkey, defeated in the First World War, her immense empire in fragments, set about transforming herself under that compulsive and ruthless westernizer, Kemal Atatürk. The Arabic script was abolished and replaced with the Roman alphabet. Kemal's strange exploits as a hatter will probably stand as the symbol of westernization carried to absurd lengths. His biographer, Lord Kinross, relates that while travelling in the West as a young man, the future president had smarted under western insults and condescension about the Turkish national hat, the fez. Later, he made the wearing of the fez a criminal offence. 'The people of the Turkish republic,' he said in a speech launching the new policy, 'must prove that they are civilized and advanced persons in their outward respect also ... A civilized, international dress is worthy and appropriate for our nation and we will wear it. Boots or shoes on our feet, trousers on our legs, shirt and tie, jacket and waistcoat – and, of course, to complete these, a cover with a brim on our heads. I want to make this clear. This head covering is called a hat.'

The home-grown colonialists

The fixation with the West did not end at independence. The elites who took power in Latin America were Europeans, and imposed European ways on their subjects. Those who assumed office in Africa and Asia were scions of the western-educated class who had turned sour on their rulers: indeed, their demands for independence were often backed up with quotes from the western political writers they had pored over in their student garrets in Oxbridge, London or Paris. As Nehru wrote, with unconscious reference to himself: 'The British had created a new caste or class in India, the English educated class, which lived in a world of its own, cut off from the mass of the population, and looked always, even when protesting, towards its rulers.' And even in independence, he might have added, towards its former rulers.

On reflection, it is obvious why few of the new ruling elites developed an indigenous model of development. Most were not themselves members of traditional ruling elites. If they owed their new-found power to anything, it was to their literacy, their western education, the familiarity with western ideas and the western-style institutions of government that they had inherited. In so far as they had clear goals, these were to transform their countries, in the shortest possible time, into western societies complete with all mod cons. And so they started building miniature western societies in the centre of their biggest cities and went on building out from there, hoping to cover their whole national territory, little realizing that it would take centuries, following this path, before the majority began to benefit.

The departure of the colonial powers had created a status vacuum, the filling of which gave a further boost to westernization. The old sources of status in ceremony, ritual and traditional power were dying. The new power strata, politicians, bureaucrats, businessmen, sought to define their status against each other by the only method all of them recognized: the flaunting of material goods of a western kind. India's political elite moved into tasteful colonial town houses – furnished in a style long dead in Britain – in the tree-lined avenues of New Delhi, while the *nouveaux riches* of younger states built themselves palatial Beverly Hills style mansions.

The growth of the modern state and economy undermined status and values at local levels, and the westernized elite now became the reference group that social climbers lower down the ladder would ape. Everyone in a position to do so tried to gain status by the conspicuous consumption of a modern lifestyle, and to acquire the necessary funds they were ready to abrogate all the bonds of traditional obligations.

In many countries the new rulers practised a brand of internal colonialism over their own people. This was, and is, at its most blatant in Latin America, where it still has a racial aspect. The new rulers who assumed power in the early nineteenth century were of European stock, and their descendants still dominate the elites. People from native Indian, or African slave backgrounds, were treated as a subject group, discriminated against, restricted to lowly jobs, forced to adopt European culture, religion and language.

The situation in Africa and Asia was not all that different. In a few countries the internal colonialism was racial too: the creoles of Liberia and Sierra Leone, the Tutsi of Burundi. In most of the rest it was cultural. The 'colonizers' were the westernized elite, whom Nirad Chaudhuri has compared to 'a separate ethnic entity with its own collective psychology'. The 'colonized' are all those groups who do not belong to the modern westernized sector. They too, as we shall see, have been discriminated against, neglected in government spending, and now show signs of becoming a sort of hereditary caste just as surely as if they really were a subject race.

Today westernization has spread into every nook and cranny in the Third World, and because of the discrimination practised against the non-westernized, it is proceeding with accelerating pace. It creeps down key arteries of indigenous society, poisoning it from within. From the top, it is disseminated through the activities and example of the local hierarchy and squirarchy. From the bottom, the young in particular have become its carriers: for them, adopting western dress and lifestyles is something like becoming a hippie or a punk rocker. It gives them a symbol of supposed superiority and an excuse to hold their parents in contempt. It is their own form of youth rebellion, but one from which, unlike western adolescents, they are unlikely to recover. The schools have been potent instruments of westernization among the young: they often impose western uniforms on pupils, and teach syllabuses emphasizing modern, urban activities and values. Young people emerge dazed and uprooted, despising their own culture.

The six-million-dollar cultural imperialist

The educational message is reinforced by adult media, which are, as communications sociologist Jeremy Tunstall has remarked, Anglo-American all over the world.

In Indonesia, and in Pakistan, Thailand, Malaysia, Nigeria, Ghana, Kenya, Colombia, Peru, the largest advertising agency is American. Three out of five top agencies are American in India, Mexico and Argentina. They use western methods, often western images. In Europe, Martini is sold with shots of rich playboys and debutantes, skiing, air ballooning, racing in light aeroplanes: if you buy the product, it is implied, you pick up some of the aura. The reference group most frequently chosen in Third World advertising is the affluent, westernized elite, and even government campaigns use the same approach. One Iranian family-planning poster I have collected contrasts a poor family, in traditional clothing, in a rundown, bare mud hut, with a vast and screaming brood, with a small family with two children in a plush suburban house with radio and TV, husband in city suit, shirt, collar and tie, wife in skirt and blouse and pinafore. Have only two children, the hidden message reads, and you too can enjoy this desirable western lifestyle. Indigenous ways are held up to scorn and ridicule — indeed, throughout the Third World traditional culture has become a negative reference group, a group that all ambitious, go-ahead people seek to escape and deny all connection with.

Not only are marketing methods western: the products they are selling are often western too — Levi's, pop cassettes, mopeds are all marketed hard. A person who uses any one of them is already assuming an element of the desired image and is more receptive to others. So the big multinationals can benefit from economies of scale, products are almost identical the world over. In November 1976 William Bourke, then vice-president of Ford's North American Automotive Operations, predicted the emergence of a single world market with a single world style: 'The day is not far off when manufacturers ... will be producing the same line of products for sale everywhere in the world, with only the most minor of variations.'

This would come about through the 'homogenizing of consumer tastes' through modern communications. If the product is not made to suit the market, the market has to be moulded to suit the product. The multinationals join forces with the national elites as agents of westernization.

Western lifestyles are also promoted through the entertainment media. Western-made films penetrate into every large city in the Third World. Ouagadougou, Upper Volta's capital deep in the Sahel, has a cinema where western thrillers and disaster movies are shown. Their influence is immediately visible, for the whole street outside is thronged every night with western-dressed office clerks, market porters and shop assistants, their mobilettes parked in dense rows.

Television plays a similar role. Poor countries who decide to set up their own TV service (whether to foster national integration or to pander to the aspirations of the elite) almost always find themselves forced, once they start broadcasting for entertainment and not merely for education, to use large amounts of foreign material, chiefly American, to fill their schedules. The American networks can make extra copies of TV videotapes at a negligible cost compared to the original cost of production. The vast economies of scale enable them to sell 'quality' products more cheaply than countries could produce their own programmes.

So programming throughout much of the Third World broadcasts the American way of life of rugged consumerist individualism. CBS programmes are distributed in a hundred countries. *Hawaii Five-0* sells in forty-seven countries and is dubbed into six languages. *Bonanza* attracts a world audience of 350 millions. In a survey of TV programming in 1970–71, media expert Tapio Varis found that 84 per cent of Guatemala's TV time was taken up with imported programmes, 62 per cent of Uruguay's, 55 per cent of Chile's, 50 per cent of the Dominican Republic's (compare the USA ratio of only 1 or 2 per cent, and Britain's of 12 per cent). In Asia, 71 per cent of Malaysia's programmes were imported, 35 per cent of Pakistan's, 31 per cent of Korea's, 29 per cent of the Philippines and 22 per cent of Taiwan's. In Africa and the Arab world, Zambia imported 64 per cent of her programmes, Iraq 52 per cent, Egypt 41 per cent and Lebanon 40 per cent. Singapore is one of the most dominated, devoting some 78 per cent of TV schedules to alien matter. It is instructive to quote a typical week's TV highlights selected by Bailyne Sung for readers of the *Straits Times*: *M'Liss, a Comedy of the Old West, Best Sellers, Jalna, Charlie's Angels, Cher, Mary Tyler Moore, Donny and Marie* (all American); *The World at War, Shoulder to Shoulder, Sykes, Play Soccer Jack Charlton's Way, The Explorers* (all British). On the film pages, advertisements for the week's shows: *Airport '77, Eagles over London, A Star is Born, The Deep*, along, it is true, with such authentic Chinese thrillers as *Bionic Boy* and *Shaolin Killing Machine*. And, if all that is not enough, you can turn to the paper's comic strip page where you will find not a single Chinese or Malay series, but the nuclear family problems and consumer behaviour of *The Gambols, Bugs Bunny, Blondie*, and *Bringing up Father* ('You're supposed to be on your way to work,' says daughter. 'Ssh ... this is a good TV programme,' grunts father.)

Over the Malacca straits in Indonesia, and you can witness an even more curious spectacle. There, American TV serials are not even dubbed or subtitled into the national language, Bahasa Indonesia. A commentator introduces them, like an Italian opera, with a summary of the plot, then off you go with *The Six Million Dollar Man*, and all non-English-speaking viewers can do is to watch the kicks, leaps and knockouts. Indonesian TV does run authentic Javanese comedies and cultural programmes of regional dances. But they also run locally made programmes in which western-dressed Indonesian crooners sing perfect imitations of American songs, squatting on motorbikes and wearing racy caps: the style and slickness of the imported programmes has to be imitated by national production too, if they are not to look naïve and wooden. Television has begun to penetrate even the remote areas of Java, where there may be just one or two sets per village, mounted on a post outside the local government offices or on the wall of an enterprising bar owner. It is a depressing sight to see these people, who are supreme artists of dance and theatre, gaping wide-eyed at western soap operas. One evening I noticed enormous crowds thronging round the public sets and spilling out of bars, and inquired what they were watching. It was a Mohammed Ali fight.

The final channel of cultural imperialism is tourism. Westerners, sick of the empty, smothering materialism of their own civilization, trek east and south on dream holidays and youthful odysseys, perhaps looking for a simplicity that Europe lost many centuries ago, and which the Third World itself is fast losing.

Destinations are attractive in the measure that they are unspoiled. Yet the very act of going to them spoils them and despoils them. The westerner goes to find somewhere uncontaminated by westernization. His visit, in itself, contaminates. He carries the virus with him. He has the Midas touch. As soon as westerners start arriving in numbers, governments, multinationals and even international development agencies rush up five-star hotels. The western tourist is unable to escape his own shadow, and a protective wall of western comforts and debased imitations of local culture grow up around him.

The contrasts are pitiful. It is a charmless sight to see fat American widows heaved up onto a camel's back in idyllic Tunisian oases or African vendors clustering like flies around topless Swedes on Gambian beaches. Gradually the village economy is distorted; the primary aim is no longer to see to its own needs, but rather to cater for the consumerist whims of foreigners. Locals leave their fields and fishing boats and become touts, flunkeys or donkey-guides. Thieves and whores arrive.

National culture is not immune. The visual and performing arts tend to degenerate from the sacred and symbolic into vulgar, commercialized spectacles and stereotyped products. The moneychangers take over the temple. As economist Jacques Bugnicourt has pointed out, tourism grows into an incitement to the pillage and plundering of local art and archaeology and the desecration of religious sites. In Nigeria, traders used to come knocking on my door at all hours of the evening and spread out their wares: the factitious side by side with the authentic, ebony-smooth heads along with rough-hewn dance masks. Traders were scouring the villages for family treasures: carved drums and granary doors, ornate spears and idols. And, because the people were poor, they risked the wrath of their gods and sold them.

Under this barrage of onslaughts, traditional cultures and social structures are diseased, dying; in many places dead. This trend has to be lamented, not just for nostalgic reasons. Just as the dwindling of animal species threatens the balance and diversity of nature, the genetic bank upon which the continuing vitality of life depends, so the disappearance of whole groups of societies reduces the cultural diversity of mankind.

Some features of traditional life deserve to go, because they conflict with justice and equity: the status of untouchables in India, the exploitation of women everywhere, the excessive authority of the head of the extended family. But surely models of development that built on the best of indigenous values could have been more widely pursued.

What the Third World needs now, for rapid development benefiting all, is redistribution, cooperation, emphasis on production, autonomy, self-help, participation. The lure of westernization has perverted development goals, making the isolated individual consumer the goal of most efforts. Western lifestyles, products and approaches – as we shall see in later chapters – generate the wrong kind of development in the context of poor nations. The western middle-class way of life is so far above the conditions of the bulk of the population in these countries that the elites can enjoy it only at the cost of grotesque inequalities and exploitation.

Western technologies of housing, industry, health, are expensive, too, and poor countries are short of funds. The choice of western approaches has meant, of necessity, that government spending was concentrated in small, high-quality packets which benefited only the few. Meanwhile, the majority languished in neglected poverty.

Part Two
Ill Fares the Land: Agriculture and Agrarian Problems

'Ill fares the land, to hastening ills a prey,
Where wealth accumulates, and men decay.'

OLIVER GOLDSMITH

4. Eco-Catastrophe in Africa

From the air, Upper Volta is a monotonous plateau of rust red and ochre peppered with the pastel green of acacia, locust bean and shea butter trees. Here and there, great spreading blotches of black where bush fires have razed the tinder-dry grass to a smoking carpet, and tiny white flecks of cattle trailing across them in lines, like rain on a window. And the villages, organic clusters of pointed, straw-roofed huts surrounded, like ewes with lambs, by granaries that are miniature models of themselves. And not a river or stream to be seen, for it is the depth of the burning dry season.

On the ground, the same endless repetition of dry bush, red dust, sand-coloured houses, women shuffling along narrow trails with water pots on their heads, men on bicycles, their heads inexplicably muffled in woolly balaclavas that must be like furnaces inside, guinea fowl scuttling in panic to get out of the way.

Giant baobabs dot the landscape with their fat, bulbous trunks and spindly branches, and strange fruit hanging down like velvet skittles on the end of ropes. Up here the rains last only three or four months, interspersed with a long dry season that shrivels and scorches plants and men. The baobab has evolved ways of coping with this, storing water in its fat girth and shedding its leaves to cut down transpiration. Grasses too are well adapted: some of their seeds have awns, like screw-drivers, that bore them deep into the ground where the bush fires cannot destroy them. They have enormous roots that can reach out for moisture far below the surface. In the dry season they become a tangled, loose, dead-looking mat of straw. With the coming of the rains, they explode out of the soil, reaching giant heights within a couple of months.

Man too had adapted to this inhospitable habitat. Not ideally perhaps, but stably enough to live that way for long centuries; that is until the population explosion destroyed the delicate balance. The traditional technique of farming here is common to the whole of sub-Saharan Africa and also to parts of Latin America and South-East Asia. The method is known as shifting cultivation or slash and burn. The farmer first clears himself a patch of bush or forest that has been left fallow for anything from six to thirty years. He cuts it with an axe or matchet, leaves it to dry for a while, then sets it alight in a great conflagration, leaving a devastated chaos of charred stumps, toppled, blackened trunks and matted grass ash. It looks like an ecological massacre, but there is some sense to it. The stumps are left in to save work. That makes ploughing impossible, but it helps to prevent erosion. Crops are planted in between. In the dry areas, these are usually in stands of a single crop: millet and sorghum for food, cotton or groundnuts for cash sale. In the rainforest areas, the cultivated plot is often a miniature model of the rainforest, with its variety of heights and species: banana palms, cassava bushes, yam vines growing out of heaped mounds. This mixed style of cropping keeps the worst of the sun's heat off the soil and breaks the fearful battering of the rains. The fertility of the soil quickly falls off after clearance – yields in the third year may be down to only one third of the first season's crop. So after a year or two's cultivation, the patch is abandoned and left fallow. A new cover of trees and bushes creeps back. This is not as high or as complex as the primeval forest, but the roots of the woody plants grow deep and draw up many of the nutrients that the rain has washed down into the subsoil. Clearing and burning does send the nitrogen in the plants up in smoke, but it frees the minerals, the potash and the phosphates, for the next crop, and free-living bacteria build up nitrogen in the soil. Burning also seems to make the soil more alkaline and more hospitable to cultivated plants. The yields in the first year of shifting cultivation can be surprisingly high, in exchange for no investment in fertilizers or animals, and much less work overall than permanent plough farming, perhaps one reason why Africa is so slow in adopting the plough. The drawback is that, at any given time, upwards of three quarters of the land is not being cultivated. The population has to be sparse, and that is probably the main reason why no advanced civilization other than the Maya was based on this technique.

Shifting cultivation was once derided by agronomists, but today it is generally agreed to be a rational and ecological way of farming in infertile tropical soils, so long as the fallow period is long enough. It is the population explosion that has turned slash and burn into an ecological tragedy, and, in the sensitive ecosystems of the dry areas like Upper Volta, into a slow form of suicide.

Everywhere in Africa, as population has grown, fallow periods – essential for the restoration of soil fertility – have shrunk. Farmers are returning to the same patch of ground too frequently, so yields fall and the soil is exhausted, sometimes irrevocably. Modern agricultural methods could compensate for this: ploughing would turn up the deeper layers of soil and enable a patch to be cultivated longer. With adequate use of fertilizer or manure, an area can be cultivated permanently. But most African farmers are still using the old methods without ploughs or fertilizer. They are practising settled agriculture with the technology of shifting cultivation. They are trying to support an increasingly dense population with methods suited for a scattered one. This contradiction, more than anything else, lies at the bottom of Africa's ecological predicament and her endemic poverty.

The creeping desert

In the Sahel, the dry region that stretches across the southern edge of the Sahara, the problem of drought is added, and soil degradation leads to the inexorable southward creep of the desert. Upper Volta is so dry that its three major rivers, the Red, Black and White Voltas (so called after hardly perceptible variations in the colour of the clay suspended in them), are indicated by *dotted* lines on the map. In the dry season, the Red Volta disappears completely, the White Volta dries up into a string of stagnant pools, and only the Black Volta, reduced to little more than a quiet stream, still crawls its way between muddy banks, the only river in the whole country.

Water is as scarce as rationed petrol in the dry season. Many village wells dry up, and women have to walk ten or fifteen miles to the nearest source. A Voltaic well engineer told me that some live so far from water that they have to set out at dusk, walk most of the evening, sleep a few hours at the well, draw their water and set off again to reach home by dawn. The *average* walk for water is five miles each way, a two or three hour haul with twenty-five kilos of water on your head for half of it. That eats up nearly four hundred precious calories every day.

The engineer's job was to bore deep concrete-lined wells through to the water table, so that village wells would not dry up. But the job was getting harder. The waters deep underground are ancient reserves built up over centuries. In the low rainfall years since 1966, they had not been topped up, so tapping them was like draining a reservoir of fossil fuel, with a limited life span. As new deep wells had been laid on for 2,000 of Upper Volta's parched villages, the water table was falling every year. Now boreholes had to go deeper and deeper, through harder and harder rock, costing more and more every time, so that the engineers were reaching the limits of their technical and financial resources.

In the north of Upper Volta lies the poorest and most densely populated region in the country. Once it was the prosperous heartland of the Yatenga, one of the two kingdoms that merged to form the Mossi empire. Ten miles or so down a bush track from the district capital, Ouahigouya, is Aorema, a dusty scatter of family compounds, each one surrounded, fortress-like, with high clay walls. I visited one of them. The head of the family was Moumouni Ouedraogo, a lanky sixty-year-old, his skin scarred with deep wrinkles and tribal markings. Inside the perimeter, the compound was subdivided into living areas for each of the five brothers who lived here with a total of nine wives and twenty-five children. The younger children were completely naked, with dry, powdery faces. One or two of them had eyes half closed up with sticky yellow matter. Three of the brothers were sitting under the straw awning outside the compound, so I sat and talked with them, an agricultural extension worker doing the translating.

Moumouni remembered that, when he was a child, only twelve people lived in his father's compound. Now there were thirty-four, with five young men working away from home in the Ivory Coast. Land in the village is allocated by the chief on the basis: to each according to his need. The bigger the family, the more land they are given to cultivate. So Moumouni, with his ever-expanding brood, was now farming a bigger area than ever before, as was almost every other family in the village. Yet the village's traditional lands had not expanded at all: on every side they were bounded by other villages. The additional land needed had been taken out of the five sixths that usually lay fallow. Fallow periods had been slowly whittled down over the decades, until they were now only four or five years, when at least twelve would have been needed to restore the exhausted fertility of the soil.

Moumouni took me on a conducted tour of his fields. Even close in to the compound, the soil looked poor enough, stony and dusty, without a trace of humus. And this was the only area they ever fertilized, with the droppings of a donkey and a couple of goats. Outside a circle of about fifty yards' diameter round the houses, the ground was a dark red, baked hard. It had been cultivated the year before but had yielded very little. Moumouni said he didn't think anything would grow there this year. Then he complained about the erosion: 'Before, it used to rain a lot but we didn't feel the hardness of the rain. Now, it rains less, but the rain is getting harder and harder.' He swept his slender hands down the gentle slope to demonstrate the sheets of water that poured off – last year, in one night they had 150 millimetres of rain – then swept them away again in despair as if to drive the problem away. The rain was not really harder. It 'felt' harder because the exhausted soil was yielding less, so there was less plant cover for the ground and nothing to break the rain's impact, beating down the soil and taking away the precious topsoil in sudden rivers formed out of nowhere. Ten years ago, Moumouni explained, some government people had come to help. They had built dykes and mounds to slow down the run off. But they had been wrongly aligned, and if anything speeded it up. Moumouni himself had stacked up a few pathetic rows of stones across the main channels.

Further out was the land which Moumouni had worked two and three years ago, and which was supposed to be recuperating. He would not go that far with us, and told us to look for ourselves. When I saw it, I knew why he could not bear to come and look at it. Parts were red and stony, baked to an iron pan, parts were covered with a smooth crust. Bushes that had been alive the year before were dead now and their branches snapped with a dry cracking noise. I broke one off and stabbed at the ground with it, but it made absolutely no impression on the rock-hard earth. One bush fire would be enough to sweep away these desiccated remains and then nothing at all would be left to stop the wind and the rain eating up the land, carving it into gulleys and later into sand dunes. Here, three hundred miles south of the Sahara proper, was an expanding advance guard, of semi-desert.

And there are many of them, like infectious spores that have been blown south and settled here and there and multiplied quietly and lethally. The same disastrous processes are at work in the whole of the Sahel from the desert fringes in Mali right across to Sudan, and down into the densely populated farming belts in the north of Ghana, the Ivory Coast and Nigeria. Like the sides of a pit dug in the sand, the Sahara is edging forward, making whole regions uninhabitable, driving people and animals south, increasing the pressure on the remaining land so that one day it too could face the same fate.

Even without the drought, the Sahel would be poor. The neat division of the year into wet and dry seasons means that, as there is no irrigation, there is no agricultural work to do for six or nine months, and the agricultural surplus is too small to support industry. So for two thirds of the year the men of Aorema have little to do except patch up mud walls that the rains have battered down, or plait ropes, mats and roofing out of the tough stalks of millet and sorghum. The dreadful unpredictability of the rain has its effect, too, in keeping men poor. Even in the fat years a farmer has to bear the lean years in mind. He will rarely grow cotton or groundnuts to earn extra cash, with which he could buy better tools or fertilizer. Instead, he will sow more grain and store it in his granary, as insurance.

In the regions of Africa with adequate rainfall, there is no danger of desertification. But the cutting back of fallow periods brings other ecological hazards. In the most densely populated parts of the Tiv area in central Nigeria, the land is cropped continuously for six years and fallowed for only one or two – quite insufficient for trees to re-establish themselves. So grasses dominate the fallow period, and *imperata* grass, with its system of deep, spreading roots, can take over and is practically impossible to eradicate. Precisely the same danger threatens in large areas of South-East Asia. One of the densest concentrations of people in Nigeria is in the Ibo heartland that was the focus of breakaway Biafra. Here geographer Barry Floyd has reported severe and destructive soil erosion, progressive loss of plant nutrients and the breakdown of soil structure.

In the better-watered areas, population has grown more rapidly and the growing of tree crops such as cocoa for cash has speeded up the tendency to permanent cultivation. Where this occurs, yields drop to an abysmally low level. As populations continue to grow and there is no extra land to bring into cultivation, the only solution people can see is to migrate. Some of them move to the free areas that are left, and they are often free because they are difficult to work or even more ecologically precarious than the places people came from. Many more join the exodus to the cities.

Nomads and flies

There is, of course, another solution. In the late twentieth century, most of Africa has still not passed through the agricultural revolutions that enabled the land to support higher levels of population in Asia and in Europe. In Asia, irrigated rice farming can be carried on for centuries in the same fields with no loss of fertility. In Europe, arable and livestock farming were integrated, allowing cattle to be used for ploughing, manure, milk and meat. And fallow periods were cut out altogether by crop rotation, which gave the fields a change and a rest.

Africa is technologically the most backward of all three developing continents. Yet to compensate for the accidents of geography and geology she ought to be the most advanced. Nature has placed considerable limitations on agriculture here. Only one fifth of the surface area of Africa is potential farmland, and of this 57 per cent is made up of the reddish soil latosol, out of which the rains have leached the most valuable nutrients leaving an acidic soil high in iron and aluminium, which cultivated plants do not flourish in. Another 20 per cent is made up of desert soil, similarly starved of essential plant foods. Africa ought to be using a good deal more fertilizer than Europe to achieve similar yields. In 1975, developed countries used an average of 100 kilos of fertilizers per hectare, Asia twenty-one kilos and Latin America thirty-two kilos. African countries used an average of only 5·6 kilos. Pests, diseases and weeds, encouraged by heat and humidity, can destroy more than 40 per cent of the crop in the fields, yet pesticide application is minimal. After the harvest, perhaps another quarter of the crop may be lost in storage, eaten up by insects, rodents and microbes. Storage facilities may be first-rate for commercial crops. For the farmers' own food they are primitive. The decorative granaries of the Sahel are elegant and aesthetic, but their mud walls and straw roofs offer little protection against rats and termites, nor do the wattle and daub yam barns of the rainy areas. Water is another obstacle in Africa. Over half the continent is arid or semi-arid. Even in the sub-humid areas, plants may transpire more moisture than the rain brings for six to ten months of the year. All but the humid regions – many of which are sparsely peopled – would need extensive irrigation works if they were to grow crops all the year round. Yet in the late sixties only 1 per cent of the cultivated area was under irrigation.

Arable and livestock farming in Africa have been kept asunder by the accidents of entomology and anthropology. Across a wide belt round the waist of the continent, the tsetse fly reigns, carrying trypanosomiasis or sleeping sickness, to which cattle are even more susceptible than men. Only a few dwarf breeds are immune, and they are not popular because they produce little meat and even less milk. Mixed farming in the tsetse zones will have to await the eradication of the fly — a complex and expensive undertaking that could take decades — or the development of effective vaccines. Outside the tsetse domain, mixed farming has not developed because arable farming and pastoralism are quite separate occupations carried on by separate tribes or groups, in most of Africa and in parts of western Asia. (See Map 6, pages 464–5.)

The separation makes ecological sense in the dry areas. The tropical grasslands are a far cry from the lush green pastures of Ireland or New England, where a herd of cows can fatten on a few fields. The edible vegetation is sparser and an animal has to wander far to fill its stomach. Moreover, grass cover shifts with the season, moving north with the rainbelts and bringing a flush of green to the tinder-dry Sahel, then shifting south again as the rains go south. The borderland between permanent farms and desert proper is fit only for pasture, and herdsmen must, of necessity, move with the herds. Some of the sedentary tribes in Africa own cattle, but many entrust them to the specialist pastoral tribes such as the Masai in East Africa and the Fulani in West Africa. Our Mossi friend Moumouni owned a cow (he used to have four before the drought). But he handed it over to a Fulani tribesman for pasturing. In exchange, the Fulani had the right to keep the cow's products, its milk and dung. If Moumouni wanted manure from his own beast, he would have to buy it off the Fulani, and though his land needed it now more than ever before, he could afford it less.

The pastoral tribes are not efficient livestock farmers, though they are certainly picturesque. I first met the Fulani in northern Nigeria, where they were wintering among the complex tapestry of tribes around Lake Kainji. Investigating what looked like a primitive haystack, I found it was a Fulani tent — they build fresh ones out of straw wherever they go. The men were out with the herds. The women left in the camp offered me a gourd full of fermented milk. Generally the pastoral tribes, with plenty of dairy products and meat or blood, get a better diet than the sedentary farmers. And, as meat is in great demand in the cities, their incomes are higher too — often two or three times those of the agriculturalists. Fulani women, noted for their slender, fine-featured beauty, often wear the family savings on their person: gold sovereigns on plaits in their hair, big Maria Theresa silver dollars hung round their necks for brooches.

Their techniques are as unproductive as their farming counterparts. A herder will often keep more cattle than he can successfully fatten simply to enhance his standing in the community. The cattle suffer from high death and disease rates — only half the calves may live to reach maturity, and even then take twice as long to fatten up as European cattle. In West Africa the biggest meat markets are several hundred miles from the pastoral zones, in the cities near the coast. Fulani herdsmen in their pointed straw hats and white shifts drive their cattle to local markets, where the great Zebu beasts, their humps toppling over, wait in the scorching sun. Middlemen in kaftans stand around under the shade of umbrellas, feigning disinterest — but at the end of the day only the scrawniest specimens will be left. From dozens of markets the cattle are gathered for the exhausting trip south. The lucky ones go by rail in wagons bristling with horns like beds of nails. Many clash their way through dry scrub and woodland, hoofing it for hundreds of miles, arriving at their destinations with bellies hanging like hammocks between protruding thigh and shoulder bones. They can lose a quarter or more of their laboriously gained weight on the trip, and grow stringy and tough — as anyone who has broken a filling on a West African steak will tell you.

Management of herds and ranges could be vastly improved: the whole of the ranges could be replanted with pasture legumes like *stylosanthes* which fixes its own nitrogen, provides a good feed, resists trampling and maintains soil fertility. But the ranges are communal property and no one really owns them. No one has any direct incentive to improve them. Only governments could do the job.

The common land

Traditional forms of land tenure brake technological progress among the farming tribes, too.

The African way of landholding has many virtues. As one often-quoted Nigerian chief poetically remarked: 'The land belongs to a big family of which many members are dead, some are living, and innumerable others are still to be born.' In the traditional view, a man cannot own the land, because he did not make it: it was always there, a gift from the gods, in trust for the lineage. A man can own the fruit of the earth – crops and trees which he himself planted and tended. But he cannot dispose of his plot or sell it, there is no individual title to land, no market in real estate. As in Aorema, land is usually allocated by village chiefs, and each family is given as much as its members need to cultivate. There is no question of anyone getting extra and farming it with hired labourers.

And so, in the traditional system, everyone has more or less equal access to the land and its produce, and no one is landless. Incomes are egalitarian, though a man with two or three wives and four or five strong sons will obviously do well for himself. But his sons will inherit only a share of his movable wealth. Side by side with the landholding system, the extended family cares for the old, the sick, the widowed, who cannot themselves farm the land.

For social justice, this system could hardly be improved upon. But it has a major drawback from the technological point of view. If a man does not own his land, and indeed even shifts his plots regularly, he has no incentive to make permanent improvements or investments in the land, such as erosion control or irrigation. There is no stimulus for technical innovation. With a small, stable population, that does not matter at all. With a population greater than existing technology can support from the land, it becomes a matter of life and death.

The traditional landholding system is now breaking down in many parts of Africa, and with it the social justice that it guaranteed. Private property in land is emerging, but in most areas it does not seem to have speeded up technical progress fast enough to cope with population growth. European rule delivered the traditional system its first heavy blows. The colonial administrators arrived with concepts of private property derived from Roman law. Chiefs were encouraged to sign away land that appeared to be unoccupied, but was in fact fallow. They had no right to do so, but they were, like most human beings, susceptible to material inducements. Large-scale alienation of village land took place in southern Africa and a good deal in East Africa, wherever whites found the climate tolerable enough to settle. In humid West Africa, the white man's grave, the pressures were not so strong. Some alienation took place in French West Africa, especially for plantations in the Ivory Coast. But hardly any happened in the British possessions. Lever Brothers tried their best to get land for plantations in the 1920s, but enlightened local administrators resisted. Sir Hugh Clifford, governor of the Gold Coast, wisely commented, 'A plantation system is not a society, it is an economic agglomeration created for the pursuit of profit. It substitutes itself for those primitive societies which in sickness and in health sustain their members.' It was one of the more honourable moments of colonial history. But the pressures towards individual ownership continued. As population grows, farmers return more and more frequently to the same plot and develop a recognized right to use it. The spread of tree crops with a life of a decade or two, such as cocoa, coffee and oil palm, pushes the process further.

Full private property in land tends to develop where population density gets so great that more or less permanent farming goes on. It is true that in the countries where land tenure has come closest to freehold property – in Kenya and the Ivory Coast – commercialized farming has advanced furthest. But private property in land – as the next two chapters will show –

is an extremely dangerous institution for the welfare of the poor. It leads to social polarization, increasing degrees of inequality, and grinding poverty among those without adequate access to land. Eventually it leads to the emergence of landlessness. As the 1957 working party on African land tenure in Kenya prophetically noted, 'The best way to deprive a peasant of his land is to give him a secure title and make it freely negotiable.' Kenya has encouraged the development of private land ownership, and the result has been a considerable degree of inequality. In 1970 just 3,175 large farms, owned by Europeans, individual Africans, corporations and some cooperatives, occupied 2.69 million hectares of the best land, while the country's 777,000 smallholders were crowded into only 2·65 million hectares. Even among the latter there were great disparities: the 52 per cent with farms below two hectares occupied only 15 per cent of the land, while the top 7 per cent took up more than a third of the total. The Kenyan government has tried to control land sales and purchases and to prevent rural indebtedness of the kind found in Asia. But in the long run polarization into landed and landless seems inevitable. Already marginal smallholders in Kenya are leaving their wives to cultivate the home plot while they migrate in search of seasonal work. Further population growth tends to place in jeopardy even the technical benefits of commercialization and private property. Mixed arable and livestock farming has been emerging among Kenyan smallholders, but it tends to retreat as more of the land is needed to grow subsistence food and less can be spared to graze cattle. West African farmers often cultivate their cash crops with the very latest techniques, but grow their own food in the old primitive ways – and as families expand, the area under cash crops dwindles.

The technical solutions exist to make African agriculture more productive: mixed farming, growing of irrigated rice in river valleys and swampy depressions, reseeding the ranges with pasture legumes, much wider use of fertilizer. In a few areas and in pilot projects, these things are already happening, but the scale is not wide enough to make much difference to the poor majority. They do not have the reserve funds needed to make these investments. They are trapped by poverty on the wrong side of a wide technological abyss which they cannot leap over. And so they get poorer still.

To break out of the trap they need help, and their governments need more aid. Africa also desperately needs a cutback in her population growth, yet of all the developing continents she has the fewest family planning programmes. And somehow the incentive to improve land and technique has to be provided without destroying the social justice that the traditional system of communal land ownership provided. The communal spirit that is the heart of the African village needs to be channelled into cooperative forms of ownership and work, not dissolved into competitive individualism.

5. Polarization in Asia

Under the steep volcanic cones of central Java, the lush landscape is alive with figures. Little better than beasts of burden,
women bend under bundles of fodder. Huge, roofed carts
lumber along, pulled by yoked white bullocks, ambling slower
than a man's walking pace. Every inch of the soil is growing
something – even the narrow paths between the paddy fields,
less than a foot wide, are planted with soyabeans or cassava.
In this rural area people are more densely packed – up to two
thousand per square kilometre – than in many western cities.

A paddy field, drained of water but still tacky underfoot, is
being harvested. There are perhaps fifty women here in their
batik sarongs, tight-fitting jackets in pastel shades of pink,
blue and brown, and coolie hats (even in poverty Indonesians
never lose their elegance). The area they are working in is no
more than thirty metres square: a combine harvester driven
by one man could clear an equivalent space in just a few
minutes. The women have small knives known as *ani ani*, made
of a razor-sharp straight blade set into a short bamboo stick.
They cut the drooping ears of rice one by one, six inches from
the top, leaving the stalks in the ground.

A more laborious and less productive technique could hardly
be imagined, yet it is not without its rationale. The stalks are
left to be ploughed in for the next planting: they provide
humus and nutrients. The use of the *ani-ani* creates the maximum number of jobs. In traditional Javanese society village
women have an undisputed right to harvest any farmer's fields.
In exchange, they get one ninth of the crop, but by haggling
and cheating in the bustle of activity (no one can keep an eye
on fifty women at once) they slip the heavier heads in their
own sacks and push their average share up to one sixth. The
system guarantees that everyone, however little land they
themselves own, gets at least some share in the produce of the
land.

Paddy growing, the staple of Asia's most populated areas, is uniquely able to absorb an expanding population. Where slash and burn eventually leads to ecological disaster as population grows, or at best a permanent decline in yields, irrigated paddy has gone on producing the same or increased yields from the same land for centuries, even millennia. The secrets of its success are still not fully understood, but the water seems to be the crucial factor. Water protects the soil against heavy rain, keeps the soil temperature down and circulates the nutrients. More important, it fosters blue-green algae which fix nitrogen from the air, rather like the bacteria in the root nodules of beans, and the rice can use this for growth. As this is a free fertilizer, paddy production can go on for years with no decline in soil fertility, even without chemical inputs.

And paddy responds to loving care in a way that no other crop does. The more labour you devote to it, the more yield it will produce, and the ultimate limits of that increase are so high that most of Asia is still a very long way from reaching them. More work can be put into paddy in any number of ways: growing the seedlings in nurseries and transplanting them, planting in carefully spaced rows, weeding more thoroughly, making even slight improvements in water control.

Paddy has soaked up the massive population increases in China, on the Ganges and the Mekong, in Java, by the process that American anthropologist Clifford Geertz has called agricultural involution. Evolution has been characteristic of progress in the West: that is, technical improvements leading to higher productivity of the land and of the worker, and therefore producing higher incomes per head. Involution is technical change that pushes up the productivity of the land alone by absorbing more and more workers into more and more labour-intensive work. With paddy, this leads to higher overall food production, but, as the population goes on increasing, declining production per person. Involution leads to a gradual drop in incomes per head and a declining agricultural surplus, and, as we saw in China, it inhibits the development of industry.

Indonesia, with its infinite multiplication of minute chores in the fields and its elaborate system of work-sharing, is the classic case of involution. Everyone gets a share in the fruit of the land, but that share very slowly gets smaller and smaller and people sink into collective poverty: they all go down with the ship together.

This morally superior system is now collapsing under the onslaught of western technology, commercialism and bare materialistic greed. The spread of the Green Revolution, with its high-yielding seeds, fertilizers and pesticides, has promised much greater rewards to the minority who have enough land to produce a surplus for sale. But the greater the rewards, and the greater the temptations of consumerism, the less the lucky ones are willing to share with those who have little or no land. After all, one sixth of an expanded Green Revolution crop is very much more than before.

So new, economically more rational but socially irresponsible systems are spreading to replace the old harvest share and displace the people who reaped it. The farmer who tries directly to resist the invasion of customary village harvesters is liable to be victimized or ostracized. So an alternative system known as *tebasan* is catching on: this involves selling the crop as it stands in the fields, a week or so before harvest, to a third party from outside the village. This third party brings in a gang of his own people working for a smaller than customary share, usually one eleventh, or even for casual wages. This allows the farmer to escape both his social responsibilities and the social consequences of ignoring them. The farmer or contractor can push up his own income even further by making harvesters use the sickle instead of the *ani-ani* knife. This cuts the average number of harvesters needed by more than half. It is technological progress combined with moral and social regression. The truly rational farmer recoups even more of his crop if he sends it to a large mill instead of getting it hand-pounded by village women. But the mill may need only one employee to do the work of ten or more hand-pounders.

So the few reap the benefits of agricultural advance, while the many reap the costs. Almost everywhere in non-communist Asia it is the same story of commercial and technical progress, coupled with an increase in landlessness and poverty, and the death of the traditional systems that provided social security for everyone.

Pauperization and debt

The facts are alarming:

*In the Punjab, where the Green Revolution and tractorization have spread furthest in all India, the proportion of landless labourers rose from 17 per cent of the rural population to 23 per cent in the sixties. In 1960, one in five was living below a very modestly drawn poverty line. Ten years later, the proportion had doubled.

*In Western Uttar Pradesh, landless labourers made up 11 per cent of the rural population in 1961, and twice that level in 1971. In Bihar they shot up from 30 per cent to 48 per cent over the same period. Over the whole of India, 24 per cent of the rural population were landless in 1961, and 38 per cent a decade later.

*In Bangladesh, the proportion of landless labourers rose by half between 1951 and 1967, while their real wages more than halved, from 2.66 rupees per day in 1964 to 1.28 rupees in 1975 (at constant prices).

*In the Philippines, at the beginning of the century, four out of five farmers were full owners of their land. By 1960, less than half were.

Asia was, traditionally, a continent of smallholders. Even in 1960 the distribution of land was much more even than, say, in the Middle East or in Latin America. Except in a few areas, really big landowners are few and far between (though one acre of well-watered paddy may be equivalent to a hundred acres or more of Andean pastureland). Of the holdings above one hectare, only one in five hundred was bigger than fifty hectares and these occupied only 9 per cent of the area. The

78 per cent of holdings below five hectares took up 41 per cent of the area.

The original egalitarian pattern of smallholdings may have developed out of the communal ownership of shifting cultivators, in the way that is happening now in Africa. As population expands and cultivation becomes permanent, the original equal share in the land becomes private property. Private property in land leads almost automatically to increasing inequalities and the emergence of landlessness, even with a static population. Coupled with the institution of moneylending and rapid population growth (around 2 per cent a year in rural Asia) the process is much speeded up.

Some extra land is being brought under cultivation in Asia, but as more than four-fifths of the suitable area is already in use, there is not much scope for this. So the average amount of land per head is declining. In 1975 there was only 0·31 hectare of farmland per rural person – 14 per cent down on 1960 – against 0·72 ha in Africa and 1·1 ha in Latin America. The customs of inheritance in Asia (as in most of the Third World) call for a shareout of property among a dead man's heirs. This usually means that farms are constantly being fragmented into smaller and smaller holdings, often broken up into many separate patches acquired through marriage alliances.

The fertile valleys near Kandy in central Sri Lanka are the heartland of the dominant Sinhalese culture. Here the paddy land is broken up like a jigsaw puzzle by hundreds of *bunds* or low walls, defining plots so minute that often there is no room for a bullock and plough to turn in them. They have to be hand-hoed with mammoties by men in brilliant white loincloths, up to their crotch in mud. In just eight years from 1962, smallholdings of one acre or less in Sri Lanka rose from 43 per cent to 65 per cent of the total number of paddy holdings, and their average size declined from four-fifths to half of an acre. Many men are cultivating half the area their fathers had, because the land was divided between two brothers. This decline in size makes the smaller owners extremely vulnerable. In many areas the majority of plots are too small to feed a family and the owners are forced to earn money from labouring. It only needs one year's poor rainfall, an attack of rice stemborer, an accident or serious illness to push a man over the precipice into debt.

Nor a borrower be

Indebtedness is an endemic ailment in rural Asia. The two main reasons for going into debt are, first, to keep alive until the next season — nearly three quarters of working households in Bihar, for example, take loans for consumption purposes. Second, to marry a daughter or bury a parent.

Ceremonies are of central importance in the traditional societies of Africa and Asia. They indicate the passage of individuals from non-existence to birth, from childhood to adolescence and to parenthood, from life to death. They are inescapable obligations, and the way in which they are carried out is carefully scrutinized by everyone else in the village, jealously comparing the cost, the costumes or the amount of food available for guests. Competition in ceremonies is unavoidable, and failure to live up to the current standard involves serious loss of face and lasting shame.

In Bali wherever you go you come across ceremonies. There are ceremonies for birth, after forty-five days of life, at puberty when the teeth are filed, at marriage and at death. And there are collective ceremonies every 210 days at each one of three village temples and three field temples. A family may easily be involved in a ceremony a month, and at the very least this will involve offerings of rice and coconut wrapped in palm leaves. Weddings are very expensive. Dewagde Darma, a fifty-year-old farmer who owns a mere half hectare of paddy, was spending £200 ($400), equal to eight months' income or many years' savings, on his son's wedding. Cremations are nothing short of ruinous: decorative paper towers and horses have to be built, entire villages fed, *gamelan* orchestras hired and priests' fees paid. Six months before my visit Dewagde and his brother had spent two and a half million rupiahs (£3,500 or $7,000) for the cremation ceremony of his grandfather, who died forty years ago. They had waited that long to save the money, rather than go into debt.

Many Balinese, however, do resort to debt. The usual way in Bali is to pawn your land for five years or so in exchange for the cash. The moneylender takes the crop from the land as his interest. One middle-aged headman I met, Idewa Gde Putra, had recently spent 300,000 rupiahs (about £400 or $800) on his daughter's wedding, amounting to two years' income. He was now planning to pawn all his land – one third of a hectare – because he needed another 150,000 rupiahs to contribute to the cost of cremating two relatives. Idewa would be allowed to work his own land in the meantime as a tenant, and take half the crop. If he does not redeem the debt, he will be landless. Dewoputtu Tinggal, a slim twenty-five-year-old, had become landless after pawning his land to pay for the birth ceremony of his first child. The men who lend the money are usually owners of two hectares or more – on paper, that is. Because of the land they have taken in pledge, they effectively control and enjoy the profits of much more than that. As land diminishes in size, the numbers needing to borrow increase faster than the willingness to lend: so population increase leads to higher interest rates, or worse terms for the loan.

Most parts of the world have seen an inflation in the cost of traditional ceremonies. A Nigerian can bankrupt himself buying beer for all the people who turn up to a parent's funeral. The new rich throw huge feasts to impress everyone. Other people feel obliged to compete and put themselves into debt to do so. Even traditional ceremonies are perverted into mechanisms of impoverishment, once gross inequalities start to develop.

The small man is discriminated against by official banks: he stands no chance of getting a loan out of them for consumption purposes. So, if he cannot raise money from his relatives, he is forced on to the loan shark market. The money is usually made available by large landowners, and the debt business swells their income even further. Rates are ruinous – in one survey in Sri Lanka they ranged from 40 to 170 per cent. An average rate of anything between 25 and 60 per cent is usual.

Meanwhile the official banks are lending to the big landowners at much lower rates, between 7 and 18 per cent. The big man can get even bigger by exploiting his privileged access to government credit and relending to his less fortunate neighbours.

At interest rates like these, the debt itself becomes an even bigger millstone round the poor man's neck than the misfortune which caused his original deficit. The third most common reason for borrowing is to pay off earlier loans: debt brings more debt. With debt added to deficiency, the poor man is even less able to meet his needs and sinks further into debt. Eventually he is forced to sell all or part of his land to pay off his owings.

All over Asia smallholders are being pauperized and turned into landless labourers. As labourers they are no less liable to debt, but have nothing to offer as collateral except their own bodies. And so, although it is illegal in most places, the practice of bonded labour is quite common in Asia (and for that matter in Central America, Brazil and Bolivia). If a man is unable to pay off his debt (as the poorest often are) he works gratis for his creditor in lieu of interest. By this method he may never pay off the capital and remain in a perpetual state of virtual slavery. In India bonded labour is outlawed by the constitution, but persists just the same. A typical example, quoted by the Indian Institute of Social Sciences: one man borrowed a mere 200 rupees (about £12 or $24) at 25 per cent interest, and was unable to keep up the payments. So he was forced to work for two hundred days in the year for his creditor and still had not repaid the capital at the end of it. Other cases from an Uttar Pradesh village: one man borrowed 500 rupees (£32 or $64) to buy food, for which he served seventeen years of bonded labour; another borrowed 300 rupees for a wedding and served eighteen years. Bonded labourers are no better than tied serfs: they cannot even leave their village without the creditor's permission. And whatever their own priorities, he has first call on their labour on any given day.

The dynamics of inequality are inherent in the institutions of Asian society: private property in land, equal inheritance and debt. Traditional society had ways of minimizing the impact of these processes, such as the harvesting rights in Indonesia or the *jajmani* system in India. Under this, the land-owning caste of each village gave a share of the crops to the landless castes in exchange for labour or services. In one village, for example, the barber would get, every spring harvest, seven pounds each of barley, millet, unhusked rice and corn on the cob, and fourteen pounds of corn, from each of his patrons. In exchange he would shave their faces and armpits and cut their fingernails twice a week, cut their toenails once a fortnight and their hair once a month. The relationship of patron and client was permanent and hereditary, and payment was in kind, not in cash. Though a small number of castes owned the land, almost everyone had access to its produce. As the anthropologist Louis Dumont has remarked, here 'We are not in the world of the modern economic individual, but in a sort of co-operative where the main aim is to ensure the subsistence of everyone in accordance with his social function.'

The colonial experience exposed traditional societies all over the world to a new virus, every bit as lethal as the smallpox in the blankets given to American Indians: that virus was materialistic greed and commercialization. Self-sufficient villages were often compelled to grow cash crops to get money to pay colonial taxes. Roads and railways allowed the world market to extend its tentacles into the remotest areas and started the process of tearing apart the bonds of tradition. That process is now being speeded up by the commercial opportunities of expanding food markets, and the opportunities for profit of new technologies. Gresham's law of economics states that a baser currency will always drive out and replace more valuable coinage wherever it is introduced. In the same way the cash nexus is replacing the dictates of traditional morality throughout Asia and Africa. Payment in wages is squeezing out payment in kind. That would not matter so much if the wages were equitable or even adequate. But they are not. As we shall see in Chapter 20, absolute poverty is on the increase in Asia. The bulk of this poverty is found in the rural areas, among those with no land or not enough land to feed themselves. The process of pauperization among the landless follows automatically, given population growth and the failure of governments to create enough employment in rural areas. If they are tenants, there are more of them wanting land than there is land available, therefore rents go up and the share left for the tenant's own needs goes down. If they are labourers, there are more of them seeking jobs than there are jobs available. Therefore wages fall. Those are the simple laws of supply and demand.

Nowhere in Asia have these catastrophic dynamics proceeded so far as in Bangladesh, whose predicament illustrates the fatal consequences of the logic inherent in Asian society. Squeezed into a tiny 55,593 square miles, an area slightly bigger than highly industrialized England (population 46 million) are some 85 million people, nine tenths of whom live on the land. Water is Bangladesh's greatest benefactor – and her persecutor. Two of Asia's mightiest rivers, the Ganges and the Brahmaputra, deposit here the rich minerals washed down from the young rocks of the Himalayas, annually renewing the soil's fertility. Yet for four months of the year much of the land is submerged too deeply to grow any kind of crop, and over the drowned fields ply barges that cannot have changed in style since antiquity. Upwind, six standing men sweat and tug on broad oars. Downwind, they ride on billowing sails sewn together from tattered fertilizer sacks. The households or *baris*, built on slight elevations, barely keep their heads above the waters.

Land hunger has reached acute proportions. At Bangladesh's low average yields of half a ton of rice per acre, a man would need about 1·8 acres of land to maintain the average-sized family of six at subsistence level. At least two thirds of households have less than that amount: 11 per cent have no land at all, not even for a house, while another 47 per cent own less than an acre, and their average holding amounts to just 0·23 acres (the size of a patch thirty-five yards square). Two processes could have compensated somewhat for the increase in population: the bringing of new land into cultivation, and an increase in yields. But there has been practically no expansion in the cropped area over the last decade, and yields have risen by only 5 per cent while population has grown by 25 per cent.

People have become so desperate for land that they have settled in areas of the delta and islands which may be flooded or hit by cyclones several times a year. They build only the flimsiest of shelters, knowing full well that they will be destroyed before long. If they get a warning of a cyclone or a tidal wave they will clamber onto their thatched roofs and strap themselves and their families down, in the hope that the rushing waters will carry them away and put them down safely. Bangladesh's violent, wandering rivers every year eat away large chunks of land, leaving their owners homeless and destitute. In other places they recede leaving silt banks of new, fertile land known as *chars*. These become the object of bitter and violent struggles for possession, invariably won by the rich man who can bring along the biggest contingent of armed relatives, supporters and hired thugs.

Landlessness on the current scale in Bangladesh is a fairly recent phenomenon. Almost every landless peasant you meet either once owned more land himself, or his father did. Subdivision by inheritance has gradually whittled down the average size of plots. As these shrink below the critical level for subsistence, the owner becomes increasingly vulnerable. If he cannot find enough outside work – or if disease or disaster strike – he will have to mortgage his land for a loan and risk forfeiture, or sell it off bit by bit to buy a temporary respite, ensuring short-term survival at the risk of long-term ruin.

Abdurrashid Ali Khan is a diminutive fifty-year-old from Sivalaya district whom destiny has cursed with four daughters, who can bring in no money and will cost perhaps £60 ($120) each to marry off. Khan's father had just enough land to get by – one and a half acres. But he had three sons, and on his death the land was divided equally between them, giving each one just half an acre. Unable to find enough work to make up his family's needs, Khan was forced to sell off his land, piece by piece, in order to keep alive. Now he owns only the land his house is built on, and sharecrops one acre and a cow.

Sale of land is the inevitable outcome of the economics of poverty in Bangladesh as a rough family budget shows. The average family of six members needs five pounds of rice per day for a survival diet of only 1,700 calories per person. Total requirements: 1,800 pounds of rice per year. The average marginal peasant's holding of 0·23 acres would yield only 200 pounds of rice or less. Annual deficit: at least 1,600 pounds of rice. Cash needed to buy it, at current market prices of 1·5 to 2 taka per pound: 2,400 to 3,000 taka (£80 to £100 or $160 to $200). Add 30 per cent for other essentials such as fuel and enough clothing to hide your nakedness and nothing more. Family income needed for survival: 3,000 to 4,000 taka. Assuming the average peasant may be lucky enough to find eight months work a year, at the daily wage of around ten taka per day he cannot expect a cash income of more than 2,000 taka. Annual deficit: between 1,000 and 2,000 taka. Now the price of one acre of land in Bangladesh in 1978 was around 30,000 taka. To meet his deficit, therefore, the average marginal smallholder would need to sell off 0·03 to 0·06 acre, or between one eighth and one quarter of his entire land, each year. And that was in 1978, after three or four years of good harvests and rising real incomes.

In the first half of the seventies an unprecedented series of disasters added to the pressures on marginal farmers, though they were only a more widespread form of what can hit any poor man at any time. In November 1970 a 125-mile-per-hour cyclone killed upwards of 200,000 people and made a million or more homeless. Civil war followed in March 1971, killing an estimated half million people and causing damage costed at $1·2 billion. Drought in the 1972–3 growing season cut the harvest from an expected 11·8 million tons to 9·8 million tons. In 1974 famine came in the wake of disastrous floods, anything from 50,000 to 500,000 people died, another 1·3 million tons of grain were lost and $3·5 billion of damage done. All these events piled up on the unfortunate Bangladeshis as if they were cursed by God, increasing the pressure to sell and mortgage land. Farmers' crops were slashed at the same time as opportunities for agricultural labour were drastically reduced. So land sales rocketed from 94,100 in 1971 to 453,200 in 1974, dropping slightly to 378,700 in 1976. In the six years from 1971 761,000 acres were sold. Assuming the sales were concentrated among owners of less than an acre, this suggests that the marginal farmers sold off half their land in those apocalyptic years.

Middle peasants – earning their own keep on two to five acres of land, and constituting around 20 per cent of the rural population – may have emerged relatively unscathed, though it has to be remembered that when a middle peasant dies leaving more than one male heir, his sons will automatically become marginal peasants.

The winners in this infernal chess game, picking off the poor pawns as they fall, have been the rich peasants, which in land-hungry Bangladesh means those 6 per cent of rural households with more than five acres each, who owned 43 per cent of the land in 1977. Many of this class had been rent collectors for the Hindu *zamindars* or landlords whom the British created in Bengal. When the Hindus fled at the partition of India in 1947, these and other big fish illegally seized the vacated farms and have since occupied other state land. Population increase and natural disaster have enabled them to expand their holdings further by buying up the land sold by the poor. Hence a dual process of polarization is going on here, and in the rest of non-communist Asia. At one end of the scale, smallholdings are becoming increasingly fragmented and landlessness is increasing. At the other, there is increasing concentration of landholding among the larger surplus peasants.

This concentration confers considerable economic, social and political power which the landlords have used to consolidate and accentuate their advantages. They tend to monopolize government services – and use them to exploit the poor. Fertilizer, usually in short supply, is sold at a premium by government officials to whoever can pay most – and that excludes the poor. Bank loans go almost exclusively to the larger peasants. One group of twenty-six virtually landless sharecroppers in Savar district told me that they found it impossible to get a bank loan – either they did not have enough land for collateral;

or the land titles were in their fathers' or grandfathers' names because they couldn't afford the fees and bribes for the land registry; or they could not afford to take a day off work to go to town, or to pay the backhander which bank officials invariably demanded as the price of giving a loan. So the poor had to borrow from the rich, at rates equivalent to 250 per cent a year. Though the lending of money for interest is contrary to Moslem precepts, the landlords circumvent this by accepting a compulsory 'gift' in rice, equal to the sum required.

Tubewells have become another instrument of oppression. The government has been building these in large numbers for groups forming themselves into cooperatives. Usually these co-ops are made up of the larger landlords. They then proceed to charge exorbitant rates for the use of the tubewell water. The annual cost of running a typical tubewell to irrigate around 200 acres was 15,600 taka – this includes 4,200 taka in wages for the guard and pump attendant, who would invariably be members of the landlords' families. The local co-op was charging water rates of 110 taka per acre, thus making a profit of 6,600 taka a year (about £220 or $440) which was divided up among the fifteen co-op members. In ways like this even government investment in rural areas, on behalf of institutions that are supposed to be for the common good, is perverted so as to accentuate inequality and exploitation.

Finally, the big landlords buy the favour of police and judges. I once asked a Bangladesh supreme court advocate if the police were usually on the side of the rich. 'Not usually,' he answered: '*Always.*' This partiality of the law is used to gain protection for a third process – besides sale and fragmentation – that is depriving the poor of their land: that is, expropriation by force or fraud.

Hassan Ali, a thirty-five-year-old farmer from Savar district, mortgaged one sixth of an acre of land, worth around 4,000 taka, for a 1,200 taka loan. The moneylender, a big local landlord, made him sign a blank sheet of paper, on which he then wrote in a debt of 1,400 taka. When Hassan had collected enough money to repay the landlord, with interest, the latter refused to take repayment and insisted on keeping the land instead. Hassan was forced to go to court and had to sell more land to pay 500 taka (about £16 or $32) in bribes. But his adversary had greater resources and won the case, thus acquiring the land at less than one third of its market value.

Mohammed Ayubali, a landless labourer from crowded Comilla district, still remembers with bitterness how his father was cheated of his land twelve years ago. A big landlord had sent some thugs to seize part of a neighbour's holding, and Ayubali senior had turned out to help fight them off. To get his own back, the landlord adopted a different tack and accused Ayubali's father of injuring his cattle. The police came to the house, manhandled him to force him to defend himself, then arrested him for assault. Ayubali senior was jailed, and his cattle and house were seized. He had to sell his land to pay legal fees, but died of a heart attack before the case was resolved.

The increase in landlessness in Bangladesh has not been matched by any equivalent increase in employment on or off the land. Job-creating investment has lagged: Bangladesh's investment is made possible only by foreign aid. Her own domestic savings rate is often negative – that is, people are consuming more than they produce – as the marginal farmers sell up in order to survive. Most of the surplus in the pockets of the rich goes into unproductive uses such as buying up land from the poor. The net result is a massive and growing labour surplus. Workers from the same area compete against each other, and against even more desperate men who migrate seasonally from flooded areas. So wage rates are forced down – in 1974–5, real wages had fallen to 45 per cent of their already low level of a decade earlier, though they had risen back to 65 per cent in 1976–7.

In 1978, at the time of my visit, daily wage rates were around ten taka a day (33p or 66 cents US), enough to buy five pounds of rice or keep a family of six barely alive. But for four months of the year, most labourers are without work. Mohammed Ayubali had not worked for two months when I met him, and had been living off savings accumulated in the previous season. He was only spending four or five taka a day.

He eats barely one pound of rice a day, enlivened only by a couple of hot chillies, while his wife and two children share a pound and a half between them. To do sustained agricultural work, he would need to eat double that amount. Because of his poor nutrition, he has grown weaker and weaker and is now capable of only light work, which pays even less wages. Unaware of the real cause of his condition, he attributes it to a vasectomy operation he underwent a year earlier.

The landless who are lucky manage to get land to share-crop. Once again, there are so many of them clamouring for land that landlords can dictate their own conditions. My group of twenty-six landless peasants complained that the poorest among them could not get land to tenant, as landlords would let only to peasants owning a bullock and plough. Landlords took a customary share of 50 per cent of the crop – but as the costs of fertilizer, seed and water have to be entirely borne by the tenants, the sharecroppers' net income amounts to only one third of the produce of the land they work. Some landlords were changing from crop-share contracts to short-term cash-rent deals for one year or even a single crop, so they could raise the rent regularly. Rough calculations suggest that peasants on this type of contract were receiving as little as a quarter of their own produce.

Paradoxically, the worse the agrarian situation gets, the more powerful the big landlords get and the more distant seem the prospects for reform or revolution. There are no nation-wide organizations of poor or landless peasants in Bangladesh. What few sporadic local conflicts there have been have always ended in defeat for the poor. Because their poverty is the greatest threat to their solidarity, setting them in competition with each other for the benefits – jobs or sharecrop land – that the rich increasingly control.

One step forward: the Green Revolution

Agriculture in Asia has not been technically stagnant as has been the tendency in Africa. It started from a much more advanced base, with plough cultivation in many parts, irrigation and widespread use of manure. Its farmers are adaptable, and those of them in a position to do so have been very quick indeed to take up innovations. The Green Revolution helped to boost food production, created more jobs on the land, and set some areas such as the Punjab and Haryana, on the road to industrialization.

Plant breeding by man has been going on continuously for perhaps ten thousand years, ever since the first wild strains of wheat, rice and corn were domesticated. In the Third World it is still going on even among the poorest farmers, who are perpetually improving their seeds, picking out the healthiest and fattest plants as parents for next season's crops.

The native varieties this selection has produced are well adapted to the traditional conditions they have to grow in. They have large, spreading roots, as the soil is often low in nitrogen. They are partly resistant to many local problems such as diseases or periodic droughts. But they are poorly suited for the most pressing problem in overpopulated lands: increasing the yield for a given area. They cannot be grown close together, or their roots compete with each other for nutrients. When they are fertilized, they tend to put on useless weight in leaves and stalks rather than into food grains. So they deprive each other of sunlight and develop long, thin stalks that lodge, that is, topple over before the grain is ripe.

Throughout the colonial period western scientific research almost totally neglected the food plants on which three quarters of mankind depended for survival. Then, in 1943, the Rockefeller Foundation and the government of Mexico set up a programme to develop new tropical varieties of wheat that would respond properly to fertilizer. It took them ten years of sifting through thousands of varieties, collected together from North and South America, South Asia, the Middle East and East Africa, to develop a dwarf variety that converted fertilizer efficiently into food grains rather than more stalk or leaves and did not topple over with the weight. It was a cross between a native Mexican strain and a North American semi-dwarf wheat, itself derived from a Japanese variety known as Norin.

The new wheat helped Mexico – which imported half her grain requirements in 1940 – to become self-sufficient by 1956. In 1970 her average yields were four times the 1940 levels, reaching 3,200 kilos of wheat per hectare. By 1966, high-yielding strains of wheat had been developed that were suitable for Asian conditions, and seed stocks were exported to Turkey, India and Pakistan. Wheat yields doubled in India between 1964 and 1972, and helped to turn her wheat-bowls, Haryana and Punjab, into her fastest-developing states.

To follow up the wheat success story, Rockefeller combined with Ford Foundation in 1960 to establish the International Rice Research Institute at Los Banos in the Philippines. IRRI collected ten thousand rice varieties from all over the world and bred and interbred them to develop maximum response to fertilizer, small leaves and short stalks. The institute arranged a strange marriage of Peta, a tall vigorous variety from Indonesia, with Dee-Geo-Woo-Gen, a dwarf rice from Japan. Their offspring was known as IR8, the famous high-yielding hybrid that launched the Green Revolution. Subsequent research has produced even better varieties. IR8 had the drawback that it was more susceptible to common rice pests and diseases than many native varieties. Successive strains have been bred that resist more and more of these afflictions. A recent prodigy is IR 28, resistant to many of the ills that rice is heir to: blast fungus, bacterial blight, grassy stunt virus, tungro virus, green leaf hoppers, brown plant hoppers and stem-borers.

The new seeds had an immediate and startling impact on food production when they were launched in 1966. Rice production in Sri Lanka soared from 649,000 tons in 1966 to 913,000 in 1968, and in Pakistan from two million to over three million tons. In actual use on farms, the high-yielding varieties gave between 20 and 35 per cent more than traditional strains. Among farmers with enough water and credit, the seeds spread like a bush fire. World-wide, the area planted to HYVs grew exponentially, from 58,000 acres in 1965–6 to 1·7 million acres the following year, 6·7 million acres in 1967–8 and 33 million acres in 1972–3. In just four years, from 1967–8, the area under the new seeds expanded from one fifth of the agricultural land in the Philippines to nearly two thirds. By 1974–5, 62 per cent of the wheat area and 26 per cent of the rice area of south and east Asia were under HYVs. But in many areas the seeds overstretched themselves, and spread to places without sufficient water. Under these conditions they perform worse than the old faithful local varieties. But in other places, where farmers were poorer and could not afford the extra fertilizer involved, they did not reach anything like their potential coverage: in 1970–71 only 15 per cent of India's rice land was growing them, and only 11 per cent of Indonesia's.

The miracle seeds did a great deal of good. Countries that had been chronic beggars in the food market, dependent on handouts from the cornucopia of the USA, came much closer to self-sufficiency. With food supplies for once growing faster than demand, prices for staples came down in real terms or at least remained stable.

The high-yield varieties *in themselves* have a potential to increase employment opportunities in the areas where they are introduced. They absorb anything from 10 to 60 per cent more man hours than traditional varieties. This is because they have to be carefully planted in straight rows rather than broadcast haphazardly. They get more intensive applications of fertilizer and more meticulous weeding. Because they cannot stand flooding or drought like the old varieties could, they have to be coddled with more finely tuned water management. They also help to eliminate that ancient curse of agriculture: seasonal unemployment.

The dry season was traditionally a time of inactivity, devoted to feasts and festivals, when what meagre surplus there was would be consumed with joyous abandon. Even in ambitious irrigation schemes that stretched the water over more of the year, only one crop could be grown because traditional varieties took up to six months to mature. The new seeds matured in only 120 days. This allowed two crops to be grown in a year, or even, in areas with water all the year round, three crops in fourteen months. The new disease-resistant strain IR 28 can mature in a mere 105 days, increasing even further the cropping intensity. So, in the areas with sufficient water, the annual burden of work no longer peaks at harvest time and drops to nearly nothing thereafter, but is more evenly distributed through the year. Perhaps more important still, growing two or three crops a year on the same land is equivalent to growing one crop on three times as much land. Multiple cropping actually multiplies land, just as surely (and much more cheaply) than opening up virgin territory. The burden of population on land is eased and the pressures for migration to the cities reduced: the landless have more work and the marginal farmers can feed a family on a much smaller area than before.

These are the potential benefits in theory. In practice the benefits have been distributed according to the parable of the talents, which seems to govern so much of life in the Third World: 'Unto every one that hath shall be given, and he shall have abundance; but from him that hath not shall be taken away even that which he hath.' The larger and richer farmers acquired the extra profits, while the landless and smallholders benefited little and dryland farmers may even have suffered in competition.

The reason for this perverse effect lies partly in the physiology of the new seeds, and partly in the anatomy of the unequal society they took root in. High-yielding varieties are aristocratic plants, fastidious, highly strung, hypersensitive. They demand good soils, copious sunshine, enough but not too much water. Because they are short and stocky, they can easily be 'drowned' if the water level rises too high, so careful irrigation control is needed. And, of course, they demand heavy doses of fertilizer, for they are, above all else, very efficient converters of fertilizers into food. They can absorb three times more fertilizer per acre than traditional varieties and produce twice as much extra grain per pound applied. Without the magic ingredients, they are like the emperor without his clothes, reduced to the status of ordinary mortals. No extra fertilizer, no extra food.

Because of their water requirements, high-yielding varieties accentuate the injustices of nature and chance. Dry areas with only rain-fed farming could not grow the first generations of new seeds. International research is only now beginning to improve dryland crops – cassava, beans, rain-fed rice. Even in irrigated areas, gaps widen between those who can irrigate their fields long enough for only one crop, and those with enough water for two or even three crops.

But even inside areas with the same natural endowments, the rich have benefited much more than the poor. In theory, the technology of HYVs is scale neutral, that is, it can be put to just as good effect on tiny farms as on huge ones. In practice, a farmer who wants to grow them needs extra cash for fertilizer, insecticides, small irrigation improvements and wages for the additional labour he needs to take on. He will more than recoup these costs from the extra harvest yielded: but in the meantime he needs credit to tide him over till then. The big landowners invariably get precedence for credit from official sources. They are more 'credit-worthy' because they have a bigger collateral to offer, but equally important, their economic power gives them political and social pull with local government and bank officials. At the other end of the scale, the smaller a man's land, the less likely he is to get credit. Tenants and sharecroppers, with no title to their land to offer as collateral for a loan, have serious problems getting any credit at all. They are dependent on their landlord to provide the extra inputs needed. As his part of the bargain he will often insist on increasing the rent for tenants and for sharecroppers on pushing up his share of the crop or converting it to a higher rent in cash. As for landless labourers, the only benefits they can hope to gain are through the additional employment available. But there may be such a surplus of them that wages do not increase as a result. And as we shall see, the mechanization that has often accompanied the Green Revolution may wipe out as many jobs as the new seeds create, or more. Access to the advice and help of government extension workers, and even to supplies of the new seeds and fertilizer, may be just as unevenly distributed as credit. Government programmes in the early phases often concentrated quite deliberately on the best-endowed areas, believing they would produce the greatest quantity of extra food, and on the richest farmers, believing they would be more adaptable to new methods, and more influential in persuading other farmers to adopt them. As economist Ingrid Palmer has pointed out about the Philippines: 'Prime consideration was not based on need, but on the chances of duplicating the glittering laboratory successes under cosseted field conditions.' This meant picking out the best-favoured areas – which were already enjoying higher yields and greater wealth than the rest. So the gap between rich and poor regions widened. It meant picking out 'progressive' farmers (usually the richest), and giving them a package of new seeds, chemical, credit and advice. The idea was that the new seeds would propagate themselves by the demonstration effect – when conservative neighbours saw the fantastic harvest their go-ahead colleagues reaped, they too would want to follow suit. Because of this unequal access to credit, supplies and advice, the poor and the small everywhere tended to introduce the new technology later and less than the rich and the big. In the Kandy district of Sri Lanka, for example, only a quarter of farms under two acres had land under the latest high-yielding varieties in 1972, against nearly two thirds of the farms above six acres. Farmers already lucky enough to belong to major irrigation schemes were more than twice as likely to be using the latest varieties than those in minor schemes.

The incomes of farmers growing the new seeds can be anything up to double their incomes with the old varieties. So the rich get richer. And the poor can easily get poorer: the increased rice production brought about by the Green Revolution may bring the price of rice down in real terms. So dryland farmers, or smallholders still using the old varieties, may earn less for their crop than before and become even more marginal and more vulnerable to losing their land.

So it is wrong to blame the technology of the Green Revolution for all the social ills that have accompanied it. It has increased regional inequalities. But within regions, it has been the pre-existing social and political inequalities that have diverted the benefits into the hands of the few.

The mean machine

Throughout labour-rich Asia, machinery is being introduced to save labour. Food production is increased – but the ability of the poor masses to buy it is reduced. Starvation spreads in the midst of plenty.

Technical advances that improve the productivity of the land, such as new seeds, fertilizers, irrigation, actually create more jobs as well as more food. These are the kind that developing countries ought to be pursuing. But individual farmers are introducing innovations that increase the productivity per worker. These produce more food at the cost of destroying jobs.

We have already seen the sad impact of sickles and rice mills in Indonesia. In this continent where there is a vast surplus of workers crying out for employment, mechanization is eliminating jobs at every stage of food production from ploughing and irrigation to threshing and milling. Tractors are among the worst culprits. Surveys have found that they cut the amount of labour required for land preparation by around one third. Farmers seem to be introducing them, not so much to save on labour costs, but to allow them to prepare land more quickly between successive crops. In Sri Lanka a small tractor can plough an acre in six to nine hours, against twenty hours for a pair of buffaloes and 128 hours for a man with a mammoty hoe. Tractors are spreading faster in Asia than on any other continent. Numbers in Africa rose from 250,000 in 1965 to 400,000 in 1975, and in Latin America from 370,000 to 580,000. In Asia the numbers rose from 330,000 to 1·21 millions in the same ten years. The fastest rises followed the Green Revolution. This speeded up mechanization for two reasons: first, it provided the extra profits farmers needed to afford tractors, and second, it made the element of time more crucial in getting a second or a third crop into the ground each year. So in India the number of tractors rose from 66,000 in 1967 to 215,000 in 1975; in Pakistan from 12,500 to 38,000; and in Sri Lanka from 9,700 to 15,800.

A study of the effects of tractorization in Pakistan illustrates the stark contrast of gain for some and loss for others. In 1965, the World Bank loaned some $17 million to Pakistan to be reloaned to farmers to finance farm mechanization. Only larger farmers were eligible for the loans. The tractors proved a superb investment: the rate of return on these farmers' outlay was a handsome 57 per cent, and as a result of their increased incomes they were able to expand their average farm size from forty-five acres to 109 acres. But only one acre in five of the extra was previously uncultivated. Over half was land that the farmers had previously rented out to tenants, or land bought from other, usually non-tractorized farmers. The farmers, now able to work a much larger area with a smaller workforce, evicted an average of more than four tenants each. The study concluded that each tractor had destroyed an average of five jobs. Overall result: incomes and wealth of a few individuals massively boosted, food production increased, but many people deprived of their access to land and work. The impact of mechanization in labour surplus areas is clearly socially destructive and must increase poverty and speed up the exodus to the cities.

So tractors not only eliminate jobs: they also seem to be powerful engines of inequality between owners and non-owners. In Sri Lanka hiring rates are so high that a tractor can pay for itself in less than two years, producing returns of 50 or 60 per cent. 'Credit-worthy' farmers could borrow money to buy one at only 15 per cent interest rates. In one survey, tractor owners were found to have earned enough extra cash to double their landholdings within a few years, usually at the expense of non-owners. These were going deep into debt to pay the extortionate hiring rates, and the tractor owners were often acting the role of usurers as well. Tractors were creating what one writer described as a 'new feudalism of technology'.

In Asia and the Middle East, even water provides jobs for the men who lift it onto fields. Pumpsets have been the tractors of water. In one south Indian district, for example, the number of electric pumpsets rose from nil to 120,000 in just fourteen years. Pumpsets have their own particularly vicious way of increasing inequality: in areas with inadequate rainfall they mine the underground water so fast that the water table drops and only expensive tubewells can reach down to it. The hand-dug wells of the poor dry up. Pumpsets cleverly transform water, a gift of God, into a privilege accessible only to the already privileged.

Innovation in agriculture is, of course, essential if food production is going to keep ahead of or level with people production. But innovation in Asia (and for that matter in Latin America and to some extent in Africa) has been introduced in an unequal society, in unequal ways that have increased inequality and poverty. The solution to the problems thrown up by the Green Revolution and mechanization must lie, not in resisting progress, but in land reform, equal access to credit and advice, and encouraging labour-intensive ways of boosting food production.

Green Revolution into Red?

The father of the Green Revolution, plant geneticist Norman Borlaug, won the 1970 Nobel Peace Prize for his contribution to enlarging the world's food supply. But the Green Revolution and mechanization have opened up great gulfs in rural society. They have brought social upheaval and often violent conflict into the countryside. The Green Revolution, in many places, has turned red, red with blood, and red with the radicalization of the peasantry.

Increased profits and the decline in traditional morality have lead to more and more bitter battles over the division of the spoils. Battles between landlord and tenant, as the landlords try to monopolize the extra profits to be got from the new technology by evicting tenants and rehiring them as labourers. Battles between landlords and landless, as labourers, seeing the wealth generated by the Green Revolution and wanting more of it for themselves, try to force landlords into increasing their wages. In rural Asia there are always false problems diverting the poor's attention from the central conflict with landlords: communal scapegoats such as the tribals or Moslems in India, the Chinese traders in Malaysia or Indonesia. But open class conflict is now emerging.

In Indochina the increasingly intolerable agrarian situation won support for communist guerillas. In the Philippines, as debt turned owners into tenants on their former land, peasant rebellion spread. In India embryonic peasant movements have emerged and violent clashes between landless labourers and landlords are increasing in frequency. Eastern India's Naxalite movement gained most publicity with its programme of exterminating the leading landlords in each village. But small-scale confrontations occur almost daily in many states, often misinterpreted in the Indian press as caste conflicts because usually a single caste owns all the land and another caste, often untouchable or tribal, makes up the bulk of the agricultural labourers.

One of the most horrific of these incidents occurred in 1968, in the East Thanjavur district of Tamil Nadu state. When the landless labourers formed a union to press for higher wages, the landlords got together into an association to organize resistance. Whenever the union called a strike, the landlords would bring in labourers from other villages, and, inevitably, clashes would break out between strikers and strike breakers. The landlords offered to rehire the labourers, but only if they disbanded their union and paid fines of 250 rupees each (equal to about three months' wages). The labourers refused, and in the heated discussions an agent of the landlords was killed. So the landlords organized a revenge expedition, piled into trucks, armed with sticks, swords and guns, and descended on the labourers' hamlet of Kilvenmani. They rounded up men, women and children, drove them all into one hut, and set fire to it. More than forty people were burned alive. The Madras High Court acquitted all twenty-five landlords accused of the crime − but sentenced the eight labourers involved in killing the landlords' agent to long terms of imprisonment.

Similar clashes have occurred in many states:

*In south Gujarat untouchables have been killed by landlords or by crop guards (landless labourers hired to prevent other landless labourers from stealing crops). In return labourers have broken up threshers and tractors.

*In the Cuddapah district of Andhra Pradesh, *harijans* had been allotted plots of fallow land by the government. As access to land would reduce the *harijans'* dependence on wage labour, local landlords drove them off their plots. In July 1974, 500 armed members of the landowning Reddy caste attacked the untouchable village of Ramanpalle, wounding thirty villagers and burning 118 huts to the ground.

*Also in July 1974, four landless labourers of Devbaath in the Punjab were murdered by landlords of the dominant Jat caste as they were meeting to organize a strike. The police had been asked in advance to give protection, but arrived fifteen minutes after the shooting.

*In a Maharashtra village studied by sociologist Maria Mies, the landowning caste of Gujars had acquired the land in the last century by abusing their position as rent collectors under the British. The local population of tribals or *adivasis* became landless labourers. In May 1971, during a famine, several of them went to the biggest local landlord to ask for grain. He gave them four kilos each, but then called in the police and accused them of looting his granary. The police arrested the tribals on their way home. The Gujars turned up in force and demanded that the police open fire on the *adivasis*, and when the police refused, opened fire themselves, wounding many and killing one. In 1972 the tribals formed an organization to push for higher wages and the return of land fraudulently acquired by the landlords. They began cultivating a disused forest reserve. But repression won through. Local police were doubled in strength and evicted the *adivasis* from the forest. The Gujars imported labourers from outside the district. The movement's back was broken.

The situation in many parts of Asia is moving towards Latin American degrees of polarization on the land, between prosperous landlords enjoying the benefits of modern technology on the one hand, and on the other the mass of rural labourers and marginalized smallholders. The same mechanisms of repression are evolving: the poor are denied access to land and forced to rely on wage labour. Landlords resort to direct violence to repress any resistance or organization among the peasants, and the local police and judiciary act as their accomplices. The peasants are weak precisely because they are poor. They have no money to buy guns or to buy off the police. They have no reserves to sustain a strike, no strike pay or social security. They are hungry, and the hungriest of them can always be tempted to break strikes or work for less than the others. Their poverty prevents them from organizing effectively to improve their wages, and because they are disorganized they remain poor.

6. Land or Death in Latin America

In rural Africa, the roots of poverty lie in the soil and man's relationship with it, the fatal impact of population and farming methods on a poor land. In Asia, poverty and growing inequality are the inevitable outcome of population growth, land shortage and the dynamics of rural society. But in Latin America, the origins of poverty and inequality are in the ancient and continuing inhumanity of man to man, in naked, ruthless and often violent exploitation. The term feudalism has often been used to describe the powers of big landlords in Latin America over labourers, tenants and smallholders. But feudalism, in medieval Europe, was a reciprocal affair. Serfs would provide their lord with labour and produce, and in exchange he would protect them from attack. And there were customary limits which exploitation could not cross. Latin American feudalism is a one-way business. The peasant has duties, the landowner rights. The peasant gives, the landowner takes. Even legal limits to exploitation are studiously ignored, because at local level the landlord *is* the law. The only limit is set by the fact that the landlord needs a continuing supply of cheap labour: the labourer must receive enough income to survive and to reproduce himself. Not enough to stay healthy, or to save many of his children from premature death.

The violent heritage

The explanation for Latin America's unique degree of inequality, exploitation and injustice has to be sought in the colonial past. For, incredibly, the society of conquest still survives today in most rural areas, more than four and a half centuries after the event. The conquistadors, Cortes, Pizarro and their followers, came to the Americas in search of wealth, status and power. They had seen men become noble, win fame and fortune, in the reconquest of Iberia from the Moors; the

New World offered a fresh opportunity to do the same. The conquerors came to settle, but unlike the lower- and middle-class Europeans who colonized North America, they did not come to work, but to live, in true noble style, off the labour of others. Naked pillage was their first strategy. When they had stolen the entire accumulated wealth of the Aztecs, the Incas, the Chibchas and other empires, they turned to more long-term enterprises: mining silver and gold, and carving themselves great estates out of the best of Indian land, a process 'legalized' in grants from the Spanish kings known as *mercedes reales*.

But land is useless without labour. Most of the history of rural Latin America is the history of the stratagems by which the conquistadors and their heirs secured a continuous supply of cheap and obedient labour for the land they had expropriated. In the Caribbean and the coastal areas, massacres and epidemics wiped out the local population, so African slaves had to be imported to work on plantations. In the interior, especially in the Andes, where the original Indian populations did survive, the problem was how to convert an independent peasantry living in communistic communities into a class of virtual serfs. The first of the institutions invented for this purpose was the *encomienda* or entrustment: each of the leading conquistadors was allocated a quota of Indians from whom he could demand labour and tribute. In exchange, he was supposed to teach them the rudiments of Christianity and the superior virtues of European civilization. The Spanish queen Isabel created the *encomienda* in an edict of 1503 which encapsulates the history of the continent: 'As we are informed that because of the excessive liberty enjoyed by the Indians, they avoid contact and community with the Spaniards to such an extent that they will not even work for wages, but wander about idle, and cannot be had by the Christians to convert to the holy Catholic faith ... I order you, our governor, that ... you will compel and force the Indians to associate with the Christians, and to work on their buildings, and to gather and mine the gold, and other metals, and to till the fields and produce food for the Christian inhabitants and dwellers.'

Indians were rounded up, often tortured and murdered to enforce compliance. Because of abuses, Charles V of Spain abolished the *encomienda* in 1520, but it has persisted, under a dozen different disguises, down to the present day. The most usual device was to deny Indians access to sufficient land for subsistence, thus forcing them to come and work for the Iberians. In Spanish America, the Indians were concentrated into *congregaciones*, in Brazil into *aldeias* or villages. Ostensibly this was so that they would be closer together for the priests to work on converting their souls, but the real purpose was to give the whites a chance to seize their land. The inland equivalent of slavery was peonage: Indians were given the right to cultivate a small plot on the worst land, in exchange for agricultural and even domestic work on the landlord's estate, and labour to build and maintain roads, bridges and so on. Under the Incas and the Aztecs, unpaid communal labour on the roads was traditional: the conquistadors took over and perverted this work for the common good for their own private ends. It still persists, legally or illegally, in many areas. In Ecuador it is known as *huasipingo*, in Chile it goes under the name of *inquilinaje*. In pre-revolution Peru, for example, it involved working 160 days a year on the landlord's land and giving unspecified extra labour as and when needed as nightwatchman, house servant, pig attendant and firewood collector. In north-east Brazil, tenants and sharecroppers were subjected to eight to fifteen days' free labour a year on the landlords' fields, over and above their rents. This system was known as *cambão*, the yoke, because, as the peasant organizer Francisco Julião wrote: 'The yoke ox and the peasant lead the same lives, bound, staggering, worn down by a task which only finishes for the one in the slaughterhouse and for the other in the grave.' The liberal regimes of the nineteenth century passed legislation restricting the worst of these forms of personal servitude, and abolishing slavery. The landlords ignored the laws, and introduced indentured labour and debt bondage to take the place of slavery. Peasants would be given loans to pay for food and clothing, which had to be bought at inflated prices in the landlord's own shops. The loans would be repaid with labour, but they never grew any less, and when a man died his debt would be inherited by his son.

Side by side with the huge landed estate, the *latifundio*, has evolved the *minifundio* or tiny smallholding, usually too small to support a family. These two extremes are almost inseparable in Latin America, and there is very little in between them. The *minifundio* is the reverse side of the coin, the residue left over when the great estates had engulfed all the land they wanted and pressganged all the labour they needed to work it. Smallholding stems from two roots – one is the class of common Iberian soldiers and later poor settlers who were not 'entrusted' with armies of Indian labourers and hence took only as much land as they could work themselves. The other is the land remaining to the Indian communities. Originally this was held in common and worked in equal parcels, rather as it was in traditional Africa. But much of it was divided up into small private plots with negotiable freehold titles by the liberal reformers of the nineteenth century. Many of the better *minifundios* were swallowed up by the *latifundios* through purchase, encroachment or real estate fraud. The rest survive, diminishing in size with each generation through division for inheritance.

It is important to remember with Latin America that inequality did not evolve gradually, and by mechanisms many people reluctantly accepted as fair game, as it has done in Asia and is doing now in Africa. It originated in the forcible enslavement of Africans and the violent expropriation of Indians, and has been maintained ever since by naked violence.

Poles apart

Wealth and income are polarized in rural Latin America to an extreme found in no other part of the world except that other society founded in violent injustice, South Africa. The vast majority are either landless labourers or owners of land so marginal that it cannot support a small family. A 1966 survey of seven nations by the Inter-American Commission for Agricultural Development found that 61 per cent of farm families in Argentina came into this category, as did 68 per cent in Brazil and 70 per cent in Chile and Colombia, and 88 per cent in Ecuador, Guatemala and Peru. Landless labourers make up more than half the active population in Chile, Uruguay, Costa Rica and Argentina, and between 40 and 50 per cent in Colombia, Mexico, Jamaica and Nicaragua.

Landownership is no guarantee of livelihood. In Ecuador, Guatemala and Peru nine out of ten farms were too small to support a family with two working adults. These sub-family farms were squeezed onto between 7 per cent (Peru) and 17 per cent (Ecuador) of the total farm area. In Colombia two thirds of farms were below subsistence level and occupied only 5 per cent of the land.

At the other end of the scale came the large estates (big enough to employ twelve or more people). Nowhere did these make up more than 7 per cent of the number of farms. But they occupied between 37 per cent (Argentina) and 82 per cent (Chile and Peru) of the total area. The average large estate in this category was 500 times bigger than the typical sub-family farm in Colombia, 570 times bigger in Brazil, 590 times in Argentina and 900 times in Peru. In Ecuador it was 1,500 times bigger, in Chile 2,200 and in Guatemala 27,000 times.

Incomes are distributed no less unequally. In Chile the bottom 70 per cent of the rural population got only one third of the total income. In Colombia the lowest 85 per cent received just 9 per cent of the income in one zone. The average large landowner had anything from eighty to two hundred times the income of the average labourer.

Brazil, land of Latin America's economic miracle, São Paulo, bristling with skyscrapers and factories, and deafened with the din of interminable traffic jams. Rio, where playboys on 500 cc motorbikes roar up and down the promenade at Ipanema beach, past the brilliant white marble, glass and steel façades of the wealthier apartments.

And land of grinding poverty: knocked-up timber shanties on steep hillsides around Recife; mud huts, misery and demoralized, inebriated *machismo* in the rural north-east, where life is frozen in the social relations of a violent past.

In Serra Pelada, a small hamlet in the state of Rio Grande do Norte, the adobe and bamboo shacks of the workers straggle along the dirt road, penned outside the barbed wire round the big estates and their palatial ranch houses. In a rough field, a gang of six labourers are clearing weeds with their hoes. Every one of them is emaciated, with wiry calves showing under rolled-up trousers, and skinny, sinewy torsos. Working in a row, they hack the scrub back along a broad strip. There is no vigour in their movements, no enthusiasm. Their faces are lined, immeasurably sad. At the end of the strip they trudge back to the bottom of the field and start again. All of them have patches on their clothes. Two have shirts torn almost into shreds.

Like all the labourers of Serra Pelada, they have no land of their own, not even a garden patch by the house where they could grow beans and cassava. The state has benevolently decreed a minimum wage of thirty cruzeiros (about £1 or $2) per day. In practice this minimum is really a maximum. No landowner in the area will pay more. Effective trade unions and strikes have been banned under the military government since 1964 – the landlords' right to exploit the workers is backed by the full force of the state. And the population boom has weakened the workers in every way in their unequal battle with the landowners. To feed their huge families, most families subsist on cassava flour, pure calories with no protein. The men are physically weak, and there are many more of them than there are jobs. Landowners employ a skeleton staff of full-time workers, taking on extra hands as and when they need them for seasonal chores. Only at peak times can a labourer get a few weeks' solid work at a stretch – the rest of the year he may only get two or three days a week after endless treks around the ranches, cap in hand. The landlords evade the minimum wage law by offering workers contracts, for example, sixty cruzeiros to clear a field that will take three or four days' work. If the worker can do it in less, well and good. If, like most, he is not getting enough calories for sustained labour, he will earn half the minimum wage. Because there is a large labour surplus, the landlords can always find takers to accept almost any wages or conditions they care to impose. And they themselves make sure there is a labour surplus, by keeping vast stretches of land abandoned under weeds and shrubs. If all this vacant land were worked, there would undoubtedly be enough employment for all the local men. As it is, people are dying of malnutrition and its effects while good land lies waste next to their homes.

The bald granite outcrop overlooking Serra Pelada, which gave it its name, has now brought an additional source of employment. Men chisel blocks out of solid rock for sixty cruzeiros a hundred stones. Women and children hammer the rough blocks into smaller chips and get twenty-five cruzeiros for a wheelbarrowful, or two days' work. The quarry owner sells the blocks for two or three times what he pays for them. His contribution is nil, except for ownership of the bare rock that is being quarried: the purchase of the land was nothing other than the purchase of the right to exploit the labour of local villagers. The Brazilian system rewards handsomely those who control capital or land, at the expense of those who do not.

Things are bad in Serra Pelada. The visibly decaying district capital of Itaipu is no more than four streets around a square, and a railway station where only one train passes each day. Fifty families every year abandon the struggle and head for the cities of Natal, Recife or São Paulo. The mayor is a forty-eight-year-old former labourer, Geraldo Luis de Oliveira, whose screwed-up face, Coca-Cola cap and cheeky manner earned him the nickname of Mountain Hare. He is desperately concerned about local poverty, so acute that children are regularly abandoned (usually more a city problem). Geraldo has personally adopted and reared four such children. Beneath the huge portraits of Presidents Medici and Geisel in his living room, he told me that local men looking for work often sold themselves into debt bondage just to get a job to feed them. Labour contractors from the booming Amazon basin would pass through, offering 'free' transport, food, shelter and clothes in exchange for two years' bonded labour without wages. At the end of this period, the man would in theory be free. In fact he would have run up more debts for food supplies and remain in bondage until he got too old or sick to be able to work well. (I was told in the Amazon basin that if a man tried to escape and was caught, he would often be killed.) The Mountain Hare informed me that only the week before a lorry-load of men who had sold themselves into bondage left Itaipu for the Amazon.

There is, in Itaipu and places like it, little sign of peasant resistance to their subjection. Repression has done its job and is reinforced by physical and spiritual weakness. The people here are extremely open, yet I wondered if their honest answers to the questions of a European were not just another symptom of ancient habits of compliance and passivity.

The *latifundio* has succeeded in guaranteeing large, secure incomes for its owners: but it has been a dismal failure at adopting new technology to boost food production. Only a minority of large estates have been able to adapt themselves to the mechanical and managerial techniques of modern farming, despite the fact that they have the funds and local influence necessary to do so.

So the familiar dualism of Africa and Asia is present here too. In the Magdalena valley, Colombia, you can see four-wheel-drive tractors ploughing hundred-hectare fields, combine harvesters trundling through man-high maize, and crop-spraying planes taking off from private landing strips – while ragged sharecroppers and smallholders pause over their hoes or wooden ploughs to watch them fly over. In most Latin American countries there is on the one hand the modern estate, with rational management aiming at profit, using all the latest seeds, fertilizers, pesticides, irrigation techniques and mechanical aids, partly to scupper a restive labour force. But still in a minority. And on the other hand the traditional sector made up of *minifundios* and *latifundios*, using the Iberian ox-drawn scratch plough or even the hoe and foot plough of pre-Columbian days.

The *latifundio* is certainly not lacking in funds or local influence to help with modernization, so why does it not invest in modernizing itself? The answer lies precisely in the extreme degree of exploitation of labour under the *latifundio* system. This guarantees a high income to any owner, whether he is an efficient farmer or not. Investment in maintaining or increasing the degree of exploitation can pay off just as well as investing in modernization: landlords often have private armies of hired thugs ready to intimidate the peasant who dares to try to organize or to improve his conditions. Or they can bribe the local police and law courts to do the job for them. Like the landowners of Serra Pelada, they deliberately keep much of their land uncultivated – in the seven countries it surveyed, the Inter-American Commission for Agricultural Development found that on average five out of every six hectares of estate land were unused.

That staggering figure should alert us to the fact that the *latifundio* is not a profit-seeking, economically rational institution. The income it provides is so high that there is little incentive to increase it further. Land is owned primarily as a source of social prestige and political influence. City professionals or businessmen often feel obliged to have their *finca* or *hacienda* up-country. Land has long been a provider of instant status, as well as a safe hedge against the insane rates of inflation that often reign in Latin America. And landownership brings political pull, because the landlord often controls the votes of his tenants and labourers. Modernization, with efficient administrators instead of slave drivers, and rational hiring and firing instead of a captive serf population, would in fact undermine the social and political rationale that motivates most landowners.

Attempts to change the system, if only for the sake of modernizing agriculture, have nearly always been rebuffed, because representatives of landowners often control political power too. The system was so unequal that an industrial bourgeoisie could not, until very recently, emerge to challenge the power of landed interests. This was because the poverty in which the majority were kept restricted the potential market for manufacturers.

Life on a postage stamp: the minifundios

The minute smallholding has been just as much of an obstacle to agricultural progress. With overworked soil supporting an increasing burden of population, smallholders do not have the capital to buy better equipment and inputs, and the political system often blocks their access to credit.

Minifundistas crowd onto marginal land, steep hillsides, eroded moonscapes. In north-east Brazil they spread out into the parched, inhospitable *sertão* or backlands, where poverty has spawned millenarian religious movements like the rebellion of Antonio Conselheiro, described in that great classic of Brazilian literature, Euclydes da Cunha's *Os Sertões*.

On the northern shores of Lake Titicaca, 12,500 feet up in the Andes, cold winds sweep over the barren, treeless *altiplano*. Quechua and Aymara Indians have lived here since time beyond memory. Legend has it that here the sun sent down two of his children, the first Incas Manco Capac and Mama Huaco, to teach men the elements of civilization. Around AD 1,000 the lake was the centre of the mysterious advanced societies that built the ruined city of Tiahuanaco and the *chullpas*, towering cyclopean tombs that haunt the hillsides by grim Lake Sillustani. The area was once prosperous. Ladders of ancient stone terraces climb up the steep slopes almost to the peaks.

Now they are abandoned, and the Puno region is one of the poorest in Peru, with an income per head of one tenth of the Peruvian average. The smallholders here began as Indian communities, but their land was divided into individual plots under misguided nineteenth-century legislation and has now reached an advanced state of fragmentation.

Carmen Zea has around a hectare of arable land. Aged sixty, he does not have the straight nose of the typical Indian: there is Spanish blood there, somewhere back along the line. He is reluctant to be photographed, for his sweater is full of holes, his ragged trilby hat is caked with sweat and dust, and he is barefoot. His land is split up into several widely scattered plots. To cultivate them he uses an ancient wooden plough with a flat iron tip, pulled by two oxen. He uses no fertilizer. He keeps his cattle's dung to burn as fuel.

To supplement the meagre crop of potatoes and *quinhua* (a cereal) produced by the fields, Zea and his family have several sidelines, none of which pay more than a pittance. They were all busy at it when I arrived. Zea's wrinkled wife, wispy grey hair straggling from under a battered grey bowler hat, was spinning wool from a hank onto a primitive wooden spindle. Zea himself was spinning too, pivoting the spindle in the broken bottom of a round pot. His twenty-four-year-old daughter, in pigtails and bowler, was laboriously weaving strips for a poncho on a low handloom pegged into the ground, and his grandson, shirtless under a thin jumper, pants covered in a dozen patches, was beating reeds between two stones into strands that would be woven into ropes.

Zea also keeps livestock: four cattle and ten sheep. The pasture land is poverty stricken – a few clumps of wiry *ichu* grass widely scattered between expanses of thin moss and bare ground. Through the dry season the cattle have to be fed with donkey loads of *totora* reed from the Indians who live on floating islands of the stuff in the middle of the lake. Zea calculates that it costs him 18,000 soles (at that time around £160 or $320) to feed up a heifer or bullock into a saleable two-year-old. On the market a first-rate animal will fetch 20,000 soles, but Zea thinks he will be lucky if he can get back even the cost of his feed. So the family are poor. The adobe walls of their huts – shaped into curious pyramids to insulate them against the extremes of hot days and cold nights – are cracking and crumbling. Revolting pieces of pig meat are hanging to dry over a rope slung on the wall: a lower jaw, an upper jaw with eyes attached, and hunks of desiccated skin and fat. 'We are in a sorry state,' Zea lamented. 'The rains are two months late, I've not been able to plant my potatoes and I think some of the sheep may die this year. There's no pasture for them.'

To keep alive, Zea had to sell one of his bullocks. I went with him to the cattle market at Huancané. Here, on a hilly patch of bare red rock, peasants rosy-cheeked from the wind and small-eyed from the sun sit with their cows on the end of a rope, and swig local gin from tiny metal cups. Many are under the same pressure as Zea: they have no choice but to sell, and there are too many cattle for sale. The buyers from the coast know it's their market and are picking only the best animals at low prices. Zea got a single offer of 16,000 soles for his black and white bullock and despite long bargaining the buyer would not go one iota higher. Zea turned him down, waited a couple of hours more in gradually deepening despair, then gave up and went home, knowing that he might have to sell at a loss at the next market. Puno province would not be rich at the best of times: but its poverty is aggravated by these city traders who buy cattle and wool cheap and sell clothes and tin roofs dear. As the region has absolutely no industry, much of its surplus is siphoned off by the industrial cities of the coast. There is nothing left to invest in improving agriculture. No wonder so many of the young people are heading for the shanty towns of Lima and Arequipa, leaving an ageing population behind.

Counter-reformation on the land

The conditions of the rural majority in Latin America have ceased to be tolerable. The spread of education and literacy has made peasants aware of the welfarist rhetoric of their governments, and they want a share in the benefits. Their expectations have been raised and will not subside again. As a result, the agrarian situation has become the most explosive political issue in the continent. On the pattern of the successful Cuban revolution, rural guerilla forces sprang up all over the place in the late fifties and the sixties, in Peru, Colombia, Venezuela, Bolivia, Guatemala, Nicaragua. Many of them collapsed through sectarianism or were decimated by effective repression by US trained and equipped armed forces.

But the issue has not gone away and increasingly the trend is to organize peasants into trade-union style associations to press for land reform, acting as pressure groups and defenders of peasants' rights. Most of these groups are careful to remain within the law, but they often meet with repression in spite of that.

The mood among governments has changed, too, as urban, industrial and technocratic interests have gained more influence and press, if not for social justice, at least for a rational, commercial agriculture free of feudal taints. Even the hardliners realize that total repression is not the answer. Repression works out much cheaper if it is combined with token reform. And in the early sixties, the United States, afraid that revolution might spread over from Cuba, tried to push governments in the direction of reform. The Charter of the Alliance for Progress, signed at Punta del Este in 1961, called for 'the effective transformation of unjust structures and systems of land tenure and use'. It was one of the first expressions of the view that has now become accepted wisdom, that social reform is just as important as economic growth.

Many governments, afraid to lose economic and military aid, complied on paper with the Charter requirements. There was a boom in land reform legislation and land reform institutes mushroomed in every capital. But – except in a few countries such as Peru, pre-Pinochet Chile, pre-Banzer Bolivia – the reality fell far short of the promise. Land reform remained a slogan, or a cunning stratagem to quieten down the rebellious peasants while giving as few concessions as humanly possible. The phenomenon known as 'counter-reform' was born. Economist Ernesto Feder defines this as the bundle of policies or practices which tend to undo land reform or prevent it from happening. Tokenism and counter-reform have been the order of the day in most Latin American countries.

Colombia's land reform is a typical example. It was instituted to defuse guerilla actions and spontaneous peasant rebellions, which in the 1950s and early 1960s succeeded in setting up autonomous zones in the central provinces. The first land reform law was introduced in 1960. It was a purely cosmetic measure; but it raised expectations among the landless, and peasants started invading and occupying the estates they worked on. The government responded with a two-pronged approach. With one hand they threw a few more crumbs before the peasants, with an extension of the land reform laws in 1968 and again in 1974. And with a boot, in the shape of the army and police, they stamped down fiercely on occupations wherever they arose. And they set up a government-sponsored peasants' organization, the National Associations of Peasants (ANUC), to channel peasant energy away from violence into harmless pleading and petitioning. The system, as at the end of 1976 when I visited Colombia, was one of diabolical cunning. Even the officials of INCORA, the Colombian Institute for Agrarian Reform, admitted that it placed all the cards in the hands of the landowners. There is no ceiling on landholdings, above which expropriation would be automatic. In practice, INCORA will only step in to try to buy a property if the peasants of an area organize themselves into a branch of ANUC and formally request to be given land. This takes time, and limits land reform to areas of active discontent. INCORA then undertakes a thorough and expensive agronomic, geological and social survey of the area and decides whether it is suitable for a 'project'. If it decides it wants to buy land, it first has to approach the landlord and negotiate a price with him. Usually, only those with poor land or especially tiresome labourers are willing to sell voluntarily.

If the landlord does not want to sell, the matter goes to law, which is long, laborious, formalistic and nitpicking. Some cases have dragged on for eight years. The law is so weighted in favour of landlords that for every ten properties INCORA has tried to buy (and these were all estates that, on the face of it, seemed candidates for takeover) it has been able to acquire only one. The legislation has more holes in it for landlords to escape through than a colander. For example, 'well-exploited land' is exempt. To be considered well exploited, an estate has to be producing only 80 per cent of the average regional yields, and these are low because landlords understate their production figures to avoid tax. Even if a piece of land is badly exploited, the owner can still save it if he dreams up a plan of improvements: 95 per cent of the lands INCORA surveys end up by being considered well exploited.

The few landlords who cannot squeeze through any of these

holes have other tactics at their disposal. From 1968, landowners who let their land to tenants became more liable for
takeover. The landowners' answer: evict the tenants and rehire them as labourers. In the five years after 1968 there were
twice as many evictions as in the previous twenty-five. The
evicted tenants swelled the surplus army of labourers and kept
wages down. So a law designed to improve the peasants' lot
was, characteristically, perverted so as to worsen it.

Some of the files at INCORA's headquarters on the outskirts of Bogotá consist of several volumes a fist thick. The
story of one of these, relating to a typical *latifundio* in the
provinces, shows what is really happening in rural areas, and
the deceits, confusions and confrontations in the battle between landlord and landless. INCORA first inspected the
estate in July 1969 and found a prime candidate for expropriation: 208 hectares, supporting only 182 cows, and slowly going to rack and ruin: 'Some pastures could hardly be found
for weeds. The whole estate was dominated and drowned by
them.' Ten tenant families occupied eleven hectares, farming
between a quarter hectare and two hectares each. But delays
followed, and two years later the landlord, a Mr Rayos, personally approached INCORA and invited them to pay another
visit. The tenants had disappeared. There was no sign of them,
their houses, or their crops. They were said to have left their
land voluntarily, and the local police inspector obligingly confirmed this – though how he happened to be there to witness
their departure was not explained.

In fact, the tenants had not disappeared, they had been temporarily evicted. Soon afterwards, they were reinstated on
shorter and more oppressive contracts, by which they could
use the land for a year and a half on condition they handed it
back cleared of weeds and sown with guinea grass. There were
now sixty-one families, farming less than half a hectare each.
By November 1971 they had resolved to form themselves into
a branch of ANUC, led by Melqueades Roa Silveira, aged
thirty-eight, father of six. In February 1973 they wrote to
INCORA asking it to buy the estate: 'We haven't a metre of
land to work on, but we want to be useful to society and to

help alleviate the national food shortage. We hope our plea will be heard.' Six of the twenty-four signatures were blotchy purple thumb-prints.

The owner replied denying that they were his tenants, claiming they were illegal invaders: 'The peasants say they signed a contract. This is a lie as the contracts cannot be located. I swear on my word as a gentleman that I did not sign a contract with them.' Rayos alleged that the peasants had killed his cows, and no less a personage than the mayor of the local town obligingly confirmed that he had found a yearling bullock with its head cut off, a buried heifer and other animal remains. This allegation may have been true, because at the same time the peasants had gone to the police accusing Rayos of unleashing his cattle onto their crops to harass them, and they might have killed the animals in retaliation. At the court hearing the judge sided with the landlord (as the police chief and mayor had done before him). He found that the peasants themselves were responsible as they had left the gates open. His judgement is worth quoting to illustrate the legalistic jargon that helps to exclude the poor, the ignorant and the illiterate from the process of law: 'If it is necessary that there should be the real or presumed existence of an illicit deed for a penal investigation to proceed, it is obvious that if an investigation has started in the absence of this prerequisite, or once started its non-existence has been established, then a negative phenomenon of processability is produced.'

By now INCORA had reopened the case and in March 1974 made another survey which recommended the estate as suitable for a project involving 206 families. Desperate by now to rid himself of the troublesome tenants, Rayos appears to have tried a new form of harassment. According to the peasants, he paid thirty or forty other families to invade the land and drive the rightful tenants out. The mayor did nothing to stop this, and had to be reminded by the Procurator General of Colombia of his duty to protect tenants.

But the hired stooge invaders had not left. In November 1974 Melqueades Roa Silveira wrote to the President of Colombia, complaining that Rayos was trying to provoke them into fighting with the new invaders. This would give the police an excuse to intervene and drive them out of their homes. (This is a common tactic in Colombia.) Not to be outmanoeuvred, Rayos also wrote to the President, complaining that INCORA was supporting a bunch of criminals, and that he had to sell his cattle off at derisory prices to stop them being murdered. He prefaced his plea for presidential help with the tell-tale remark: 'We are decisive supporters of your government and we brought our humble votes to establish it.'

In August 1976 INCORA offered Rayos 2,000 pesos an acre (about £40 or $80) for his estate. Rayos refused, claiming it was worth eight times as much. When I left Colombia an INCORA lawyer was wading through the three-hundred-page file to decide whether to go to court or not. Seven years after the first visit, and the legal battle had not even begun.

I have quoted the case at length because it illustrates the resources landlords use in their fight against tenants and land reform laws, not only in Latin America but in parts of the Middle East and Asia too. They can usually rely on local police, local judges, local administrators to back them up. They do not hesitate to break the law if necessary, and usually get away with it. And rural poverty is so desperate that there are always enough peasants willing to fight their own kind rather than the landlords, just to get a living to keep alive a bit longer. In this case the peasants had the help of an association, ANUC, and a relatively incorruptible national institution, INCORA. More often than not, poor peasants would stand alone against the combined weight of the establishment.

It is no accident that Colombia's land reform law gives landlords so many loopholes. Many of the legislators who drafted it are landowners, or at the very least depend on the votes that landowners can deliver. And so, like legislators in other Latin American countries, they can do little to infringe landlord power, and so they go on being dependent on it.

The lucky few

Even in a token land reform like Colombia's, some peasants are lucky enough to be the tokens. Some 120,000 families had been given land by 1976. Most of this was carved out of the vast uncultivated areas owned by the state in the grassy plains of the *llanos* or the virgin Amazon rainforest. A few peasants even won land near their own villages and formed cooperatives to work it, but there were only a few dozen of these in the whole country. They get credit, supplies, organizational help and advice unstintingly. They become model pilot projects, while the majority of their brothers remain in neglected poverty.

One of these projects is El Alivio in Tolima province, site of some of most violent conflicts between peasants and land-owners in the fifties and sixties. The name means repose and the setting fits it: cradled in the Magdalena valley between two arms of the northern Andes, reached by a stony lane flanked by hedgerows where flocks of green parrots feed. When I arrived the president of the cooperative, José Presiado, a vigorous forty-year-old, was hosing down the estate's new tractor and harrow outside their shiny new barn. There are ten associates, with another sixty-eight dependants, growing rice on seventy acres of good irrigated land.

All of them are former day labourers. They were given the estate in 1972, after years of protracted struggle and repeated invasions lasting for a few days each. Wives and children used to come along too and were beaten up and thrown into police lorries along with their husbands. Presiado himself spent two months in gaol as an 'inciter of disorder'. 'We were all earning about forty pesos a day (75p or $1.50) and working only fifteen days a month. We lived in shacks with only one room, on the edge of the road or in a gully, because all the good flat land was taken for crops. We occupied only the estates belonging to doctors or lawyers in Bogotá: they had many hectares lying neglected while there were families dying of hunger.'

Today the farmers of El Alivio are doing very well for them-selves. They get two crops of rice a year, fetching them an annual net income of about £500 or $1,000 each. They own outright all their machinery, having paid off the loans. Each one has built himself the house of his dreams. The co-op secretary, José Mendoza, has seven rooms, portable TV, kerosene fridge, smooth concrete floors, three-piece suite and a well-stocked larder. There is piped water to a communal washing area, septic tanks for sewage, sizable vegetable gardens growing maize, beans, pumpkins. All the children were in school – before, none could afford the books or food. If anyone was ill, they all chipped in to pay the doctor's bill – as labourers they could not afford any treatment at all. Their prosperity showed just how much change could come over peasants' lives in Latin America, given real land reform and efficient farming. Yet there was a touch of sadness in their new lives. 'We have got our piece of land,' said Presiado. 'But we remember that our comrades still have none.' Out of seven hundred members of the local peasants' association, only seventy had benefited from this and other schemes. El Alivio was an oasis of prosperity and equality in a desert of continuing poverty and injustice. Its members were in a moral dilemma. 'Some Marxist students came here to visit,' Presiado told me. 'They said we were becoming petty bourgeois, that we shouldn't live like this, we should give it all up to go on fighting. Why? We live better now because we are working for ourselves. But we pay for José Mendoza to do a lot of work organizing the other peasants.'

Tokenism thus raises a few peasants above the many, co-opting the most militant leaders into the middle classes. A few sacrificial landowners' heads get tossed into the arena. But even the few who are forced to sell out get compensation, which they can go and invest in urban real estate, and become landlords again to the millions who have migrated to the cities because they could not survive on the land.

The settlers

The most common form of token reform in Latin America is no reform at all. It involves settling landless or marginal peasants on unused virgin land – instead of giving them the under-used land on the big estates. It requires no sacrifice from the landlord class. It lets the head of steam blow off the areas of most acute poverty – while doing nothing to change the feudal relations within those areas. Colombia, Venezuela, Peru, Bolivia and Brazil all have extensive colonization programmes, and the vast Amazon basin has been the main target area.

It was no accident that the Amazon area was never occupied by the conquistadors or by large numbers of spontaneous settlers. Seething with dangerous reptiles, insects and diseases, it is probably the most unhealthy place in the world. The soil is mostly infertile laterite, though there are narrow belts of alluvium along the river valleys that may be used for rice-growing. Aerial surveys have shown that only 4 per cent of soils in the region have even medium fertility. Clearing the forest is a laborious business, and once the tree cover is removed, soil degradation can progress rapidly.

This is the area Brazil has chosen to prove that it gives 'access to the land' to its poor peasants.

The forest is an endless woven carpet of dense, dark green crossed by the broad meanders of great coffee-coloured rivers. Signs of human activity – small patchwork clearings, curls of smoke and the thin red lines of dirt roads – are dwarfed against this immensity. But they are spreading fast. The Brazilian Amazon has the feel of a tropical wild west: boom towns strung out along dirt roads, ponies hitched to rails, ten-gallon hats and leather boots, and cowboys driving herds of cattle. But the backdrop is not wide-open spaces, but liana and creeper-strangled rainforest, and the steers are humpbacked zebu.

Settlers have been coming here for centuries in a slow trickle, erecting ramshackle homesteads in defiance of hostile nature. In the late nineteenth century the rubber boom brought in entrepreneurs, desperadoes and semi-slave *seringueiros* or rubber tappers. Others came to pan for diamonds or to collect brazil nuts from the majestic *castanheiros* that tower head and shoulders above the other trees. But settlements were sparse, scattered along the banks of navigable rivers, isolated by immense tracts of impenetrable jungle. The Amazon basin remained an unconquered mystery. The military regime took power in 1964 largely to prevent land reform in the north-east. It saw in the Amazon a pie-in-the-sky to offer the oppressed peasants to take their minds off rebellion. Moreover, it wanted to open up the vast region with its wealth of natural resources. And so, in the late sixties, the epic highways were driven through the forest from Cuiabá to Santarem, from Belém to Brasilia.

The five-thousand-kilometre Transamazonica, longest of them all, climbs and dips between thick stands of forest and glinting swamp. Exotic butterflies flutter as thick as fallen leaves and hairy green spiders crawl across the narrow two-lane track of red laterite dirt. Traffic is still only a trickle of dusty ranchers' Chevrolet pick-ups and timber trucks and every now and then a great yellow monster of a bulldozer flattening out the ruts and dents torn in the road surface by torrential downpours.

The colonization effort here is planned and executed by the National Institute for Colonization and Agrarian Reform (INCRA). Its local headquarters in the booming frontier town of Maraba are besieged daily by dozens of would-be settlers in battered hats and creased trousers, from Rio Grande do Norte, Ceará, Pernambuco, Bahia. In the whole Amazon basin INCRA has an unimaginable 350 million hectares, about two fifths of the area of the United States, under its jurisdiction. Some twelve million of these are now being settled in integrated colonization projects. It all looks impressive enough on paper. The director of the Maraba project, Dr Carlos Alberto, unfolded a coloured map of the 260 kilometres of highway he controls, to explain. For ten kilometres on either side of the road are small yellow rectangles showing the 100-hectare plots that are being given to individual families. Scattered here and there were green squares representing service areas where agricultural technicians, health posts and schools are concentrated.

Settlers must be over twenty and under sixty-one, with some experience of agriculture. They can buy the land for a give-away price of forty-seven cruzeiros (about £2 or $4) a hectare.

If they have no savings they can get a low-interest twenty-year loan. For the first six to twelve months they get a wage so they can feed their families while waiting for the first crops to ripen. Certainly most of the settlers have the right kind of origins. They are a hardy breed, like Sergio Silvapinto, a broad, sinewy Negro of forty-nine, who was a landless labourer in the state of Maranhão. For the past five years he has been the proud owner of 100 hectares of virgin rainforest. He started modestly, with five hectares, just to feed his family while he cleared more land. Now he has spread out into forty hectares, and grows rice, bananas, cassava, pineapple, lemons and beans, and grazes twenty-five head of cattle. Francesco Carvalho, a nervous, angular white of fifty-five, was a smallholder in the parched *sertão*, the backlands of the north-east. 'It's so dry that the *sertanejo* becomes obsessed with water,' he explained. 'I was ready to go anywhere at all in the world where it rained more. This land here – fifty hectares of it – is worth more than five hundred of *sertão*. Here I've got my five thousand coffee bushes and soon I'll be driving my own pick-up truck.'

The Brazilian colonization programme is a model exercise in the wrong way to alleviate rural poverty. The 100-hectare plots are so large that only a tiny minority can benefit. A family can only work, with its own labour, about ten hectares or less: so the settlers who have been lucky in the draw are taking on the many unlucky ones as labourers – Sergio Silvapinto employs three brothers, friends of his from back home, who are waiting in the long queue for a farm. So the old system of landlord and landless labourer is being re-created in the jungle.

And this is only the sector designed for smallholders. The lion's share of the Amazon, ninety kilometres deep behind the ten-kilometre smallholder strip, is being sold off in county and country-sized lots to private companies – many of them foreign – for exploration, mining, timber production or ranching. People like US entrepreneur D. K. Ludwig, who has bought up more than a million hectares of land on the Jari river to grow rice and timber and employs 8,000 workers. If the whole area had been allocated to smallholders or cooperatives, it could have had some effect on rural poverty. Instead, it was carving out of the trackless wilderness a replica of the exploitative system that dominated the rest of Brazil. But there is another factor of global importance: the clearing of the jungle is threatening the delicate ecology of the rainforest, one of the world's lungs replenishing its oxygen supplies. INCRA's rules specify that half the land should be left under forest or should grow tree crops. But it is impossible to police such a vast area. The jungle is being felled and fired indiscriminately and cattle are grazed on the impoverished scrub that grows to take its place. The highways cross endless wastelands of charred stumps. The graceful brazil nut trees, protected by law with heavy fines, stand dead, white and leafless, ghostly skeletons of the massacred jungle.

7. The Shrinking Earth: Ecological Threats

In 1977, the Food and Agriculture Organization and Unesco jointly published an alarming map of the spread of deserts across the world. Shaded in orange, pink and red were all the areas in danger of desertification. The coloured patches covered a major part of the developing world outside the rainy equatorial belt. In Latin America they stained north-east Brazil, central and northern Mexico and stretched right down the Andes as far as Chile. They ate into the Horn of Africa and much of the south-west of the continent. And without interruption they reached half way round the globe in a broad swathe from the Atlantic coast of the Sahara, right across north Africa and the Sahel, through the Middle East and Persia to Pakistan and north-west India.

There could be no more graphic expression of the ecological dangers that threaten so much food production, so many livelihoods in the developing countries.

The world is losing precious agricultural land at twice the rate that new land is being broken for farming. An area bigger than Great Britain is disappearing every year. Soil is being exhausted, eroded, blown away at the rate of two and a half billion tons per annum. By the end of the century the world may have to support one and a half times its present population on only three quarters of its present cultivated area.

In his report on the state of the environment in 1977, United Nations Environment Programme Director Mostafa Tolba warned that, if present trends continue, there would be only 0·15 hectares of farm land per person by the year 2000, half the 1975 level. Productivity would have to double merely to allow people to get the same amount of food as today. These were the figures on which he based that calculation: in 1975 there were 1,240 million hectares under cultivation. Over the next twenty-five years, perhaps another 300 million new hectares may be opened up. But over the same period 600 million hectares – half the entire 1975 cultivated area – may be lost. Of this, half will probably disappear under the ink-blot spread of cities, which are expanding horizontally twice as fast as their populations are growing, and over some of the best agricultural land at that. The other 300 million will be the toll of soil degradation.

At least half of the total erosion will be in the world's 45 million square kilometres of potentially productive but eco-logically precarious drylands, which stretch through a hundred nations. About 700 million people live in this zone, almost all of them in devolping countries, and 80 million live in areas that are currently undergoing rapid desertification.

Everywhere the deserts are advancing. In Sudan the southern edge of the Sahara moved south by 100 kilometres between 1958 and 1975. The Thar desert in Rajasthan is expanding by half a mile a year. The deserts don't march forwards on a solid front, like an army. Patches appear, like those at Aorema in Upper Volta, around centres of population or watering holes, then spread, link up with others, and finally merge into the desert itself.

The chief agent of what has been called a leprosy of the soil is man, the impact of his activities on highly sensitive and delicately balanced ecosystems. The prime factor in the process is population increase. The number of people in the Sahel, for example, is doubling every twenty-five to thirty years. We saw the consequences of this among settled farmers in Chapter 4: the cutting down of fallow periods, a progressive decline in the vegetation cover, increasing erosion. As population goes on growing, cultivation is pushed into areas that are entirely unsuitable for agriculture, and there the process progresses even more rapidly.

The pastoral nomads and their animals are the other pro-tagonists in the tragedy. Their populations have been increas-ing too, a little more slowly than the farmers, but too fast for the land. Four or five head of cattle are required to maintain each person, so this automatically means an increase in the livestock numbers. But other factors have expanded the herds beyond the limits of good sense. Improved breeding and veterinary services have cut down the great epidemics that kept herds in check. Pastoralists – as we saw with the Fulani – are not noted for rational herd management. The animals are their wealth, their status symbols, their insurance policies. In years of good rainfall they expand their stocks to insure against drought: but it is a policy that does not pay off. As they start to cull the herds in dry years, meat prices may fall, so they are reluctant to reduce numbers enough. Gradually far more animals build up than the system can maintain, and it breaks down under the strain.

In a misguided attempt to improve pastoralists' incomes and to boost meat production, governments sank wells and built watering places – but not enough of them. As a result, the herds tended to congregate around them, concentrating the pressure in just a few areas instead of spreading it evenly. Many of the wells are now surrounded by sterile rings upwards of fifteen kilometres wide. An area of sandy pastureland can be transformed into a barren dune landscape in two or three years by overgrazing. Put simply, this means that the animals eat vegetation more quickly than the earth can regenerate it. Tough woody species spread that are unpalatable to the cattle, hence increasing pressure even more on their favourite grasses. Herders make things worse, deliberately starting great bush fires in the dry season. These bring out a few tender shoots of green for the starving animals, but weaken and destroy plant cover. So the soil is more exposed to sunlight, and soil humidity declines, making life even more difficult for the plants that remain. The animals' hooves do their bit too, loosening and compacting the soil, making it less porous to water. So when it rains, less water gets down into the soil, more runs off. As the final link in the chain, with fewer plants the soil reflects back more and more sunlight – that is, its albedo increases. The ground heats up less, and since rain is caused by warm, moist air rising, there is even less rain than before.

The disappearing forests

There is a third factor besides farming and herding in the spread of man-made deserts: deforestation. The progressive destruction of the Third World's stock of trees is damaging not only in dry regions: everywhere it occurs it can accelerate the decay of the soil and reduces its capacity to feed and employ people. It can reduce rainfall and lead to drought. More of the rain that does fall runs off into rivers and streams, taking topsoil with it. This leads to silting downstream, the dilapidation of irrigation systems and an increase in floods.

The world's forests are shrinking at an alarming rate. It has been estimated that between 1900 and 1965 perhaps half the forest area in developing countries was cleared for cultivation. The 935 million hectares of closed tropical forest still left may be disappearing at the rate of 1·5 per cent to 2 per cent a year. Unless careful management policies are introduced, this could lead to their total disappearance within fifty or sixty years. Studies from individual countries confirm the overall picture. In the hilly Azuero peninsula of Panama more than two fifths of the forest was removed between 1954 and 1972. In Brazil a quarter of forestry reserves had been cut down by 1974. In 1975 Brazil's forests were being cleared at the rate of 62,500 square miles a year. If continued, this would destroy the Amazon forest, believed to provide a quarter of the world's oxygen supplies, in just twenty-seven years. Comparison of aerial photographs of the Ivory Coast taken in 1956 and 1966 showed that nearly a third of the forest cover had disappeared in those ten years. By the mid-seventies only five million hectares of forest remained of the fifteen million that the Ivory Coast had at the beginning of the century. Many of the disappearing forests are being cut down for firewood. The Food and Agriculture Organization estimates that some 86 per cent of wood cut in the developing countries is used for fuel. A total of 1,220 million cubic metres goes up in smoke every year, about half a cubic metre, or a medium-sized tree, for every person.

Wood is an inefficient source of energy: when used in cooking, which takes up half the wood used, 94 per cent of its heat value is wasted. It is a poor fuel, yet the poor have no alternative to it. Kerosene is too expensive, especially after the oil price rises, and you have to buy costly equipment to burn it. But firewood itself is now getting dearer, as supplies dwindle and people have to trek further and further from the villages to get a load. In Nepal, where it used to take an hour or two at most, collecting wood is now a whole day's labour. As all available trees near centres of population are stripped and felled, the price of firewood has risen steeply. Labourers in Niamey, Niger, are reportedly spending one quarter of their incomes on wood. This predicament is what environmental writer Erik Eckholm has called the poor man's energy crisis.

Deforestation speeds up the process of desertification. In some parts of Africa the fuel shortage is so acute that even crop residues and stubble – formerly left in the field to provide some modicum of humus to bind the soil – are now uprooted and burned. In mountain areas trees and shrubs may be the only thing holding earth on the steeper slopes. Remove them, and the soil goes with them. In the eastern hills of Nepal the topsoil has been almost completely washed away and two fifths of the cultivated fields have had to be abandoned. As firewood dwindles the soil is hit in indirect ways. Peasants turn to burning cowdung as fuel instead of using it to maintain soil fertility. This changeover has been completed in most of India, where carefully moulded cowdung patties, their lentil discs neatly impressed with finger marks, decorate the walls where they are pushed up to dry like some new kind of stucco. At the beginning of the century dung made up only 5 to 10 per cent of Indian domestic fuel consumption. Today it represents three quarters. More nitrogen and phosphorus goes up in cowcake fires than the total Indian production of chemical fertilizers. On overcrowded Java forests have been massacred to open up new plots, as land hunger pushes peasants to cultivate fields higher and higher up mountain slopes. Only 12 per cent of the island now has tree cover. In central Java steep forested inclines have been reduced to powdery, crumbling cliffs. The Indonesian government is making strenuous efforts to reforest the hills, and has outlawed shifting cultivation. But the cutting still goes on.

Silt and salt

Soil lost from the watersheds and the mountains washes down in the rivers. In reasonable quantities it can be beneficial. The plains of the Ganges owe their continued fertility to mineral-rich alluvium from the young mountains of the Himalayas. The Greek historian Herodotus called Egypt the gift of the Nile, but if it is, that is courtesy of Ethiopia, whose lost top-soil goes to replenish Egypt's.

But the accelerated erosion brought on by deforestation brings down more silt than downstream systems can cope with. In Java, silting has reduced the capacity of many irrigation canals by as much as a half, and two thirds of the irrigation network is in urgent need of rehabilitation. Effective irrigation is crucial to increasing food production in developing countries. Silt cuts down the amount of water that can be delivered to the fields, or destroys the farmers' control over that water. Dozens of dams built at huge expense have seen their capacity dwindle as silt builds up in the lakes behind them. Colombia's Anchicaya dam lost one quarter of its capacity in the ten years after it was built in 1947, because of the tree-felling activities of marginal settlers who had arrived upstream. Taiwan's Shishmen reservoir, built to last seventy years, lost nearly half its capacity in five years. Flooding adds the finishing touches to silt's destructive work. Silt pushes up the level of river and canal beds to the point where they often overflow their banks and rise above defensive dykes built to contain them. The disastrous floods that inundate northern India every year or two are partly due to Nepalese deforestation. Not only is the silt load increased, but more water drains off the denuded hills than before. And so the Ganges and her tributaries like the Kosi and the Gandak in Bihar inundate, at monsoon time, fields and villages alike.

Another threat to irrigated land is salinization and waterlogging. Many of the irrigation canals in the Third World are unlined, so that, instead of draining away, water seeps down into the ground and raises the level of the water table below. This lifts the harmful salts that rain has leached down into the subsoil, up into the root zone where they stunt plant growth and reduce yields. In the Punjab seepage has raised the water table by seven to nine metres in just ten years. In India as a whole, 15 per cent of all irrigated land has been damaged by salinity, along with one fifth of Pakistan's land and as much as a quarter in Iraq. Other affected areas are the Peruvian coast, north-east Brazil, central and northern Mexico. In all, perhaps 300,000 hectares every year are being lost to salinization and waterlogging – and these are irrigated hectares, equivalent to as much as a million hectares of dry land or the area of Lebanon.

The ecology of poverty

All the threats to the land, with the possible exception of salinization, are caused by poverty and overpopulation and, in turn, they accentuate poverty. Nomads overstock their ranges as an insurance against drought, and thereby directly increase the dangers of drought. Peasants overcrop and underfertilize their soils to keep alive, and the resulting exhaustion impoverishes them and their land further. Lack of money for kerosene forces them to cut down forests and burn valuable manure, ruining the land and pushing their incomes down even lower. Man and the land in poor countries are locked in a destructive and seemingly inescapable relationship, in which they are spiralling down, in self-fuelling motion, towards mutual destruction.

Land is essential for food and for work. Loss of land is one of the processes undermining the livelihoods of the rural poor in the Third World. We have seen the others at work in all three continents: the dispossession of smallholders. increasing landlesness, mechanization, increasing population. Taken together, these trends add up to a rise of terrifying proportions in the numbers of families unable to find enough work to feed themselves.

The impact of these processes could have been lessened by the right kind of social reforms and investments. First and foremost, by radical land reform and the establishment of co-operatives, giving everyone who lives on the land access to the land and its produce. Then by channelling investment towards small subsistence farmers to improve the productivity of their land so they do not have to rely on the labour market. By giving the small man the equal access he has a right to, to government services, credit, supplies, advice. By carefully controlling the spread of mechanization, job-destroying machinery being made more expensive, and job-creating, labour-intensive methods more attractive. In co-ops, mechanization becomes a benefit, not a threat, as the extra income is equally shared and the workmen freed can be employed in small-scale manufactures.

In most countries government policies have been the direct opposite. Land reform has been reticent, not radical, and landlords have usually been able to evade or frustrate it with the connivance of corrupt police and government officials. The lion's share of investment has gone to a few favoured areas and to better-off farmers. Public investment in agriculture has not been evenly spread, but spent in large packets on relatively small numbers of people: the model pilot projects with prosperous, neatly dressed workers, which visiting dignitaries are ferried round while carefully hidden down the road the many are ragged and starving. Expensive settlement schemes provide the lucky few with everything: land, roads, clean water, supplies, credit, schools, health clinics – while the unfortunate majority are left with nothing.

More serious still than all of this is the fact that the rural sector as a whole has been starved of funds, while the cities and modern industries were coddled. No wonder the rural poor, disinherited by a conspiracy of man and nature, fled to these selfsame cities. There they did see the expected pavements of gold – imitation western cities and imitation western factories – but these were for the privileged minority, not for them. They were left to house and employ themselves as best they could. The rural poor became the poor sub-proletariat of the cities. There was no room for them at anybody's inn.

Part Three
Hell is a City:
Urbanization and Industry

'The British have exploited India through its cities, the latter had exploited the villages. The blood of the villages is the cement with which the edifice of the cities is built.'

GANDHI

8. Exodus: The Rural Poor Vote with Their Feet

A donkey cart trots down a road in north-east Brazil, headed for Recife. The husband rides up front. On the back, piled high, are chairs, mattresses, pans, clothes, wife, children and on the top a green parrakeet in a wooden cage.

At Hooghly station in Calcutta, the down train arrives from Delhi, Allahabad, Lucknow, Benares, Patna and stations south. Among the crush of humanity that falls out of the opening doors are ragged Dick Whittingtons from the flooded north or drought-ridden south of Bihar, from poverty-stricken Orissa and crowded Uttar Pradesh, clutching cloth bags or battered cardboard suitcases.

And every day at the vast lorry parks of Lagos or the bus stations of Lima, young couples reach up while porters fling down their few possessions from the roof.

Migration for work is accelerating in the Third World. Some of it trickles into areas more favoured by nature or government investment; most of it floods towards the cities. A few migrants may be following some vague dream of the big city' and a sophisticated lifestyle. The majority are driven by the necessities of survival. The land cannot provide them with a job, so migration is like a plea for employment, a courageous expression of the willingness to work more than the poor soil or the unjust society of their home areas will allow them to. Migration is a symptom of rural poverty and of urban over-privilege.

All roads lead to Rome: the rural dynamics of all three continents push people to migrate. In Africa the exhaustion of the soil is the spur: poverty may be shared, but when food yields fall too low, some of the people on the overcrowded life raft have to leap overboard and swim towards uncertain shores. As the smallholdings of Asia and Latin America shrink below survival size, some of the heirs to the land must forgo their right to an equal share, and head for the cities. And as the number of labourers increases and the number of jobs dwindles through mechanization, the landless too have to look elsewhere for work. The result is identical, whether landownership is tribal and communal, private and fragmented, or large and capitalistic.

It is not easy to migrate. It means going into exile, leaving your home village, leaving the supportive network of the extended family, leaving the complex culture of status and ceremony in which you hoped one day to play your part. It is a last resort, when all else has failed.

Migration for work begins as a temporary phenomenon. In central Java, almost every able-bodied man spends several months of the year away from home. Supar Kristanto lives in Gunung Kidul, a dry area that gets only a few months rain a year. Everyone here is poor, everyone is on the lookout for extra work. Supar owns only five hundred square metres of land, no more than a garden around his house. There is no hope of regular employment as an agricultural labourer in the area, so he is forced to go to Jakarta, selling cooked food from a little stall. He comes back once a month, bringing back five thousand rupiahs (£6 or $12) each time. Rajil, a twenty-five-year-old with one child, owns half a hectare: but you need about a hectare and a half in this area to be self-sufficient. Four times a year he goes to the regional capital of Jogjakarta for two or three weeks at a time. There he joins the throng of cycle rickshaw drivers who line every street. Competition is so stiff that he is lucky if he earns 500 rupiahs (60p or $1.20) in a day. He spends his nights sleeping on the three-foot-long seat, legs up: it saves money and protects the rickshaw against thieves.

The building sites of Bombay or Calcutta are full of seasonal labourers. They live in ragged tented camps like the hordes of Genghis Khan. The landless labourers of Rajasthan move to Delhi or Ahmedabad for the dry season, when there is no work to be had on the land — and their women and children go too. The women, in their dark green and maroon and orange saris, can often be seen on roads or building sites, pick manfully in hand or basketful of stones gracefully balanced on their heads, while their children are left to play among the rubble.

Even permanent migrants are reluctant to sever all ties with their home areas. In India it is common for men to leave their families behind in the village while they work in the city. Calcutta is full of single men. A thriving trade in prostitution has grown up among women factory workers. It is a tragic encounter of their poverty and the men's loneliness.

In a seedy suburban sidestreet, a row of cobblers squat in lotus position by their lasts. They are landless labourers from Bihar, of the untouchable caste of the Chamar or leather people – it is considered polluting to touch the hide of dead cattle. One old man of sixty, a carpet of white hairs on his chest, sits by his tools. A few hammers, knives, punches and needles are his total working capital. He spends his day on the pavement mending shoes. Some days he earns nothing at all, some days five or ten rupees, depending on trade. His night is spent on a string bed inside a tiny windowless cell four feet wide and seven deep, where his few bits of clothing are slung over a string on the wall. His wife stayed in their home village, and he visits her perhaps three times a year, when he can afford the fare. Once a month he goes to a scribe outside the central post office, who fills in a money order for forty or sixty rupees (£2–£3, or $4–$6) made out to his wife. It isn't much of a life, but back in Bihar he would be lucky to earn half as much as here, and hard put to keep body and soul together.

The world-wide trek for work

National boundaries are no deterrent to the determined migrant. A steady stream of workers, most of them from rural areas, flows north and west from the Third World into the rich First World. In the sixties, the UN-affiliated International Labour Office estimates, 5·1 million migrants from poor countries joined this long trek for work. In 1979 such migrants may have totalled 10 million.

The United States and Canada gained a net official inflow of four million foreign workers, and on top of that several millions of Mexican wetbacks waded across the Rio Grande to become underpaid farm labourers or join the urban underclass. German industry hired some 600,000 Turks, many of them to man the soul-destroying assembly lines of its auto industry: in 1973 9 per cent of the German workforce was made up of foreign nationals. Germany used them like ballast in an air balloon, taking more on board when the economy was booming, jettisoning them to gain height when things were bad. The migrant workers of the Mediterranean allowed Germany to export its unemployment problems. France depended equally on Algerians and Moroccans – in 1974, 5 per cent of Algeria's workforce was in France. Britain, in the boom days of the late fifties and early sixties, took on board migrant workers from the countries its colonial policies had helped to ruin. The 1971 census showed 1·16 million residents born in the New Commonwealth, mainly from India, the West Indies, Pakistan and Bangladesh. Many of them joined the sub-proletariat, taking on the humble and low-paid work that native Britons would not touch. As the West staggered through the prolonged depression of the seventies, racialism strengthened. Ethnic tensions in the rich countries were the expression of global inequalities, a microcosm of the north–south conflict come home to roost.

But considerable migration for work goes on inside the Third World. Wherever a poor country that has not got enough work to go round lies next to a richer country that is in need of manpower, this human traffic goes on as naturally as heat flowing from a warm room to a cooler one. In South America alone there are three million migrant workers. Landlocked Bolivia and Paraguay each have around 700,000 workers away from home, mostly in Argentina. Oil-rich Venezuela (average income $2,570 in 1976) has attracted 600,000 workers from neighbouring Colombia where incomes are only a quarter as high. Large numbers of Asians now work as labourers in the Arab oil states. In West Africa, migrant workers number six million and make up a massive proportion of the workforces of sending and receiving countries. Some 43 per cent of Mauretanian and Togolese workers work abroad, as do a third of Upper Volta's. The Ivory Coast would collapse without the 55 per cent of its workforce who are foreign migrant workers, and the Gambia

(25 per cent migrants) and Ghana (22 per cent) would also be badly shaken.

The Ivory Coast and Upper Volta are inextricably linked by migrant labour. The Coast relies on Voltaics to work the plantations of coffee, cocoa, oil palm and coconuts on which it has based its successful economic growth. Per capita incomes have grown and grown, reaching $610 in 1976, the highest non-oil income in sub-Saharan Africa. Upper Volta has stagnated, with per capita incomes of $110. Her shaky balance of payments depends on foreign aid and the remittances of her workers abroad. In 1973 they sent back around $30 million, or $40 to $50 each.

The whole business started under the French, who turned Upper Volta into little more than a reservoir of slave labour. Workers were conscripted into forced labour gangs to build the roads and railways. Upper Volta itself was neglected, so that the richly endowed but underpopulated Ivory Coast could be developed. After the French left, migration continued, on a voluntary basis: it had become almost a tradition among the Mossi, an obligatory rite of passage between adolescence and manhood. Young Voltaics are expected to spend four or five years in the Ivory Coast. The practice reduces the number of mouths the land has to feed, and brings in extra capital which could not be generated from the poor native soils. It also eases the intolerable tensions that build up between father and son in the strongly patriarchal Mossi society.

The Ivory Coast calls like a siren. Those who have not yet gone there develop dream fantasies about its paved roads, its street lights, its floodlit stadia, its sheer greenness – dreams that reflect sadly on the parched poverty of their own land. Returned migrant boast of their exploits – some even hire *griots* or troubadours to go before them into their village chanting their praises, as if they were heroes back from war. The travellers ostentatiously ask for change of one thousand franc notes, pay the family's poll tax for the year as if it were nothing, wear western clothes, carry radios, ride bikes and speak French to confound their friends. Girls are attracted to their veneer of sophistication, and mock at those who have not yet made the trip. 'He who has not travelled is like a man who has not been circumcised,' goes a local proverb. Eventually the pressures tell on the non-migrant and he just has to go too.

The reality he finds is, of course, not so glamorous. At best, he works hard and saves hard, though he may do both harder than his body can stand. There is the story of one Voltaic worker on a pineapple plantation who thought he would save on food by eating nothing but the fruit he worked with every day. After six months, the acid, proteinless diet killed him. Every penny of his wages for the entire period was found in his pockets.

Joseph Yameogo, a twenty-three-year-old Mossi, lives in a tiny mud-floored room in a swampy shanty suburb of Abidjan. In his five years in the Ivory Coast he has tried out many jobs: plantation labourer, houseboy, nightwatchman, washer and greaser, factory hand. He says the main purpose of his travel is to save up enough money for a bicycle. He is luckier than many Voltaics in the big coastal city. Discrimination against Voltaics is quite common. As urban unemployment rose among native Ivorians, so did resentment against migrant workers. After demonstrations, local employment exchanges stopped placing Voltaics in industrial jobs so now they can only get low-grade ones. The Mossi, so dignified, decent and hardworking in their own country, acquired a reputation for drunkenness and crime in the Ivory Coast as police mugshots of sad, demoralized faces with Mossi names like Traoré or Ouedraogo cropped up with unfailing regularity in *Fraternité Matin*, the daily newspaper.

In the mid-seventies Upper Volta suspended all official labour migration to the Ivory Coast, after the Coast had refused to increase the minimum plantation salary and to deduct compulsory savings from the Voltaics' wages and send them to Upper Volta. So illegal migration and labour piracy started up, as happens wherever laws and regulations hamper the flood of poor people looking for work. Most of the big plantations in the Ivory Coast now employ full-time labour recruiters. I met one of these pirates on a big oil-palm estate, a bulky bald fifty-five-year-old with a short grey beard. He described his methods: 'I have to get off the train at the frontier and cross on foot between the guard posts. Then I walk from village to village. Everywhere I ask to see the chief. He collects people together. I tell them about the good wages, the nice hospital, the modern houses on our estate. For every man who comes with me, I give the chief a thousand francs (about £2.50 or $5).' On each trip he recruits about forty men and pays their fare to the border, where a lorry is waiting to take them south.

Islands of privilege: the cities

Inevitably, in these days of nation states, the majority of migrants head for the cities of their own country. It is an exodus of epic, historic proportions.

In 1940, Third World towns and cities housed 185 million people. By 1975, the number had risen to 790 million. Well over half the increase was due to immigration from rural areas. In 1960 the United Nations estimated some 9·2 million people a year were flooding into the Third World cities – some 25,000 people every single day. By the early seventies, 12 million people a year – 33,000 a day – were arriving.

Not that the rural areas became depopulated: far from it. Their populations continued to increase faster than available jobs, and in absolute terms their numbers grew faster than the cities, from about 1,350 millions in 1950 to 2,060 millions in 1975. But the cities' *rate* of growth was two to four times faster. As a result, the share of the rural areas in total population declined from an average of 84 per cent in 1950 to 73 per cent in 1970. That left southern Asia and Africa still about four fifths rural, but Latin America was three fifths urban (it had been three fifths rural in 1950).

What is it that gives the cities of the Third World their immense gravitational pull? Is it the poverty of the surrounding rural void – or the cities' own inherent attractions? The question whether migrants are pushed by penury or pulled by wealth is academic. They are two ends of the same continuum. The city seems wealthy precisely because the land is poor, the land seems poor in relation to the city's wealth. It is the comparison that works on the minds of the rural poor – though in many areas their minds may be wonderfully concentrated by the prospect of imminent starvation.

In western countries, there is very little difference between urban and rural incomes, and even less when the relative costs of living are compared. In the Third World, urban incomes are, on average, two and a half times higher than rural incomes. The greater the income difference, the steeper is the gradient of the slope pulling people into the cities. These differentials are generally highest in Africa, where cities have grown fastest.

In the early sixties, economist Paul Bairoch has estimated, non-agricultural incomes were fifteen times agricultural ones in Gabon, nine and a half times in Liberia, eight and a half times in the Ivory Coast. In Asia differentials were less glaring, but still considerable, with urban incomes 6·3 times rural ones in Thailand, 4·6 times in Cambodia, 2·4 times in the Philippines and 1·9 times in India. In Latin America the biggest gaps were in Venezuela (5·3 times), Bolivia (4·2 times), Mexico (4·1 times), Haiti (3·9 times) and Guatemala (3·8 times).

Income is not the only important differential. Another is the grotesque gap between city and countryside in the provision of all kinds of government services, health, sanitation, schools, electricity, clean water. All these factors represent a kind of invisible or social income, and migrants are well aware that they improve their life chances and those of their children.

Take clean water, for example. In Africa 36 per cent of the urban population has reasonable access to a safe water supply, against only 21 per cent of the rural. The urban over rural advantage is 67 per cent to 30 per cent in Latin America, and 47 per cent to 19 per cent in South and East Asia.

The risk of epidemics may be slightly higher in crowded urban areas. But that does not justify the concentration of all the hospitals and a major part of the doctors in the biggest towns. In the Philippines there are seven times as many doctors per person in the towns as in the rural areas, in Ghana and Senegal ten times more, in Haiti twenty-five times, in Thailand thirty-one times and in Kenya fifty-seven times.

What of that bright symbol of modernization, electricity?

Peasants prize a domestic supply highly. It is as sought after, as long saved up for, as a tin roof. In any village or rural town a bare bulb burning out of a booth shop, while all around burn oil, is a sure sign of status. Electricity frees the peasant from the tyranny of early bedtime. It is the essential precondition for further progress to a fan, a fridge or a record player. But it can also help a village to develop small-scale industry. While all modern cities and most large towns are supplied with electricity in developing countries, only a small minority of villages are. In 1971, 23 per cent of Latin American villages were electrified, in Asia 15 per cent, in Africa only 4 per cent.

Perhaps most important of all these non-monetary advantages of the cities is education. Rural areas in the Third World are lucky if they have a school within a two-hour walk. In the poorest countries only 36 per cent of rural schools provide the full basic primary course, against 53 per cent of urban schools. Virtually all secondary schools are in towns. Any peasant who places a high value on educating his children will see the city as the best place to do this. And there are few people in the Third World who do not see education as the road to riches, or at least the way out of poverty.

The unfair channelling of public investment into the cities reaches scandalous proportions in most developing countries. For example, the Ivory Coast's development plan for 1967–70 allocated 8,000 francs CFA per resident in Abidjan for roads, sewerage, water and electricity supply, primary schools and dispensaries. Other urban areas were allocated 6,000 francs per head. For rural areas, the allocation was only 400 francs. In all developing countries, four fifths of the $980 millions spent on water supply improvements in 1970 went to the urban areas, which had only just over a quarter of the population and were already much better provided than rural areas.

Excess provision of government services in cities also attracts an unfair share of private-sector jobs. As the cities alone can offer the roads, power, communications and water that industry needs, as well as the desirable suburbs that executives expect to live in, the overwhelming bulk of modern industry has been concentrated in a few large urban centres in each country. Industry and administration in their turn attract service jobs. Private industry pursues profit and cannot be expected to locate its factories so as to achieve the greatest happiness of the greatest number. But how are we to explain what British economist Michael Lipton has called the urban bias of government policy in the Third World? Why do governments discriminate – there is no other word for it – so obviously and shockingly against the rural majority of their citizens?

The colonial powers began the process, providing themselves, in their city bases, with the services and salaries they were used to back home. At independence, the national elites could have taken the view the big cities were already well enough provided for and the rural areas should now get their share. But the elites had been brainwashed into a fascination with all things western, and wanted to build up the western enclaves of their country. And when nationals took over administration posts from whites, few of them had the self-restraint to accept lower incomes more in line with the ability of their country to pay. In the private sector, urban salaried workers have been able to obtain higher incomes because they are more easily organized than scattered peasants. Factories and cities are more complex organisms than self-sufficient villages, more easily disrupted by syndical action.

The concentrated city masses as a whole are engaged in a sort of unspoken collective bargaining with their governments: put up prices too far, and they riot until they are brought down to an acceptable level. Since ancient Rome the urban mob has been one of the most dangerous and destabilizing elements in any state, and it is best to placate it if you hope to keep on holding the reigns of power. But there is a question of balance; the price of food is also the farmer's income. The urban mob, simply by virtue of its concentration near the seat of government, is better organized to get its way over food prices than scattered and usually unorganized peasants. And so governments usually keep food prices artificially low, thus depressing incomes in the rural sector.

Relations between town and country in the Third World are

rather like those between rich and poor countries. The rural areas tend to have poor terms of trade – that is, their produce fetches excessively low prices compared to the cost of the cities' products, whether these be plastic bowls, tractors or administration. And the reasons for these poor terms of trade are exactly comparable with those for Third World products in general. The rural poor lack the muscle of organization and coordination with which to extract higher prices.

The city's advantage, then, is due to a conspiracy between governments and their employees and organized workers to increase their own incomes at the expense of the rural masses. As Tanzania's President Julius Nyerere has remarked, much of the money spent in towns comes from foreign loans that have to be repaid with foreign exchange, and that is usually obtained by exporting the farmers' produce. The farmers bear the costs, city dwellers reap the benefits. 'If we are not careful,' Nyerere warned, 'we might get into the position where the real exploitation in Tanzania is that of the town dwellers exploiting the peasants.' That position has already been reached in most developing countries.

Migration, then, is a form of voting with your feet, of demanding a seat at the table where the feasting is going on. It happens because development is uneven and the benefits of growth are so unevenly spread. It is a protest against inequality.

But the process of migration can itself damage the rural areas further. They do gain something: the pressure for limited land and jobs is reduced, and migrants send home cash that helps eke out low village incomes.

Against that, the rural areas are losing their brightest and best, the most educated, progressive, adaptable, young and vigorous elements to the cities. Surveys show that the typical migrant is aged between twenty-five and forty. Four fifths of migrants to Bombay are of working age – against an average of only half of India's total population. The village is left with fewer breadwinners to support its children and old people. Migrants are also better educated. A joint UNICEF/International Labour Organization survey in the Ivory Coast found that the more educated a man was, the more likely he was to leave the village. Overall, around a third of young rural-born men had moved to towns, but among those who had completed primary school the proportion was 61 per cent, and of those with above primary education no less than 93 per cent had decamped to the cities. Migrants appear to be more intelligent and adaptable than those who stay. A survey in Huaylas, Peru, compared migrants with their brothers who had remained behind and found that people regarded the migrants as more independent, intelligent and diligent at study than the non-migrants — precisely the kind of people who could have helped the villages to adopt the new technologies they need if they are to develop.

Young people who have spent years in education expect a certain status in return, but because of urban bias there are few or no jobs in the villages that can offer such status. Villages are short of schools, health clinics, roads — and so they are short of jobs as teachers, nurses, engineers. Investment in the rural areas would create more such jobs, and keep more of the talent in the villages. As things stand, the rural areas bear the cost of raising people to working age, and the city reaps the benefits. The city expropriates the human capital of the land. It is an invisible but heavy burden, added to all the other injustices.

How long will they keep on coming?

The promised land that migrants hope for turns out to be a mirage for many of them. Though their income will usually be better than back home, they are likely to end up earning a subsistence living as a hawker or casual labourer — that is, if they can get any work at all. They are almost certain to find themselves living in sub-human conditions of overcrowding and insanitations, worse than anything in Dickens's London or Jakob Riis's New York.

So why do they keep on coming? Is there perhaps an equilibrium level of human degradation, a set of physical conditions so appalling that no more migrants will be willing to tolerate them? The lesson of Calcutta, where families live in concrete tubes in the middle of the road, seems to be that there is no such level.

The answer has to be sought in economics. Early theories held that there was a labour shortage in the urban areas which pushed urban wages up way above what people could earn in the rural areas. This brought more and more migrants flooding in to the cities, which increased the labour supply and should therefore bring wages down. When the wages had dropped to the level of rural incomes, migration would stop.

In reality, as we have seen, urban wages are high not only because there is a shortage of skilled labour but also because of discrimination by government and the superior organization of workers. Wages remain high even though unemployment in urban areas of the Third World has never been higher.

The most sophisticated explanation of migration that holds the field today is known as the Todaro model after its economist author. According to this theory, migrants are well aware that the fence of high unemployment stands between them and the attractive urban wages they have heard about. But they will go on heading citywards as long as their present income is lower than their expected income in the city. The expected income is the likely urban wage multiplied by the chances of earning it. Take the typical example of a country where the average rural income is $100 (£50) and the average urban income is $250, but where urban unemployment is running at 20 per cent – so the chance of getting that wage is only eight out of ten. The expected income is therefore eight tenths of the average wage, or $200, still well worth migrating for. In this typical country, it would go on paying people to migrate until urban unemployment reached the astonishing level of 60 per cent (a level actually attained in some squatter areas).

One may quibble about the exact equilibrium level that will finally halt the migrant hordes. But the grim implication remains: the rural exodus is likely to continue for a very long time, as long, in fact, as urban areas stay so much richer. If it is not halted by a more or less immediate programme to bring rural incomes much closer to urban ones, it will be halted instead by the rise of urban unemployment to intolerable levels that will threaten the stability of nations, and therefore world peace.

9. The Promised Land: Skyscrapers and Shanty Towns

In the press of pedestrians on Bogotá's main artery, Carrera 10, a smart young professional raises an arm to halt a cab. His palm stretches out and his grip on the neat, leather-cased folding umbrella he carries is loosened. Suddenly, like a greyhound from its trap, a tattered, barefoot figure in a jacket three sizes too big shoots out, weaves under the man's arm, wrenches free the umbrella and is away, weaving expertly among the rush-hour traffic, forcing a big orange bus to an emergency stop with a wail of brakes and horn.

That was the first glimpse I caught of Fabio, just eleven years old, whose innocent, cartoon-like face under a basin of raven black hair looks three years younger still. He left home when he was eight because his stepfather used to beat him with an iron bar. Since then he has been one of Bogatá's army of five to ten thousand – no one knows exactly how many – urchins or *gamines*, who live, sleep, beg, sing, steal, fight, love, hate and often die on the streets of a heartless city. In this naked confrontation of the poor with the affluence of the rich, the *gamines* offer a parable for all Third World cities.

Like all such agglomerations, Bogotá is a schizophrenic, Jekyll and Hyde place. Steel and darkened-glass skyscrapers rise around the flyovers and landscaped palms of the Parque de la Independencia, while half a mile away timber and cardboard shanties tumble down the steep hills that form a backdrop to the city. Rich Bogotá has managed to sweep the habitations of the poor way out of sight. But the poor will not starve on the fringes while the rich feast. They invade the centre in their rags and dirt. Beggars line the pavements under the chic shops of Carrera 7 and Avenida Jimenez. A red-faced woman coughs and points to the baby asleep on her shoulder and holds out her hand for money, importunate, insistent, desperate. A cripple paints surrealistic scenes to collect money to pay for an operation. An emaciated man in his fifties, drowned in a brown poncho, strums a guitar while his ten-year-old daughter scrapes a plastic pipe with a knife and her baby sister shakes a maraca. Expressions of unutterable misery on the father's face, and distracted, hungry anxiety on the girls', belie their carnival rhythms. Then there are the rubbish people, a legion of the damned, almost as ragged and dirty as the trash they collect from the city's dust and waste bins. Women heaving great sacks of cardboard on their backs, and daub-faced boys heaping garbage from the lamp-post containers onto ramshackle pushcarts, mingle and jostle with jumpsuited secretaries and well-dressed bank employees. They roam the smart suburbs, collecting garbage before the municipal cart comes around, and the conscienceless rich – rich enough to afford £10 ($20) for a full bottle of whisky – have the unbelievable effrontery to make the scavengers pay if they want the empties.

The rich created this problem. The lawyers and businessmen who own estates up country and pay their labourers so little that they have to leave for the cities. The speculators who jerry-build city slums without light, roads or water and charge rack rents for the privilege of living in them. The rich brought the poor here, and perpetuated their poverty once they got here. Perhaps it is only fitting that they should not be allowed to feel comfortable in their wealth.

The *gamines* are the vanguard of this great army of the poor. They harass the urban privileged like horseflies, constantly reminding them of the poverty they represent. They leap onto their buses and sing tragic songs for money. They beg, hand outstretched and bottom lip curled down, dirtying clean suits with their grubby hands. Above all they rob, mug and terrorize the middle classes and tear from them the possessions they have bought with the surplus squeezed out of the poor.

These little Lords of the Flies live in *galladas* or gangs of ten to twenty-five members, each with its own territory and sleeping place, and an older leader who has won his position through a dozen street battles, like a stag wins his herd. Fabio belongs to the Hot Pipe Gang. Francisco, aged twenty-one, is leader of the pack. Half his front teeth are missing, knocked out in a brawl. His leadership gives him the right to command, to sit back while others do the hard work of stealing, and to take the lion's share of the proceeds. I sat with him in the heart of his territory on Carrera 10 while he explained the tricks of his trade: 'The best way to steal a watch is to stand by the traffic lights in the rush hour and look for some fool with his window down and his hands on the steering wheel. You wait till just before the lights are changing, then whip his watch off and run for it. He will never come after you, with all the other cars blowing their horns at him to move off. On the streets we work in threes or fours. When you have snatched a wallet or a bag, you pass it to one of your friends and run off, so if they do catch you, you are clean. When people run after you, your friends trip them up or threaten them or sometimes stab them. Believe me, if you get robbed, the best thing to do is to leave well alone and forget about it. The easiest people of all to rob are ladies carrying parcels. You just stick a pin in their bottom and they drop everything. We sell our stuff to the second-hand shops. They give you ten times less than the thing is worth, but on good days you can live well. Today I've got two thousand pesos in my pocket (about £40 or $80).'

Late one night I toured the urchins' sleeping places with a social worker. They had made their little dens wherever they could. One tiny boy was curled up inside a cardboard box in a shop doorway, alone. Another gang lived in a concrete shaft leading down to the city sewers, with rats for sleeping companions. The Twenty Fifth Street Gang had built themselves a rough shelter of branches and leaves on a vacant lot. Finally we came upon the Hot Pipe Gang and I learned how they got their name. Eight or ten of the youngest ones were curled up, one on top of another, round the warm base of a lamp-post that was heating up from an electrical short circuit inside. In each place the same huddle of grubby, nervous faces old before their time, the same rags and bare, black feet. The same smell of sweat and marijuana. Almost all the *gamines* are on drugs, including cocaine and heroin – Colombia is one of the chief sources of supply for northern America. One high the boys have invented for themselves is sniffing petrol fumes. It ruins their lungs, but gives them, so they say, a warm feeling that carries them through the chilly nights. Drugs deaden the pangs of hunger – and give them the courage needed for robbery.

The life of the *gamin* is a child's heaven and hell. He enjoys an unlimited freedom that most children only dream of. He travels from town to town, from adventure to adventure, like Huckleberry Finn. The city is like a jungle for him: he is some times a beast of prey, sometimes a scavenger living from the dustbins behind restaurants. He bathes naked in public fountains and hitches free rides on car bumpers, displaying due contempt for accepted ways of the impressive modern city reserved for the privileged. But street life can be as dangerous as guerilla warfare. All *gamines* brush frequently with the law and often cool their heels in prison. They are forever being knocked down by cars as they dash among the traffic – little Ernesto, aged eight, hobbles around on a makeshift crutch, his tiny leg marked quite clearly with the zigzag track of a bus tyre. But the *gamin*'s worst enemies are other *gamines*. Most of them carry knives and razors, and fights are a daily hazard. Perhaps half of those I met had prominent wounds or scars. The chest of one fourteen-year-old was a gnarled mass of scar tissue where a 'friend' had jokingly poured petrol over him while he slept and set fire to it.

The *gamin*, like the slums he comes out of, is the symptom of a diseased society. Most urchins are the children of rural migrants, driven out of the countryside by the forces described in Chapter 7. They head for the cities hoping to improve their conditions. Many are illiterate, and have no skills to sell that the modern sector needs. Rents, even for hovels without light, sewage or water, are high. True squatters, in self-built homes and paying no rent, are found only in a few scattered pockets on impossible slopes that no speculator could develop. Any squats on suitable sites are soon driven off by the police, though they ignore the equally illegal constructions of the speculators. So little money is left for food or clothing. Many families subsist on tortillas, soup or *panela* (sugar water). The home becomes an overloaded lifeboat with dwindling supplies, and members of the same family fighting each other like rats for them. Many of the *gamines* I met had left home after a savage beating, often for 'stealing' food from the cupboard. One boy had his hand burned with a match for taking a piece of cheese without asking. Another was tied to a tree and horsewhipped.

The poor Colombian family is not held together by strong bonds at the best of times. The majority of couples are not legally married. The culture of *machismo* (the only dignity a poor man has) pushes the men towards cruelty inside the home and infidelity outside it. In the city the pressures for family collapse increase: fights over food, over money, over inability to find a job. Broken homes are the rule. Single mothers may abandon one or more of their children if they cannot feed them. Or bring in another man, who, in the *macho* culture, is expected to detest his stepchildren (as they will detest him) and beat them. The child may already have a taste of street life, having been sent out to sell cigarettes or clean shoes to bring in extra money. He knows he can make a living on the streets, perhaps even a better living than at home. So off he goes.

The *gamines*, of course, do not realize they are the product of social injustice, nor do they realize that their activities are a sort of chaotic revenge for that injustice. They are waging a selfdefeating, individualistic war of crime, when the problem requires disciplined, organized struggle. But they represent, more clearly than anything else, the split in the Third World between the modern city of the urban privileged, and the vaster city of the poor camped at its gates.

The dual city: skyscrapers and squatters

That split originated once more in colonial times. Pre-colonial cities grew up as markets, centres of religion, trade or administration. Sometimes they were parasitic, the seats of conquerors, for the extraction and conspicuous consumption of tribute exacted from subject peoples. Most had grown organically from the societies of which they were part. But the Europeans were not like other conquerors. They were not rough barbarians like the Arabs, the Mongols or the Moguls, come to enjoy the wealth of agrarian people and to adopt their ways. Utterly convinced of the superiority of their own culture, they built themselves models of their cities back home. From Lima's Plaza de Armas to Dalhousie Square, Calcutta, the European colonial city was a little seed of Europe transplanted to exotic soil. Apart from a few minor allowances for rain and heat, it altered itself hardly at all. It was alien and uncompromising, the visible focus of a culture that was equally unwilling to compromise.

Nevertheless, natives were needed, as porters or tea boys or junior clerks. And so, where it was not appended to an existing native city, the colonial city secreted round itself a border of native hutments. This was the origin of the dual city. Economically, the colonial city was essentially parasitic, the place where the economic surplus extracted from the colony was collected together for shipment back to Europe. Gandhi was well aware of this role: 'The cities are a creation of foreign domination,' he wrote. 'Today, the cities dominate and drain the villages so that they are crumbling into ruin.'

The parasitic character of Third World cities persisted after independence. The blood of the villages is still the cement with which the edifice of the cities is built. Indeed, the real problem of hyper-urbanization did not appear on the scene until after the colonial masters had left. By and large, they had prevented migration by physical means. They had not encouraged the development of industry. They had educated only so many natives as they could employ in their own service. Independence gave a massive boost to the cities of the new states. Civil services expanded, new capitals were built in some countries. Massive investments were poured into the establishment of new industries in the cities, and education spread the values of westernized city life to increasing numbers.

And so the urban areas of the Third World have swollen like boils. In 1920 the urban population of the less developed regions was around 100 millions, making up only 28 per cent of the total urban population of the world. By 1940 the number had grown to 185 millions, more than doubling to 419 millions by 1960. By 1980 the urban areas will contain some 970 million people, more than half the world's urban total, and fifteen of the twenty largest cities in the world will be in developing countries. Though India, for example, is still an overwhelmingly rural country, with an urban population of around 120 million in 1976, it is in absolute terms more urbanized than any country in the world except the USA and the Soviet Union.

The rate of growth of the Third World's towns and cities has accelerated, like the suicidal collapse of matter into a black hole. In the twenties they were growing at 3 per cent a year, speeding up to 3·9 per cent in the fifties. In the 1970s they were expanding at 4·3 per cent a year. At every point city growth far outran the general population boom. Urban population multiplied eight times between 1920 and 1975, while the total population rose only two and a half times. Third World cities are now growing at twice the pace of western cities at a comparable stage of economic development – a pace equalled only in the United States in the decades of flooding immigration between 1850 and 1920. The growth rate for individual cities, especially capitals, has broken all records. Almost without exception, the fastest-growing cities are in Africa. Between 1960 and 1970 Kinshasha's population expanded at 12 per cent a year, Abidjan's at 11 per cent, Monrovia's and Blantyre's at 10 per cent. Dar-es-Salaam and Rabat grew by 9 per cent a year, Nairobi, Lagos and Lomé at 8 per cent.

In Asia Seoul led the pack at 8·5 per cent a year, followed by Kuala Lumpur at 6·5 per cent, Bangkok at 6·2 per cent and Karachi at 5·6 per cent. The fastest growers in Latin America were Belo Horizonte (8·3 per cent), Bogotá (7·3 per cent), São Paulo (6·4 per cent), Mexico City (5·8 per cent) and Lima (5·1 per cent). These were the primate cities, many times bigger than their nearest rivals in each country.

After two or three decades of independence the cities of the Third World are still the dual cities of colonial days. The central area of any primate city is almost indistinguishable, apart from the beggars, from its modern western counterpart. Jakarta's highways sweep from the giant freedom monument of Merdeka Square past five-star hotels and banks to fashionable residential suburbs. The smart bungalows of Chico in Bogotá could be the outskirts of Bonn. Singapore's industrial estates could be those of any western city, while the blocks of flats for Abidjan's salaried workers would not stick out among the council estates of Britain.

But the modern city centre reminds one of a film set for a western, where the buildings have only fronts propped up with joists, and behind them is the bare desert. It is a small island set in a sea of misery. Where London has a green belt of farmland, Third World cities have vast black belts of poverty, monstrous accretions of virtual ghettoes for the excluded and unwashed.

The urban bias of investment does not extend to these encampments of the poor outside the city walls. Few of the schools, clinics, roads and sewers with which the modern sector is so well provided are located here. The slums are as underprovided, as discriminated against, in relation to the modern city, as the rural areas are to the towns. In Lusaka, capital of Zambia, for example, the nearest clinics to squatter settlements are on average thirteen kilometres away, and a slum child has only one sixtieth of the chance of getting a primary school place that a child from an 'official' quarter has. The squatters must queue for water at standpipes serving a thousand people with a slow trickle, or buy polluted water from vendors at ten times the price the modern city resident pays for his metered domestic supply.

So even within cities, the location of facilities makes the privileged even more privileged, and the poor even less so. It makes privilege and underprivilege inheritable: the children of the poor are more likely to get diseases and disease-generated malnutrition from dirty water, they are less likely to attend and complete school.

The squatter areas are growing even faster than the booming cities they surround. Slums, shanties, bustees, *barrios, favelas, pueblos jovenes, villas miserias, bidonvilles*: every language has a name for them. The United Nations secretariat has estimated that squatter settlements are growing at an average of 15 per cent a year, nearly four times faster than the overall city growth rate. For example, Ankara grew at 5·3 per cent a year between 1960 and 1970, while its squatter areas grew at 12·6 per cent. Mexico City grew at 2·8 per cent a year between 1952 and 1966, but its shanties spread nearly ten times as fast. Lima's population increased by 9 per cent a year in the twelve years from 1957, while the *barriadas* mushroomed at 64 per cent.

In most cities the major part of the increase in overall population went to swell the underprivileged squatter settlements. These now house more than two fifths of the population of the major Third World cities, but in many places much more than that: they contain 46 per cent of Mexico City's population, 70 per cent of Casablanca's and Ouagadougou's, 80 per cent of Douala's and 90 per cent of Addis Ababa's.

No city in the world, however rich, could build modern houses, pave roads, dig sewers, lay water pipes and electricity cables as fast as people are arriving. And these are not rich cities. The flood of immigrants bursts all the barriers of planning and legislation. They ask for no one's consent to come, they just arrive. They do not ask official permission to knock up a ramshackle home to live in or let out, they just get on with it. So the cities spread amoeba-like in places undreamed of in most planners' philosophies, over low-lying marshes and 60 per cent slopes, between railway lines and onto stilts over stagnant lagoons.

Each city has its own peculiarities, its own history and character, its own patterns of residence and tenure. To get the feel of these peculiar animals, you have to explore them one by one. I have space here for only two, one a city in its earliest infancy, the other in the late stages of decrepitude and decay.

The urban village: Ouagadougou

You would never guess that Ouagadougou was the capital city of Upper Volta. One peace corps volunteer allegedly scootered straight through it thinking he was still on the outskirts. Cars are few and far between – mopeds are the status symbols of the city's middle class of government employees. Modernity is only a thin veneer. There is only one dual carriageway, flanked by an open sewer where graceful herons wade. The focal crossroads, grandly named the Place des Nations Unies, is simply the point where six quiet roads meet, without kerbs, crossings or street lights. The central market, a huge cavernous hangar presided over by a long row of vultures, is surrounded by a confusion of low wooden stalls: old women selling shrunken baboon heads, butchers with near-black meat, ready cooked by the heat, hills of grain, and a herdsman bickering over the price of three strands of rope for his goats.

Ouagadougou is a nascent metropolis housing only 150,000 people in 1973. It is a good place to observe the earliest phases of urban growth. Land is scarce in the official, planned city because of the cost and slow pace of laying pipes and roads. There is a brisk black market in building lots here, theoretically limited to one per family. But there is as yet no shortage of land outside the central area. The land here is tribal. Settlers in Africa may ignore state laws, but they always respect custom: a newcomer must report to the traditional land chief and ask for a small piece of land to build on. Permission is usually granted free, though the chief may expect favours in return and small gifts at festivals. But tenancy is insecure. Settlers are aware that the chief can turf them out unceremoniously if he takes a dislike to them. There is no crowding as yet, and broad rutted paths separate the random scatter of compounds. These are ample, walled miniature fortresses, in pure village style, with three or four little circular huts around a broad central court for people to cook, play or work and pigs to scuffle and chickens to scratch. Water is one of the worst problems, along with lack of work. Everyone digs his own well, but in the dry season these dry up and water has to be bought from vendors who trundle around brightly coloured oil drums mounted on wheels: water costs 25p or 50cts a barrel. As for sanitation, most people go to the fields. The more enterprising may dig a latrine pit, but many site it so close to their well that the field trip would certainly be more healthy.

There is, of course, poverty.

Issaho Kandibi is a big-boned Mossi in his forties. He has a wife and four children and is looking after his brother's wife and her four children. The compound is spartan, the family's material possessions can be counted on the fingers: a corrugated-iron door on the round hut where Issaho sleeps; a fifteen-year-old bike with only the central spindle left of the pedals – bought with the savings of a spell in the Ivory Coast; and five chipped enamel bowls near the blackened wall by the fire. Everything else is home-made, including the children's toys. Assetta, aged eight, pushes along an old wheel rim with a piece of cane. Six-year-old Adissa plays with half a rubber ball. The younger children are completely naked, the older ones wear baggy second-hand knitted bathing trunks.

The children line up under the shade of a thatch roof and wait, quiet with hunger, while Issaho's wife serves up lunch, a plate of blackeye beans. The adults eat only once a day, usually millet paste with a red-hot spicy sauce. If they can restrain their appetite and keep back a little to mix with water the following morning, they can have some breakfast too.

Issaho's home village, Tengango, has gone through the familiar process of dwindling fallows and soil degradation. There was a time when he could grow enough millet to sell a third or a half for cash, which would pay his poll tax, buy meat and kerosene, and leave a little so he could chip in his share at relatives' funerals or weddings. But now the fields do not produce enough to live on, and for three months of the year he has to buy extra millet. He was forced to move to the city to survive. He still keeps his fields, and goes back home to work them in the four wet months, sleeping in a hut to guard the crops against trampling Fulani cattle. The rest of the year he lives in Ouagadougou.

He has given up wandering forlornly round offices, markets and warehouses trying to pick up odd jobs. Instead, like so many slum dwellers, he employs himself. He sells bundles of rushes for roofing, at 250 francs each (about 50p or $1), and panels of woven millet stalks for doors or walls, at 400 francs each. He works meticulously and with pride. The demand in expanding Ouagadougou is much higher than back home, enough to give his family a cash income of about £55 or $110 a year. Buying water in the dry season drinks up about $40 of that.

Despite his poverty, Issaho has retained his dignity and uses his ingenuity as best he can to make ends meet. I asked him if he earned enough to cover his needs, and he surprised me by saying that he did, because he didn't want to have 'more than his class'. But he did admit that if he wanted to eat two or three times a day instead of once, he wouldn't have enough.

In spite of the poverty of the majority, there is little exploitation here. No one is yet speculating in misery. No one pays any rent for the land or the house they have built themselves. People settle near neighbours from their home area. Like many middle-level towns in other countries, Ouagadougou is as yet no 'great wen of all' as William Cobbett called nineteenth-century London. It is still little more than a collection of urban villages, retaining most of the appearance and much of the social cohesion of the rural villages on which they are modelled, as most newcomers settle close to relatives or acquaintances from home.

Things may not stay that way. If Ouagadougou follows the pattern of other African cities, as demand for land increases, local tribes or chiefs may become land speculators and charge rents, or sell land. Longer-standing residents may set about building additional houses to let. And, once introduced, rents will no doubt inflate. But there is time to prevent these things. The iniquities lie in the future for Ouagadougou.

Calcutta: the packed and pestilential town

Long before the sickness became generalized, Calcutta was already suffering all the symptoms of hyper-urbanization. It was the first of the great urban chancres of the Third World.

On 24 August 1690, Job Charnock, a servant of the British East India Company, cast anchor on a mudflat in the River Hooghly, little knowing that this would one day become the densest concentration of suffering humanity in the world. For four years he had been the company's agent at a Mogul trading centre upstream, but the Mogul viceroy of Bengal had laid siege to the place, so Charnock was sent to find another base for the lucrative trade. The site he chose was surrounded by insalubrious swamps which would later spread malaria and give the city the flooding problem with which it has had to live ever since. But commercial and strategic considerations came uppermost in Charnock's mind. There was a deep-water anchorage for ocean ships, and the swamps provided protection against local nawabs who might turn hostile at any time.

Calcutta grew rapidly into the foremost trading outpost of the largest empire the world has ever seen. For 140 years from 1772 it was the capital of British India, and accreted all the services needed to administer the biggest of all Britain's colonies. It was the railhead for India's transport network: all lines of communication converged on it. Way back in the eighteenth century Robert Clive was already writing, 'Calcutta is the most wicked place in the universe.' Kipling's verse could apply to so many Third World cities:

> Chance-directed, chance-erected, laid and built
>> On the silt,
> Palace, byre, hovel – poverty and pride –
>> Side by side;
> And, above the packed and pestilential town,
>> Death looked down.

In the 1900s Calcutta became the centre of the jute-processing industry, which pulled in many rural migrants from the areas ruined by British administration. Engineering followed, to provide the mills with their machinery. Hindu refugees, fleeing from East Bengal when India was partitioned in 1947, provided the last great wave of migrants.

So Calcutta was bloated like a child with kwashiorkor, not healthy flesh or fat, but a watery, diseased oedema. I had seen a good deal of the Third World and of India before I visited Calcutta. But it was still a culture shock to arrive there, in a hot and damp rush hour, as dusk fell. It is the nearest human thing to an ant heap, a dense sea of people washing over roads hopelessly jammed as taxis swerve round hand-pulled rickshaws, buses run into handcarts, pony stagecoaches and private cars and even flocks of goats fight it out for the limited space. The trams and buses sag on their springs, people crammed in more densely than British captives in the Black Hole: twenty or thirty standing inside, six clinging to handrails outside the door, three or four on the back bumper, two on the spare tyre and the odd athlete suspended by nothing more than his finger tips from a window frame. A young woman in sari, her head leaning on her hand with an air of sleepy melancholia, reached for breath out of the window, though the air outside was almost as dank and malodorous as inside. She summed up my first feelings. After a few days of acclimatization, I got used to it all and began to admire the guts and gusto of the eight million people who survive in greater Calcutta.

Calcutta's slums or bustees house about a third of the city's inhabitants. Haransar Para is typical, a dark huddle of ramshackle buildings by the black, sluggish waters of East Canal. They have been here long enough for landlords to improve them. Many are in brick or concrete with tiled roofs, others exotic two-storey structures shakily constructed of corrugated iron on a wooden frame. The dwellings are arranged around a central courtyard. Each court has one service privy which must serve fifty people or more: it is no more than a hole in a concrete slab with an earthen pit underneath, its contents all too visible to users, and smellable from every room. Each family has only one room eight or ten feet square into which as many people may be crammed, along with their pots and pans, their bicycles and their gaudy pictures of Ganesh and Parvati. Haransar's narrow, unlit alleys are unpaved. Even in the dry season they have to be crossed by precarious rows of half bricks peering out of murky ponds. In the monsoon the whole place is awash and some homes are two feet deep in water, with families taking permanent refuge on their wooden beds raised four feet off the ground for this purpose. The contents of the privies float about like toy rafts.

Bustees are not, strictly speaking, squatter settlements. They are legal and above board. The land is rented from its private owners by middlemen or *tikka* tenants, who usually own the actual buildings and live there themselves, in conditions little better than anyone else. Residents pay their rents to the *tikka* tenant, and these are quite modest – between 75p and £1.25 ($1.50–$3) per month.

Yet there are those who cannot afford even these rents. For them, there are the camps, often situated by canals where people can wash and excrete. Walls of rough driftwood planks, roofs of sacking held down by bricks, these tents are the homes of ragged legions of rickshaw drivers and construction workers.

And there are the street dwellers. An Indian information official – most concerned, for it was at the time of Mrs Gandhi's emergency, to project a good image – explained to me that these people did not actually live on the street. 'It gets very hot here in the nights, you see, so some people like to put their beds out of doors.' He knew I didn't believe him, but at least he'd done his duty. The street dwellers are variously estimated to number anything from 40,000 to 200,000. You see them curled up on a straw mat or a piece of cardboard by the odd aluminium pot. Along the staid colonial shopping arcades, under the subways, camped on a roundabout by the gigantic pylons of Howrah bridge. A random line of them under a high wall by the riverside warehouses of Strand Road: a family of three living in a tiny shelter of torn khaki canvas slung over bamboo poles, not more than four feet square. A woman dreaming on her *charpoy* string bed, baby at her side with a tattered shirt over its face, pots, pans and boxes stuffed under the bed. A large family of eight under an awning, their tea cups neatly hanging from a string tacked to the wall. All this in full gaze of passers-by and a noisy flow of traffic. Street life is, by definition, a life lived in public.

Each one of these faces hides a personal disaster: a fifteen-year-old boy whose parents died of cholera four years earlier. His uncles neglected him so he left his home village for Calcutta, and he earns two rupees a day collecting rags and scrap paper. A twenty-five-year-old woman whose husband deserted her, so she had to move out of their bustee room. Now she lives on the pavement near the railway station, working as a domestic servant in the daytime and at night as a prostitute. A widow of forty with five children: when her husband died she couldn't work the family smallholding and bring up the children, so she fell into debt and had to pay it off by selling house and land. Now she lives on a platform at Ballygunge railway station where she has to pay protection money to thugs to stop them driving her away. She supplements her meagre servant's pay by begging.

Street dwellers are like wild birds: they have their own particular ecology, their favoured nesting sites and feeding grounds. You find them close to the markets, bazaars and warehouses, where they might pick up the odd day's work; or near the temples, where they can beg from people feeling pious; or by the station where they arrived; or under a wall or fence, giving some minimum of shelter and protection against the elements. Their mode and place of residence is inseparably linked to their income and livelihood: they can't afford house rents near their place of work or source of income, nor can they afford bus fares from further out where rents might be lower. Many of them were swept away to the outskirts under Mrs Gandhi's emergency, but if they are moved, their precarious ecological niche is wrecked and their very survival is threatened. There can be no solution to their accommodation problem without a solution to their economic problem.

Hobson's choice – or why squatters squat

While western cities are thinning out as people move to the suburbs, Third World cities are growing denser, infilling their empty spaces, building layer on layer of unsafe structures. In Istanbul tents sprout under the crumbling walls of ancient Byzantium and three-storey wooden shacks are sandwiched between modern blocks of flats in defiance of all building regulations. In 1970, 2·2 million Turks had to live here in the same space that housed only 1·3 million ten years earlier. In Asian cities, a hundred people are crowded into each hectare, as against only forty-five for western Europe and seventeen for the United States.

One-room dwellings are the rule in squatter areas. The extended family, with grandparents, grand uncles, brothers and all their wives and children in the same compound, tends to break up here into its constituent nuclear units: two parents and their children. In Tehran more than nine out of ten squatters live in one-room units with an average of only three square metres space per person. Personal space in Calcutta is cut even further – eight square feet per person is not uncommon. In the Karachi slum of Usmania Mohajir, two fifths of the dwellings have more than six people per room (the average British home has 0·6). Overcrowding imposes mental strains, family tensions increase, rivalries between brothers and sisters get more intense, privacy is an unknown luxury. Overcrowding adds to the other stresses of dirty water and lack of health posts and school, depressing the productivity of breadwinners and pushing the children towards educational failure. The poor live in places that are likely to consolidate and perpetuate their poverty.

And they know it. Everyone likes a nice house and clean water, and wants their children to go to school. The poor live in slums for a simple reason: they have no choice. They cannot afford decent housing of the kind most public authorities and private developers choose to build. They cannot afford it because they are poor. They spend anything between one half and three quarters or more of their incomes on food alone. To buy better housing would mean slicing into food budgets already pared to the bone. If the choice is hunger or a leaky roof, they have to put up with the leaks. And they are poor because there are not enough paying jobs to go round. The slum problem is the visible expression of the Third World city's economic crisis.

Instead of building accommodation to suit the purse of the poor, most governments and councils have built to excessively high western standards, using expensive materials and construction methods. Most public housing in the Third World is another example of inappropriate technology. Only a few oil-rich states can really afford to provide western-style housing for all their city dwellers. For the rest, the high cost of this choice means that only limited amounts can be built – and that only the urban privileged, the government employees and salaried workers, can afford to buy or rent it.

A study by the World Bank of six developing cities shows that a major proportion of urban households cannot afford to buy on a mortgage or rent even the very cheapest public housing units. The proportions excluded ranged from 35 per cent of the people of Hong Kong, through 47 per cent of Bogotá and 55 per cent of Mexico City, to a full two thirds of the populations of Madras, Ahmedabad and Nairobi. The costs of modern-sector housing in many Third World cities now equal or exceed those in some capital cities of the West – a salaried worker in Abidjan may be paying as much in rent as a British council house tenant, out of a quarter of the income.

Soaring land prices contribute to the high cost of housing. The cost of land on the expanding periphery of Calcutta went up by 1,300 per cent between 1950 and 1965. Land prices have risen twice as fast as consumer prices in Tehran and Seoul, three times as fast in Mexico City, five times as fast in Jamaica. When public services – surfaced road, water, light – are extended to a new district, land prices can easily quadruple. As soon as a place becomes habitable, the urban masses can no longer afford to live there. Land prices have been inflated by speculators cashing in on the sheer pressure of demand: the endless floods of migrants looking for a place to live – and fighting an unequal battle with national and multinational companies, hotels, banks and so on for land near the centre. As jobs tend to be located centrally, the poor are pushed further and further away from where the work is, so either their chances of employment are reduced, or they have to spend a huge proportion of their wages on transport.

Nationalization of urban land could prevent the worst excesses of land price inflation, by which urban landowners are being made into millionaires not by their own enterprise but by the total economic situation of their country. Land could then be allocated on welfare grounds, not on the basis of who can pay most. But urban land reform is not even on the drawing boards of most Third World governments, possibly because land speculation is one of the most profitable sidelines for many top civil servants and politicians.

The final solution: removal of unauthorized structures

National and city governments have been the main architects of the slum problem, because they have failed to invest in rural areas, to keep people in the villages. They have failed to invest in job creation in the cities, to give city dwellers an adequate income, and they have spent their scarce funds on over-expensive housing. Migrants migrate, and squatters squat, simply in response to the circumstances created by their rulers: they have to survive, and they have to live somewhere. But many governments have failed to understand the causation of squatter settlements, and have treated them as a sort of deviant behaviour, a housing crime, an ugly eyesore that can be swept away provided you can mobilize enough bulldozers and policemen for the operation. Not satisfied with neglecting them, some governments have chosen to harass and persecute the rural poor camped outside the city walls or on its very streets, as if they were besieging armies and infiltrators.

Too many governments have chosen to remove the symptoms rather than the cause. In Manila, Colombo, Tripoli, Nairobi, squatter settlements have been flattened. In India, Mrs Gandhi's son Sanjay spearheaded a 'moral crusade' against slums and street dwellers. As British writer David Selbourne reports, from March 1976 Bombay's 75,000 beggars and hawkers were mopped up in mass arrests, some of them taken to forced-labour camps designed 'to lead the able bodied to a life of self-respect, dignity and rehabilitation'. The Maharashtra government appointed a special police force to protect all vacant lands from squatting and to demolish new hutments. Delhi started on a drive 'for the removal of encroachments and the demolition of unauthorized structures', razing to the ground the sardine-packed streets and bazaars of old Delhi and trucking the inhabitants to dumping grounds far from the city, abandoning them without light, water, sanitation, transport or jobs.

The Ivory Coast's vigorous demolition programme was inspired by laudable motives of improving housing conditions, yet its effect was quite the opposite.

Chic, flash Abidjan has become the siren of West Africa. The Manhattan skyline of its Plateau district rises over streets resounding with the horns of Peugeots, Mercedes, Alfa Romeos. French boutiques sell the latest Parisian fashions.

Like Calcutta, Abidjan was an artificial creation. The site was chosen as a port and terminal for the Niger railway that curved down from Niamey, Bobo-Dioulasso and Bouaké with the produce of a far-flung empire.

It was not chosen for its capacity to carry a huge metropolis. No one could have foreseen its vertiginous growth, from a mere 58,000 in 1948 to 250,000 in 1963 and more than a million in the late seventies. Today, its spread across islands and lagoons has led to immense imbalances in the location of jobs and homes. A green belt of forest reserve did nothing to halt the growth: squatting burst out again beyond it, at Abobo, where an unofficial city shows every sign of outgrowing its official sister. A typical Abobo resident may be ten miles and three expensive changes of bus away from his job in Vridi and spend two or three hours a day straphanging. Traffic jams are chronic, for Abidjan has 70 per cent of all the cars in the Ivory Coast but only 13 per cent of its population. This is how cities in poor countries come, prematurely, to suffer the tribulations of commuting familiar in rich countries.

The land was once tribal land belonging to the Ébrié, but it was unacceptable for a capital city to grow according to the whims of land chiefs, so the Ébrié were bought out long ago. This move did not bring with it the expected control over the city's expansion. Little flocks of shanties spring up in the most unsightly and unhealthy places. The thriving community of Marcory Potto-Potto is built on swamp. Its passages are permanently flooded, and taxis refuse to negotiate the knee-deep potholes and mudbaths of the access track. Only a few houses are in traditional style of clay over a lattice of bamboo. Most are curious disinherited structures, reminiscent of the artist Kurt Schwitters' garbage collages – grey wooden planks shored with bits of corrugated tin, packing crates still marked with their destinations, and other *objets trouvés*. Here bachelors and families live in single rooms off shared courtyards. And next door, picturesquely scattered and plaited with pink bind-weed, is a large colony of tiny tin shacks which appear to be inhabited exclusively by women. I later learned that here lives a major part of the city's downmarket prostitute population.

Most of the residents here pay rents to the petty landlords who knocked the shacks together. The landlords have no title to the land, no right to be occupying it, no right to be charging rents. The tenants are exploited and have no security of tenure.

Abidjan has pursued a policy of building a large amount of new public housing to near-western standards. But because of the high cost it cannot hope to house the backlog of shanty dwellers, let alone keep up with the inflow of newcomers arriving at the rate of two hundred every day. To provide sites for the new estates, shanty settlements have been bulldozed out of the way and their inhabitants dispersed to fend for themselves as best they can. In just five years from 1969, the dwellings of one in five of Abidjan's families were demolished. Most of them were not rehoused, but simply dehoused.

The displaced shanty dwellers have no priority for rehousing, because they had no formal title to the land they were on. They are, like anyone else, free to apply for a new flat or bungalow – but few of them can afford the rents. The fate of Port Bouet is a sad moral tale for Third World slums. It was a fishing village, fronting the Atlantic surf along a steep beach. Behind this, a lively mixed settlement of migrants had grown up, with large houses built solidly of rough wooden planks. All the thoroughfares were lined with the plethora of small trades that all squatter settlements foster: charcoal merchants, fish smokers, cabinet makers, bike repairers, sellers of fifty-seven varieties of cooked food.

All that was left of Port Bouet when I visited it was a small triangle, soon to be demolished in its turn, that looked as exposed as Custer's last stand. Surrounding it, behind a no-man's land of rubble, was an advancing line of modern blocks of flats. The cheapest rents were around four times what the average shanty family was paying. And the new, planned, sanitized area will no doubt comply with job-destroying western-style zoning regulations that keep out the mass of informal trades and the considerable employment they generate.

The former inhabitants of Port Bouet were scattered all over the other squatter areas of Abidjan. In a marshy wilderness of shacks renamed Port Bouet Two, I met one family that had been displaced three times by demolitions, and even their present resting place was on someone's schedule for clearance. The head of the household was a divorced lady with two children. She had been offered a piece of municipal land to build on, but could not afford the high contribution required of her. She was paying a fifth of her £18 ($36) a month income from selling cooked rice in rent for a one-roomed wooden shack, part of which fell down even while I was talking to her.

It is easy to see why governments do not like squatter settlements. They are invariably insanitary (but that is the government's doing) and usually overcrowded. Because they are cities of the poor, they harbour more than their share of petty thieves, drunks and murderers (though the big-time criminals live in the modern city). They flout property rights. They are illegal or at best outside the law. They are rushed up in defiance of all regulations on planning, safety and public health. They are a snub in the face of bureaucracy and authority; an anarchic gesture of freedom.

But they do have considerable virtues which are only just beginning to be recognized. Rents are non-existent, or at any rate far lower than in the modern sector, so families have more to spend on food. People can build their own houses to suit their ideas of comfort or household arrangement, and to a standard they know they can afford. As and when they have the cash to do so, they can improve their home, adding another storey, or replacing a wall of old tea chests with bricks.

Spontaneous settlements allow people a freer choice of where to live. Usually rural migrants will settle near relatives or people from their home area, so the squatter belt becomes a string of urban villages where people can preserve at least some of their culture, their ceremonies, their networks of mutual help and support. This can cushion people against the isolation and alienation of fragmented city life. Finally, squatter settlements are not covered by inappropriate western planning ideas of zoning, separating residential and industrial areas – ideas, incidentally, that have suppressed the emergence of much employment in small business in the West too. Shanties are places of work as well as of residence.

All these virtues exist side by side with the real vices: overcrowding, insanitary conditions, lack of facilities, insecurity of tenure. The ideal approach to the squatter problem is to preserve the virtues while eliminating the vices. The squatter phenomenon is inevitable for the foreseeable future, and has to be accepted as such. Existing shanties – all but the most squalid – should be left standing with their low rents, their job opportunities and their community links. But they can be upgraded very cheaply, with roads, sewers, water, light, best of all with the voluntary labour of the squatters themselves. Incoming migrants can be provided with sites on which to build their own houses with a bit of expert guidance, sites where the essential services are already laid on or are installed by the squatters. Some governments have now accepted this principle: Zambia, Tanzania, Malawi, Senegal, Turkey, Iraq, India, Pakistan all have substantial programmes. Squatters can be given security of tenure and urban housing land nationalized to prevent rent inflation. Schools and health posts can be evenly spread throughout the city, not reserved for official areas. These measures will not make model garden cities, but they will create appropriate cities. They will provide the migrants with a more healthy and dignified environment where they and their children have more equal chances in life.

City incomes of the poor can be improved by providing more labour-intensive workplaces. But, ultimately, the only way of halting hyper-urbanization is by reducing the obscene gap between city and rural incomes, investing in improvements that will help to keep the rural poor on the land. The problem of overblown cities, in other words, cannot be solved until the problem of underdeveloped rural areas is attacked.

10. Workless of the World: Success and Failure of Big Industry

'It is machinery that has impoverished India. By reproducing Manchester in India we shall keep our money at the price of our blood.'

GANDHI

All day long men crowd around the inquiries grille at Calcutta's central employment exchange, which must have one of the largest number of unemployed on its books in the entire world. At the time of my visit in 1976, there were 201,052 people on its register, and they were fighting for just 8,469 vacancies.

It does not say 'Abandon all hope, ye who enter here' over its forbidding wrought-iron gates, but perhaps it ought to. Inside, an air of gloom and desperation reigns. The murky rooms, lit by naked, smoke-blackened lightbulbs, are lined with aged green filing cabinets, every drawer bursting with the yellowing files of half-forgotten applicants. Young men thrust their forms at junior clerks, full of hope and urgency, as if the clerks could hand out jobs in return. Others tap away at typing tests, forced at last to prove in action the grandiose claims on their application forms. Outside, a few enterprising touts have solved their own unemployment problem by ministering to that of other people: they sell the *All India Employment Gazette*, or cyclostyled application forms for specific jobs recently advertised in the papers. It is all a forlorn quest. Most of the applicants are condemned to spend the afternoons looking at the pictures outside cinemas, unable to afford the entrance fee, or trudging from one 'No vacancies' sign to the next, living by cadging off relatives and performing menial domestic chores in return.

In 1977, the International Labour Office estimates, some 331 million people – two fifths of the entire labour force in the non-socialist Third World – were unemployed or underemployed. Of these, perhaps 40 millions were totally unemployed, a rate of 5 per cent. Unemployment in cities is much higher than this average suggests. Urban unemployment in Algeria was over 26 per cent in 1966, 20 per cent in Morocco (1960), the Ivory Coast (1963) and Guyana (1965), in Jamaica and Burundi 19 per cent (1960 and 1963). One survey of thirty-four countries, using figures from various years in the sixties, found that the urban unemployment rate was above 10 per cent in twenty of them, above 15 per cent in eight and topped 20 per cent in four.

In many countries open unemployment has risen steadily, hardly falling even in upturns in the economic cycle: India's 2·6 million registered unemployed in 1966 climbed steadily every year, reaching 9·6 millions in 1976. Sri Lanka's 225,000 rose to 546,000 over the same ten years. But open unemployment is only a small part of the employment problem. It tends to be a city phenomenon – that is where the labour exchanges are, if any, for people to sign on and be counted. And it is an affliction more of the middle and lower middle classes. The real poor cannot afford to be unemployed, nor can their relatives afford to keep them.

Underemployment is much more widespread and hits mainly the rural areas and the urban poor. The I L O estimates that it affects 290 million people in the non-socialist Third World, and of these, 250 millions are on the land. Unemployment is easily understood: if a man has no work and is seeking a job, he is unemployed. Underemployment is a more tricky concept. Many idle rich are severely underemployed. A man is also, strictly speaking, underemployed if he has only modest needs and can satisfy them by working only part of the time. Underemployment, for those with an adequate income to meet their needs, may be a luxury to be savoured, not the curse that it often seemed to hyperactive, puritanical European colonialists.

Underemployment, as a *problem* to the man suffering it, is inseparable from poverty. Problem underemployment occurs when a man is working less than normal and is seeking additional work. Even if he works full-time, he is considered underemployed if his income is inadequate to meet his basic needs.

Of all the many problems that beset the Third World, the employment problem is probably central. Even the food problem which occupies so much of popular debate in the West is at bottom a question of providing the poor with the work and income to enable them to buy the food they need. If the record of job creation to date has not been impressive, the task that lies ahead looks positively frightening. Between 1975 and 2000, on a medium projection, the labour force of the developing countries will grow from 1,125 millions to 1,907 millions. Asia's workforce will expand by 60 per cent, Africa's by 86 per cent and Latin America's by 103 per cent, over 1975 levels. If we add to the increase in the labour force the 331 millions who are currently unemployed or underemployed, this leads to the daunting conclusion: *more than one billion new jobs have to be created in the Third World before the end of the century.*

The record of the past is not encouraging. The sixties and early seventies were relatively good times: industry expanded rapidly, while the new strains of seed allowed many (though not enough) smallholdings that would have become unviable to go on supporting their owners. But even in this period the creation of new jobs did not keep pace with the creation of new people, and unemployment increased. In Colombia, for example, the labour force grew at 3·5 per cent a year while jobs for them expanded at only 2·3 per cent. In Sri Lanka new jobs were created at the rate of 2 per cent a year, but the labour force grew at 3 per cent.

Overall, the Third World labour force was growing at 1·66 per cent a year in the early sixties and 1·97 per cent a year in the early seventies. In the future, it will speed up to 2·1 per cent a year between 1980 and 1985, reaching an all-time peak of 2·23 per cent ten years later. Even if the impossible happened and population growth were to halt overnight, the workforce would still go on growing for fifteen to twenty years, until the baby boom had worked its way through to the labour market. If jobs could not be created fast enough at a time of rapid economic growth and slower growth of the labour force, what chance is there of keeping pace in the future?

None at all, if present policies continue.

We have seen how the land is failing to absorb extra workers because of soil exhaustion and mechanization. Part cause in the agricultural problems was the fact that governments channelled a grotesquely excessive share of their scarce investment funds into industry and the infrastructure it needed.

What then, of this great panacea and panjandrum? It grew fast – yet its performance was disappointing. It paid its workers relatively well, but it failed to employ enough of them. It did not drag the backward rural areas bawling and screaming into the twentieth century, as leaders had hoped it would. Indeed, it helped to ruin them. As the great spearhead of modernization it was cracked up to be, it was a disastrous flop.

It is important to understand the reasons why. The first and most straightforward is that it started from a very small base, so that even great leaps forward could not make it expand fast in absolute terms. The second is that, as in every sector we shall be looking at, inappropriate western models were followed. The latest, large-scale, capital-intensive machines were bought, needing only a few machine minders to keep them running. As they were so expensive, and funds were so scarce, this meant that only a few workplaces could be created. The average cost of a workplace in a small-scale enterprise ranges from $50 to $200 in Africa to between $1,000 and $3,000 in Latin America. Jobs in large-scale enterprises cost five to ten times as much, and hence, given a limited budget, can employ only one fifth or one tenth as many people. This philosophy of 'big is beautiful' brought high incomes for the few that worked with the new machines, while throwing out of work the many who did not. Like mechanization on the land, large machines were engines for increasing inequality and poverty.

Colonial de-industrialization

Industry started from a small base partly because Europe wiped out what industry did exist before her arrival on the scene. It had always been small-scale and decentralized. On the one hand, village crafts, smithing, pottery, spinning and weaving, carpentry, masonry, basketwork – little of which would be sold outside the immediate vicinity. On the other hand, the skilled artisan trades producing luxury goods for kings, courtiers, bureaucrats and temples. There was little competition: handicrafts were produced by families for their own needs, or by semi-hereditary castes. There was, as Swedish economist Gunnar Myrdal points out, no spur to efficiency or improvement of technology. Nor did that matter, until the arrival of the Europeans. Nowhere was there a large proportion of the population engaged in manufacture, though India and China had built up important manufacturing industries, which might, eventually, have taken off.

They did not, because as Europe became industrialized, she de-industrialized the rest of the world. In many cases there was a deliberate policy of preventing local entrepreneurs starting up manufacturing in competition with the industries of the colonial country, and even of stamping out those already in the field. It was not through fair and free trade that the West came to dominate industry in the early years. In Britain, for example, the wearing or selling of silks and calicoes from India, Persia and China was prohibited. Britain consciously destroyed what industry India had by restricting her exports of manufactures, prohibiting the export of British textile machinery to India, and flooding India with imports from Britain. British goods were allowed to move freely from one Indian princely state to the next, while locally made goods had to pay internal customs duties at every frontier, which made them dearer. India's textile industry was ruined. Cotton spinning virtually disappeared from the villages. Millions of spinners and weavers lost a major source of income. In 1908, when Gandhi advocated a return to hand spinning as a 'panacea for pauperism', the art had almost completely died out and the Mahatma could not even find a single spinning wheel to work with. Only a long search through the great textile state of Gujarat finally unearthed some wheels that had been consigned to the loft as useless lumber. Until the early nineteenth century, India had been a textile exporting country. The British made her an importer. The value of her currency declined along with the purchasing power of her inhabitants. It was, in the end, a self-defeating policy, for as Karl Marx pointed out in 1853 –

in a comment that is still relevant today – 'You cannot continue to inundate a country with your manufactures unless you enable it to give you some produce in return.' Likewise, Spain and Portugal did not encourage the emergence of industry in Latin America. For a long time the colonies there were forbidden to produce anything that was already being made in the mother country. A burgeoning manufacturing industry began during the Napoleonic wars, when trade with the Iberian peninsula was cut off. This could have provided the basis for industrialization of the kind that began at this time in North America. But the groups that seized power in the newly independent Latin American states of the early nineteenth century, and maintained it thereafter, were the landowners, the producers of raw materials and the commercial bourgeoisie who exported these and imported the luxuries required by the local rich. The embryonic industrialists wanted protective tariffs to get their factories going, but the ruling groups did not want the dearer imports this would have meant, nor were they interested in developing the home market for manufactures by increasing the incomes of the peasants. And so Latin America prematurely adopted the British expounded doctrine of free trade. Her industries could not compete with cheaper British and US manufactures, and did not get off the ground until well into this century, when the Great Depression once again interrupted trade with the West. The free trade virus also killed off nascent industries and old traditional ones in the non-colonies such as China and Japan, who were compelled by military force to open their frontiers to western manufactures. Only Japan, of all non-European countries, succeeded in overcoming the obstacle course set by the western industrial powers, and finally industrialized.

Independence: rapid strides ahead

Despite these initial handicaps, Third World countries have, in the last two or three decades, succeeded in expanding their industries with remarkable speed. Even allowing for the fast rate of population increases, manufacturing output overall, and per person, has grown faster than any western nation (except the USA) achieved in the days of their own industrialization. In the boom years of 1953 to 1970, total industrial output grew at an annual rate of 7·2 per cent a year, per capita output by 4 per cent. Britain, at her fastest stage of growth between 1800 and 1850, achieved a growth rate of only 3·6 per cent in total manufacturing output, or 2·2 per cent in per capita output.

Third World industry continued its beanstalk-like growth in the seventies, averaging 7 per cent a year between 1971 and 1975, only 1 per cent short of the ambitious target set for the United Nations' second development decade. Even in the bleak oil-crisis-shadowed years of 1973 and 1974, when western output fell back, developing countries' output continued to plough ahead.

Industry in the Third World countries has usually developed to a common pattern known as import substitution, by which domestic manufacturing is built up to replace imports from the West, behind a protective fence of often extremely high tariffs. The first industries to develop are usually those processing locally produced, perishable materials, especially food: baking, food processing, canning, soft drinks, beer. Next come industries using bulky, locally available materials, where high transport costs make foreign goods too expensive: cement, bricks, sanitary ware, furniture. The first steps into consumer durables come with the assembly business: local workers not yet skilled enough (or without the local back-up of subcontractors) to produce the components for cars, fridges or cookers assemble kits of components shipped in from industrialized countries. Gradually the locally made content of these products is increased, creating jobs in component making, tool and die-and-mould making. Finally, but only in a few countries, a capital goods industry making machinery may develop, and the state might develop iron and steel industries to feed these. The import substitution game can take a long time to pay off, or even to reduce imports. The reason is that all the machinery for industrialization, all the knowhow and spare parts, and often a lot of the raw materials such as plastics or special metals, have to be imported.

A newer strategy which found increasing favour in the seventies was export-led industrialization. This tried to get over the problem of small home markets by turning out, usually with the help of western multinationals, manufactures for the western market, profiting from the developing country's vast supply of cheap labour. The South-East Asian nations have pursued this approach in clothing, shoes, consumer electricals and electronics from hair-dryers to calculators and cameras. But the strategy has its problems: it too involves dependence on western imported technology. As its products must compete in the international market place with the most sophisticated western goods, it demands a good supply of skilled workers and effective marketing – two factors most Third World countries lack. Its worst drawback is that it may be self-defeating: in the seventies it helped to awaken increasing protectionist feelings in western countries, which slapped import quotas and restrictions on many Third World manufacturers.

One of the greatest success stories in rapid industrialization was Singapore, which transformed itself within the space of only ten years, from 1965, from a trading base to the only non-oil Third World country with a per capita income ($2,700 in 1976) ahead of several European countries. National income grew at the astonishing rate of 17 per cent a year in the first half of the seventies, while manufacturing jobs nearly trebled from 79,000 in 1968 to 207,000 in 1977. Factories mushroomed on the former mudflats of Jurong, where an entire modern city, with workers' flats, executives' houses, parks, golf-courses and motorways sprouted from a wilderness in the course of five to seven years. The bulk of the new investment was foreign: European, American and Japanese multinationals moved in in droves. Rollei, wiped out in Germany by Japanese competition, opened up a camera factory. Philips, likewise hit in Holland and Britain, opened up four factories producing anything from domestic electrical goods to telecommunications equipment. Mighty Mitsubishi opened a ship repair yard and trained its own workforce in its highly idiosyncratic Japanese management style – office workers all dressed in grey overalls to emphasize unity with manual workers, knee bends and arm stretching sessions for everyone, twice a day. Local entrepreneurs profited from orders from the multinationals, and from the increased spending power of their employees. Ngai Mee, for example, makes gaily coloured wrappers for chocolates, biscuits and toffees. But even the smallest piece of their machinery is imported. The six-colour printing press they are so proud of comes from Japan, where several of their workers had to go to learn how to use it. The tool and die firm of Nam Tat had only seven employees in 1968, now it has a hundred. It produces plastic injection moulds of gradually increasing complexity, as its skills develop.

Building up the skills to man industry is a slow process. A skilled engineer takes four years to train, and another skilled engineer has to be taken out of production to do the training. Creating the kind of schools that foster mechanical, practical minds can involve restructuring the entire educational system away from the traditional academic bias. More advanced skills have to be learned abroad in the industrialized countries, an expensive business which only a few students at a time can profit from. Nam Tat's most recent order, when I visited them, was for a complicated casing for a General Electric radio alarm. The Singaporean who did the design job had ten years' training behind him, including a couple of years abroad, and Nam Tat had imported a hugely expensive Swiss spark erosion machine to do the more sophisticated work. But some jobs still are beyond their capabilities. The general manager of Philips Singapore showed me a vast range of their products that were assembled locally, from TV sets to fan heaters, but most of the components or moulds had to be imported. He slapped a neat orange hair-dryer with sleek, curving shapes: 'It would take years for them to develop the engineering skills to develop that here,' he said. The success of Singapore tempted many other countries to believe they could follow in its footsteps. But it was a forlorn hope: the multinationals need only a limited number of platforms for their cheap mass-produced exports.

So most of Third World industry, for all its rapid growth, remains at a relatively low stage of development, almost totally dependent on western knowhow and technology. Its share of world manufacturing output has remained virtually static for twenty years since 1955, at around 7 per cent of the total. The real advances are being chalked up by only a handful of countries: South Korea, Hong Kong, Taiwan, Singapore, India. In 1971, Latin America turned out 55 per cent of the manufacturing outputs of the Third World. Just three countries — Brazil, Mexico and Argentina — were producing nearly two fifths of the Third World total.

Seven-league boots and tiny feet

And despite all the effort and sacrifice, industry has been unable to absorb even the increase in the labour force, let alone take in the millions displaced from agriculture. In the sixties, for example, the labour force increased by 165 millions, but industry employed only 54 millions of these.

Because of the small starting base, impossible growth rates would be needed if industry were to absorb most of the increased working population. In 1970 industry employed only 22 per cent of Latin American workers, 17 per cent of Asians and 11 per cent of Africans. By 1975, overall, perhaps 18 per cent of the workers in developing countries were in manufacturing — and the workforce as a whole was increasing at 2 per cent a year. To take in these two extra workers for every hundred, the eighteen jobs in industry would have to grow by more than 11 per cent a year. Only a handful of countries managed to expand their industrial workforce by more than 10 per cent a year in the first half of the seventies: Nigeria, Singapore, Kenya, Haiti, Iraq, Korea, Tanzania and the Philippines. In countries containing half the Third World population, industrial employment grew at 4 per cent a year or less. Allowing for productivity increases, industrial output in the Third World would have to grow at perhaps 20 per cent a year, around three times faster than at present, to absorb the extra workers who will come onto the labour market. This is totally impossible: thus pointing to the importance of creating a major part of the new jobs that will be needed on the land.

Nevertheless, manufacturing industry could have absorbed far greater numbers than it has done, and spread the wealth it creates far more widely and equitably, if it had chosen the right kind of labour-intensive technology. Instead, as most leaders were obsessed with catching up with the West, they wanted the very best available western techniques. Western technology, naturally enough, has been developed for western social and economic conditions: a large, skilled industrial workforce, high wages and welfare benefits, and plenty of capital. Under these conditions, it made sense to adopt labour-saving, capital-intensive technology, though even in the West this process is now going further than our social systems can tolerate, leading to rising unemployment even in years of expansion. And this is the technology that most developing nations, with their throngs of work-seekers, subsistence rates of pay and chronic shortage of capital, have imported. Productivity — that euphemistic expression that so often means redundancies — grew as fast in the Third World as in the West, at around 4 per cent a year. So, while manufacturing output grew at around 7 per cent a year in the sixties, employment in industry grew at only 3 per cent. That gap was due to the introduction of more and more efficient machines. Industrial workers were becoming more and more productive, and many of them more and more highly paid as a result. Yet at the very same time the great horde of the unemployed and underemployed, poor beyond western imagination, was swelling. What good was it to them that better-quality goods were being turned out at lower prices? They had no money to buy them at any price.

Buying western technology with little thought for its effect on employment has been a bad deal for the Third World. It did not reduce, but increased their dependence on the West. Often it did not cut imports and even increased them. It worked at only a fraction of its capacity. And often it threw out of work, by what Gunnar Myrdal has termed the 'backwash effect', as many as or more people than it could employ. Gandhi was well aware of the dangers of western technology half a century before concern about appropriate technology became fashionable. 'Men go on "saving labour" till thousands are without work, thrown on the open streets to die of starvation,' he wrote in 1924. Or again, 'How can a country with crores (tens of millions) of living machines afford to have a machine which will displace the labour of crores of living machines?' Gandhi saw quite clearly that mass production (which he defined as 'production by the fewest possible number') could lead in the Third World context to mass unemployment and the concentration of wealth and power in the hands of the few.

More recent experience has confirmed his insight. The International Labour Office economist Keith Marsden quotes the appalling but characteristic case of a country where a new plastic shoe industry was set up. Two expensive plastic injection machines were imported at a cost of $100,000 (£50,000). The PVC material for the shoes also had to be imported. The factory employed a total of forty workers, who turned out some one and a half million pairs of plastic sandals a year. They sold well, because at $2 (£1) a pair they were no dearer than cheap leather ones, but lasted much longer. They soon supplanted leather shoes on the market, and made a fat profit for the manufacturer and decent wages for the workers. Meanwhile the five thousand artisans who used to make the leather shoes found their business drying up and were finally flung onto the human scrapheap, together with their suppliers of leather, hand tools, eyelets, lining, laces and lasts. Overall result: forty jobs gained, perhaps eight thousand jobs lost. Import bills increased (the leather used to be supplied locally). Inequality and poverty given another boost. Marsden quotes other sad examples of inappropriate western technology: the $2 million date-processing plant that lay idle for two years because no one knew how to repair it; or the Latin American sweet factory that was inactive for most of the year because 80 per cent of its sales were made in the few weeks before a religious festival.

Advanced technology has directly contributed to the excessive growth of cities, both in the relatively high incomes it generates for its workers, and by destroying the village crafts that used to provide a good deal of employment. Whereas village industry is evenly spread, large-scale technology brings centralization and concentration. It demands to be set up in the urban centres with the roads, water and power that have not reached the rural areas. It expropriates the work of the villages and removes it to the cities, forcing villagers to follow it. And yet it demands skills they do not possess, and can only employ a few. It deprives them of livelihoods, turns them into human flotsam and jetsam, the lost lumpenproletariat of the slums.

The stranded whale

One of the most ironic results of using rich man's technology in poor countries is that it lies idle much of the time, like a great whale stranded in a freshwater pond. Millions are unemployed, while machines stand silent.

Before the depression of the seventies created overcapacity in western industries such as steel, oil-refining, plastics, ship-building and cars, most branches of western industry operated at 80 to 100 per cent of capacity. Even the lower end of that range would be considered an outstanding performance in a developing country. Survey after survey has revealed the appalling waste of expensive plant in the Third World: Indian industry running at 75 per cent of capacity, West Pakistan's at 64 per cent, Afghanistan's textile mills at 43 per cent. Sudan's ministry of planning estimated that utilization of capacity rarely exceeded 50 per cent and in the private sector typically ran at 15 to 30 per cent. A four-country survey of 1,451 firms by the World Bank found average capital utilization levels of between 35 per cent (Israel) and 50 per cent (Malaysia). Because of this, there are many fewer jobs available than if the plants were running at full tilt. The International Labour Office states that making full use of existing capacity could take up between 40 per cent and 100 per cent of open unemployment in the modern sector.

Waste of capacity is the visible symptom of a whole range of ailments afflicting industry in poor countries.

Firms that use foreign machinery and imported raw materials naturally need foreign exchange to buy these, but because of the foreign exchange nightmares that beset practically every developing country, foreign exchange is more precious than gold and there are endless difficulties in obtaining it. Nearly two thirds of firms in a Tanzanian survey said that part of their overcapacity was due to inability to get hold of enough foreign exchange. One firm had been set up to make fishing nets. It used foreign machinery and made the nets out of nylon, which had to be imported, whereas Tanzania is one of the world's biggest producers of sisal. Inevitably, the firm ran into foreign exchange problems which halted its imports of nylon. Its expensive machinery could not be converted to sisal, and so stood idle. Quite apart from getting money to pay for imports, importing anything in most developing countries is often a nightmare of labyrinthine bureaucratic procedures – again, partly because of the balance of payments problem and the desire to cut imports to essentials. Import licences can often be obtained only after long delays. Customs officers can be as strict as the gatekeepers of heaven (unless you suitably grease their palms). Three or four sets of every conceivable document are required and final clearance – even when the thing has arrived – can take months. When I went to live in Nigeria, I sent an expensive tape-recorder on ahead, air freight. It did not re-emerge from the customs sheds until twelve months later, when I was leaving. Not only factories, even development projects using foreign technology are held up. The Kaliprogo irrigation project in Indonesia had three British trucks out of action for three months waiting for a drive gear.

Another hitch is that capital-intensive western technology needs a reliable infrastructure which is often lacking in developing countries. It relies on inanimate rather than human energy – and as fuel gets more and more expensive, that choice becomes less and less rational. Moreover, the power stations, too, are pieces of foreign technology, and suffer from the same problems. Power cuts due to lack of maintenance, excess loads or tropical storms are one of the facts of life in poor countries, which is why in most hotel rooms you will find a little stack of candles in reserve. Seven out of ten Tanzanian firms suffered from unannounced supply interruptions. One in three complained of water shortages. Repair and maintenance is always a problem, both because spares suffer from the foreign exchange problem and because even when they arrive there may be no one around who can fit them. Shortages of skilled labour and efficient management also play a part.

But there is another reason for overcapacity which points straight to the core of industry's problems in the Third World. It is that the average developing country has a home market for manufactured goods that is too small for the available western-made manufacturing plants. In many countries the market is small numerically – two thirds of Third World nations have populations below ten millions. More significantly, the market is small in terms of effective demand: not enough people can *pay* for the products of industry, though they may well need or want them. Even some of those who can pay may be out of reach of underdeveloped marketing networks. In Tanzania, there were people crying out for this or that product, yet it couldn't be got to them because of bad roads or sparse retail outlets.

Western firms in the business of machinery and plant building are geared up for the dominant western markets, which are large, with well-developed home and foreign marketing networks. Western firms usually need plants with large capacities, machines that can handle a rapid throughput of raw materials. Very often the smallest size of plant available from western catalogues is too big for the market demand in a poor country.

So why, if large-scale western technology is so obviously inappropriate, is it so widely used? Partly at least because it is the only technology there is. National research and development capacities in most of the Third World are extremely rudimentary — once again, because the market for research scientists is small, but also because higher education is less developed and frequently weighted towards the impractical humanities. The research spending of the big western multi-nationals probably outweighs that of practically every developing country.

Then there are the spurious attractions of modernity. Many Third World leaders regard the small-scale, intermediate technology that some United Nations agencies now recommend as second rate, second best: they want the best. Bigness has political advantages too, of a primitive kind: a minister looks more impressive opening a giant steelworks than a small engineering workshop.

Technology is partly determined by taste. In colonial days, European things acquired an aura of glamour and prestige and came to be preferred to native styles — as if by imitating the white man's outward appurtenances one could pick up some of his mysterious power and arrogance. So the maharajahs modified their manners and traded in their elephants for Rolls-Royces and Cadillacs. Tastes are inseparable from social inequalities: the westernized elites indulge in the conspicuous consumption of western products, so everyone else apes them. Stylish cars cannot be produced in tiny labour-intensive workshops.

Indulging westernized tastes entails producing western-style goods (if you don't a competitor or importer will). And that automatically involves using western technology, usually capital-intensive, to produce them. So the choice of social model imposes the choice of consumer goods, which imposes in turn the choice of machinery to produce them with.

Multinationals, which account for a great deal of private investment in the Third World, almost always use capital-intensive technology. They want to turn out a standard, brand-named product, so they use the same machinery in poor countries as they do in rich. More generally, capital-intensive techniques may be artificially fostered by certain distortions in the economic policies of most developing countries. Many of these make capital appear to be cheap even though there is a chronic shortage of it, and labour appear relatively dear even though it is in chronic surplus. National currencies are often overvalued, which makes foreign-bought machinery cheap. Official interest rates may be excessively low, encouraging businessmen to invest in new plant. And the wages commanded by industrial workers may be too high because local firms have to compete for skilled men with multinationals paying higher rates. Private firms may mechanize, too, to avoid the troubles of a militant workforce, or the mistakes of an untrained one. All these factors combined add up to a strong incentive to buy more machines and employ fewer men: a country wanting to create more jobs would need to reverse them. So eventually the large new factories post notices saying 'No applicants' and, since many applicants can't read, hire factory guards and build large security gates to keep out the stream of desperate and demoralized work-seekers hammering on the door.

11. The Barefoot Businessman: Traditional and Small-Scale Industry

'A man on foot is automatically suspect.'
JEAN COCTEAU

The Victoria memorial gleams white under the hot sun in Calcutta's Maidan, and the black statue of the imperial queen, squat and scowling as ever, heats up. At her feet, a snake charmer lies in wait for the passing prey of tourists. I look easy game. He stares at me with black-rimmed eyes and fumbles at a flat, round basket. 'See snake sir, quick quick.' His hands tremble with haste and anxiety that he may miss an opportunity to earn, as they pass by like oases in a long desert day of waiting and hoping. Finally he whips off the top, grasps for his pipe and starts up a slow wailing dirge. The snake lies still, as if dead. He clouts it with the back of his hand, blows his pipe furiously, cheeks distended to bursting, weaving his head from side to side, but still the snake will not budge. He keeps banging it on the head with his pipe until it stirs and half rises and peers at him with a look of irritated boredom.

By his side his daughter has a long, furry mongoose with a pointed nose, clinging to her shoulder. The charmer notices my attention wandering: 'Okay sir, you want to see mongoose and snake fighting, only thirty rupees.' He opens a second basket and roots nervously through half a dozen squashed reptiles, drags one out and straightens it a bit. 'No thank you,' I reply. 'It may kill the snake.' 'No no, not kill.' 'I haven't got time.' 'It will be very very quick.' 'I'll give you five rupees for what I've seen.' 'Okay, give me ten rupees and you can see fight.'

The snake charmer, like the majority of non-agricultural workers, belongs to the informal sector, that great mass of untrained, underpaid toilers who are unfortunate enough to be excluded from the bright new modern sector of industry, government work and western-style services. He may do a bit better than most, provided enough tourists stroll by and other snake charmers keep away. But he shares with all the informal sector the insecurity, the dependence on chance demand and chance encounters, the almost daily exposure to disaster. The land has less and less room for the poor, the modern sector cannot use them. Yet they have to earn a living somehow. Traditional manufacturing used to offer them a niche, but today it is dying on its feet, and the death of such talent and hard work is a tragic spectacle throughout the Third World. So the disinherited are shifting their ground, moving into what one could call spontaneous business – all that multitude of trades half way between tradition and modernity that springs up unbidden among the marginal masses of the cities.

The death of tradition

Traditional manufacturing and services had many virtues. For the most part, they were decentralized into the villages, evenly spread across the country. They provided much-needed extra employment in rural areas – even today non-farm activities employ between a quarter and a half of the workforce in rural areas. They offered work for the slack season when there is little to do on the land – in this period of the year, they may make up three quarters of all employment. And they are still an important source of additional family income to supplement the meagre earnings from agricultural work. This is especially important for the landless and the smallest landowners. In five Pakistan villages surveyed in 1968, non-farm work provided one quarter of all the income of farm families, but for the smallest farms it provided two fifths. In north Thailand three quarters of the income of the smallest farmers came from this source.

Clearly, any threat to non-farm work in rural areas is a double threat to the incomes of the most vulnerable groups. And threat there is. In one sphere after another, city-based industry has destroyed the livelihoods of village artisans. Nigerian village potters become redundant as cheap plastic bowls and buckets flood the market, and blacksmiths are pauperized as farmers turn to mass-produced hoes and matchets. Families in the Peruvian *altiplano* abandon their handlooms as women buy their woollen skirts at market, ready made, from the factories of the coastal cities.

Not all non-farm work in rural areas is in manufacturing, of course. Almost equal amounts may be created by trading and services, and lesser proportions by construction and transport. But these activities can flourish only if agriculture and rural industry are flourishing. All the principal branches of rural manufacturing are threatened. Perhaps a third of its workforce is in textiles, clothing and leather work. Another sixth may be in each of food processing, wood and furniture, and metalwork. All these activities are precisely those in which Third World countries start up their first industries. The growth of modern industry has dealt a heavy blow to the villages.

But traditional manufacturing exists in towns too. Indeed, many towns have, in the course of history, become great centres for a particular craft such as brasswork, jewellery, ceramics or carpets. It is not just village enterprise, but the whole of the traditional sector that is dying, leaving its workers to seek work elsewhere, or remain jobless and impoverished. Its central problems are low productivity in relation to the competition from factories; low quality, in the eyes of consumers brainwashed into believing that standardized factory products are superior (and, it is true, in some cases they do last longer or work better); and lack of organization and marketing.

Take the crafts of Kashmir. The Moguls retired to this mountain paradise to escape the oppressive heat of the Gangetic plains in early summer. They and their courtiers provided a ready market for Kashmir's specialities: papier-mâché boxes lacquered with flowers and leaves and animals, wood carvings, jewels made from jade, sapphires, rubies from near-by Ladakh. The British colonial rulers continued the tradition of holidaying in the temperate climate of the hill stations. As they were not allowed to buy land here, they had themselves built luxurious houseboats on the reedy banks of lotus-carpeted Dal

Lake. They too patronized local crafts – brought to them by traders on *shikara* boats. When the British left, the market dried up, and tourism has not replaced it.

Kashmiri carpets are skilfully built up on great vertical frames, each tuft individually hand-knotted. The traditional patterns are inscribed on yellowed parchments, in an esoteric script that the carpet weavers can read fluently, even though they may not read or write their own language. Wages have sunk so low in relation to the cost of living that a family man cannot survive on them. Most of the adult men in the trade have left for other jobs – they can earn double as unskilled road labourers. They have been replaced by their own sons. Young boys aged seven or eight upwards crouch by the looms all day long, their tiny fingers working with unbelievable speed. Using these methods a medium-sized carpet can take anything from one month up to nine months or more for the closest knotted silk. But when factories can turn out passable imitations at much lower prices, who will buy the labour-intensive Kashmiri carpets, however beautiful? The only market now is among tourists and western buyers from upmarket shops. Traditional carpets seem to be in chronic oversupply as so many villages in the Middle East and western Asia are making them. There is no way the trade can continue to employ so many people and go on paying them a living wage.

Low productivity and changing tastes threaten another venerable and skilled craft: Java's batik industry. As westernized tastes spread and traditions weaken among the young, women are turning away from hand-made batik sarongs to machine-printed cloths from India or Hongkong. Batik is too labour-intensive to survive the competition of machinery. Each piece of material has first to be washed alternately in alkaline water and coconut oil, left in the sun to bleach to the delicate creamy tint of batik cloth, starched in rice water, then pounded to soften it. After this, the artist sketches the pattern in charcoal on the cloth. Then the women take over. In the batik sweat-shops of Jogjakarta's back streets, they kneel or squat gracefully around little stoves, warming pans full of melted wax. They dip in their *tjantings* – bamboo-handled copper cups with a capillary spout – and apply the wax meticulously to both sides of the material. This is then dipped in cold water to harden the wax, and immersed in baths of die, previously brewed up in bubbling stone vats. The wax is removed by washing several times in petrol and hot water, and the white areas thus exposed are dyed again in a second or third colour. One labour-saving innovation has been introduced: most of the cloths for women's sarongs are now waxed by *tjap* – a copper pattern mounted on a wooden block, which is heated, dipped into wax, and printed onto the fabric by hand. Even with this change, batik cannot stave off the challenge from cheaper machine-made prints. Sadly, it may eventually survive only in a truncated form, catering for local ceremonial occasions, western high-fashion tastes and the tourist trade.

Because of the low productivity of labour in traditional industries, they can compete with factories only if their wages are extremely low too. But lack of organization is another cause of poverty, especially under the widespread putting-out or homework system. In many cases this is dominated by middlemen who supply the raw materials at excessive prices and buy back the finished work at too low prices, squeezing the poor worker in the middle to the margin of survival. Again and again one is astonished by how little homeworkers – often women and children working in spare moments – earn for considerable amounts of work. The wife of a landless labourer in central Java took two weeks to make a floormat of palm leaves, working an hour or two every day. The selling price: just 300 rupiahs (40p or 80 cts). In north-east Brazil women hand-sew entire tablecloths, or patiently crochet complex lace patterns with half a dozen needles at once, for the equivalent of 5p or 10 cts an hour or less. A study in this area found that the full-time work of six handicraft homeworkers would be needed to get an income equal to the legal minimum wage.

Middlemen can force homeworkers' incomes down by their superior organization. They control the sources of raw materials and the market outlets. They act in collusion. The artisans or homeworkers are scattered and unorganized. They have no contacts of their own to buy supplies and sell their produce. They need the money immediately and cannot hold back their goods to push the price up. Indeed, they are often in debt to the middlemen.

Agra – famous for the Taj Mahal – is also India's foremost centre for hand-made shoes, with perhaps 80,000 craftsmen involved in the trade. Every day the cobblers bring some 75,000 pairs of shoes to the wholesale market, but the buyers are in a stronger position; there are fewer of them so they have a monopsony – a buyer's monopoly. They have funds behind them and can tide over a while without buying, whereas the cobblers have to sell there and then to get money to buy food to keep alive and more leather to keep working.

The death of the traditional sector, and all the disruption and human suffering that involves, is not entirely inevitable. Significant parts of it could be rescued, albeit with a smaller workforce. Governments could help it to compete, pump in funds to help it improve its technology, product quality and marketing, organize producers to freeze out parasitic middle-men.

A few governments have pursued imaginative policies of this kind. Most have worked on the theory that the traditional sector will wither away naturally and its workers get absorbed into the modern sector. They are certainly right on the first count, but dangerously wrong on the second. So, instead of building on existing skills and traditions, most governments have pumped all available funds into large-scale modern in-dustry. Instead of gradual organic growth, there have been abrupt discontinuities.

The westernized modern sector is killing the traditional sec-tor. The displaced workers of the latter have not, for the most part, found work in the modern sector, but have shifted into the informal sector. Here too they suffer from government neglect, low productivity, low pay, lack of organization. But they move into activities that are not so inevitably doomed by changing tastes. The enterprising village blacksmith will not lie down and die with his fellows, but give up making matchets and start repairing pumps and tractors.

The barefoot businessmen

The bustling market of Bouaké, second biggest city in the Ivory Coast, hums with activity. Diviners sit crosslegged on collapsed boxes, waiting to tell your future. Traditional medicine men sell rams' horns, snakes' heads and desiccated chameleons. The tiny glass booth of Watch Doctor Monsieur Emmanuel Ipadé is decorated with childish paintings of giant watch faces, while over a boy tailor dreaming at his treadle sewing machine, a sign proclaims: 'Pop fashions here, dress yourself at Mr O Dao's.' Meanwhile King Hairdresser invites you in for a crop – take your pick of the exotically named but uninviting convict-style profiles painted on his door: Mirano, 75 style, Afro, Hercules, Casino, Ghana style, Santiago, Cockroach or the two-penny all off, Ordinary. Round the corner they are doing a brisk trade in used cardboard for packing or making houses with, and you can even buy empty bean cans, shampoo jars and White Horse whisky bottles to keep your savings, cooking oil or plastic flowers in.

This is the spontaneous business of the informal sector, varied, inventive, booming in numbers if in nothing else. A survey of Bouaké in 1969 found more than 3,100 informal enterprises in the city. Among them were: 513 tailors, 440 weavers, 459 taxis, 425 rickshaw men, 259 masons, 207 prostitutes, 136 car and bike repairers, 131 joiners and carpenters, 112 restaurants and bars, 87 hairdressers, 60 blacksmiths, 54 jewellers, 43 watch repairers, 36 photographers, 15 hair dyers and ten bootblacks. Today the number of businesses will have doubled or trebled.

Spontaneous business is growing even faster than the cities themselves: 12 per cent more hopeful entrepreneurs every year join the crowd in Kumasi, seat of the Ashanti kings, 25 per cent more in Freetown, the perpetually rainy capital of Sierra Leone.

According to the International Labour Office's definition, an enterprise should be classified as informal if it employs only a handful of workers, on low incomes, using rudimentary equipment, and works outside the framework of laws and regulations. The informal sector covers services – shoeshine boys, cigarette vendors, sweepers, porters, scribes – and manufacturing, anything from palm-leaf roofing panels and twig brushes to religious objects. Jakarta's *makan* sellers, pushing their little carts with glowing charcoal fires warming soups and fried pancake rolls by the light of storm lamps, are into food processing just as surely as a canning factory – so are the corn-cob roasters of Africa or the sweet and biscuit bakers of the Middle East.

The informal sector employs a large proportion of the urban population. Surveys from Bombay, Nairobi, São Paulo, Abidjan, Jakarta and cities in Peru put its share of city employment at between 40 and 60 per cent. And, as the rural exodus continues, this share is unlikely to decrease. Most migrants start off their working city lives in this sector and, conversely, a majority of informal-sector workers are migrants. Four fifths of Lima's hawkers and nine tenths of Jakarta's come from outside these cities. After a few years in this kind of work, a migrant may have learned enough of the city's ways and made enough contacts to land a steady job in the modern sector. Many migrants will find themselves trapped in a life of poverty and insecurity, although in most cases they are still better off than if they had remained in their rural area of origin, at least in monetary terms.

A survey in Lima, Peru, found that three quarters of street vendors were earning less than the government's minimum wage, indeed an unlucky 13 per cent of them were actually making a loss. Most had gone into trading for the simple reason that they could find no other work. After a difficult period, they began to make some kind of living and developed their own style of expertise: knowing which street corners or thoroughfares produced the richest crop of customers at different times of day. Their incomes were low not because they didn't work hard – more than half of them were putting in forty-five hours a week or more – but because there were too many competitors. Productivity was low as they might have to wait an hour or two between each customer. Nearly half of Jakarta's one million workers are in the informal sector. The

70,000 rickshaw drivers buzz around like wasps and earn, on average, less than £50 each ($100) per year. Unknown to them, the city's official plan predicts that by 1980 'the function of the *betjak* rickshaw as a means of transportation would become non-existent'. Two thirds of the city's 30,000 hawkers were found to have a daily turnover of less than £6 ($12). A similar proportion were so abysmally poor that virtually 100 per cent of their income was spent on food. Three quarters of them had turned to hawking because there were no other jobs available.

Migrants are much more likely to be poor and underemployed than natives of the cities they have come to: in São Paulo 44 per cent of migrants had monthly incomes below 200 cruzeiros in 1970 (about £20 or $40 at the time), against only 29 per cent of non-migrants. Nearly one migrant in three was underemployed, but only one non-migrant in five. Migrants – though more educated than the neighbours they left behind – were less educated than life-long city dwellers, so the latter were more likely to pick up steady, well-paid jobs in the modern sector. A 1970 survey in Peru found that 59 per cent of informal-sector workers earned below $47 a month, compared with only 18 per cent in the formal sector.

Their poverty is due to two factors: first, as we shall see, governments have shamefully neglected this sector, leaving it with primitive technology, management and marketing, and low productivity. Second, there are far too many informal-sector workers chasing far too little work. There is not much work because there is not enough spending power among their customers, poor like themselves. And there are too many work-seekers because of the never-ending flow of refugees from rural poverty. Because of this massive growth of people seeking work in the informal sector, and because of lack of investment in it, there is a danger that it will go the way of so much smallholder agriculture, towards what might be called industrial involution: supporting an ever-increasing population with a steadily declining income per head.

The virtues of spontaneity

In spite of all this, the informal sector has considerable hidden potential.

The modern sector is out of bounds for most of the poor. It cannot and often will not give them work. Nor will it provide for many of their needs, as they can afford few of its products and even less of its services. The dualism found on the land is here again in the cities. The modern sector is the economy of the privileged. It employs them, houses them and pays them enough to afford its products. The informal sector is the economy of the poor. Through it they house themselves and employ each other and produce goods and services they can afford. There is precious little contact between the two economies.

The greatest advantage of spontaneous business is that it requires an absolute minimum of capital and skills. The barriers to entry are so low that virtually anybody can set up in business. So the informal sector mobilizes the savings of the poor, spares them the indignity of begging others for work and allows them the liberty (with attendant risks) of being self-employed. Two out of five Ivory Coast entrepreneurs had a capital of less than 10,000 francs CFA (about £25 or $50) and only one in five had more than 50,000 francs. Almost all of them had got the money together themselves or borrowed it from relatives and friends. The informal sector requires no diplomas, no degrees or school leaving certificates — bits of paper the poor in any case do not possess. Two thirds of its workers in Freetown, for example, had no schooling at all, along with two fifths of its entrepreneurs. Most of the rest had not completed their primary schooling. Nine out of ten skilled informal-sector workers in Kumasi had picked up what they knew on the job. That does not mean they had no training. Recruits are often taken on as apprentices, becoming almost part of the family, sharing the boss's house and table as well as his workshop. The sector offers the cheapest and simplest models for improving the skills of the workforce, a precondition for improving their incomes.

The sector does provide real and necessary services and products, too. When I was in Nigeria, bush garages were a handy institution whenever the car broke down (which, given the state of the roads at that time, was frequently). The premises: an inspection pit dug in the ground under a bamboo shelter to keep the rain off. The equipment: a few spanners, sandpaper, tape and several old wrecks cannibalized for spare parts. The staff: a ragged, oily crew of teenagers and young men willing to learn. They would rush out eagerly as you chugged to a halt and after half an hour's improvisation and experiment with a few bits of wire could usually get you on the road again.

There is, hiding its light under the informal bushel, probably the greatest reservoir of adaptiveness and invention that exists in developing countries. While western consultants and agencies are urging Third World governments to adopt small-scale appropriate technology, the barefoot businessmen are actually putting many of the precepts into practice. The technology they use is of necessity small-scale and labour-intensive, since they have so little capital. They use local materials because they can't afford or get licences for imports. Recycling of waste is a speciality at which they are past masters. In Ouagadougou they make passable flip-flop sandals out of old car tyres and donkey harnesses out of rusty bike chains. In southern Peru I met one old village blacksmith forging bright new kettles, pans and funnels out of polished-up used tin cans. In Calcutta I came upon a tiny workshop cutting up old cooking oil containers and working them into neat round tins for rough local *beedi* cigarettes.

Development agencies now recommend the use of second-hand equipment for some industries: it is much cheaper than new, and usually provides more jobs. Calcutta's Daramtolla Road is lined with little engineering shops that have been doing just that for decades, working on small contracts for bigger firms or garages. 'Sri Kali Engineering Works, repairers of petrol engines,' says one sign over a ten-foot-wide booth. Or the next: 'Das Engineering Works, mechanical engineers and labour contractors, specialists in vibrator machine milling and vertical milling jobs and general orders.' Most of the proprietors here seem to be men who picked up their skills in a factory, saved up and bought old lathes or drills for the odd two thousand rupees (around £100 or $200), rented a shopfront, hired some likely lads, and trained them up themselves.

Most informal-sector business is physically located in the squatter and slum areas. Haransar Para, the Calcutta bustee we looked at earlier, is a hive of industry and trade. Teenage boys nail together tea chests on an empty space where another family graze two muddy-black water buffaloes and sell their milk. A gang of grubby, khaki-clad mechanics sandpaper an ancient car ready for a paint job. A laundryman pulls the tabs off vests and *dhotis* while a brush vendor calls from house to house.

Indeed, spontaneous business is the exact economic parallel to spontaneous settlements. The same forces give rise to both. The urban bias of investment generates higher city incomes, which pull in the marginal rural poor. But that investment, in jobs as in housing, is used up in expensive western-style packages that can only benefit the few. The many are left to house themselves, and to employ themselves. As long as rural incomes are so far below urban, and as long as the obsession with western architecture, tastes and technology continues, the informal sector will go on growing. There is no chance of it fading away for a very long time to come.

Logically, governments should face up to that fact and make the most of it. Informal businesses are the ideal place to try out small-scale, intermediate technology approaches. Their machinery can be improved, their owners can be provided with credit and trained in better management, quality control and marketing, their workers' skills upgraded. They could be tied in with the modern sector by encouraging big factories to subcontract work out to them. This whole vast mass of self-improvement could be built on to provide an unprecedented groundswell of manufacturing and services in the city economies of the Third World.

In practice, from most governments spontaneous business gets the same treatment as spontaneous housing. It is seen as a transitory, deviant sort of activity; a nuisance that contributes little to the kind of economy political leaders want to build up; and, like the shanties it is housed in, a hazard to public health and political stability.

At the best it is ignored and neglected. It enjoys none of the access to official credit, cheap foreign exchange and government assistance that big business can count on. Banks will advance money to the small informal-sector businessman even less readily than to the smallholding farmer. He has no collateral apart from his cranky old machines or tumbledown shack. He keeps no books other than those in his head. All in all, he is a decided credit risk. Only 4 per cent of Kumasi enterprises and 2 per cent of Freetown's had had loans from banks or official credit agencies. Without credit, the small man finds it much harder to improve his business and is usually doomed to stay small.

Into the bargain, he may suffer a good deal of government discrimination, restriction and even outright harassment. Official standards of quality or safety are set artificially high, with the modern sector in mind. The informal sector cannot hope to comply, and hence is excluded from many markets. Spontaneous businesses are no better provided with services than are slums: the majority have no roof over their heads or are housed in tents or shacks. Most have no water or electricity – essentials for manufacturing activity. City governments copy western city ways and insist on licences, which are often restricted in number. Few small businesses apply for them and even fewer obtain them. Hence they are often, strictly speaking, illegal and even more exposed to risk and uncertainty than they need be. They become sitting ducks for the extortions of corrupt officials and policemen. If they will not pay these under-the-counter taxes on their activities, they are liable to be moved on, perhaps even to get what little capital they have broken up. Whenever a slum is demolished, the bulldozers are knocking down not only wood, cardboard and tin, but dozens of businesses with their laboriously built-up good will, and hundreds of jobs.

12. The Curious Economy

Altogether we are dealing with a rather curious animal in the economy of a typical Third World country. It does not much resemble the well-proportioned horse of the healthy industrialized country, muscular and balanced. It is much more like a giraffe. Its parts look somehow out of scale, lopsided and prone to falls, or like an advanced case of hydrocephalus, with swollen head too heavy for the thin body to carry and draining its vitality.

To put it in context, one ought to sketch, in oversimplified form, the main features in the development of the great industrial powers. In Britain, for example, the industrial revolution was firmly built on the foundations of an agricultural revolution, and the productivity of the land grew side by side with that of industry. Industry can grow only if there is a growing agricultural surplus: farmers must produce a good deal more than they themselves need, so the city workers can be fed. Industry, likewise, can prosper only if farmers have surplus income which they can spend on manufactures.

Western industry, inevitably, began on a small scale and large-scale industry emerged only gradually as technology evolved, based firmly on knowhow and skills acquired in earlier stages. Western cities, in turn, expanded in proportion with the growth of industry. By and large a non-agricultural job was created for every agricultural job that disappeared.

Western countries had their own miniature population explosions too, but none of them so rapid as in the Third World today, and generally in line with the expansion in food and employment. When jobs did not suffice, the surplus people were exported to the wide open spaces of North America and Australasia.

Finally, as agriculture and industry both grew more productive, and could feed and supply the population with a smaller effort, they could support a growing tertiary sector not producing anything, but providing services first for work, and then for leisure.

That does not mean that industrialization in western countries was achieved painlessly. The sufferings that the British working class went through were certainly as bad as most now found in the Third World: poor peasants were expelled from their villages by the enclosure movement, handicrafts were wiped out by factories, industrial workers and their wives and children were forced to work long hours and live in conditions of appalling sanitation. But development did follow the logical sequence, and each phase was built on the solid foundations of the preceding one.

In the developing countries the elements did not develop in the same sequence, but grew as it were out of turn. Industry was forcibly developed without adequate agricultural surplus to support it, developed consciously and deliberately by leaders impatient for results, copying the surface appearances of western economies while ignoring the processes by which they had been created. Another society that created industry by force in a somewhat similar way was Soviet Russia, and there industrialization was not achieved without the most appalling rural suffering. Large-scale industry was developed, before small-scale industry in each country had provided the indigenous pool of knowhow and skills in which it would flourish.

And so a modern sector was thrust into the nest like a cuckoo, and began to kick the native fledglings out of the nest and grow fat on the mother's desperate efforts to feed it. This parasitic sector was located in the cities. The vast income differentials — artificially imposed by rulers — between this sector and the impoverished countryside sucked people prematurely into the cities. Third World cities grew much faster, numerically, than industry.

At the same time, the beast's head, the tertiary sector, swelled out of all proportion to the body. In 1960 the developed regions had an average of one worker in manufacturing for one in services. Only in Asia are these two sectors balanced. In Latin America and Africa there are three service workers for every two in industry. This premature swelling of services was due to two other conditions: one, the government sector was overgrown, and overpaid, beyond the capacity of the economy to support it without sacrifice. Two, the migrant masses, unemployable in industry, took refuge in hawking, whoring and the like.

Simultaneously with all these imbalances, population was booming and adding complications to all the other complaints. It expanded faster than the growth of paying employment. It did not emerge organically out of these societies, but was imposed on them before they were ready for it. So the increases in agricultural productivity that were achieved were eaten up by extra people.

These are the five fundamental imbalances of the typical developing economy: industrial development without adequate agricultural development, large-scale industry without the prior development of small-scale, urbanization outpacing industrialization, services growing too fast for the productive base of agriculture and industry, and population growth racing ahead of employment growth.

Four out of the five can be blamed on discrimination in government policy: not simply urban bias, but, more generally, bias against everything that was not up-to-date, 'progressive', western – bias against the rural sector but also against the poor urban sector, because the goal was bright new cities and factories. Internal colonialism, in other words, of the westernized over the non-westernized.

The priorities are, at last, changing. Some governments, and the majority of United Nations agencies and bodies such as the World Bank, now realize that the balance has to be shifted towards developing agriculture and increasing the incomes of rural and urban poor. The majority, however, still seem to have made only marginal adjustments to their dream of building little western consumer societies on tropical soil.

Part Four

The Lost People:
The Underdevelopment of Man

'Through me you pass into eternal pain, through
me you pass among the lost people.'
Inscription over the Gate of Hell

DANTE, *Inferno*, Canto iii, 2-3

13. Sins of the Fathers: How People Underdevelop

Francisco's mother Fatima is small for her age. She is visibly weak, distant, yet easily irritated by the children. Years of pregnancy and menstruation, along with an iron-poor diet of maize, have made her chronically anaemic. Her husband Jaime is a landless labourer, with a low, erratic income barely enough to keep them all alive and clothed. No one eats enough, and when there's not enough to go round Fatima goes without, even when she's pregnant. And that is frequently, as the couple use no form of contraception. They have had ten children, six of whom survived to adulthood.

Fatima went through several periods of undernourishment while Francisco was in her womb. There were times when Jaime could not get regular work and everyone went hungry. Fatima also had several attacks of stress and anxiety when Jaime beat her. Francisco probably suffered his first bout of growth retardation, both mental and physical, before he even saw the light of day.

He was born underweight, and his brain was already smaller than normal size. For the first few months he was breast-fed and suffered few infections, as he was partly protected by the antibodies in his mother's milk. Then he was weaned onto thin gruels and soups, taken off the breast and put onto tinned evaporated milk, thinned down with polluted water from the well. His diet, in itself, was inadequate. Then he started to get more and more infections, fever, bronchitis, measles and regular bouts of gastro-enteritis. With well-fed children these pass within a few days, but in his case they went on for weeks and sometimes a month or more. In these periods he could tolerate no milk and few solids, and so was given weak broths, tea or sugar water. By now he was 25 per cent underweight. Because of poor nutrition, he was even more susceptible to infection, and each time he was ill, he lost appetite and ate even less. Then he got bronchitis which developed into pneumonia.

But Fatima borrowed money off a relative, went to town and got antibiotics for him.

So he survived. But malnutrition made him withdrawn and apathetic. His mother got no reward from playing with him, so he received little of the stimulation his brain needed to develop properly. As he grew older, infections grew less frequent, but by the time he went to school, aged eight, he was already a year behind normal physical development and two years behind mentally. The school, in any case, was a poor one, with only three classes, no equipment, and a poorly qualified teacher. As Francisco was continually worried about whether and what he was going to eat that day, he was distracted, unable to concentrate, and seemed to show little interest in schoolwork. The teacher confirmed that he was a slow learner, and could not seem to get the hang of maths or reading and writing. As the family was poor, they did not want to keep him on at school. He was doing so badly anyway that there seemed no point. He did a year, then was away for three years helping an uncle who had a farm, then did another year, then left for good, barely able to read or write more than a few letters. He soon forgot what little he had learned. So, like his father, he began tramping round the local ranches asking for work. Without any educational qualifications or skills, that was all he could ever hope for. And because so many were in the same boat, pay was low. When he was twenty-two he married a local girl, Graciela, aged only fifteen. She too had been undernourished and was illiterate. She soon became pregnant and had to feed another organism inside her before she herself had fully developed. Graciela had heard about family planning from a friend, but Francisco would not let her use it and anyway she was not sure she wanted to. So, by the age of only twenty-five, Graciela already had five children and had lost two. The children had every prospect of growing up much as Francisco and Graciela did, overpopulating, underfed, in poor health and illiterate.

Francisco's case illustrates perhaps the greatest tragedy of Third World poverty today: the underdevelopment of man himself. Poor people never reach their full human potential in physical strength, intelligence and wellbeing. They are trapped in a pattern of overlapping vicious circles. Overpopulation begets poverty, which begets hunger. Hunger leads to sickness and sickness to malnutrition, in a spiral that can end in death or permanent disablement. Both result in brains starved of nutrients and of stimulation, and in educational failure. And that leads to low-paid work and more poverty. Most tragic of all, the underdeveloped man and woman have underdeveloped offspring. The sins of the fathers are visited upon the children. Poverty becomes hereditary.

And generates national poverty. In earlier chapters, we have looked at the inadequacy and misdirection of investment in physical capital on the land, in cities and in the workplace. But the human capital of a poor country is just as important, perhaps even more so. Malnutrition, disease and ignorance create a weak, unskilled workforce, not productive enough to generate a surplus, not educated enough to improve its performance.

Investment in men can pay as good a rate of return as investment in machines. A well-fed, healthy worker is capable of producing far more than the small cost of keeping him well fed and healthy. A farm worker can get more produce out of the land if he has been taught the most effective techniques. Industry can expand faster if the education system has provided it with the right mix of trained manpower. More than any other single factor, relevant, practical education can enable men to transform their own environment. Population programmes, too, are an investment in human capital. They ensure that fewer or more widely spaced children are produced, so each stands a better chance of developing his potential.

In the next four chapters I shall be looking at the state of human resources in developing countries, at population, nutrition, health and education. All four spheres are closely linked, as Francisco's story shows. And they are linked, too, with the development of agriculture and industry, and with the distribution of wealth and power to which I shall turn in the final section.

In each sphere, the developing countries set out with immense initial problems. But the way they have been tackled until very recently did little to alleviate poverty and much to increase inequality. In food, the sheer quantity of production has been the focus, ignoring the central question of how it is to be distributed. In health and education (as before in housing and in industry) inappropriate western models have been followed, so the privileged minority benefited while the poor majority was ignored. Both privilege and underprivilege have been reinforced according to the parable of the talents, until there is a real danger of the poor becoming almost a hereditary caste, perpetuating its poverty unto the third and fourth generations.

14. *The Sorcerer's Apprentice: Population*

'God made women to have children. The tree that does not bear fruit should be cut down.'

JIUSEPPA SOARES ACOSTA

Outside her hut in north-east Brazil, Maria Nazaré de Souza sits stiffly on a neighbour's chair – she has none of her own – and blinks at the photographer's flash gun. Ranged on both sides of her are her children. Six of them are standing, stiffly. The two youngest, aged two and three, cannot walk or stand, so one sits on Maria's lap, the other on a sister's arms.

Maria would be pretty, but her cheeks are sunken from fasting and her eyes staring from crying herself to sleep. She has on a short black dress, which bulges out over the swelling of seven months of pregnancy. The black is mourning. Her husband died three days ago, aged only forty-five. He had cut his leg while clearing a patch of ground, and the wound became gangrenous. He was only a day labourer, earning fifteen cruzeiros a day (about 60p or $1.20) on the two or three days a week he could get work. They could not afford medical attention.

The mayor of the local village brought the photographer along. He is going to try to get her picture published in a newspaper and to organize a collection. Maria would depend on what people gave her. Her eldest boy was fourteen, and he would have to work like a man to try and support the family, but it would be some years before he could command a man's wage. With all those children depending on her, how could she manage, she asked. They could hardly cope when her husband was alive, and he was strong. She seemed to be overcome by a sense of utter helplessness and abandon, like a piece of driftwood on the tide. She broke down and wept on her neighbour's shoulder.

Life for those with husbands is little better. A mile away Iracema Gomez sits in the shade of the overhanging roof of her hut. Eleven of her thirteen children are buzzing around in the warm evening like a swarm of flies, and a teenage daughter, old enough to start child-bearing herself, nurses her mother's latest arrival. Iracema has little time for each of them, even though she devotes her entire life to child-bearing and child-rearing. Her stocky, wiry husband Francisco is lucky by local standards: he has a three-year tenancy on a hectare of land and gives 40 per cent of the produce to the landlord. That enables the children to have at least pants to cover their nakedness, though their bellies are clearly more full of worms than of food.

Francisco is forty-five, Iracema thirty-eight. She still has time for another two or three pregnancies, perhaps more. I asked Francisco if he wanted any more children. 'I would stick at thirteen if I could,' he said, 'but I can't, you know what I mean? Not until I'm older anyway. I'm still young, my wife is young, what can you do? You can't help yourself. So one of these comes along every thirteen months or every seventeen months. Well, I always say, at least it shows my parts are in working order.'

Families with children into the double figures are very common in north-east Brazil. Rural mothers in this state, Rio Grande do Norte, have an *average* of more than seven living children. A quarter of them have ten or more. And that is not counting the dead ones. You often meet women like Luisa Gomez, a slight, small thirty-nine-year-old. She married at fourteen. Since then she has been pregnant sixteen times, once every eighteen months. For half of her adult life she has been pregnant, and for the other half breast-feeding the most recent addition. Only six of those sixteen are still alive. There were three stillbirths and seven died in their first year. Ten wasted pregnancies. Seven and a half years of drain on an already weak organism, for nothing. Worse than nothing, for all the anxiety, all the care, all the concern, and then the grief.

Life goes on like that. Before the first one is even on its feet, the next is on the way. Housework becomes a crushing burden with no labour-saving devices to help out. Feeding the family is like cooking for a works canteen. And with each successive birth the figure collapses a little further, the breasts sag and a paunch develops, making the women look pregnant even when they are not. Privacy, time to yourself, time to rest even, is an unheard-of, undreamed-of luxury. Bearing and rearing children, every girl is told, is a woman's only function. And because to believe otherwise would be to condemn herself to utter despair, the woman accepts the idea: and teaches it to her daughters.

The death slump

These are the human realities of the population explosion, not only in Brazil, but in Bangladesh, Egypt, Nigeria. Wherever growth rates are high, families are poor and women's lives are limited and miserable.

The raw data are no less uncomfortable. At the turn of the century the developing nations contained just over one billion people. The second billion was added over the next sixty years. The three billion mark was passed in 1977. Five billion will be reached around 2000, when the world will total six billion.

So the pace of growth has been hotting up. In the early 1900s, the population of what is now the Third World was expanding at only $\frac{1}{2}$ per cent a year. This speeded up to 1 per cent a year between 1920 and 1950; from then the growth rate has soared: 1·9 per cent in 1950–55; 2·13 per cent in 1955–60; 2·27 per cent in 1960–65; 2·3 per cent in 1965–70. In the first half of the seventies the rate passed through a plateau. But it is scheduled, according to the United Nations' medium predictions, to reach an all-time peak of 2·37 per cent a year between 1980 and 1985. From then on it may finally begin to climb slowly down.

In the meantime, the growth rates of the developed countries have been slowly grinding to a halt. As a result, the poor countries account for an increasingly massive proportion of the world's population. Until about 1960 they represented two thirds of the total. By 1980, they will make up more like three quarters, and after the year 2000 the developing nations will constitute four fifths of mankind.

The population explosion was not due to any boom in births, but to a slump in business for death.

Europe had its own milder version of this during the industrial revolution. Ever since the first agricultural revolution, Europe's population had risen almost imperceptibly slowly, with high birth rates balanced by equally high death rates. From the eighteenth century on, improved nutrition from increased food production, followed by advances in public health and medicine, started to pull the death rate down in one country after another. In England, for example, it fell from thirty-five per thousand in 1740 to twenty-six per thousand in 1800, twenty-two per thousand in 1850 and fifteen per thousand in 1900. The birth rate by contrast fell much more slowly: as late as 1870, it was still at thirty-five per thousand, declining slowly thereafter to about twenty-five per thousand in 1910 and sixteen per thousand in 1930. In every country of the world, natural population increase is brought on by this opening gap between declining death rates and more slowly falling birth rates. Eventually birth rates drop far enough to match death rates, and population growth levels off. This process is known as the demographic transition, and it can take a long time – in England, it lasted perhaps two hundred years.

The Third World has been in the thick of its own demographic transition, infinitely more traumatic than the West's, for more than two decades, and for most of them it is likely to last at least another seventy years on the most optimistic forecasts. No developed countries have had to face such staggering rates. At their fastest rates of growth, most were expanding at between 1 and 1½ per cent. The United States grew at 1·6 per cent a year for most of this century, but had vast open spaces to fill, fertile soils and abundant natural resources. Western population growth rarely exceeded the capacity of agriculture to feed or industry to employ the increase. In the nineteenth century Europe industrialized with its population growing at only 0·6 per cent a year, around a quarter of the rate that developing countries now face in the early eighties.

Western growth emerged organically from within. But the Third World was dragged into the demographic transition and had population growth imposed on it from without, before it was ready.

In nature, abundant fertility is a blessing. Every species of animal produces far more young than can hope to survive to maturity. So every turtle mother lays dozens of eggs in the sand in the hope that one or two may flop into the sea without being eaten by gulls on its way. High fertility guarantees that enough individuals will get through to carry on the precious genetic inheritance of each species, improved because natural selection has weeded out the weakest. Numbers are kept stable, over the long term, not so much by each species itself as by the whole ecosystem, by natural enemies large and small, predators and diseases. When these natural controls are removed, population explosions and eco-disasters can occur.

In traditional human societies, numbers are kept in check by wars, famines and epidemics. Before the days of nation states, if one group grew faster than its food supply, then it could simply up sticks and migrate, or conquer itself some extra *lebensraum* at the expense of its neighbours. The colonial powers came along and shattered these regulatory agencies. Tribal and princely wars were suppressed for the good of orderly trade, and a *pax colonialis* imposed. 'Barbarous' customs like infanticide, blood feuds and suttee – the self-cremation of Hindu widows on their husband's funeral pyre – were stamped out under the rule of western law. Roads and railways were built, allowing food to be transported from surplus regions to areas of famine. In Indonesia and in India irrigation systems were built which boosted food production and with it population – Java's 1800 population of five millions grew to thirty millions a century later.

All these factors set the Third World on the first stages of its demographic transition long before any significant medical advances had been made. But it was medicine that speeded up growth rates to their present ruinous level. After the Second World War a new medical technology joined the battlefront against disease. First sulfas, then antibiotics filtered down to the people not just through health services, which did not touch a major part of the population, but through village pharmacists. DDT came into action against malaria-carrying mosquitoes, vaccination campaigns protected many children against the ancient infant-killers.

The result was that Third World death rates plunged into a steep decline. From around thirty-five per thousand just before the Second World War (England's level of two centuries earlier) they fell to sixteen per thousand in the late sixties. It took just thirty years to halve the toll of mortality. In England the same decline was spread over a century and a half. Meanwhile birth rates carried on merrily at high levels: still at forty-two per thousand in 1950–55, dropping only slightly to forty per thousand ten years later and 37·5 per thousand in the first half of the seventies.

Death control without birth control: this, in a nutshell, has been the population problem of the poor countries.

It is only natural that birth rates take so very much longer to fall than death rates. Death rates drop because of external factors outside the control of individuals. But if birth rates are to fall, people have to change their own behaviour, grow out of the ingrained patterns evolved over centuries. Political revolutions can happen overnight; technological revolutions in a few years; but social revolutions take decades. The delay, sometimes fatal, is called cultural lag. People in the Third World developed attitudes and institutions to encourage such high birth rates for a specific reason: to cope with high death rates, and especially to offset high infant mortality. In the late 1930s, around 230 children out of every thousand born alive would not live to see their first birthday. Even today, in many African countries the infant mortality rate is still 180 per thousand, or higher, and in the poorest areas disease or hunger can carry off up to half the under-ones. In the face of this heavy toll, couples produce extra children knowing that many will fall by the wayside. 'The first two are for the crows,' says an Iranian proverb. The Chinese have their own version: 'One son is no son, two sons are an undependable son, and only three sons can be counted as a real son.'

The maintenance of high birth rates is not left to chance. Ways of guaranteeing them are built into the social structure, in early marriage, praise for fecundity in women, concepts of virility in men. Such expectations are drummed into every growing child, and few grow out of them fully. It can take a generation or more to shift such attitudes.

The growth strategy – or why people want big families

'Eighteen goddess-like daughters are not equal to one son with a hump.' *Chinese proverb*

In most of southern Asia, Africa and the Middle East, birth rates have not come down for a disturbing reason: people actually want large families, and believe it is in their interests to have them. Too often it is assumed that people out of reach of clinics, condoms and pills are like rabbits, helplessly generating uncontrollable numbers of offspring. They are not. Every culture has some method of family planning, whether it is abortion, infanticide, prolonged breast-feeding, or the universally known methods of coitus interruptus and abstention. These were the means by which European countries dragged their birth rates down long before the advent of the sensitized sheath or the pill. Of course they are not entirely reliable: they demand considerable self-control, and men will be men. They may produce an extra child over the odds every now and then. The fact that they are not more widely practised points to an uncomfortable conclusion: these people are planning their families. And they are planning large ones. Surveys of couple's ideas of an ideal family size often uncover alarming results in many areas. In Mysore, India, for example, even urban families thought an average of 3·7 children would do them nicely, while rural families wanted 4·7 children.

In surveys carried out in the *developed* countries in the sixties and seventies, women indicated a mean of between two and three and a half as their ideal family size, and the proportion wanting five or more children nowhere exceeded 9 per cent. In Third World surveys, ideal family sizes ranged from a low of 3·8 in rural Thailand, between four and five in Chile,

Indonesia, Korea and the Philippines, and 5·1 in West Malaysia. The proportion wanting five children or more ranged between 21 per cent (Taiwan) and 66 per cent (Indonesia). African women wanted the largest number of children: their ideal family sizes ranged from 5·7 for Nigeria, through 7·5 for rural Ghana, to 9·4 in one Kenyan survey. The proportion wanting five or more children in African surveys ranged from 61 per cent to 100 per cent. A 1973 survey of Yoruba women in Nigeria asked women how many children they thought would be too many: the mean answer was 8·5. Improved infant mortality does not appear to promise a worthwhile decline in ideal family size: asked how many children was the best number to have if they were sure that all would survive to adulthood, the Yoruba women's mean response was 5·7.

These are regions where men envy the father with two or three strong sons and women are jealous of the mother who bore them, because such families often command extra power, wealth and status. The drop in infant mortality has presented everyone with an unprecedented opportunity to be as prolific as those they envied. Except that when *everyone* is standing on tiptoes, no one can see any better.

Throughout these culture areas the extended family is a kind of private corporation through which the needs and ambitions of its members are fulfilled, and usually, as in the business world, in competition with other corporations. In the traditional struggle for land and power, the bigger corporations stand a better chance of winning. In most of traditional Africa the man with three or four sons is allocated more land to work. The increased surplus they produce enables him to marry a second or even a third wife, and these will compete with each other as to who can beget more sons. Like IBM or General Motors, a man pursues a growth strategy, but instead of accumulating capital, he accumulates people. As the head of a vast army, his influence and chances of power in the community are considerably increased.

In Asia and the Arab world, life is even more of a competitive struggle, red in tooth and claw. Disputes over land boundaries, water rights, debts, are commonplace. Rather than resort to corrupt police or courts who might, after all, decide against them, people often take the law into their own hands. In this situation, sons are potential fighters in factional feuds. And the more children you have, the more alliances you can contract, through marriage, with other families, whose resources, wealth or power supplement your own.

Having a large family has an economic as well as a socio-political rationale. Here one of the most pressing considerations is insurance against old age. Social security gets only 5 per cent of the gross national product in developing countries (against over 15 per cent in Europe) and that is largely confined to the modern sector. A large cross-national survey in Asia found that, while most urban middle-class families would not rely on their children for financial help in old age, between 62 and 90 per cent of poor urban and rural families would do so. Among rural Thais, 60 per cent quoted economic benefits as the major advantage in having children. Only 14 per cent cited happiness, love or companionship.

Children are also labour power. The western concept of childhood as a time of play and freedom from responsibility does not exist outside the elite of developing countries. A growing infant graduates, around the age of four or five, into miniature adulthood. At first he will be entrusted with minor jobs calling for little strength or skill. In southern Peru melancholic, barefoot girls herd the family llamas. Boys mind cows in India. All children are expected to do any amount of chores helping out mother at home, or father in the fields. In the towns they are sent out hawking or begging: I have seen little girls of eight selling sunflower seeds in Turkish cinemas at midnight, boys of nine selling ball pens in Nigerian lorry parks, Indian boys of twelve making shoes for 13cts (6p) a day. From the age of thirteen, the child becomes a full unit of labour power. In 1979, the ILO estimates, 55 million children were at work in the world.

The profound sexual inequalities that persist in most of the Third World mean that, in the calculus of costs and benefits that couples make in planning their families, sons far out-weigh daughters. In the Hindu religion only a son can perform the funeral rites for the father's soul: an orthodox man must beget a son, or risk rebirth in a lowly form like a snake or a pig. In almost all cultures sons carry on the family name and fame and inherit the estate. In Asia sons attract dowries. Anyone who has only daughters is quite likely to face financial ruin, anyone with nothing but sons can make a considerable profit from that fact alone. Men earn more than women – so sons bring in more cash before they are married and can provide better for their parents in old age. No wonder Indian brides are greeted with the traditional wish: 'May you be the mother of eight sons.'

But one son is not enough. As long as infant mortality is high and there is any risk of your losing an only son, you have to have two. A survey in the Indian state of Gujarat found that couples planned their families so as to ensure that at least two sons survived to support their parents in old age. One mother explained that the ideal family would be two boys and one girl, but to make sure of two surviving sons you could not afford to have less than five children surviving beyond the vulnerable ages below ten. Every street in the village had families whose sons had all died, and these cases were quoted as cautionary tales. In Gujarat an old couple can rely on a daughter and her husband to support them if they have to, but it is considered extremely shameful to do so and every meal has to be paid for in humiliation.

'No sons begets many children,' runs another Chinese proverb: the family that has no luck at first has to keep on trying for male children. The Asian cross-national survey quoted earlier found that a third of rural families in the Philippines, two fifths in Korea and nearly a half in Thailand would simply go on trying, no matter how many daughters they got in the meantime, until they had at least one son. Even those who would eventually give up would not do so before they had had three or four daughters in a row.

But what of the growing disadvantages of having too many children, so obvious to an outsider? It seems curious that the peasant is willing to see his land shrink to nothing as it is divided up by inheritance – or that he can afford to raise a large litter on a paltry and uncertain labourer's income. These things are costs — but in the poor man's own accounting system, they are outweighed by the benefits.

At Khanna in the Punjab, small landowners were aware of the problem of land fragmentation through inheritance. But Harvard sociologist Mahood Mamdani found that they considered this a problem for their children, not themselves. Their chief concern was surviving in the present. They did not possess machinery and so at harvest time many of them needed a good deal of extra labour. Feeding an extra son at home worked out at one quarter of the cost of hiring outside workers.

The smallholders also hoped that if their sons worked hard, or got paying jobs in the near-by town, they could save up enough money to buy extra land. This would get their heads above the dangerously close waters of total ruin — and overcome the fragmentation problem. Everyone could point to one or two families who had pulled this off by having many sons.

The landless poor, in town or country, saw similar advantages in large families. The more potential wage earners there were, the greater would be the family's surplus, they argued, since the overheads of rent and housing were fixed.

Both these viewpoints would have a certain validity in a booming economy with rapid increases in the productivity of the land. But where, as in most of the Third World, population growth is outstripping the growth in rural and urban employment, they are irrational and dangerous. Labourers will get lower wages because of an oversupply of labour. The land produces diminishing returns for each extra person who works it. This is not even a zero-sum game where one man can win what another loses: it is a minus-sum game where practically everyone loses.

In this kind of social situation population programmes have not met with much success. The Punjabi town of Khanna was the site of an intensive family planning programme, including education and house-to-house supply of contraceptives. The crude birth rate did fall from forty per thousand in 1957 to thirty-five per thousand in 1968, but the programme directors concluded that this was due to a rise in the average age of marriage. The programme had not persuaded anyone to have smaller families: all it had done was to shift couples who had already been practising birth control by abstention or withdrawal onto more modern methods. Mamdani discovered that many villagers would accept the pills out of courtesy, then throw them away. One family had even built a little sculpture out of the boxes. The programme workers were met with considerable but concealed scepticism. People thought they were American spies, or tax collectors. Anything seemed more sensible than the true explanation: that so much money was being spent to get them to have fewer children, when they all knew it was better to have more.

Clearly these people who insist on producing children in vast numbers are not insane, nor are they fools. They are acting according to what they themselves see as their best interests in the competitive society they live in. But these individual interests are in conflict with the interests of the society as a whole.

The large family brings private benefits. In most places it still costs less to raise an extra child than the potential gain from his labour, his marriage alliance, or his support in old age. It is a profitable venture; it brings in a worthwhile return for the investment.

Against this there are massive social costs: land erosion, fragmentation of holdings, unemployment. But the family itself – even if it is aware of the causal link between its own behaviour and the social effects – does not have to bear the costs directly. It exports them, dumps them on the village or the national doorstep, or on the future. The land fragmentation problem will hit your children – let them worry about it when you're dead. They can always head for the city. In the last resort the whole village can export its population problem.

This collision of private and public interests is found in some typical western enigmas. Every household wants a car to increase its freedom and mobility, but when too many people have one they get stuck in traffic jams, motorways are pushed through their neighbourhood, public transport seizes up and declines so that eventually people take far longer to get to work than their grandfathers did on the trams. Because everyone strives for individual freedom and mobility, eventually their freedom and mobility are restricted more than ever before. So it is with children. People have large families in a bid to escape poverty, yet their poverty is increased because everyone else is following the same strategy.

Only a handful of family planning programmes have yet confronted this central point. Unless attitudes to large families, and the costs and benefits of having them, are changed, making contraceptives available may provide a social service but it may not have a significant impact on the birth rate in many countries.

Cannon fodder — or how people are stopped from having small families

'Suffer the little children to come unto me, and forbid them not, for such is the kingdom of heaven.'   *Saint Mark's Gospel*

The desire for large families is not universal in the Third World. In all continents there are individual families rich enough, and poor enough, to want to limit the number of their children, and to feel that it is in their economic interests to do so. And in many places social pressures do not push so unanimously towards the large family ideal.

In Latin America the family is rarely the extended, corporate entity of Africa and southern Asia. The melting pot of races has produced a continent of *mestizos* (white–Indian half castes), mulattoes (white–Negro) and *zambos* (Indian–Negro). Adult children tend to form new households when they marry, and even the nuclear family is unstable among the poor. Ever since Spanish soldiers took Indian women as their brides, cohabitation has been as commonplace as legal marriage. In these conditions grandparents and siblings may not be around to take some of the weight of rearing children off parents' shoulders, nor can they count unconditionally on support in old age. Grinding poverty and acute shortage of work has always made children a considerable burden among the poor. In all developing countries migration to the cities is producing family circumstances similar to these.

In South-East Asia the status of women is often higher than, for example, in southern Asia. In some places they inherit an equal share of family property. So here the fertility drug of striving for sons is not so strong.

In many countries the poor who do want small families face strong institutional obstacles, either preventing them from getting hold of effective means of birth control, or playing on their consciences, making them feel it is wrong to limit their families.

In an overcrowded world, many governments and organized religions are still alarmingly pro-natalist. More people are cannon fodder in rivalries with bordering states; statistical fodder to boost a tribal or ethnic group's self-importance in national affairs, or a nation's status in the international community; even their souls can be ammunition to fire heavenwards.

Despite the sorry consequences of population growth which we saw in Part Two, many governments remain unconcerned. No less than sixty-four out of 130 countries surveyed by the Population Council in 1976 had no official policy to reduce population growth and gave no support to any kind of family planning activities. The Cameroon government considered its country to be underpopulated. Malawi, tens of thousands of whose workers have to slave in South Africa's mines for lack of jobs at home, prohibited the wide dissemination of family planning services and information. In Upper Volta, where the disastrous consequences of population growth on the land are all too plain, the military government did not support family planning and contraceptives were unavailable in rural areas. In Burma family planning clinics were banned and the import of contraceptives illegal. In eastern and southern Asia, where the population problem is most acute, over 90 per cent of the population lived in countries with an active population policy. But only 36 per cent of Latin Americans and 8 per cent of Africans were lucky enough to do so.

The attitudes of religious hierarchies are an equally powerful obstacle to the spread of family planning: perhaps more so, as they influence the policies of governments as well as the behaviour of ordinary people.

Hinduism and Buddhism are for the most part neutral, though the doctrine of non-violence brings problems for abortion, and the belief in reincarnation poses some conundrums. If someone is destined to be reborn in your child, perhaps birth control interferes with the process. And if the population begins to decline, there might be more souls wishing to reincarnate than available bodies. In Bali, priests had already had to find theological answers to a more immediate problem: as the population increased rapidly, where were all the extra souls coming from? They found authorities for the view that a single soul can reincarnate in several bodies. This theory can be neatly reversed to account for population decline: several souls can reincarnate in a single body.

Islam and Roman Catholicism both appear to be potent forces maintaining fertility at high levels. The areas with the fastest population growth rates in the world lie in the Moslem belt from North Africa, through south-west Asia to Pakistan and Bangladesh, and in Central and South America. In these areas birth rates are usually a good deal higher than one would expect simply from the level of income in the country, and the decline in birth rates has lagged behind the fall in death rates even more pronouncedly than elsewhere in the Third World (see Map 5, pages 462–3).

The theologians and theoreticians of Islam are by no means unanimous in their views on family planning. The 1975 meeting of the World Moslem League declared roundly that birth control had been 'invented by the enemies of Islam', and urged the faithful to 'procreate, avoid abortion and reject the pill'. Against this, many influential Moslems from Egyptian professors of Islamic law to grand muftis in Jordan and leaders of Koranic school teachers in Bangladesh have spoken out in favour of family planning. Though both sides base their arguments on the pronouncements of Mohammed in the Koran and other sacred books, opponents cannot point to any specific prohibition of family planning and have to argue from the supposed implications of remarks such as 'It is I alone (Allah) who ensures livelihood for your children,' or 'Kill not your children for fear of want,' or the expansive, 'You shall procreate children and grow in numbers. Because I shall take pride in the innumerable number of my followers on the day of judgement.' Supporters of family planning cite quotations such as: 'We used to practise coitus interruptus during the time of the Prophet while the Koran was being revealed. The Prophet came to know of this, but he did not forbid us'; or the even clearer advice of Mohammed to a man who said he did not want to get his maidservant pregnant: 'Practice coitus interruptus with her if you wish. What is preordained for her will certainly befall her.' Barrier methods such as condoms or foams are simply modern versions of withdrawal, and no more sinful, simply because they were not specifically mentioned in the holy books, than the use of cars instead of camels, or kerosene in place of candles. While infanticide and the taking of human life is expressly forbidden, most authorities agree that the human soul does not enter the body until 120 days (or some say ninety) after conception. Hence abortion before that date is permissible, as are methods that prevent the implantation of the fertilized egg, such as the pill or the IUD.

The real problem is not so much what enlightened authorities believe or what the holy book says, but what ordinary Moslems believe and what religious leaders in the villages, the *imams, maulanas* and *madrasa* masters, teach their followers and pupils. They are often limited in their knowledge of the sources, and rational arguments bear less weight than dogmatic, unsubstantiated assertions and emotional appeals. I discovered this in an extended conversation on family planning with the *muezzin* (the man who calls the faithful to prayer) of a tiny mosque in the village of Agarogram in Comilla district, Bangladesh. He wore the regulation outfit of skull cap, kaftan, green dhoti and spade-shaped beard. Aged fifty, and father of ten children, he had clearly followed his own precepts. Family planning is against the religious law, he told me. God made us all, God has abundant mercy and he will feed us. Even before the creation of a man in his mother's belly, God has provided for his food, clothing and education. I asked him if there were many landless labourers in the village who could not get enough work to feed their families. He readily agreed that there were, and also conceded that excess population was the main cause. Then how has God provided for these people, I asked. If God allows this to happen, it means he wishes it to happen. Perhaps he wants to punish us, who knows his purpose? But does God not allow you to use your intelligence to avoid suffering? If a car comes at you, are you not allowed to jump out of the way? Certainly we are, God has given man his intelligence for that purpose. Then can you not use your intelligence to avoid the suffering of too large families? Not if to do so we have to violate religious regulations. What regulation is it against? God gave us the Koran, our holy book, and in that there is no instruction to plan your family. But is there any instruction against planning it? Not specifically, but Allah wished Moslems to spread and multiply and family planning wishes to reduce the numbers. God has already created every soul, and who will come and who will die he has planned up to the last day when every man will face judgement. It is not for us to interfere with this. But if God has foreordained a birth, will a man be able to prevent it with contraceptives? He did not think so. If God has decided it is time for you to die, then should you take medicines to try to keep alive? When medicine goes into your body, it seeks God's permission to act, and if it is your time to die, the medicine will not do you any good. Is it not the same then with contraceptives – if God has decided you will have a child, they cannot stop it happening? That may be so, but we are not allowed to use them. Violating these rules is a sin and a man will be punished.

It is not reason that is arguing here. If you press the opponents of family planning, you usually find that the emotional stance underlying their opposition is the fear that contraceptives will encourage 'immorality' and pre-marital sex. That could undermine the entire sexual politics of society from arranged marriages and parental authority, to father's control over daughters and men's control over women. It is these fears that explain the strength of opposition. The fear of eternal damnation, unsupported by any specific religious text, is no more than a rationalization.

Just as strong as direct teaching is the indirect effect of the status of women on fertility. The status of women is low in most traditional societies. Their lack of access to work outside the home and to independent sources of income gives them no channel to seek status and security other than by mothering many children, preferably sons.

In theory the status of a woman in Islamic law is not too oppressive. She has the right to inherit property, though only half the share of her brothers. Her consent is required for an arranged marriage, and she may divorce her husband, as he may divorce her. But in practice the situation of women in Islamic societies is probably worse than in any other major culture, and in Bangladesh it approaches the intolerable. Purdah is not enforced with the strictness of the Arabian peninsula. The head-to-foot veil is becoming uncommon, but women still draw the top of their saree over their head and hold a corner in their teeth. They affect a giggly and hysterical shyness, disappearing when a strange man appears in the compound, turning aside when a man passes them on a narrow village path, looking positively panic-stricken if he addresses a question to them. In neighbouring India, women work in the paddy fields and even on construction sites. In Bangladesh a woman will only work outside the home if the direst need drives her to it. Women do not usually attend any religious, political or social gatherings, they are rarely seen in urban centres, and their husbands even do all the shopping.

Hence a woman is entirely dependent on her husband for food and money. On marriage, she moves to her husband's family home where she becomes the very lowest member of the pecking order. The only way she can gain status and power in the family is by producing sons.

But even the protection offered by marriage is insecure in Islamic society. A man can divorce his wife simply by saying 'I divorce thee' three times in front of witnesses. As many as one in six marriages in Bangladesh may end in divorce. As women find it much harder to remarry than men, female divorcees outnumber males by eight to one. Many men, I am told, make a business out of getting married, collecting dowry and gifts from the father-in-law, then divorcing and getting married again. And with high rates of mortality, many women are left premature widows – there are three million of these in Bangladesh, against only 415,000 widowers. Unable to work outside the home, and with little hope of remarriage, the divorced or widowed woman is in an extremely precarious economic situation. In the cut-throat struggle for survival that is social life in Bangladesh, she is quite likely to be robbed or cheated of her land if she has any. Her only hope of security lies in having as many sons as possible. Sons will work the land for her, and defend her against depredations. Not surprisingly, surveys in Bangladesh have shown that women's ideal family size is significantly larger than that of men. Their low socio-economic status will have to be substantially improved if their fertility – at present their only road to status and security – is to be reduced.

The opposition of the Roman Catholic hierarchy to effective family planning has been more united, and made more impact on policy than the Islamic opposition. Islam is a rather democratic religion in which each believer relates directly to Allah, but Catholicism implicitly gives the priest considerable powers over the believer's eternal soul, through absolution and excommunication, and these claims are taken very seriously by poor people. The Catholic women of Latin America have been placed in the intolerable dilemma of choosing between the welfare of their soul in the after life, or the welfare of their families in the present.

At the core of official Catholic views is the 1968 papal encyclical *Humanae Vitae* (On Human Life) which came out against the use of any artificial means to prevent procreation. Pope John XXIII had earlier set up an official study commission on family planning, which decided in favour of a more liberal attitude. In his encyclical, Pope Paul VI overrode the findings of this commission. The tortuous and sometimes contradictory logic of *Humanae Vitae* is not easy to follow. In essence, it states that God created the act of love for a dual purpose: first, to create children, and second, to unite the spouses in love. He deliberately fused these two aspects in such a way that they were inseparable by natural means. This was a sign that he did not wish man to separate them by interfering with nature. 'Every conjugal act must remain open to the transmission of life,' read the key sentence. Boiled down to practicalities, this meant that only the so-called rhythm method was acceptable: couples wishing to limit their families should restrict intercourse to the natural, God-given period of infertility.

Critics – many of them Catholics – were quick to point out the weaknesses in these arguments. The deliberate use of the infertile period consciously separates the two functions God linked in the act of love. Moreover, why should the Church reject interference in the natural process of procreation when it tolerated other unnatural intrusions into God-given human biology via modern medicine and surgery? Many Catholic theologians, individual priests and some national hierarchies claimed that the encyclical was not an infallible pronouncement, but merely a personal statement, a note of guidance, and that the final choice lay with the conscience of each couple. But most Church hierarchies in Latin America supported the line of *Humanae Vitae*. Governments shied at risking the vocal opposition of such a potent moulder of public opinion as the Church: even those who favoured family planning could only do so in a quiet, underhand way.

Ask any woman in rural Rio Grande do Norte in north-east Brazil how many children she wants, and she will answer 'Whatever God wills.' It is not that she personally welcomes the large number that invariably results; but she can see no practicable way of avoiding them. The idea that she herself could control her own fertility, leave off being a baby factory for a few years and give her existing children a chance is too revolutionary for her to contemplate. But if you really press her on her ideal family, she will give you a surprisingly low figure. Maria Vincentia Marinho is a slender old matriarch of eighty-eight who lives in a house only a few feet away from the surf where *jangadeiros* launch their triangular-sailed fishing rafts. She had nineteen living children, and has more than three hundred direct descendants down to great-great-grand-children, and she is very proud of the size of her family. 'No one will destroy us, ever,' she told me. 'Our votes alone decide who is going to be mayor here.' When I asked her how many children she would really have liked, if she had been able to choose, she said four.

In Rio Grande do Norte, an unholy conspiracy of male *machismo* and Church dogma has lined up against the women's desire to have smaller families. Brazil's family planning associ-ation, Bemfam, launched a programme here in 1973 to give the women an alternative. Local volunteers such as nurses and teachers distribute pills and educate women about the need for them. By 1976 one in four of the 350,000 fertile women in the state, from the rippling sugar estates of the coast to the tinder-dry scrub of the hinterland, had been con-tacted at least once. But the programme did not catch fire, as some of the more successful ones have done. In 1976 only just over one in ten fertile women were being supplied with con-traceptive pills, and less than two thirds had taken them reg-ularly for more than a year. Part of the problem lay in the fact that Bemfam did not have enough money to do the job properly. A programme based on the pill needs a very effective follow-up service, because a lot of women get headaches when they start their first couple of courses, and in a poor area with malnourished, anaemic women side effects are likely to be more pronounced. Women with headaches or dizziness need information, reassurance, perhaps a change to a lower dosage of oestrogen. But Bemfam was short of doctors as back-up in cases of serious complications. Often when women did not return for new pill supplies, the unpaid distributors did not chase them up to find out why, and acceptors were lost.

The Brazilian government gave Bemfam nothing except criticism, saying it was run on foreign funds and aimed to re-duce the country's growth rate (2·8 per cent in the late seven-ties, doubling every twenty-five years). With 112 million inhabitants in 1977, it was already the world's seventh most populous state, but it wanted more population growth to make it a major world power and to people the vastness of the Amazon basin. The Church was indirectly responsible for the government attitude. In other respects, the Brazilian heirarchy is very radical, and frequently attacks the country's rulers on their social and economic policies. The government did not want to antagonize the Church even further by taking a contrary stand on this sensitive topic.

But the Church's direct influence on local attitudes was more damaging still. The women of the north-east compensate for their grinding poverty with an intense, fervent religious faith. Not that they go to mass much, but they know they ought to. And they have a vivid, concrete idea of paradise as a realm of happiness and light opening up at the end of life's dark tunnel, and an equally palpable idea of hell as a place of real physical torment. The Church exploits this religiosity to attack family planning in general, and the Bemfam programme in particular. It backed *Humanae Vitae*, but clothed its attacks on birth control in left-wing rhetoric. The media constantly quoted prominent churchmen in the state. Dom Eugenio Salles said that birth control campaigns were a conspiracy of the rich industrialized nations to keep down the poor countries so they wouldn't have to redistribute the world's wealth. The rich elite of Brazil wanted family planning too, he said, to combat the threat of growing numbers of the poor clamouring for social justice. In reality, population growth produces a reserve army of unemployed and reduces the power of the poor, but no matter, for it is not reason that is arguing here. Fallacious arguments like these are common in nationalistic and left-wing circles in many countries.

The archbishop of Natal, Dom Nivaldo Monte, joined in the chorus, claiming that the pill provoked 'irreversible bio-psychic ailments' and was 'biologically and scientifically condemned'. Population growth produced a preponderance of youth, and that was a good thing: 'A country of old people is a country marching to its destruction.'

Perhaps the most effective enemy of the programme was an

ancient Italian monk who toured the salvation-hungry villages, preaching the imminent end of the world to open-air crowds of thousands. He would rant against permissiveness, pop music and women in trousers. But he reserved his special venom for the pill. Every woman who used it would go straight to hell when she died, he promised, and her husband with her.

And the women believed him. When I met Niosa Lopez de Sousa, she had just had her fifteenth child and was still bulging with the after-effects. She was only thirty-three, but had been married at fourteen. The new baby was in a cradle in a bare room, and the ten living children came and peered at it and asked if it was a doll. Niosa once took just five pills to see what they were like, but she got headaches and stopped. 'The pill is a sin,' she explained. 'The bible says so. God ordered people to multiply – if there was no procreation, there would be no people.' She had to find some rationale for all this effort and suffering. 'It is a big sacrifice, raising so many children. But I just have to depend on God's will. All my problems come from that.' Jiuseppa Soares Acosta lives in a tumbledown shack in a dusty street on the outskirts of Ceará Mirim, a provincial town. She too has had fifteen pregnancies, though she is only thirty-five, and now has a paunch that makes her look permanently pregnant. Only five of her babies survived. The youngest, a puffy, nine-month-old boy, has an infected ear that suppurates, but she cannot afford treatment: 'If you don't have the ten cruzeiros for the hospital, they'll let you die there on the doorstep.' She took the pill for six months, three years ago, but got headaches. 'I was dizzy, running around the house like I was mad. It was a sin, I know it was. I think that when I die it will be the biggest sin I have to answer for. God made women to have children. The tree that doesn't bear fruit should be cut down.'

The Church's ally in this battle against the liberation of women is the powerful *machismo* of the Latin male. One reason birth rates are so astonishingly high in the continent is that most men will not use the traditional methods of withdrawal or abstention. They will have sex whenever they want it, and that is that. If the woman doesn't want to, she may well be forced to. Worse, the *macho* male wishes to prove his virility not only to himself or to his wife, but also and perhaps primarily to other men. The only verifiable way of doing so is by getting women pregnant. 'Some men only believe they are men if they have a child every year,' one woman lamented. 'I have to take the pill secretly. If my husband knew he would kill me.' I have met women with black eyes acquired in precisely this fashion. Bearing children, moreover, ties a woman down while leaving the man free. It restricts her freedom to go off with other men, and finally makes her unattractive to them, Because *el hombre muy macho* is as jealous as he is unfaithful.

Consider the situation of a woman about to take the pill for the first time. She knows she needs it, but at the same time she feels guilty. God may punish her – and her husband may beat her into the bargain. But she takes her heart in her hand and swallows the pill. Then she gets headaches – intensified by her anxiety and her physical weakness. The headaches seem like God's warning. If she persevered for a month or two, they would probably go away. But all she can think about is the pain and confusion now. So she stops taking the pill.

And she tells tales, and the tales get amplified. In the medical post of a fishing village I met one woman of twenty-eight who had three living children and wanted no more. But she would not take the pill because she was afraid it would make her hair fall out. Another woman, aged forty with five children, believed it would send her mad. Apocryphal tales abound: one user was said to have given birth to a child, and when it opened its tiny hands for the first time, they were full of pills. A common belief is that the pill works by accumulating into a malignant bolus in the womb that can only be removed by surgery. This ties in with the most widespread fear of all: that the pill causes cancer. Rumours are often believed more readily than direct personal experience. One man in this same village told me that his wife took the pill for a whole year with no side effects at all, but stopped after hearing all the tales about its dangers.

So nine out of ten women remain in their bondage, and each

of their average of seven children is weaker, worse fed, clothed and educated as a result. The poor women of Latin America are martyrs to theological niceties conceived far away from the hovels and shanties where their consequences are suffered, in guilt, pain and poverty. Fortunately, in 1978, the Brazilian government changed its stance, accepted the need for family planning and even started its own high-risk pregnancy prevention programme.

In 1978, ten years after *Humanae Vitae*, came the first tentative and ambiguous signs of a thaw in the Vatican's icy attitude to family planning. The Kenyan government had decided to integrate Catholic hospitals into the state medical services, which meant that Catholic doctors, nurses and administrators could find themselves obliged to follow government policy on family planning, and to cooperate in providing artificial methods of contraception. To provide guidance on this quandary, the conference of Catholic bishops in Kenya commissioned a paper by Father H. Lotstra, which was submitted to the Vatican, and approved as a worthwhile statement. Quietly and indirectly, this acquiescence opened the way for local branches of the Church to take a more permissive attitude, though it was later hedged with reservations.

Lotstra commended the natural rhythm method as being most in keeping with the moral law and with human dignity, but he acknowledged that it demanded effort and self-sacrifice. Couples were faced with a conflict of duties: 'On the one hand they have a moral obligation not to frustrate the natural openness of their sexual union to procreation. On the other hand they feel equally obliged not to endanger the stability of their union by renouncing the sexual expression of their love or the good of their families by having more children.' The decision on what method to use was for each couple to take in their own conscience, but if they chose an artificial method they should not be condemned: 'There should be no room for disturbing guilt feelings or ecclesiastical sanctions.' Lotstra went further, suggesting that Catholic medical workers could cooperate in the government's family planning programme. They should explain all the available methods, their advantages and disadvantages, and point out the moral advantage of the rhythm method. 'But in the last analysis, he will respect the couple's decision and he will help them to implement it.'

The passing of this document by the Vatican indicated that it might be thawing and accepting the critics' argument, that *Humanae Vitae* was not an *ex cathedra* pronouncement, which could be ignored only at spiritual peril, but more a note of guidance. While it would make it easier for liberal hierarchies to give governments more leeway in adopting effective national programmes, everything would still hinge on local attitudes. The reactionary village pastor could still use his claim to power over souls, the hierarchy still use their power and influence to discourage artificial methods. A much more positive statement from the centre would be needed before women in need everywhere would feel genuinely free to adopt effective methods.

On the septic ward: the abortion epidemic

The church plays a prominent part in another Latin American tragedy: illegal abortion.

The rise in abortion is a global trend. In the Third World it is, paradoxically, a hopeful sign. It is a drastic method of controlling births after the event, among women who have not yet found an effective prevention. It shows the lengths to which women will go to limit their families, and is a sure indication that they would be receptive to family planning programmes if any were provided. Yet abortion is still illegal or highly restricted in most of the Third World, and in 1977 only ten Third World governments had abortion laws or policies that could be termed liberal. The practice remains most restricted in Latin America (where only Cuba has a liberal policy); the attitude of the Church is the main cause.

The official Catholic view, shared this time even by the opponents of *Humanae Vitae*, is that it is a mortal sin to take a human life, and that life begins as soon as the ovum is fertilized by a spermatozoon. That cuts out abortion at any stage of the pregnancy. And for many churchmen, it also cuts out intra-uterine devices, as these are believed to prevent the fertilized egg from being implanted in the womb, and hence are a form of abortion. Church and state have laid an inescapable trap for the poor women of Latin America: they have withheld the proper means for preventing pregnancy, and also made the last resort of health and sanity, abortion, illegal. But the women's need is so desperate that increasingly vast numbers are willing to break the law. As with all laws against what sociologists call victimless crime from gambling to prostitution, all that happens is that the activity goes underground and flourishes in a perverted form, polluted by extortion, intimidation and appalling conditions. In Lima, Panama, Buenos Aires and Asuncion, between a half and two thirds of all women aged thirty-five to forty-nine have had at least one abortion, and the number of abortions per thousand live births doubled or trebled over five years. In Bogotá, Colombia, where abortion is totally illegal, the rate rose from 115 per thousand live births in 1964 to 147 in 1968, and a 1975 survey found a rate of nearly one abortion for every two live births. In the Uruguayan capital Montevideo, abortions are estimated to outnumber live births by three to one.

As there is no official control over health standards, illegal abortion always leads to a high proportion of complications, even in rich countries, let alone amid the proliferating microbes and poor sanitation of the Third World. In Bolivia, women with complications from illegal abortion make up more than 65 per cent of gynaecological and obstetric admissions to state hospitals. Nearly a quarter of all deaths in El Salvador's maternity hospital had the same cause. Nine out of ten women admitted had used no form of contraception.

The Materno-Infantil, Bogotá's biggest maternity hospital, is a gaunt, dungeon-like building with a flaking façade and echoing corridors, not the nicest of places to bring your baby into the world. One in five of the 30,000 admissions a year is a case of post-abortion complications.

Next to the intensive care ward with its rows of cots and undersized, ailing, wailing babies is a silent ward. Here the patients are sleeping or gazing vacantly, and some of them are weeping. There are no babies. This is the septic ward, which handles the worst cases of post-abortion complications. In the sister's room a purple log book is kept registering the bare facts about those who died. Each dry, clinical entry summarizes an unwritten tragedy:

'30/10/76, Fanny Osorio, thirty-seven, of Bogotá, married, cause of death, septicaemia and peritonitis; 2/11/76, Anna Lucia Garson, twenty-two, single, of Guayabal, cause of death, stage IV sepsis and pulmonary embolism; 8/11/76, Pedraza Transito, eighteen, single, cause of death, stage III sepsis.' And so on, with an entry every few days.

Even as I visited the ward, in one bed a young woman began to writhe with pain. She dropped onto the stone floor, groaning, haemorrhaging yellow liquid. An abscess, the aftermath of a botched abortion, had ruptured. Two nurses rushed over and heaved her back onto the bed, limp as a rag doll in her stained shift. Her head lolled to one side, eyes glazed over, and saliva crept from her half-open mouth.

Luisa was lucky. They brought her round and by afternoon she was well enough to talk to me of the experiences that led up to her admission. Now aged twenty-six, with one child of five years and another of six months, she had never used any form of contraception since her marriage at sixteen. Her husband earns around £30 ($60) a month, and like most Bogotanos, rich or poor, they pay out half of their income in rent. Two months before, she had realized she was pregnant again.

'My husband wanted me to have an abortion. I said let's have this one other child, but he wouldn't have it. We had big rows, he got very angry and violent with me. I pleaded with him and wept and said please don't make me have an abortion. But he forced me to, he threatened to leave me. How could I stay alone with the children? Who would have paid the rent? How could I get a job if I was pregnant?' She waited for the nurse to change her drip feed, and her eyes watered as she reflected. Then she described the operation, performed for a fee of about £10 ($20) by a *señora* in the back room of a dress shop.

'She put me on the bed, and gave me a herbal tea. Then she put a pillow on my stomach, so I couldn't see what was going on. It hurt so much, as if she was using a knife. Afterwards I went back home but I started feeling bad, very bad. I had fever. My husband paid for a taxi and I went back to see the *señora*. But she pushed me and maltreated me, and gave me some pills. The fever only got worse. I was vomiting and had stomach pains, I was crying with the pain. Eventually my husband brought me here and they told me I had an infected ovary that will have to come out. That doesn't matter because I don't want any more children, but I would rather have had this baby than go through what I have suffered.'

The problems arise inevitably from the illegality of abortion. Most of the abortionists have no medical knowledge, and sanitation in the slums where most of them work is bad. Dr Armando Lozano, head of the septic service at the Materno-Infantil, told me, 'A few of the *señoras* use traditional methods such as quinine water – preparations that are either poisonous to the woman as well as the foetus, or useless. The majority use a hollow rubber or plastic tube and poke through it with things like umbrella spokes, knitting needles, or even sticks and bits of wire. As a result, we get women in here with ruptured wombs, rectums, intestines, bladders. One girl came in with her womb, intestines and kidneys slashed as if she had been carved up with a kitchen knife. The conditions of cleanliness are subhuman. There is no disinfection or sterilization. Septicaemia, abscesses, peritonitis are common consequences, and most of our patients have to have their womb or ovaries removed. This is often a terrible tragedy for them because from then on they think of themselves as incomplete, and their husband may no longer consider them a whole woman. Many couples have broken up because of this.'

An illegal abortion is a profound personal crisis for the woman, compounded of physical pain, fear of death, guilt, anxiety over detection or the future of her marriage and the fate of her other children. Economic pressure, combined with ignorance of contraception, is the most common reason for seeking abortion. Another patient in the ward, Francisca, was the victim of rape, but Colombian law does not allow abortion even for this. Just fourteen, she has the lozenge eyes, raven-black hair and round cheeks of the near full-blooded Indian. 'I have six brothers and sisters,' she told me. 'We live with a relative because my mother is dead and my father didn't want us. This type came into the house when I was alone doing the washing. He was a married man, old. He pushed me into the pile of laundry and said, if you don't let me do it, I'll kill you.' She found she was pregnant, so her eldest sister got an abortionist. Francisca started haemorrhaging straight away. When the bleeding showed no signs of stopping her sister brought her to the hospital. The abortion had not even been complete – the foetus was still there, but the womb had become infected and would probably have to come out. The doctors, in law, would be risking prosecution in order to save her life. And Francisca, who had only just entered her child-bearing age, would never be able to be a mother.

Another ward patient, Maria, a pretty and flirtatious twenty-five-year-old, is typical of Colombian women in her chequered personal life, her sporadic and ill-informed use of contraceptives, and her explosive fecundity. Married at fourteen (the minimum age is only twelve, which doesn't help to limit population), she had two children in quick succession. When she was sixteen she had an IUD inserted, but didn't get it renewed. As IUDs come out after a few years, at nineteen she had a third child, then a fourth which died. At twenty-one she was pregnant again, but her husband left her so she got an abortion. When she met another man, three years later, she didn't want to use the pill because she thought it was a harmful drug, so she used the rhythm method. This proved its unreliability (critics say you can't regulate love by the calendar or the thermometer), she got pregnant again and had her second abortion, which landed her in hospital with a kidney infection.

None of these women were 'taking the easy way out' or 'avoiding the consequences of their irresponsibility' – phrases that anti-abortionists often use. They had all taken agonized decisions knowing the high risks involved. The evidence shows quite clearly that women will have the abortions they need whether the law allows it or not. The purpose of the anti-abortionists – to save human life – will be better served by legalizing abortion and reducing the need for it by making contraceptives widely available. If unwanted pregnancies come to full term, the poor women of the Third World sometimes turn to far worse measures than abortion. Concealed infanticide by neglect is widespread. Few mothers are desperate or depraved enough to kill their children. But if a child gets sick, as they often do, some mothers may not do all they can to bring it back to health. I have met several doctors who told me that some mothers had seemed disappointed when they cured their children. I have met mothers living within walking distance of free clinics who would not take their ailing babies there. Infant sickness may come into a poor household as a blessing in disguise: it can be accepted as destiny or God's will. Arthur Clough's verse 'Thou shalt not kill; but needst not strive/Officiously to keep alive' is a medic's joke in the West, but an everyday dilemma for the poor women of the developing countries.

Child abandonment is extremely common throughout Latin America. The *gamines* of Bogotá have their parallels in Mexico City and Recife. In Asia children are often 'sold' into domestic service with a richer family, though the child does not become the property of the purchasers and is free to leave at any time. Another practice which is spreading is the outright sale of very young children for adoption, often in western countries where birth control and legalized abortion have cut down the previous supply of unwanted illegitimate children. This is one of the most distasteful expressions of world inequalities. But we should beware of morally condemning mothers who 'sell' their children. They genuinely believe they are helping the remaining children by reducing the number of mouths to feed, and that the child they have sold is going to have a better life than it could possibly have had with them. Rather condemn the system that pushes them into such unnatural acts. The uncaring, unequal society that tolerates such poverty.

The upward spiral: fewer children, higher incomes

Continuing population increase has a more devastating effect than the usual vicious circles the poor are trapped in. It is more like a spiral, on which the poor are moving downwards, while the less poor find themselves rising.

Families with higher income and education levels tend to have smaller families. This improves their health and productivity, and provides them with extra funds to invest, so they can further improve their income and education. Nations whose wealth is increasing rapidly tend to have slower population growth. This frees more funds for productive investment, which increases national wealth further. At the other end of the scale overpopulated poor nations and large, poor families have little or no surplus to invest in improving their incomes, so that the factors that induce better-off couples to limit their families do not come into play. So they go on having large families and get poorer – and so on.

The overall progress of development seems to brake the birth rate – and, conversely, a lower rate of population growth is an excellent tonic for economic growth. Countries of similar culture with lower birth and growth rates also tend to have higher incomes per person and all that goes with these: more urbanization, more literacy, more industry and services. But this link-up does not hold for countries with very different cultural systems: the highest birth and growth rates in the world are found in countries with Moslem culture (including the extremely wealthy oil states) and in Latin America, most advanced of the developing continents, with its *machismo* and Catholicism (see Map 5, pages 462–3).

The great success stories in population control fit in well with the idea that overall development speeds up the demographic transition. Singapore halved its birth rate in just eleven years from 1964, from thirty-six per thousand to eighteen per thousand (it took Britain sixty years to achieve this); Costa Rica's birth rate fell from forty-six to twenty-nine over the same period; Reunion's from forty-four to twenty-eight; Hongkong's from thirty-four to twenty. Colombia, Chile, Tunisia,

South Korea, Mauritius, Martinique and Trinidad and Tobago all had diminishing birth rates, by at least one point a year over the same period. All these countries are fairly high up the development ladder: the poorest of them, Colombia, had a per capita income of $630 in 1976. They are all relatively urbanized, with more than two fifths of their people living in towns. Many of them have the additional advantage of smallness: their inhabitants are easier to reach with supplies of contraceptives.

The development pill works by changing the costs and benefits of child rearing. It is not that people become any less selfish or more considerate than the growth-oriented villagers of Africa or southern Asia. They still pursue private interest before public welfare. But children become less of an economic benefit and more of a burden, and the cost of raising them in more than modest numbers comes to outweigh the expected gain. Being prolific ceases to be a profitable proposition.

One of the most powerful of the pressures development creates favouring smaller families is urbanization. In the rural context, children are needed to help out with family labour in the fields, while the communal living style of the extended family provides grandparents or sisters-in-law to help out with child care. Privacy and leisure are alien concepts: children are not regarded therefore as a bind or a distraction. And when they grow old, parents naturally live in the same house as their children, who look after them in turn. Urbanization undermines the extended family: the increasing city housing shortage tends to break families up into nuclear units of two parents and their children. It pushes rents up, increasing the pressure on family budgets and the cost of raising extra children, while the need for child labour is much smaller. As a result, the birth rate in cities is usually around six points lower than in rural areas. In a 1969 survey village women in Sierra Leone in their late forties were found to have had an average of nearly nine live-born children each, while town dwellers had had only five. In the same year urban mothers in Turkey were found to have had an average of 4·7 live births each, against 6·4 for rural mothers.

The spread of education is another important factor. It brings extra costs in school fees and books, and reduced income as the child's role of miniature workman declines. By the time your son has passed through all his grades, and spent his inevitable years of youth unemployment hanging around street corners, he is ready to leave and set up a home of his own; your return on investment drops nearly to nil. The marginal urban poor, of course, still need human insurance policies for old age; but as the modern sector absorbs more workers, social security covers an increasing proportion of the population.

The spread of education for women — previously left out of school and adult education — provides more of them with the knowhow and motivation to limit their family size. The average number of live births to uneducated urban women in Ghana, in a 1960 survey, was over six, against only one for women with secondary schooling. In the same year, an Indian study found that urban illiterate women had an average of nearly seven live births, while secondary school graduates had just two each. Other aspects of the improvement in women's status affect family size. When women work, the role of worker conflicts with the role of mother, and having fewer children helps to ease the tensions of too many demands on their time. Throughout the world, women are going out to work in increasing numbers. The process is slow in Africa and the Indian subcontinent, where women make up about a third of the workforce in the mid-seventies. In Latin America, their share rose from a very low 18 per cent in 1950 to 22 per cent in 1975. In eastern Asia, the area that has seen the biggest falls in birth rates, their share went up from 28 per cent to the near western level of 38 per cent. Most surveys have found that women who do formal work outside the home have fewer children.

The development pill, when it first goes to work in unequal societies, can accentuate inequalities, because it is the better-off who first start to limit their families and get the benefits of doing so. In the Indian village of Rampur, near Delhi, sociologist Monica Das Gupta found that the most educated caste, the Brahmins, were the first to start limiting their family size, while the least educated, the *Bhangis* (sweepers), multiplied at twice the rate of the Brahmins.

Because of their education levels, the Brahmins were the first caste to become involved in the urban economy. They managed to land more of the permanent salaried jobs, which brought good steady incomes and often a pension as well. To progress up the career structure, and to make sure their children got the same kind of jobs, they had to invest money in education: this was an incentive to limit their family size so they would have more surplus funds to invest. Families without education, initial capital to educate their children, or land, were condemned to casual jobs with low incomes that prevented them from accumulating the capital needed to educate their children. They could never break in to the upward spiral. The best strategy for maximizing their incomes and insuring against old age seemed to be to have large numbers of children. But this, in itself, made it harder for them to save enough to break into the upward spiral. So the rich got richer – and the poor got children.

But when the poor do come to limit their families, inequalities can be reduced. Excess people competing for jobs force wages down. Cutting back population growth among labourers can halt and reverse this process. The excess of tenants seeking farm land, and of urban poor seeking housing, pushes rents up and produces windfall gains for the rich: population control can reduce these pressures and prevent rents from rising so high. And where there is a labour shortage – or at least no great reserve army of unemployed – the poor become easier to organize to press for their rights. Slowing population growth in all groups not only reduces poverty, but also inequality. It has to be a prime weapon in any strategy for justice.

The downward spiral: larger families, lower incomes

It used to be a standard piece of accepted wisdom that overall development was the best way to slow down ruinous population growth rates. But for those countries really caught in the treadmill, it is no use looking to development for salvation, because the population boom is the biggest single obstacle to the economic progress that is supposed to bring an end to the population boom. It is the master lock on the national poverty trap.

The most essential ingredient in economic progress is investment, in improving land, industry, man. Developing countries already manage to save less for investment than developed ones: in the early seventies, the poor countries were saving between 12 and 18 per cent of their gross national products, while the developed countries averaged 23 per cent.

In the advanced countries, almost all the money invested can go to improving productivity in all spheres, so that incomes can rise rapidly. In the Third World, a massive chunk of investment goes into opening up new land and building new schools or factories merely to feed, educate or employ the extra people produced by population growth. It has been calculated that every 1 per cent of population growth forces a country to spend 4 per cent of its national income on this kind of 'demographic investment' – in other words, to stand still. For the average developing country, with population growing at 2·4 per cent a year, 10 per cent of GNP has to be spent on staying in the same place on the down escalator, leaving only 2 to 8 per cent for improvements. For the poorest countries, with low savings ratios and high population growth rates, there will be nothing or less than nothing left over to improve people's incomes. There will be no true economic growth at all, merely a pointless multiplication of everything at the same low level, or lower.

The International Labour Office economist Felix Paukert calculated that, for twenty-one developing countries he surveyed, population growth soaked up 70 per cent of the increase in national incomes, and only 2·6 per cent went into genuine income-improving investment. Small improvements in the population situation can bring massive benefits for the poorest countries. Take a country whose population was growing at 2·5 per cent a year, and which was investing 12 per cent of its GNP: only 2 per cent would be available for real investment.

Cutting the growth rate by only half a per cent could double the amount available for investment. But that is easier said than done, because national poverty, aggravated by rapid population growth, leads to continued rapid population growth. Because the poor families that make up the bulk of poor nations tend to have large families that keep them poor.

As we have seen, a poor family is likely to want more children simply because of its poverty. The poor have no savings and no cushy, pensionable positions, so they need children as an insurance against old age far more than do the rich. If they own land, they can less easily afford to hire workmen at harvest time, or to mechanize, so they must rely more on the muscle power of their sons. If they are landless, they need the extra income that working children and youths can bring. The poor lack education, and so are more ignorant about effective methods. Their health is bad, so infant mortality is high, and so they compensate with rabbit-like fecundity.

Having large numbers of children is often simply a strategy for survival but it prevents the poor from rising above survival level and, indeed, often comes close to jeopardizing their survival. The poor of the Third World often court long-term ruin to avoid immediate disaster. In the same way, going into debt keeps your head above water for the moment, but may plunge it below even more surely in the long run, so eating near-pure carbohydrates allows you to go on existing, yet prevents you from securing more than a mere existence. Avoiding health expenditure like shoes, or boiling water, saves money needed for food, but makes you sick more often, and cuts your income.

Overpopulation at family level means that all the income has to be poured into immediate consumption, and none is left over for investment in the fertilizers, pumpsets or better lathes that could boost productivity, or the education that could improve children's life chances.

Large families have an adverse effect on the welfare of all their members. Parents have been found to have worse physical and mental health than those with fewer children. They are subject to greater stress, are more likely to be under-nourished, and fall ill more frequently. This, in turn, affects the productivity of the bread-winners and reduces their earning power.

Large families are one of the many interlocking mechanisms we shall be exploring in subsequent chapters, by which poverty is made hereditary. Children of larger families tend to be smaller and weaker at birth. They have higher infant mortality and fall sick more often. They are more likely to be malnourished. A 1963 study in the small Colombian town of Candelaria found that only one child in three was malnourished in families with one or two children, against 44 per cent in families with five or more. Family spending on food dropped from twenty-three pesos per person in families with one child to only ten pesos for those with eight or more.

Because of malnutrition and other forms of deprivation, children from large families often have lower mental abilities, which condemn them to failure at school and low-paid, insecure employment in later life. They tend to score lower in tests for every type of mental ability: a British study in the 1950s found that children with six or more brothers and sisters scored an average thirteen points less on intelligence tests than only children. This effect is produced by two factors: the disastrous impact of malnutrition on the developing brain, and the similar results of lack of stimulation. Children from large families get less parental contact, as parents have more chores and less time to spare, and must share it round greater numbers.

Just as a population slowdown can increase equality, rapid population growth enhances inequality, forcing owners of marginal smallholdings to sell out, pushing rents up, dragging down wages and making the poor much harder to organize. And we have already seen in Part Two how population growth can pauperize entire communities through degradation of the soil, deforestation and desertification.

Bottoming-out: escape routes from the downward spiral

The overpopulation–poverty spiral is not endless. Famine and death define its lowest reaches, where it turns into a simple vicious circle. But there is another painful route out that can lead on to the upward spiral. It is that poverty itself may reach such levels that — exactly as with increasing affluence — child rearing starts to cost more than its expected benefits.

This point has probably already been reached in much of southern Asia, Java and the Nile valley. Land is becoming so infinitely subdivided that most farms cannot support a large family and are so small that a man can work it alone without the need for large amounts of family labour. And the labour surplus has reached such chronic proportions that wages are too low to support a large family.

In Bangladesh, surveys have found that the less land a man owns, the more likely his wife is to know about, approve of and practise family planning. Farmers of more than two acres whom I met were determined to have as many sons as they needed to work their land without hired labour — generally, one son for every one and a half acres they possessed — and these men did not seem particularly concerned that their sons would inherit much smaller patches than they themselves enjoyed. But at the critical size of holding that a man can work alone — about one and a half acres — and below, there was a noticeable desire for small families. But what of the theory that the landless and near-landless also want extra sons to bring in extra wages? This too begins to be inoperable as poverty really bites. In Bangladesh, it has been calculated that a male child begins from the age of twelve to repay the cost of rearing him. By the time he is sixteen, he will have repaid that cost in full, and by the time he is twenty, he will have earned enough to cover the cost of rearing another child. Now the decline in real wages produced by the labour surplus tends to lengthen the time needed for a child to repay its cost — if real wages halve, repayment time doubles. More critically still, increasing poverty has led to a situation where the poorest openly admit that while they might like to have more sons, they simply cannot afford to rear them up to the age when they will begin to earn money.

At this lowest ebb, it is possible for a vigorous population programme finally to find receptive customers. When this succeeds, the population growth rate can be brought down *before* economic development occurs, and from that point on, movement on the spiral may be reversed and the development process can proceed more rapidly and bring population growth down further.

Several poor and large countries have achieved significant drops in their birth rates since 1975, before the restraining factors associated with economic development could have come into play. These include Thailand (1976 per capita income $380), Indonesia ($240), India ($150), Philippines ($410) and Egypt ($280). Significantly, they are all countries where landlessness and shortage of employment have reached advanced levels, and they all have vigorous family planning programmes and governments committed to family planning.

Bali is an excellent example of how this process of bottoming-out works in practice.

Before 1969 there were practically no users of contraceptives on the island. In that year an official population programme was launched. By June 1977 an astonishing 60 per cent of fertile couples were using modern reliable methods such as inter-uterine device or condom – a level not far below many a western country. I asked dozens of village parents how many children they thought constituted an ideal family. Almost all of them said two: one boy, one girl.

The Balinese experience does not fit in at all with the idea that overall development is a precondition of population slowdown. Income per head is even lower than the 1976 Indonesian average of $240, as is the level of education. Only 10 per cent of the population live in urban areas, and infant mortality is still high. Bali's success story, I believe, is an example of bottoming-out of the downward spiral.

Land hunger has reached intolerable levels. The average holding is about a fifth of a hectare. A family of six would need about a third of a hectare of good land to be self-sufficient, so almost everyone has a second occupation – making bricks in wood-fired kilns, producing craft work for ceremonies or tourists. Holdings are now so small that most men can work their land alone and don't need extra sons for

cheap labour. For the same reason there is not much labouring work to be had on other people's land, so a son cannot
earn his keep by bringing in wages. Many men whose fathers
had two sons or more have seen the land shrink to postage-
stamp size in their own lifetime. Madé Mangku, aged twenty-
five, had to share his father's third of a hectare with his elder
brother. The 0·15 hectares are not enough to feed his wife and
two children, so he carves stone statues to make ends meet.
Like many Balinese, he is a gifted artist and his ornate sculptures of Vishnu seated on the wings of Garuda, king of the
birds, would grace any temple or garden. But they are not in
great demand: few tourists want to buy heavy stonework.
Mangku gets only $9 (£4.50) for a statue that takes him three
weeks to complete. His wife trades in vegetables. They could
not afford to feed a single extra child and wish to stop at two,
so his wife has an inter-uterine device.

Two additional factors have helped in the Balinese success
which are weaker in otherwise similar areas. First, the village is
a caring community in the most practical sense and neighbourhood associations help out the poor with funeral expenses, and
help the widowed and the sick. This reduces the social security
motive for having large families. Second, the tradition of cooperation extends into the fields, reducing the need for family
labour – a man will help his neighbour transplant his seedlings,
and harvesting groups cut the ripe rice, taking a share of the
crop in payment.

There are several other escape routes from the down spiral.
The first is that external aid can supply the investment for
real growth that the population boom prevents the country
itself from generating. Very large quantities of aid would be
needed. And if the usual unequal-growth strategies were being
pursued, it would take too long for the benefits to filter down
to the poor and incline them to have smaller families.

Until they reach rock-bottom, people in the lower reaches
of the whirlpool are unlikely to limit their families voluntarily
in competitive societies. The second approach would be to
force them to do so by using some degree of compulsion. The
brutal shambles of India's experiment in forcible sterilization

has discredited outright compulsion. But indirect forms such as economic and social incentives for small families, and disincentives for large, have been tried with some success, for example, in Singapore. The third approach would be to reduce the competitiveness of village life, creating cooperative structures that would give every one an interest in community welfare and could exert moral pressure on recalcitrant families. Village-level social security systems could be devised. Finally, redistribution and land reform can improve the situation of the poorest even in the absence of economic growth, and give them some of the motivation to have small families that overall development provides.

Outlook: grim

What, then, are the prospects for the population of the Third World, in the last quarter of the twentieth century?

The demographic transition is proceeding on its expected course. Birth rates in the Third World have started to come down more rapidly. The average dropped from 42·9 per thousand in 1969 to 39 per thousand in 1975. Death rates continued to come down, but not quite so rapidly: over these same six years, they dropped by 1·9 points. So the gap between birth rates and death rates that opened up to cause the population explosion was beginning to close again. From the early 1980s, overall growth rates will slowly decline: just how fast will depend on the success of population programmes and the progress of economic growth, the spread of education, the success of egalitarian policies. The three developing continents vary considerably in their performance to date, and their outlook.

Africa is likely to go on growing longer than Latin America or Asia. African parents show little sign as yet of adjusting to the fact that more of their children are surviving: in the ten years from 1960–65 birth rates declined by only 1·4 points, from 47·7 to 46·3. Death rates fell more than twice as fast, so Africa's population growth actually speeded up, and the United Nations predicts that it will continue to accelerate until

1985–90, when it will reach a peak of 2·88 per cent a year. The continent's 1977 population of 423 millions is expected nearly to double to 811 millions by the end of the century. The outlook is all the poorer because few governments show any real concern about the problem: in 1976 only four states out of forty-three had an official policy of cutting population growth.

Latin America's growth rate has already reached its peak: in the late seventies it was growing at 2·74 per cent a year. The rate is expected to decline thereafter, but only slowly, so that the 1977 population of 336 millions may reach over 600 millions in the year 2000. Birth rates came down twice as fast as in Africa, from 39·5 per thousand in 1960–65 to 36·9 per thousand in 1970–75. This was just a little faster than death rates, so growth slowed by a fraction. Prospects here are better than in Africa, though still not too encouraging: only nine governments out of thirty-three had an official policy in 1976 of slowing growth. But the situation is volatile: abortion rates show a massive hidden need for contraception, and any change in the official attitude of the Catholic Church to birth control could result in rapid change.

Asia housed 2,325 million people in 1977 – 57 per cent of the world's population and three quarters of the Third World's. This is where progress is most desperately needed. Asian birth rates declined most rapidly of all – from 43·5 per thousand in 1965 to 38·1 in 1974 – and the decline seemed to be gathering momentum. But the bulk of the progress was concentrated in East Asia, where successful family planning programmes coupled with egalitarian economic growth in Taiwan, South Korea and red China cut birth rates by eleven points in the five years from 1970. In the areas of worst poverty, south and South-East Asia, birth rates fell three times more slowly, by between three and four points. Fifteen out of thirty-two governments, containing 90 per cent of the population, are committed to slowing population growth, and the decline in growth rates is predicted to move fastest here; but the population will still expand to around three and a half billions at the end of the century.

Some commentators and media – hungry for signs of hope

on a bleak horizon – have hinged on the tiniest hints of progress as an omen that the world had solved its population problem. It has not, nor will it have even if family planning programmes reach 100 per cent of fertile women in every developing country tomorrow. The population problem, like its sister the food problem, will be with us for probably another century.

The first reason for caution is that death rates have not bottomed out by any means. They can get as low as five or six per thousand in Third World countries – lower than the advanced countries, because of the very low proportion of old people in the population. Only Latin America – apart from a few black spots like Haiti, Honduras, Nicaragua and Bolivia – has rock-bottom death rates unlikely to get any lower. Hence any drop in birth rates will be pure profit, and lead to equal drops in growth rates.

In Asia and Africa, death rates still have some way to fall, especially in the poorer countries and the rural areas. Any significant advances in health programmes could bring death rates down just as fast as birth rates are declining, and hence keep the populations growing at the same rate. Asia's death rates of around fourteen per thousand are unlikely to drop very fast – they remained almost static in south and South-East Asia between 1970 and 1975. But in Africa the rates are so high – up to twenty-three per thousand in West Africa – that they should continue to drop rapidly.

The second cause for concern is that population will still go on growing even when all the growth-oriented African tribesmen, the survival-seeking Asian rural poor and the *macho* males of Latin America have been converted to the small-family norm. If every developing country introduced compulsory sterilization for parents of more than two children tomorrow, the population boom would continue for another fifty to a hundred years before it stopped. For the greatest population threat to developing countries lies in the generation that should be their hope for the future: the young. The under-fifteens make up 44 per cent of the African population, 42 per cent in Latin America and over 40 per cent in most parts of Asia, against only 24 per cent in Europe and 26 per cent in North America. This generation is much bigger than the older generation that spawned it, and all its members still have to grow up, get married and have children.

The third worry on the horizon is that, even when populations have finally stopped growing, developing countries will still be dealing with the problems of stable populations that will be two or three times the present ones. Already the Third World has desperate problems feeding, educating, clothing, housing, finding jobs, resources and energy for their people. By the latter half of the twenty-first century there will be the equivalent of a whole new Third World, or more, on top of the present one. For individual countries, the prospect is terrifying. India's cities today are overcrowded, her fields overworked, her youth unemployed; yet she will certainly have to carry twice her present population, and possibly three times as many. Nigeria's present population of seventy-eight millions will probably reach 320 millions before levelling out. Bangladesh, currently collapsing under a population of a mere seventy-six millions, could well have to accommodate 400 millions.

These prospects mean that timing, in the battle to beat population growth, is of the essence. As World Bank President Robert McNamara has pointed out, every decade of delay in reaching replacement-level fertility (when each mother has an average of just one fertile daughter) means an extra billion or two on the world's final, stable population total. Demographer Thomas Frejka has calculated that, if the world could reach replacement-level fertility by the year 2000, the world's population would stabilize at around eight and a half billion towards the year 2100. If, as seems more likely on present trends, replacement level is not reached until 2020, then the final stable level will be eleven billions – three billion extra, or an entire 1977 Third World, because of twenty years' delay. A further twenty years' delay would produce a final stable population of fifteen billions. Before this comes about, Thomas Malthus may finally raise his voice again. So far his theory that the power of unchecked population growth needs must outstrip the power of the earth to feed man has not been validated.

This has only been possible because of the grain surpluses of North America and the Green Revolution. Both depend on fossil fuels: gas and oil to produce the fertilizers and insecticides, oil to drive tractors and harvesters. For the past twenty years, the most productive agricultures in the world have been in the business of processing oil into food. We know now that this cannot go on. Keeping Malthus at bay depends on our finding ways we have not yet found of getting high yields off the land without oil, and on the unpredictable vagaries of the world's weather machine. If a non-oil agricultural practice is not developed fast, available food per capita will start to decline. There may not be huge famines: things will more probably go with a whimper rather than a bang. In the most vulnerable and poorest areas (which lack the money to command their fair share of food supplies) death rates will start to rise again slowly. Adults may survive, functioning at ever lower levels of vitality and productivity. But infant mortality rates will creep up and those sad processions behind two-foot coffins become more frequent. For places like Bangladesh, the eastern plains of the Ganges in India, Sri Lanka and the Sahel, this is no mere scenario: it is already happening.

If man does not conquer the population problem, nature will step in and do it for him. And everywhere it will be the poorest families who bear the brunt of the attack.

15. Man is What He Eats: Malnutrition

'Der Mensch ist, was er isst.'
LUDWIG FEUERBACH

Adequate nutrition is the most basic of all human needs and rights, and hunger is the worst of all the many slings and arrows suffered by the poor inhabitants of poor countries. It weakens bodies, damages tissues. It condemns mothers to grief, and children to death or disability. It turns family life into a bitter struggle for scarce resources. And it threatens the most precious attribute of being human: an able, alert mind.

The word 'hunger' is emotive and imprecise. The overused expression 'world hunger' conjures up images of starvation, shrunken limbs, staring eyes and begging-bowls. But the truth is that though malnutrition is almost everywhere among the poor, the traveller in the Third World rarely sees people who are nothing but skin and bone. Only in extreme situations, in Biafra, Bangladesh or the Sahel, do these occur in large numbers. The everyday reality of malnutrition in the Third World is less dramatic. It is adults scraping through, physically and mentally fatigued and vulnerable to illness. It is children – often dying, not so frequently of hunger alone, as of hunger working hand in hand with sickness; but more often surviving impaired for life.

The United Nations Food and Agriculture Organization estimated that in the early seventies there were 455 million people in the Third World getting less than the minimum intake of food required to keep body and soul together in the long term. This amounted to one quarter of the total population of non-communist developing countries. Some 300 millions of them were in Asia alone.

The most widely distributed form of malnutrition is known as *Protein Energy Malnutrition* (PEM). This is found when food intake is inadequate in quantity as well as quality. Until recently more attention was paid to lack of protein, but now it is believed that most regions would have adequate protein intake if only they were getting enough calories. Lack of calories forces the body to burn up precious protein as fuel, instead of using it for building and renewing tissues.

Surveys of the extent of protein energy malnutrition have found widely differing incidences in different parts of the world. Taking an average of twenty-five surveys made over the last ten years, World Health Organization nutritionist Dr E. M. DeMaeyer found that the median value for moderate malnutrition was 19 per cent of the children of the developing continents, and for severe forms, nearly 3 per cent. The situation was worst in Asia, where 31 per cent suffered from moderate PEM and 3·2 per cent from severe. Africa came next, with 26 per cent having moderate PEM and 4·4 per cent severe. Latin America was somewhat better nourished, with a median of 19 per cent with moderate malnutrition and 1·6 per cent with severe. In particular areas the situation is much worse – 90 per cent of children in the Puno area of southern Peru were found to be underweight, a quarter of them severely so. World wide, of the three hundred million plus children under five in the Third World, perhaps one hundred million were suffering from some degree of protein energy malnutrition, seventy millions of them in Asia.

There are two main forms of PEM. *Kwashiorkor*, an acute condition, may be invisible to the untrained observer. The wasted tissues are hidden by a watery swelling, and the child may have a round, cherubic moon face. But he has little of the zest of a normal infant. He is miserable, withdrawn and inactive. He may develop darker patches on his skin, and his hair may be thin. Kwashiorkor sufferers are between 20 and 40 per cent underweight for their age.

The *marasmus* victim is over 40 per cent underweight. His diet has been so poor over a long period that his body has not been able to adapt simply by halting its growth. It has been forced to turn on itself and to consume its own tissues. So the marasmus child looks like a wizened old man or a foetus. He has hardly any fat and his muscles are wasted. His chances of survival are poor.

PEM victims are usually children, though women may suffer mild forms of it. Children get lowest priority in the share-out of family food supplies – and they are much more susceptible to disease which often starts off cases of malnutrition. But there are other nutritional deficiencies that can hit adults too. Of these, the most common is *anaemia*. Perhaps a third of all men and two thirds of women in developing countries are anaemic. Their largely vegetarian diets often contain much less usable iron than meat does, and stomach parasites such as hookworms may siphon off much of the iron that is consumed. (See Map 6, pages 464–5.) The effects are well known among menstruating or pregnant women: lack of energy, fatigue, reduced concentration. Generally, diminished mental and physical capacities. *Goitre*, due to lack of iodine in the soil, is widespread in the Andes, the Himalayas, Indonesia and in pockets throughout the Third World. Only in extreme cases does it lead to the well-known neck swelling. It can also lead to cretinism and mental retardation among children. *Xerophthalmia* is common among the poor and is due to deficiency of vitamin A, found in carrots and green leafy vegetables. Its most serious consequence is defective vision, starting with night blindness and ending with total blindness. *Beriberi*, which leads to stomach problems among children and dropsy or palpitations among adults, is found mainly in Asia. It is due to lack of the B vitamin thiamine, abundantly present in unrefined brown rice, but lost during milling and polishing of rice. It is really a sort of cultural disease due to strong preferences for white rice. The highly nutritious rice polish – which could improve the health of poor Asians overnight, at no cost – is usually fed to animals. *Pellagra* occurs mainly among people with a maize-dominated diet, and is due to a lack of the B vitamin niacin. It can lead to weakness and loss of weight, as well as dermatitis, diarrhoea and even insanity due to lesions in the nervous system.

Hunger, merely as a subjective experience, involves suffering.

It means to be in a state of perpetually frustrated desire. The poor may be so accustomed to this that they no longer notice it – they wouldn't even know what life would feel like without it. But it is there all the same. Experience of hunger in the West is, ironically, largely limited to the grossly overfed who happen to be on a temporary diet. Anyone who has been on a crash diet for more than a couple of days will know the feeling. The reader might try two or three days on 1,000 calories a day, if he has not done so already, and then attempt some complicated mental task and some hard labour like digging the garden. He will notice a slowing of his mental abilities, a tendency to be easily distracted and easily irritated, a difficulty in concentrating on his physical work. While labouring he will get tired more rapidly and need more frequent rest pauses.

But hunger is damaging, too, for its economic effects. The labour of a hungry man is less productive – so he is likely to produce less or to earn less and this will keep him poor and hungry. Food intake has a direct and obvious effect on work. The body requires a basic minimum for its metabolism and for daily chores of bare existence. This varies with age and climate. Over and above the minimum, the amount of physical work a person can sustain is directly determined by the amount of calories he eats. In the Second World War, the Germans found they could boost coal production from the Ruhr pits simply by giving the miners more food. When the daily allowance was raised from 2,800 calories to 3,200, daily output per man rose from seven tons to nine and a half tons. Engineers working on the Pan-American highway were disappointed at the efforts of the local workforce until someone found out how little they were getting to eat at home. Canteens were set up to give the men three square meals a day, and production of concrete paving trebled overnight. Another study found that manual workers needed 3,000 calories to achieve 100 per cent of their working capacity, and agricultural workers 3,600 calories. If they were expected to live off 2,500 calories a day, manual workers could only function at 58 per cent of capacity and agricultural workers at 44 per cent. Where the diet provides only 1,800 calories a day, as in the poor strata of developing countries, workers cannot develop muscle strength and precision of movement. Avoidance of physical effort, and excessive resting, become essential adaptations to chronic hunger.

If a man is self-employed, he can adjust his performance to his capacities. Even so, his productivity and income will certainly be lowered. Where a hungry man depends on wage labour, or on factory work, his low output, accident proneness and inability to keep pace with machinery or with other workers will soon be noticed, and he will be sacked. Hence malnutrition pushes men towards low-paid, casual employment or unemployment. With low incomes, they can afford to buy less food, and are caught in a vicious circle of poverty, malnutrition and impaired labour power. Malnutrition in the Third World does not begin at birth. The poor man may be starved from the moment of his conception. If so, he will come into the world stunted and retarded.

Third World children are usually smaller than western children: an average newborn baby in India, for example, weighs only 2·7 kilos against 3·4 kilos in the United Kingdom and Scandinavia. Much more serious, though, is the effect of malnutrition on the developing brain. The human brain seems to grow in two stages. In the first, lasting from the tenth to the eighteenth week of pregnancy, the adult complement of nerve cells is built up. Malnutrition of the foetus at this stage (via hunger in the mother) will result in a brain that has permanently and irrevocably fewer cells than its potential, and mental capacity is partly limited by the simple size of the brain. The second growth stage lasts from about week twenty of gestation until two years after birth. This phase builds up the myelin sheaths which insulate nerve cells and speed up the transmission of impulses. At this period, too, the interconnections between nerve cells, the axons and synapses which make the brain and the nervous system a more complex and efficient communications network, are being constructed. The growth of these interconnections depends on the availability of the necessary nutrients to help cell growth, but also on the amount of stimulation from the environment. Practice makes perfect.

Malnutrition at this second stage, especially if accompanied by lack of stimulation (as it often is), can permanently retard the development of a healthy functioning brain.

Animal experiments have shown the effects of malnutrition suffered in these crucial periods of brain growth. John Dobbing of Manchester University found a reduction in the size and weight of lab rats' brains of about a quarter. Bernard Cragg of Monash University, Australia, found that underfed rats had 40 per cent fewer synapses – the essential interconnections between nerve cells – than normally fed ones. Measurements among children have confirmed these findings. A group of Chilean babies who died of malnutrition in their first year were found to have 20 per cent fewer brain cells than normal. Joaquin Cravioto studied undernourished children in south-west Mexico and found that by the time they were three years old they were already nearly a year behind normal ones in language development. Other studies have found that children who had gone through periods of severe malnutrition performed much worse than those of their brothers and sisters who had not on a whole range of perception tests. They found it harder to relate sound patterns to visual ones, to distinguish the orientation of shapes in space, and to describe the path a researcher was moving their arm through while their eyes were closed. Perception skills of these kinds are fundamental both to productive work and to the abilities underlying the learning of reading and writing, which, in turn, are the keys of academic success.

The malnourished child is therefore more likely to become a failure at school. He is more likely to have been starved of stimulation than his normal siblings, because he tends to be withdrawn and his mother gets little reward from playing with him. He is more likely to lose learning time through illness, because he is more susceptible to infection. And he will become anxious about food, which will diminish his attention to and exploration of the external world.

In other words, he is a born school drop-out. And as education in the Third World determines pay levels even more rigidly than it does in the West, he is doomed to a life of poverty which he will probably pass on to his children, not through his genes, but through his environment. The debate as to whether environment or heredity causes intelligence differences is an artificial one; in real life environment is hereditary.

The fatal conspiracy: hunger and disease

So far we have spoken about malnutrition on its own. In practice it usually occurs in combination with ill health. Malnutrition lowers resistance to illness, and illness aggravates malnutrition. Hunger and disease chase each other down a spiral that leads to death or life-long handicap.

Cells need protein and calories to grow. Without them, essential tissues and processes cannot develop properly. Among the tissues affected by malnutrition are the mucous lining and muscular wall of the intestine. If these are weakened, food is not absorbed efficiently. By this process, hunger itself can be a contributory cause to poor nutrition. Hunger leads directly to worse hunger.

In addition, malnutrition may lead to slower production of antibodies and white blood corpuscles, resulting in lowered resistance to infection. The bone marrow, where red blood cells are produced, may atrophy and cause anaemia. And thus, even where malnutrition is not a direct cause of death in children, it may have contributed by making the child more liable to disease. Malnutrition hovers in the background of perhaps half of all illness and deaths among Third World children. A survey in Latin America showed that 8 per cent of deaths in children aged between six months and two years were directly due to malnutrition, while in 41 per cent of deaths it was an associated cause. Underfed children are more likely to catch any disease that is going the rounds. In one Guatemalan village, children with moderate malnutrition were three times more likely to get diarrhoea than well-fed children, and those with severe malnutrition five times more likely.

Conversely, illness has a drastic impact on malnutrition. Disease increases the need for food. In fever the body's metabolism speeds up and it burns more energy. Some bacterial infections eat up, through nitrogen loss, two or three kilos of human muscle, and that can only be made up by consuming more protein. But at the same time disease usually reduces the intake of food. The sick body consumes less food than normal, and does not even absorb what it does consume very well. The patient loses his appetite and cannot hold down some kinds of food. Traditional ideas on how to feed sick children often make things worse than they need be. The sick child may be put on thin gruels or even cooking water from vegetables. He gets practically no protein and probably inadequate calories too. So nature combines with culture to transform disease into malnutrition. For a child a bout of serious illness is often the first jolt that sets the ball of malnutrition rolling down the slope: this explains how one child can be malnourished and another child in the same poor family unaffected. As disease in the Third World is often due to lack of village sanitation, clean water or immunization services, government neglect of the rural poor is almost as responsible as poverty itself for widespread malnutrition among children.

The breast versus the can

Today, a man-made epidemic is worsening this hunger–disease link: the world-wide spread of canned baby milk, sold, ironically, with the message that it improves child nutrition.

Mother's milk is the cheapest and best food available for young children in the Third World. It contains the required nutrients in the right proportions, it is clean and free from pollutants and infections. It contains antibodies that give the child protection against many diseases. It is the child being weaned off his mother's breast, onto other foods, who stands the greatest risk of infection, and the most dangerous years of his life may not be the earliest months, but the period from six months to two years. The rate of incidence of diarrhoea in the Guatemalan village among children aged six to twelve months was double that among those under six months. For infants aged one to two years, the rate was treble.

The earlier a child is weaned, the greater risk he runs of serious illness. Weaning, in most of the Third World, invariably means increased exposure to polluted water. And early weaning is becoming more common in the Third World as tinned and powdered baby milk spreads. This replacement of the mother's breast by the multinationals' tin can is one of the saddest examples of misdirected 'modernization'. In the Third World context, where the majority of women do not work or work in occupations where they can easily take their babies with them, canned milk has practically no convenience value. But it is a kind of status symbol, a proof of progressiveness.

The canned milk bacillus spreads by emulation: but it is also helped along by high-pressure marketing. Even where advertisements contain cautions, surveys have shown that the message mothers pick up is that it is superior in nutritional value to breast milk. To the uneducated, its whiteness next to watery-looking mother's milk seems to confirm its greater powers. Chemists recommend it to boost their sales. Even doctors, who ought to know better, often recommend it. Once a woman has started her baby on it, her own breasts will dry up and she is forced to go on using canned milk even if she changes her mind.

The vast majority of families in the Third World live in economic and sanitary conditions that make baby milk a recipe for disaster. It has to be made up with water, which is more often than not polluted. The mortality rate among bottle-fed babies in Chile, for example, is three times higher than among the breast-fed. And canned milk is very expensive, costing £1 ($2) a week or more. Poor families simply cannot afford enough of it, and let it down with too much water. So the child's nutritional status gets worse. And so, because there's less money left over, does that of his brothers and sisters.

Large families are usually poorer and more prone to sickness than small ones: and bottle-feeding mothers are liable to have larger families than breast-feeders. The reason is that breast-feeding in itself is a natural form of contraception. It can delay the return of menstruation by as much as eighteen months and increase the spacing between births by up to two years. Dr Franz Rosa, of the American University of Beirut, has calculated that breast-feeding provides more protection to Third World couples than all family planning programmes put together. Early weaning, by contrast, cuts down intervals between births, weakening mothers and their offspring. It increases family size, cutting down the food supplies available for each person.

Bottle-feeding among the poor majority leads directly or indirectly to malnutrition and infection. Mother and child health programmes have been emphasizing the importance of breast-feeding for some years now, but, in the face of strong messages pushing canned milk, this may not be enough. Canned milk in the Third World should be available only from health clinics, for mothers unable to breast-feed. Some countries have taken the necessary strict action. In Papau New Guinea, for example, commercial baby milk may not be advertised and a mother must have a chit from a health worker to buy it.

In the shadow of the graveyard

Pamplona Alta is one of the dozens of dusty squatter towns among the desert hills around Lima. On the highest sandy outcrop, a crowded circle of makeshift crosses of wood and tin marks the children's cemetery, sad landmark of poverty. The most recent of the small, raised mounds are decked with garlands and flowers. The older ones are already merging into the sand, as if they had never existed. The passage of a poor child in a poor land is as fleeting as a bird's shadow. The very morning I visited the place, a small funeral procession climbed up through the streets of shacks. At its head, a father carries the tiny coffin of his dead child in his arms, and there is grief in his face and reproach at the injustice of it all.

Here in the real world, malnutrition emerges out of the complex interaction of economics, feeding practices and sanitation. Few of the adults of Pamplona Alta are seriously malnourished – and yet children are dying of malnutrition in their midst.

Sheer poverty does play a part. Without careful calculation and good knowledge of nutritional principles, it is difficult to get a good diet on the £6 per week ($12) that many families earn here. If the family uses canned milk, things get that much more difficult. I met one family of five children, living in a wooden shanty with flapping plastic sheeting painted black for a roof. The latest arrivals were twins, and the mother's anaemic organism could not feed both. One developed acute malnutrition and had to be sent to a charitable clinic for the tricky job of rehabilitation. The other was being fed on canned milk costing £1.20 ($2.40) for a week's supply, or 20 per cent of the family's income.

The baby's milk powder was mixed with dirty water. It never rains in Lima, and piped water only recently began reaching a few of the *barriadas*. Residents in Pamplona Alta have to buy their water from battered tankers that ply up and down the steep streets. It costs 15 soles a barrel, at that time around 15p or 30cts, and the average family needs four barrels a week – another 10 per cent of family income gone. This must be one of the few places in the world where water is the object of widespread theft. It is stolen from the rusty second-hand oil drums where families store it. The water is not clean when it arrives, and after a few days standing in the hot sun, under a flimsy covering of plastic or planks held down by stones, the bacteria multiply. Some mothers boil the water for their babies. Most don't, because fuel costs money and they can't afford it. So stomach infections and diarrhoea are common. Even breast-fed children are at some risk, since they need some water.

An episode of gastro-enteritis can be the beginning of a fatal progression. Children with diarrhoea cannot tolerate milk because they are temporarily deprived of the enzyme lactase which digests the lactose sugar in milk. The mother should gradually get the diarrhoeic child back onto milk within a few days, via soups and purées. Instead, she often keeps him on thin broths and sugar water for a week or more. His nutritional status worsens, so he is less able to resist infection and the next attack of gastric trouble lasts longer. The child's weight falls further and further behind normal with every episode of illness.

Diarrhoea often provides the break that puts even breast-feeding mothers onto canned milk. When diarrhoea crops up, the mothers stop breast-feeding – often on doctors' recommendation. Few doctors tell the mothers to keep on stimulating their breasts to keep them producing milk till the child is ready for it again. After a week without stimulation, the breasts dry up so breast feeding is no longer possible.

The cycle of infection, malnutrition and reinfection carries on and can easily lead to third-degree malnutrition, where the child is 40 per cent underweight or more. This is usually the point of no return. The Baby Jesus clinic in Ciudad de Dios takes in these end-of-the-road cases. With special feeds and intensive care it can often rehabilitate them, but as this is an expensive process only a tiny minority of cases are treated. The clinic's files make tragic reading.

Claudia Espinosa was born in January 1975. By April of that year she had first-degree malnutrition, second-degree by August, third-degree in December. When admitted to the clinic in January 1976 she weighed just 5·4 kilos (11·8 pounds) – 40 per cent below the normal for her age – and had continuous diarrhoea, swellings in the neck, a red throat and a running nose. The dietician commented 'Dietary history: maternal milk from birth to three months, then tinned milk according to the amount of money available, sometimes none. At four months, oats with water, potato purée. Ate well, but when had stomach illness (often), didn't eat. Comments: a reasonable diet, short on quantity because of lack of money.'

If poverty was the problem in Claudia's case, poor nutritional practice bore much of the blame with Elizabeth Cuba Bellido. Born 26 June 1975, she came to the clinic in March 1976 because she had had diarrhoea continuously for thirty days and had vomited all her feeds for the past fortnight. She arrived with third-degree malnutrition. She was dehydrated, had little subcutaneous fat, and her skin was covered with scars and scratches. She had respiratory and ear infections and needed a blood transfusion because she had acute anaemia.

'Dietary history: mother's milk was stopped after only one week because the mother developed mastitis [inflammation of the breast]. Doctor prescribed milk powder. Baby cared for in day by aunt. At seven months developed severe diarrhoea. All milk stopped, put onto aniseed water and sugar water, then soups. At eight months vomiting again, all feeding suspended except tea and water.' Millions of children in the Third World die every year because their mothers don't know how to cope with an attack of gastro-enteritis, whereas a simple solution of salt, sodium bicarbonate, sugar and clean water could save their lives.

At the Baby Jesus Clinic there is a small ward for the worst cases, which have to be looked after on a day-care basis. The babies in the cots are frighteningly small and scrawny, and a pair of twins – always the most vulnerable – lie side by side, miniaturized by hunger, their faces blotched with brown patches, their hair thin and almost balding.

In ways like these, malnutrition begets disease and disease begets malnutrition, and poverty leads to both just as both lead to poverty.

World cannibalism: the unequal distribution of food

It should already be apparent that the sensationalizing media view of 'world hunger' is pitifully inadequate. There is really no such thing as world hunger, but only the hunger of particular areas and particular social groups. The total food resources available in the world would be perfectly adequate to feed everyone properly if they were fairly distributed among nations and social groups.

Seen over the longer term, total food production in the world has defied Malthus's predictions that it could not keep up with population growth. In 1975, production per head was 7 per cent higher than in 1961–5. But this is the world average. The performance in the developing countries was not so good, despite impressive growth in their total agricultural production. In the 1960s this grew at 2·9 per cent a year, slowing a little to 2·5 per cent a year in the first half of the seventies, in both periods exceeding the expansion of western agriculture. But while the West's population was growing only very slowly, the Third World's was booming and consumed all the food production gains. So per capita food production grew at only 0·3 per cent a year between 1960 and 1970, and in the following five years it actually fell by 0·1 per cent a year. In Africa it fell by more than 2 per cent a year.

The 'world food problem', then, is not so much one of overall production, as one of local production and, above all, of distribution. The world's food supply is not shared out in such a way as to maximize human welfare. The distribution is just as unequal, unjust and iniquitous as that of every other element of life. The numerical spread is not so wide as with income: the top feeders may be eating only two or three times as much as the bottom. But nature herself sets limits to inequality in this sphere: at one extreme, by the sheer impossibility of stuffing much more than 5,000 calories a day down your gullet, at the other by the early death of those eatless than 1,500 a day for any length of time.

Yet food inequality is perhaps the most damaging of all the myriad forms in which inequality appears. It is inequality not in material possessions, but in human flesh and bones. It affects not just convenience, comfort or status, but survival as a full human being, or indeed survival in any form at all.

This inequality is both international and national. The Food and Agriculture Organization has calculated that in 1972–4 the average Third-Worlder got just 2,210 calories a day, or only 96 per cent of his energy requirements. Meanwhile, the well-upholstered average inhabitant of a developed country got 3,340 calories a day, or 31 per cent more than he needed. This excess over requirements represents the amount laid down in collective fat, overweight and obesity, or burned up in guilt and fear-ridden attempts to get rid of it in frenetic jogging and squash playing.

In 1972–4 people in seventy-one out of 128 developing countries surveyed were getting less than their dietary needs. This was an improvement on 1961–3, when ninety-one countries fell below requirements, but still left a lot of ground to be made up.

Protein is distributed just as unevenly. An adult man on a typical western diet rich in animal proteins, which are well balanced and easily assimilated, needs only around forty grams per day. But only two of thirty-four developed countries were getting less than eighty grams per day in the mid-seventies. The great beefsteak-for-breakfast carnivores were New Zealand (107 grams per day); the USA and Russia (105 grams); Icelanders got 114 grams. In the developing world the typical diet of the poor is of staple cereals, in which protein is not so well balanced: under such a diet, sixty-two grams of protein would be needed for the average man. Twenty-seven out of 128 developing countries got an average of less than fifty grams. And since there was a deficit of calories everywhere, much of the protein would be burned up for energy.

The overconsumption of the developed countries is intimately linked with the underconsumption of the Third World. One man's heart attack is another man's malnutrition.

Much of the best land that should be used for domestic food production in the developing countries is growing cash crops for the West: five of the most common, sugar, tobacco, coffee, cocoa, tea, are not doing the West much good either. In north-east Brazil, dense stands of thick green sugar cane wave their silvery tassles in the breeze, while the labourers who plant and cut it are squeezed onto the roadsides in their little huts and have no room even for a few vegetables. 'Sheep eat men,' the peasants displaced by enclosures of common land in England used to complain. Cash crops eat men in much of the developing world.

And meat eats men. The carnivores of the western world are also cannibals. That requires some expansion.

Meat production is not wrong in itself. There are many agriculturally marginal areas, uplands and drylands, that are fit for little else. But in Latin America, cattle are being raised on prime agricultural land for export to the West or consumption by local elites. Raising cattle is a notoriously inefficient method of getting protein off the land. Cereals can give five times as much protein per acre, legumes such as beans ten times as much. But cows don't only eat grass. A large proportion of the world's protein supplies – grains, soybeans, milk products and fishmeal – is fed to them. Nutritionist Frances Moore Lappé has calculated that a steer needs the equivalent of sixteen pounds of grain to produce one pound of edible meat, and that perhaps a third of the world's grain supplies, two thirds of the oilseeds, half the fishmeal and a third of the milk products are fed to livestock. In the United States alone, some 118 million tons of grain and soybeans were consumed in 1971 to produce only twenty million tons of meat. Figures from the Food and Agriculture Organization's Fourth World Food Survey paint an equally alarming picture. In 1972–4, 43 per cent of the world's cereal production was used as feed for livestock, whose meat was consumed largely in the West. Exactly the same proportion was available for consumption by the human beings of the developing countries, who made up nearly three quarters of the human race. In the USA, 88 per cent of cereals were fed to livestock. In every region of the world, the proportion going to fatten up meat for the tables of the rich remained the same or rose – for Western Europe, the share went up from 60 per cent in 1961–3 to 71 per cent in 1972–4.

Because of his predilection for meat, the average inhabitant of a developed country consumes, directly and indirectly, something like one ton of grain per year, and more than three quarters of that is first transformed into animal products. People in the poor countries consume less than a fifth of that amount, all but 13 per cent of it directly as cereal. Westerners who are concerned about the pressure of population on world food resources should remember that their typical family of four are consuming more grain than would a poor Indian couple with eighteen children.

Much of the protein wasted on the livestock eaten by the West comes from the poor countries: oilseeds and peanuts from West Africa, fishmeal from Peru, soybeans from Brazil and so on. I remember the hunger of little boys in Kano, northern

Nigeria – their sad faces covered in the white, flaky skin of kwashiorkor. They had learnt off by heart the common West African beggar's plea 'Dash me money', but somehow got it garbled into 'Dasimon'. I bought some cooked cassava for a snack and accidentally dropped a piece on the ground. Half a dozen of them leapt on it like a pack of wolves and fought each other desperately for it. Yet on the outskirts of the town, huge pyramids were being piled up of sacks of protein-rich groundnuts for export to the West.

One of the saddest aspects of this lugubrious business is the massive protein consumption of household pets in the West. Britain's six million dogs and five million cats consume around one and a half million tons of food a year, most of that of animal origin though some, of course, would be unfit for human consumption. The equivalent in grain would be enough to feed the entire population of Egypt. The United States has forty million dogs and twenty-three million cats. One coddled western pet probably consumes the produce of more land than the average Third World person. Dogs eat men too.

Not that westerners benefit from their dietary bonanza. Indeed, it is killing them. Excess consumption of calories leads to obesity which increases the likelihood of death from heart disease. Excess consumption of animal fats seems to do the same. The reduced intake of vegetable fibre adds to the risk of bowel complaints. The rich of the world are eating themselves as well as the poor.

The distribution of food *within* individual Third World countries is just as uneven. In north-east Brazil, the poorest fifth of urban households in one survey were getting less than 1,500 calories per capita – a level at which the human body is no longer capable of sustained work. At the other end of the scale, the richest 10 per cent were getting more than 3,300 calories per person, and the richest 1 per cent were eating 4,290. In Maharashtra, India, the poorest quarter of households got an average daily intake of 1,540 calories per person, while the richest 17 per cent got 3,000 calories or more. Schoolchildren of low-income families in Hyderabad had only 1,376 calories each per day and 36 grams of protein, while the children of richer families got 2,485 calories and 69 grams of protein. In almost all surveys, the urban poor show up as having the worst diets of all. The rural poor are usually two or three hundred calories per day better off. This is because they often have at least a small garden plot of land, or get some payment in kind. Against this, their calorie needs are greater.

Within each group, families with children have worse diets the more children they have. A survey of poor households in Colombo, Sri Lanka, found that more than half the undernourished families (getting 1,800 calories a day or less) had four or more children. Among the adequately fed households (2,800 calories or more) over half had no children at all and another third only one. Nor is there food equality even within poor families. The working men get absolute priority, and mothers and children get what is left over, which is usually deficient in calories and other nutrients. This unequal distribution is not as unjust as it may seem: it is another strategy for survival. If the working adults don't get enough food, they will be unable to work well and then everyone will starve. But if mother or children are tired and inactive, that is less crucial. The tragedy is not that this survival option is chosen, damaging the biological quality of the children, but that poor families have to choose at all.

It seems probable that the world can go on producing enough food, overall, to keep up with rising population. Fashions in international panic come and go. After bad harvests in 1972 and 1974, when fertilizer prices were sky high, there was much hysteria: famine was stalking the Sahel, the monsoon had failed in India, world cereal reserves had reached an all-time low. All the optimism generated by the Green Revolution had evaporated and it seemed that Malthus was about to be proved right. The next two years were more fortunate: there were good harvests in India, North America and Russia; fertilizer prices had come right down again. Cereal stocks were replenished. It seemed that doomsday had been averted.

But complacency is just as out of place as blue funk. Whether there is famine or feasting depends on the vagaries of the world weather machine which we do not yet fully understand and cannot predict let alone modify. If the world succeeds in keeping food *production* neck and neck with population growth, it will only be through sustained research, effort and investment.

And, unless the *distribution* of food is changed, hunger will go on spreading at the same time as food production rises.

The criminal maldistribution of the world's food resources, outlined in this chapter, is possible only because income is so inequitably distributed. The world food market matches supply with *effective* demand. Whatever those with the money to pay want, even if it is wasteful beefsteaks and dog food, they get. What the poor need, they don't get, unless they can pay for it. The world food market will not match food supply with real human needs until world incomes are more equally distributed.

Inside the Third World, as we shall see later, the rich are getting richer and the poor poorer. The poor are less able to buy enough food while the rich, with their preference for meat, distort the food market and push up the price of grains, making it even harder for the poor to make ends meet.

Other trends suggest that whatever happens to world food production, malnutrition in developing countries is likely to increase drastically if present policies continue. In the rural areas, access to even a small piece of land can improve food supply: but as we have seen, landlessness is increasing. Payment in kind used to guarantee a survival minimum, but the trend to payment in wages, plus increasing unemployment, pushes many incomes below survival level.

Malnutrition is not the result of inadequate world food production. It is the result of poverty; of gross inequality in the distribution of income and of land; of government bias against the poor in the provision of clean water and sanitation, which could prevent so much malnutrition. In the final analysis, it emerges as the result of all the processes of pauperization and discrimination with which this book is concerned, and it can only be cured by a combined attack on them all.

16. Death Control: The Diseases of Poverty

'Every dollar spent on doctors and hospitals costs a hundred lives.'
JORGE DE AHUMADA

A poor man's life is also a dangerous one. The Pena family, all nineteen of them, live in a two-room rented shack at El Codito, a hillside shanty town just outside Bogotá, Colombia. The building perches precariously within a few feet of a sudden drop into sandstone quarries below. Only a pile of brushwood for cooking prevents the young children from wandering over the edge.

The father of the family, Francisco Pena, came to the city from rural Boyaca twenty-five years ago with his wife, Amparo. They hoped to improve their lot, but, as they now admit, it got worse. Francisco works in the quarries. When he is working, he earns between 75p and £1.50 ($1.50 and $3) for a lorry load of finished stone chips or sand, which takes a day and a half to cut and break up or grind. Many men bring along their wives and children to speed up the job. But it's a risky business – chips fly everywhere, fine dust gets in the lungs, rocks fall on people. Francisco himself has not worked for six months because he tore a ligament in his arm while swinging a rock-breaking hammer.

Health hazards are built into the pattern of their lives. Their sardine-like living arrangements rapidly spread whatever diseases one of them picks up. Amparo and Francisco live in one room with eleven of their twelve children. Their eldest daughter lives in the other with her husband and their four children. This room is also used for cooking and the thick smoke from the wood fire gives the family frequent lung and eye complaints. They have a poor diet that gives them little protection against disease: maize soups, white rice or pasta, rarely any meat, beans or fresh vegetables.

There is no piped water supply for the settlement. Water

comes from a stream more than a mile away. In the evenings, children go down with battered old pans and oil cans, fill them up and stagger home with them slung from bamboo poles. The stream is grossly polluted, mostly by the excreta of residents. No sewers have been provided. Only a minority of residents have latrines, and these are no more than pits dug in the earth. I asked the Penas if they had a latrine. They did not even know what the word meant. When I clarified, Amparo replied, 'Oh no, we're only poor peasants. We just go up the road, in the bushes.' The only public service El Codito enjoys is electricity. This was not provided by the authorities, but is a pirate supply illicitly connected to the mains, for a considerable fee, by enterprising electricians.

The state of the Penas' health is shocking. Amparo, still attractive at forty-two, loses some of her charm when she laughs: she has no front teeth. Three of her children died in their first year. The survivors suffer spasmodic bouts of assorted illnesses. When I visited them the picture was as follows. The fourteen-month-old granddaughter had diarrhoea and hadn't eaten anything solid for two weeks. She tottered around with a vacant, withdrawn look. Amparo's eighteen-month-old son had a grossly distended stomach, probably due to malnutrition. The three-and-a-half-year-old had a bad scar on his leg where a pot of boiling water tipped over him (even accidents are more common among the poor). The fourteen-year-old son gets regular attacks of vomiting and coughing blood and may have tuberculosis. The family have neither received nor sought any medical attention at all for any of these complaints. Amparo complains that the health clinic, where service is free, is too far away. With the walk and the long wait, a visit might take up a day and she can't spare the time with so many people to look after. 'I'd sooner pay for a doctor,' she commented in disgust. 'But do you ever visit a doctor?' I asked her. 'No, we can't afford to.'

Disease is accepted, fatalistically, as a fact of life, inevitable, irresistible. You simply suffer it and hope you will come out in one piece at the other end.

As with the Pena family, the health problems of the rural

masses and marginal urban poor emerge from their poverty and their hazardous environment. They are compounded by their own hygiene-flouting behaviour. The health services, too distant or too costly, might as well not exist for them.

The life of man is nasty ... and short

The pattern of disease in the Third World is quite different from that in the West. The major killers in the rich countries are the diseases of affluence. Cancer causes 15 per cent of all deaths. Diseases of the circulatory system carry off 32 per cent. The pattern in the developing countries is precisely the inverse image: cancer and circulatory diseases cause only 4 and 15 per cent of deaths respectively. The chief killers in the Third World are infectious, parasitic and respiratory diseases, often helped along by malnutrition. These cause 44 per cent of deaths, against only 11 per cent in the typical developed country. Among children, they kill an even higher proportion – around three quarters in Latin America.

The incidence of illness in the poor countries is on a scale quite unimaginable to the incubated westerner. Threadworms infest one billion people, trachoma and hookworms afflict half a billion each. One survey in Tanzania found less than one person in a hundred who was free of parasites, while hookworm, bilharzia and filariasis each affected 40 per cent of the population. A World Bank study of Indonesia construction workers found that up to 87 per cent had hookworm, up to two thirds roundworms and up to 58 per cent whipworms. Leprosy afflicts ninety-three people in every thousand in the Central African Empire and fifty per thousand in Upper Volta.

As a result, man's allotted span of years is much shorter than in the developed regions, where, in 1977, a newborn baby could expect to live until it was anything from seventy to seventy-five years old. In Latin America, life expectancy at birth was only sixty-one years, in East Asia only fifty-two, forty-nine years in South Asia and just forty-six years in Africa. These figures tend to conjure up misleading images in most people's minds, of the average African flaking out at forty-six. In fact, anyone who gets through his childhood has a better chance of survival. A twenty-year-old in Colombia can expect to live until he is sixty, till he is fifty-nine in Nigeria or fifty-seven in India. In the really unhealthy places even adults die young: a twenty-year-old will die when he is fifty-one, on average, in Chad and the Central African Empire, or at forty-nine in Gabon and Guinea.

The childhood years in the Third World are not so much the happiest years of life as the most dangerous. Babies may come trailing clouds of glory from heaven, but they are all too likely to depart again prematurely. Infant mortality takes a terrible toll. The official figures record that between forty and two hundred children in every thousand die before their first birthday in developing countries. The true figures may be much higher, especially in rural areas where the child often leaves before its arrival has been duly registered. In the poorest regions it may have little better than a fifty-fifty chance of survival. So child funerals are a common sight. In Guamo, Colombia, I came across a small procession of children carrying a bier draped with white, blue and yellow ribbons. Inside, surrounded by flowers, lay the body of a nine-month-old boy. He wore a crown of gold foil on his head like a little prince. His eyes, half open, gazed emptily. He died of gastro-enteritis.

In the poorest areas, parents have learned to live with infant mortality and accept child illness and death stoically, and it is one of the tragedies of their lives that their loved ones may leave them forever at any moment. Infant death is so ordinary a part of life in western Nigeria that Yoruba women believe some children are *abiku* – born to die, continually called on by spirit companions to rejoin them in the world of the dead. A mother may suspect a child is *abiku* if it resembles a dead brother or sister, or gets sick frequently. She then spoils it, grants its every wish to persuade it to stay, or gives it a special name such as Banjoko ('Sit down and stay with us') or Malomo ('Do not go again').

Yet the child who dies early may be the lucky one. For some of those who survive, one complaint follows another without respite. One Guatemalan child whose health progress was charted in detail started with respiratory disease and conjunctivitis at the age of one month. An unbroken succession of ailments followed in its first twenty-four months: five prolonged attacks of diarrhoea, ten lung infections, four bouts of bronchitis, six of conjuctivitis, plus measles, abscess, thrush, stomatitis, burns, roundworm, salmonella, shingella and tonsillitis. Each infection led to a loss of weight which the child never had a chance to make up, so that by the age of two its weight was equivalent to that of a normal baby of six months.

As children grow older, the risks gradually diminish, but they do not disappear. An international comparison of schoolchildren found that in Bangladesh 97 per cent had worms of one kind or another, in Sri Lanka 95 per cent and in Venezuela 93 per cent. A survey in Bangkok discovered that schoolchildren aged between ten and fourteen had an average of over three diseases, defects or parasitic conditions each: two thirds had trachoma, one third skin disease, a quarter lice, another quarter bow-legs, and one in five had goitre.

The wild bunch

Individually, the diseases that afflict the poor in poor countries are a vicious crowd. The heat and moisture of the tropics provides an ideal breeding ground; the close proximity of man to the elements leaves him pathetically vulnerable to their attacks.

Disease organisms have evolved side by side with human beings. In their fight for survival they have adapted themselves to the ecology of their chosen prey, Man, to his eating, excreting, washing, working and even sleeping habits. Many of them have developed life cycles of astonishing complexity, spending part of their lives in men, part in insects, snails or other animals, exploiting not only each of their unwilling hosts, but cashing in on the relationship between them. Sleeping sickness, endemic in tropical Africa and (as Chagas' disease) in Latin America, is caused by a single-celled parasite, the trypanosome, transmitted by the bite of the tsetse fly. The fly breeds in wooded river valleys, and, as men have to live close to water, it is difficult to escape its domain.

One of the most common and complicated ailments is malaria, caused by the single-celled *plasmodium*, which is injected by the bite of the mosquito. *Plasmodium* exploits the vampiric relationship between mosquito and Man: the eggs of the female mosquito can only mature if she has a meal of human blood. Anyone who has travelled in infected areas will know the lengths to which *anopheles* will go for the sake of her offspring, and the trials and battles of wit needed to evade her. When the fine mesh protective net has been tucked under the mattress and you've snuggled down to sleep, you will hear her unmistakable whine like the distant noise of a toy aeroplane. When the mosquito is at work, saliva is injected in order to stop the blood from clotting, and with it come the *plasmodia*. They migrate to the liver where they feed and grow. Each one then divides into forty thousand merozoites, whose release into the body is responsible for the high fever of the disease. The merozoites live in red blood cells, where they grow again and each one splits into twelve more. Every time they divide another stage of fever comes upon their host. Some of the merozoites become male and female gametocytes, and these are taken up by the mosquito with her blood cocktail. Inside the mosquito the gametocytes go through a dizzying sequence of exotic transformations: they become gametes, then microgametes, then ookinetes, oocysts, and finally sporozoites. In this phase they migrate to the mosquito's salivary glands ready for transfer to their next victim. Mosquitoes can breed in the smallest pond, even a cow's hoof-print filled with water. Despite twenty years or more of eradication programmes, malaria is still widespread and, indeed, making a comeback. Some 600 million people live in endemic areas in sixty countries, and the disease kills one million children a year in Africa alone. (See Map 6, pages 464–5.)

Diseases such as sleeping sickness and malaria are known as vector-borne diseases, and depend more on their insect carriers than on human habits. Campaigns to eradicate the carriers are often the only practicable way of fighting them.

But most tropical ailments get a helping hand from the life-styles of their human victims. Leprosy, with ten or twenty million victims, is encouraged by infrequent washing. So is trachoma, which causes conjunctivitis, and eventual blindness for one in twenty sufferers. Children rubbing their fly-clustered eyes with dirty hands are especially vulnerable.

But the largest group of tropical diseases is transmitted via human excreta. The hookworm clings to the stomach wall with a fearsome set of teeth and lives by sucking blood, injecting chemicals to prevent clotting. Its eggs pass out in faeces. If people do not use latrines, the larva hatches out and lives in the soil. When the next barefooted person comes along to relieve themselves in that particular spot the larva bores through the skin of his feet. Hookworm infects up to 95 per cent of the population in many areas and is a prime cause of anaemia. Schistosomiasis, also known as bilharzia, is a water-borne disease with some 250 million victims in seventy-one countries. It lives in the blood vessels of the intestines or bladder, causing swelling and inflammation (victims in Brazil are called *barriga d'agua* or water-bellies). Eggs pass out with the urine, hatch out in slow-moving shallow water and seek out their second host – a special breed of water snail. Here they pass through another phase before becoming fork-tailed cercaria which seek out and bore into the legs of anyone standing in the water. Schistosomiasis is common where water is got from water holes, and it was common in the paddy fields of China before a massive campaign exterminated the water snail that carries it. Other faecally borne diseases, such as cholera, typhoid or dysentery, do not pass through an intermediate host like the snail, but can be transmitted directly from person to person via dirty hands, or indirectly through polluted water supplies.

The poverty–disease cycle

Illness, like hunger, is in itself an evil. It causes pain and sets the mind against the body. It undermines a man's sense of wellbeing in the world.

Illness in general can be looked on as a kind of disease that thrives in the environment of poverty and perpetuates it, so that it can multiply more successfully. Chronic disease-proneness causes poverty, while poverty provides the ideal breeding ground for disease, in a recurrent life cycle of re-infection.

Disease brings concrete economic costs to the individual, his family and his country. It reduces a man's productivity as surely as hunger does. It raises the cost of living for the victim, as he must pay for treatment, at the same time as it depresses his income as he takes time off work. If it hits a poor farmer at planting or harvest time (and it often does, as the rainy season is always more unhealthy) it may be the first step on the road to debt and landlessness. If the victim dies, the family faces the often ruinous expense of a funeral at the same time as it may be losing one of its working members.

Sick people need more food. In chronic illness scarce food is wasted because the body cannot convert it so efficiently. Parasites such as hookworms, tapeworms and roundworms are all ravenous feeders, and have chosen the human digestive system as their home precisely so that they can feed off what you eat, or off you, without effort. They may cause internal bleeding quite apart from what they consume. An infestation of *ancylostoma duodenale* hookworms can cause loss of four millilitres of blood every day – about one and a half litres (two and a half pints) every year. A study in Panama found that the extra food needed to compensate for stomach infections was $10 (£5) a year, nearly 2 per cent of the average income, and a greater burden for the poorest families. Another investigation, in Colombia, found that heavy roundworm infestation could cut the calories absorbed from carbohydrates by 30 per cent.

Disease slashes income. Acute illness may put the family breadwinner in bed, and poor people in poor countries have no social security to fall back on. An attack of malaria can keep a man off work for three days and if he is a wage labourer, he will earn nothing and his family will probably eat nothing during that time. In endemic areas, malaria is estimated to

cause absenteeism rates of 25 per cent or more. It hits school
attendance in the same way, adding to the problems of children already battling against an army of disadvantages. Workers in developing countries lose a lot more working time each
year because of disease than in western countries, where the
range of loss is between 2 and 7 per cent. In Burma and Mexico
12 per cent of working days are lost, in Egypt, Chile and
Colombia 15 per cent, in Guatemala 16 per cent and in Ecuador
29 per cent.

Chronic illness may not lay a man up, but it saps away at
a man's strength and cuts down his productivity, which may
already be low because of hunger and heat. Schistosomiasis
has been estimated to cut working capacity by anything from
15 to 80 per cent. Hookworm is said to reduce labour efficiency
in Syria by as much as a half. So the chronically sick man is
likely to be poorer than the healthy one because of lower output and higher absenteeism. In the Caribbean island of Saint
Lucia, workers with schistosomiasis infections were found to
earn 30 per cent less than those without.

In a World Bank study in Indonesia, agricultural labourers
and rubber tappers with hookworm-induced anaemia were
found to be around 20 per cent less productive than their non-
anaemic colleagues. Their foreman's views of which workers
were 'lazy' or 'weak' were found to correspond closely to the
incidence of anaemia. Workers with higher levels of anaemia
earned less in incentive payments than their colleagues, and as
a result of their lower income they consumed less calories,
protein, vitamins and iron than non-anaemic workers. This
poorer nutrition contributed to their poor productivity and
lowered their resistance to disease, hence they were more likely
to lose time off work.

Absenteeism and low productivity, on a national scale, contribute to national poverty. They mean that farms and factories
must hire more people than they really need. Since there is so
much unemployment in the Third World, this may actually
spread the work around more widely. But low productivity
means there will be little surplus for investment, and disease
in families makes it harder for them to save money for invest-

ment. Disease may also close up many areas that could be productive: river-blindness and sleeping sickness have emptied the river valleys in West Africa's Sahel region, while the tsetse fly has prevented the development of mixed agriculture in much of Africa. So disease creates poverty, while poverty, continuing the cycle, maintains the conditions that foster disease. Behind almost every tropical disease life cycle lies a set of social and physical conditions which are, for the most part, not adopted out of choice, but out of poverty. Simply wearing shoes, for example, would prevent parasites like bilharzia or hookworm from penetrating the feet. People in the Third World do not go barefoot out of ignorance or for cultural reasons – shoes are now seen as desirable everywhere, and people wear them without much thought for their health benefits. If the poor do not wear shoes, it is for one reason only: they cannot afford them, often enough for themselves, but certainly not for the growing feet of their children.

Overcrowded, badly lit and ventilated houses help to incubate disease. Measles (a far more severe condition in the undernourished child), whooping cough, tuberculosis spread more rapidly. Insects breed in straw roofs. Tetanus lurks in mud floors ready to creep in through a wound, or the severed placenta of a newborn child. Health workers urge people to get tin roofs, cement floors and windows, but most people need no persuading. These things are now status symbols throughout the Third World, regardless of their health benefit. Anyone with the spare money to get them will do so, if only to prove he can afford them. Those who stick with windowless mud and thatch do so out of poverty alone.

Failure to wash frequently may aggravate diseases like leprosy, scabies or trachoma. Yet few people are dirty by choice or nature, and their failure to wash may not be due to ignorance. In Upper Volta people cannot wash much because a woman can only bring back so much water on her head on one trip to the distant well. In squatter Lima or Nairobi, water costs hard cash, and so does soap. Wherever it has to be bought with cash or valuable time, water is reserved for the necessities of survival, drinking, watering animals and cooking.

Or take the supposed folly of not boiling or filtering water. Water filters cost money, and so does fuel. A study in the Peruvian town of Ica found that women were not boiling water because scouring the fields for diminishing supplies of firewood took time, and wood and kerosene were getting increasingly expensive.

Poor nutrition contributes to disease, but no one eats badly out of choice. It is not from ignorance of nutritional principles that Sri Lanka tea labourer lives on unleavened bread, the Brazilian sugar worker on tortillas or the Javanese smallholder on plain rice. When the poor have to spend the money, as at weddings and funerals, you find that they invariably lay on nutritious spreads including a staple cereal, vegetables and meat. They would eat that way every day if they could. Their diets are unbalanced and unprotective primarily because they are poor.

The disease of neglect

Perhaps the most devastating cause of illness in the Third World is unclean water and poor sanitation. This is the result of poverty of a different kind: poverty due to official neglect or even negligence. Provision of clean water could have saved more lives than any other single measure – yet governments chose to spend far more on doctors and hospitals. Polluted drinking water transmits cholera, typhoid and dysentery, and the drinking water of the neglected poor is almost always polluted. In southern Peru peasants have shallow, stagnant wells at the bottom of gardens where donkeys and sheep graze freely. Nomadic herdsmen in the Sahel swig water thirstily from the water hole that their cattle are trampling into insalubrious mud.

Water holes, serving as combined toilet, bath, washhouse and well, pass on other diseases. Guinea worms produce larvae in a blister on the leg, which bursts on contact with water. The larvae are eaten by cyclops – tiny copepods – and these, in their turn, are swilled up in the water jugs of humans.

As with everything else, the rural areas have been shamefully discriminated against. A World Health Organization survey found that only 29 per cent of the rural population of developing countries enjoyed access to safe water in 1975, against 77 per cent of city dwellers. Rural provision varied from a low of 19 per cent in south and east Asia and 21 per cent in black Africa, to 32 per cent in Latin America. No attempt was made to correct this imbalance, indeed government spending continued to widen the gap: four fifths of the money spent on water supply improvement between 1971 and 1975 went to the urban areas, along with 97 per cent of the investment in sewerage.

Improvement in water supply can have a dramatic effect on health. Studies in East Africa have found that laying on clean water can cut cholera incidence by 90 per cent, typhoid by 80 per cent, trachoma by 60 per cent and leprosy by half. In thirty backward rural areas in Japan, infant mortality was halved when piped water was provided.

The poor do not like dirty water any more than the rich: the apparent abandon with which they drink infected brews is due to acceptance of necessity, not preference. A clean water supply for their village is often one of their priority requests from governments. But several water projects have failed because they ignored the economics of poverty: where water charges are made, the poor are less enthusiastic and in some cases have returned to their old, polluted sources, preferring the risk of possible disease to the certain cost of payment.

Excreta disposal is a key link in the chain of transmission of many diseases. Here, too, there is the same gross discrimination against the poor, accentuating their poverty through disease. Adequate facilities are poor or non-existent in most rural areas. In 1975, according to the WHO survey, only 6 per cent of rural households in Asia, 25 per cent in Latin America and 28 per cent in Africa had adequate sanitation. Yet this was enjoyed by around three quarters of the urban population in all three continents.

Sanitation is one of the few areas where traditional beliefs are as great an obstacle to health as poverty (the other major field is the feeding of young children). The germ and worm theory of disease is not widespread in the more backward rural areas. Peruvian mothers, for example, believe that diarrhoea is caught from cold draughts. Africans are liable to think it is due to an enemy practising sorcery against them. It is not an easy task to convince people of the link between their private excretory behaviour and community health.

Take a morning stroll in any part of India and you are liable to stumble upon scores of hunched, crouching figures easing themselves on any handy patch of ground. Gandhi was revolted by this practice: 'Some of the national habits are bad beyond description, and yet so ingrained as to defy all human effort. Wherever I go this insanitation obtrudes itself upon my gaze in some shape or other,' he wrote. Yet India's insanitation is motivated by an obsessive concern with ritual purity and cleanliness. The orthodox Hindu considers contact with excrement defiling, and hence would think it filthy in the extreme to deposit it inside his own house. The proper place for it is the public thoroughfare, where untouchable sweepers can remove it. So personal ritual purity is preserved at the expense of public health. This is why Benares, the holiest city of the Hindus, is one of the unhealthiest places in India.

But even in this culture-laden sphere, practical economic considerations play an important role, as the organizers of many projects have found when they gave people latrines and found them unused. One project offered village people in Orissa, India, moulded concrete latrines for only $1 (50p). But only three hundred were bought among a population of 60,000, and two thirds of the bought ones were not used. Apart from the old problem of defilement, the main reason was that at least a quart of precious water was needed to flush the toilet. Moreover, the men working in the fields were unwilling to make the long trek home to use an installation of whose utility they were unconvinced. Toilets in Panama were reportedly used as chicken coops and grain silos. Even if they are used for their destined purpose, they can sometimes be even more of a health risk than the old habits. I have seen latrines on Sri Lankan tea estates that were so clogged and smeared with filth that no one using them without shoes could fail to catch some appalling disease.

Part of the problem here is the choice of appropriate technology. The porcelain four-gallon flush of the rich, rainy temperate regions is totally unsuited to the tropics. It is too expensive and wastes too much water. It also wastes one of the biggest potential sources of organic fertilizer in the Third World. The ideal form of sanitation would allow excreta to be collected into large village fermentation chambers where it would produce methane gas and a safe residue for fertilizer. But all that is really needed for sanitation purposes is a properly sited and managed hole in the ground far enough away from the water supply. And for that, no investment at all other than education and sweat is needed.

The story of the battle against disease in the tropics is a sorry one. The great extermination campaigns and vaccination drives saved millions of children from an early death, but left them to face a life of debilitation, because the health of the majority of adults, and the diseases that weaken rather than kill, were neglected. The population increase that resulted from death control without birth control pushed up the incidence of poverty, malnutrition and disease. And the poor got almost no health care at all.

In the rural areas of Upper Volta, one doctor may have to serve more than 200,000 people. Proper medical care is impossible. In most places it is reduced to an annual visit to each village, to inoculate the children and increase the population. It is worse than useless. I talked with the men of one large compound housing forty people. Several of the residents have been permanently brain-damaged by meningitis. Everyone gets stomach upsets the whole time. In the rainy season, when every hand is urgently needed in the fields, the situation is worse. Malaria attacks and guinea worm fevers confine men to their sleeping mats for three days at a time. I asked them if the doctor ever treated any of their complaints. The head of the family replied, without a trace of sarcasm in his voice: 'The doctor is only for children, not for adults.'

Health-care systems in most of the Third World neglect the poor, not because there is not enough money to spend, but because inappropriate western models have been followed: inappropriate in cost, in approach and in technology. Most health problems in the Third World (and for that matter in industrial countries, too) are environmental in origin. Relatively simple preventive measures can cut at their roots. Instead, expensive cures have tinkered with the symptoms, on such a small scale that only the privileged have benefited.

The good health of western societies today is less the work of doctors and hospitals than of advances in public health: improvements in clean water and sanitation due to public action, improvements in housing and nutrition due to rising incomes. Deaths from whooping cough, measles and tuberculosis, for example, came down to low levels in Europe long before effective treatments for them were devised. Even today, the diseases that replaced the older generation of killers – cancer and heart complaints – could be cut dramatically by environmental action, banning smoking, heavily subsidizing vegetable fats, banning refined white flour. Instead, costly drugs and high-technology surgery and irradiation get all the money spent on them.

Western medicine is in the business of cure, not prevention. It has always been preoccupied with the individual in isolation from his environment. It has treated him like a complex piece of machinery, like a car. Wonderful ways have been invented of fiddling about with the working parts to get the vehicle on the road again. But even today precious little thought is given to the general conditions that put the machine out of action in the first place, like the state of the roads or the quality of oil or petrol being used. Even in the West, western medicine is a very expensive and ineffective way of improving the health of the community. It is bankrupting sick people or government treasuries at the same time as the incidence of the killer diseases goes on rising.

For the poor countries of the world, the western approach to health has been a total disaster. It has focused on lavish buildings, imported equipment and drugs, and expensively trained personnel. Its cost has put health care of any kind way beyond the reach of the majority in almost every Third World country.

As public funds are in short supply in poor countries, using high-cost technology means that only minimal quantities of health care can be provided. Most developing countries devote less than 2 per cent of their gross national product to health, against, for example, 4·3 per cent for the United Kingdom and 3·4 per cent for the USSR. The amount spent per capita in the early seventies was often pitiably small: $0.14 in Kenya, $0.56 in Upper Volta, $0.80 in Brazil, $0.90 in India, against $105.16 in Britain. Yet western-style health care does not come any cheaper in the Third World – indeed in some cases it is dearer than in the West. This means that the average Indian gets about one hundredth as much health care as the Briton, though the latter, with his sanitized environment, falls ill much less frequently. The overall coverage of services is sparse. In advanced western countries, in the early seventies, one doctor served between 600 (Canada) and 760 patients (United Kingdom). Provision in the wealthier developing countries in Latin America and east Asia lags some way behind – there are 1,400 people per doctor in Singapore, 1,660 in Brazil, 2,180 in Colombia. The poorer the country, the thinner the coverage. Each doctor in Sri Lanka has 4,010 people to serve, in India 4,160. In Indonesia there are 18,100 people per doctor, in Nepal 36,450. Provision is poor throughout Africa: Senegal and Ivory Coast have around 15,000 people per physician, Nigeria 25,000, Benin 36,000, Chad 44,000, Upper Volta 60,000 and Malawi 86,000. Other services are equally weak. Where western countries have one hospital bed per 110 people or less, in developing countries there may be anything from 300 up to 7,000 people per bed. Dentists are even scarcer in developing countries. France and Germany have one dentist per 2,000 people, but India has one per 66,000, Nigeria one per 580,000, and Chad and Rwanda have one dentist per two million people.

All these figures, which relate to the early and middle seventies, are of course averages. But the minimal quantities provided are not shared out evenly. The bulk of what limited facilities do exist are hoarded in the cities, along with all the other benefits of civilization. In the rural areas of Pakistan around 1970, there were 24,200 patients for every doctor against only 3,700 in urban areas. In the Philippines, Honduras and Colombia each country doctor had to serve six times as many people as his city colleague. In Kenya, sixty times as many. Capital cities are even more favoured. They contain the biggest hospitals with the most prestigious facilities, the medical schools and the most ambitious doctors. There is one doctor per 1,350 people in Port au Prince, Haiti, against one per 33,000 in the rest of the country; one to 4,000 in Dakar, one to 44,000 for the rest of Senegal. One third of all Colombia's doctors practise in Bogotá, which contains only one eighth of the total population.

It can be argued, of course, that scarce facilities have to be built somewhere, so they might as well be built in the towns where rural populations can easily come in if they need to. But in reality they cannot, and do not come, along dirt roads often impassable through rains, with no public transport. They will not come for anything but matters of life and death, because transport and treatment often costs more than they can afford (free health care is rare in the Third World) and their time costs them money. They are not going to neglect their fields for a day to go and have a guinea worm removed.

Studies in several Third World countries have shown that western-style health facilities are inaccessible to the poor majority geographically, economically and socially – by distance, cost, and culture or language. Urban health facilities do not serve the people of whole regions, but only those in the immediate environs. An Indian survey found that nearly two thirds of patients at a health centre came from less than a mile away, and for every extra half mile of distance the proportion of the community using the centre fell by half. Beyond four miles, less than 1 per cent of people were using it. In Ghana four fifths of the in-patients at five major hospitals came from the towns where the hospitals were located.

There are times of crisis when even the stoic, fatalistic

peasant would have recourse to modern medicine if he could, but the far-flung sufferer is going to be in a sorry state when he reaches hospital in the back of a bone-shaking lorry.

Except in countries with effective, barefoot doctor style programmes, the rural majority are not covered in any way by modern health services. A Punjab study of 5,000 cases of illness found that only one in ten were treated by government services. Three out of ten were treated privately, mostly by traditional healers. The rest got no care at all. In Colombia over a third of the population was estimated to have no access to the health services in 1975. In southern Peru, the proportion without access was 56 per cent. Even in the well-provided cities, most of the poor do not use health facilities because they are not located in squatter areas, or cost too much. In New Delhi, only 7 per cent of illness comes to the attention of the medical services. In Cali, a large Colombian city with one doctor per 900 people, three fifths of slum dwellers never used a health centre, and two out of every five children who died had no medical attention in the two days before their death.

Governments must bear most of the blame for this situation. They have misspent their scarce funds on facilities for the lucky few. But there are two other starring villains in this melodrama: doctors, and drugs.

The medical Mafia: doctors and drugs

The typical Third World doctor is an intriguing piece of very inappropriate technology. He is about as helpful in improving his countrymen's health as a tiny fleet of Rolls-Royces might be in providing transport for the masses. Until the last few years he was modelled in almost every detail on his western counterpart. Usually he is trained in dealing with acute medical problems using surgery or drugs, and his training is grotesquely expensive. For example, in 1965, when it cost $19,630 (£10,000) to produce one medical graduate in the USA, the cost in Guatemala was $19,000; in Jamaica and Kenya $24,000; in Colombia $29,000 and in Senegal $84,000. At the end of his training, the doctor will often be better equipped to handle western complaints – of the kind his elite private patients also happen to suffer from – than the assorted worms, fevers and nutritional deficiency states that afflict the vast majority of his country's population. If he is very bright, he may even have spent a period perfecting his knowledge of western ailments in France, Britain or the USA. The end product is a man with skills that can be sold almost anywhere in the world, to the highest bidder. Because he knows this, and his employers know this, he has to be grossly overpaid to keep him in his own country.

Yet wild horses will not drag him into the 'bush' where he is really needed. From a career point of view, the city has the facilities he believes he needs. From a personal point of view, it is the only place where he can earn the extra income from lucrative private practice which he thinks he deserves, and the only place where he can impress the elite he belongs to with the conspicuous consumption of his gains. His ethic enjoins him to alleviate suffering, yet (with a minority of admirable exceptions) he shuns the places where suffering is greatest. It is not human need that determines the service he provides, but ability to pay. He goes where the money is, and he need not worry his professional conscience about that, because where the money is, there too are the best facilities for pursuing what he considers 'excellence'.

The money is in the rich cities of his own country. But, even more so, in the rich countries of the world. After his country has crippled itself to train him, he is quite likely to take his expertise off and use it in Europe, North America or Australasia. The migration of the Third World's doctors to richer pastures is perhaps the biggest flow down the brain drain. A World Health Organization survey of the problem found that, in 1971, the developing countries lost 63,000 doctors to the West and received back only 1,300 in return. The poorer the country, the more it was likely to lose its doctors: nations with per capita incomes of $800 (£400) or less had between 10 and 60 per cent of their doctors working abroad. Those with incomes between $800 and $2,000 usually had less than 10 per cent. Countries with per capita incomes of more than $2,000 were net gainers of doctors.

Haiti had more doctors working abroad than at home. The Philippines had a net loss of two thirds of its stock of doctors. Jamaica, Paraguay and Syria lost between two fifths and a half, while Barbados, Guyana, Sri Lanka and Thailand all had more than 3,000 doctors working abroad. More Thai doctors were working or studying in the United States than were staffing all the provincial health centres in Thailand, four times more, in fact, than the entire annual output of doctors from the country's medical schools.

The western countries at the other end of this human pipeline received, ready-made and at little or no cost to themselves, a substantial proportion of their own needs for trained personnel. In 1970 the United Kingdom had 21,000 foreign doctors, most of them from the Commonwealth. British hospital services would have collapsed without them, as Britain's own doctors were flowing down another brain drain to North America. The United States had 68,000 foreign doctors in 1972, nearly a quarter of its total supply.

This whole lamentable traffic is a measure of the irrelevance of medical education, in most of the Third World, to the Third World's own health needs. We have seen how radically different are the disease patterns of rich and poor countries. If the medics of developing countries were properly trained to treat the majority of their own people, their skills would be that much less saleable in the West.

But the rich countries profit in other ways from the ill health of the Third World. Very few developing countries have facilities for manufacturing drugs, so the drug business is monopolized by the multinationals. Drugs can take up to 40 per cent of the national health budget in developing countries. High drug prices, and the promotion of an unnecessary variety of brand-named products, push up the cost of medicines. Drug prices are often higher than in the West. For example, when a hundred Polycillin were selling for $21.84 in the USA, and $8.23 in the UK, they cost $41.95 in Brazil. Pharmaceuticals in Colombia were estimated to cost 155 per cent more than world market prices. Valium was selling at eighty-two times and Librium at sixty-five times the international market price. Economist Constantine Vaitsos has calculated that excessive drug prices may have cost Colombia something like $20 million in foreign exchange in 1968. The usual justification of high prices is that they are essential to finance research and development of new drugs. Yet there is no guarantee that profits earned in the Third World will go into research likely to benefit the Third World. On the contrary, the chief ailments of the world's poor receive scant attention compared to the diseases of the rich. The reason is simple: drug research, like food production, is geared not to human needs but to the effective demand of the market. The poor do not have enough buying power to influence what gets produced.

But that is not the only respect in which developing countries get a rough deal. The Director General of the World Health Organization, Dr Halfdan Mahler, summed up some of the questionable practices at the World Health Assembly in 1975: 'Drugs not authorized for sale in the country of origin – or withdrawn from the market for reasons of safety or lack of efficacy – are sometimes exported and marketed in developing countries. Products not meeting the quality requirements of the exporting country, including products beyond their expiry date, may be exported to developing countries that are not in a position to carry out quality control measures.'

Drugs are pushed just as hard in the Third World as in the West. More money may be pumped into promotion than into research. In some cases doctors have been offered inducements of free medical equipment or holidays. Advertisements, promotional literature and explanatory leaflets often make claims for drugs' curing powers that would not be tolerated in their country of origin. The Parke-Davis product Chloramphenicol, for example, is an antibiotic indicated for some serious bacterial infections in the United States. In Mexico and Central America it is recommended for a range of other conditions so broad that it sounds like the wonder drug: dysenteric infections, tonsillitis, pharyngitis, urinary, uterine and ophthalmic infections, brucellosis, phlebitis and yaws. In the

USA, a series of possible adverse reactions are listed, including nausea, vomiting, headache, mild depression and confusion — and caution is urged in prescribing the drug during pregnancy or lactation. The doctor is advised to avoid repeated doses and to discontinue as soon as possible. None of these warnings are mentioned in Central America or Argentina.

Most sinister of all is that, as regulations on the testing of drugs are tightened up in the rich countries, the Third World is becoming a vast laboratory of experimentation on human guinea pigs, at earlier stages of drug development than would be permitted in the West.

All the activities listed above are legal in the countries in which they occur. Each state is free, the drug companies argue, to pass its own protective laws on pricing, taxation of profits, quality and date regulation, and compulsory provision of information. And it is true that they are free to do so, just as a poor man is free to wear a Saville Row suit. But the fact is that at present the vast majority of countries do not have enough trained pharmacists to carry out quality control and to check the information provided by the companies.

Hope for the future must lie in regional cooperation among developing countries to pool their scarce manpower and set up their own manufacturing capabilities for drugs whose patents have expired. WHO is promoting the use of a simplified list of two hundred essential drugs, which would allow products to be bought in bulk and cut down the work of evaluation. WHO has also organized a certification scheme by which drug exporters should obtain a certificate from their governments stating that the product is authorized for sale at home. But membership of the scheme is voluntary, and it can be evaded by shipping drugs through non-member countries. The best way of cutting the cost of drugs, however, is to spend much more on disease prevention.

The health services as a whole need to be remodelled along the lines proposed by the WHO for primary health care, as an encouraging number of countries are now beginning to do. This involves delivering a basic level of service to the villages and slums by means of modestly trained barefoot doctors, selected from the community itself, and provided with essential supplies. Great emphasis would be placed on preventive measures through promotion of better sanitation, nutrition and family planning. Costs can be reduced and consciousness raised by involving the people in voluntary work. Higher levels in health services would be reoriented to service the lower, with resources and training diverted away from the urban privileged to the poor masses, to achieve what WHO director general Halfdan Mahler has called 'justice in health'.

In health, as in so many spheres of life in developing countries, there is a dual system. On the one hand is modern western-style medicine, with expensive drugs and expensive doctors, affordable only by the rich, or urban salaried workers covered by health insurance schemes. On the other, the poor masses, abandoned to their own devices, forced to medicate themselves direct from the chemist's shop, to resort to traditional healers, or, most frequently of all, to suffer disease patiently and hope it will eventually go away. The few get high-standard service, partly paid for out of government revenue raised from the whole population. That service – and the clean water and sanitation with which the areas where they live are provided – improves their productivity at work, raises the educational chances of their children, helps to make privilege hereditary.

Meanwhile the poor majority are lucky to get any health service or sanitation at all, and their lack of it helps to condemn them and their children to continuing poverty.

17. The Alienation Machine: The Uneducated and the Miseducated

'The more a person studies, the more foolish he becomes.'
MAO TSE-TUNG   FROM   LAOU TSE   C6TH BC

Pablo Cruz Guayara learned the importance of being literate the hard way. For sixty-two years he'd muddled through life well enough without being able to read or write. Thirty years ago, he and a friend bought seventy-five acres of poor, eroded land in the Magdalena valley, Colombia, and divided it between them. Then for three decades they worked their farms, growing cassava, beans, plantains and maize for their own families and tobacco for the market. Life was hard, but Guayara managed. He still lived in the one-roomed bamboo-and-mud thatch-roofed house, but he could afford a crate of Coca-Cola every now and then. He even bought a tractor, though his land was so fragmented by cliffs, gullies and streams that there were only a few fields he could use it on, and he regretted the purchase. A smart salesman had persuaded him he needed it, and as he couldn't read the brochures himself, he hadn't been able to check properly.

Suddenly out of the blue, in 1975, he received a legal document, hand-delivered and sealed in red wax. He had to get a friend to read it to him. It was from a powerful local businessman, claiming possession of Guayara's land. It seems there had been irregularities in the old contracts by which Guayara and his partner had divided up the land they bought. As they were both illiterate, they had not checked the documents. His partner died without a written will, and the son and heir fell into debt and mortgaged his land to the businessman, giving up the deeds as security. But he couldn't keep up the payments, so the land was forfeit. And the deeds also covered Guayara's land.

Guayara contested the case – and lost. He appealed to a higher level, and lost again. When I met him, he was appealing, without much hope, to the highest court in the land. He had already spent £500 ($1,000) in legal fees, and had to sell off eight acres of undisputed land, which he had purchased more recently, to pay them. He showed me his papers and handed me a bundle of tax forms and assorted transactions as confirmation that everyone had treated him as the owner of the land for years. He knew I would be able to read them. He could only look on and nod. Because he and his friend were illiterate, Guayara was now going to lose the land he had martyred himself and his family to save up for, the land he knew like the palm of his hand, the only basis of his status, his pride, even his survival.

Cualberto Altamira, who lives in a wooden shack roofed with polythene in a Lima squatter settlement, also has cause to lament his illiteracy. A few years back, when moving to Lima, he lost his papers, and if your papers are not in order in Peru, you are a virtual outcast. Without his marriage certificate he couldn't get an official permit for his house. Without his military service booklet he couldn't get a regular job. Without his birth certificate he didn't even exist. Altamira went to a backstreet lawyer who gave him some replacement papers for £10 ($20). It was only when he showed them to a prospective employer that he discovered they were irregular – the military service booklet was a school exercise book. He has now been to see a properly qualified lawyer who says a set of papers will cost him £80 ($160), equal to three months' wages. As he can only get casual work two or three days a week, because he can't prove military service, he has no idea how he will save this money. He is trapped in a limbo of official non-existence.

It was only after meeting these two men that I fully understood the meaning of illiteracy. It is not only a disqualification from better-paid employment in offices or factories. It is not only a cultural deprivation, an exclusive from national life, and in some countries even from voting. It is also a political fact, a handicap for disadvantaged individuals and groups in the bitter struggle for advantage and survival in the Third World. To be illiterate is to be helpless in a modern state run by way of complex laws and regulations. The man who cannot read or write is at the mercy of those who can. He is totally dependent on the sometimes questionable honesty and competence of lawyers and officials. He cannot read signs or official announcements. If he wants a job, he can't look in the classified columns, he has to go round on foot and hope he will stumble across something. If he is a farmer he has to rely on other people to tell him new seeds are available. He knows little of his rights, and even less about how to assert them. He is a sitting duck for exploitation and fraud. He may be able to count his small change – but he can be cheated out of his inheritance.

Illiteracy is a personal tragedy, and a powerful force in preserving inequalities and oppressions. Its extent in the modern world is one measure of the ground Third World education still has to cover. During the decade of the sixties, which saw tremendous efforts to combat this scourge, the overall proportion of illiterates in the adult population fell from 59 per cent in 1960 to 50 per cent in 1970. But because of population growth, the number of illiterates actually increased, from 701 millions in 1960 to 756 millions ten years later. In 1970 illiterates still outnumbered literates in the developing countries by ten millions. By 1970, only Latin America had succeeded in reducing the absolute number of illiterates, and still had 24 per cent of adults who could not read or write. In Asia 47 per cent were illiterate, in Africa a daunting 74 per cent.

Illiteracy, like other forms of educational disadvantage, weighs heaviest on the groups who are already disadvantaged in other ways. Rural areas have a much higher proportion than cities. In Morocco in 1971, for example, only half the adults were illiterate in towns, against 88 per cent in the rural areas. In El Salvador, one in three city dwellers could not write, compared with two out of three rural inhabitants. Illiteracy is concentrated among lower-income groups, the marginal masses and women. While only 40 per cent of men in developing countries are illiterate, the proportion among women is 60 per cent.

In all this, illiteracy is simply the most acute expression of a more general deprivation: the lack of education among the poor, either of an academic kind that would give them equal opportunities in the employment race, or of a practical kind that would enable them to improve their land or their workshops. Education is not only the key to personal enrichment. In the Third World context, it should be the central mechanism by which entire villages and urban communities learn to develop themselves, their productive potential, and their resources.

Instead, it has turned into yet another device for ensuring high rewards for the few and continued poverty for the many. It is an alienation machine, distancing young people from their families, and from manual work, making them turn their backs on the villages that so desperately need their promise, vigour and adaptability. It does not even turn out enough people with the skills that the modern sector needs, but produces a large class of disoriented drones and impractical mandarins.

The numbers game

If education has failed in most countries as a tool to aid development and equal opportunity, it is not because governments did not expand it fast enough. Education has been a boom industry in the Third World. The achievement in numerical terms is considerable. In 1960 45 per cent of primary age children and 21 per cent of secondary age were in school in the less developed regions. By 1970 62 per cent of primary and 32 per cent of secondary age children were enrolled. In absolute numbers, progress is even more astonishing: from 99 million primary pupils in 1960 to 171 million in 1970; 36 million secondary students jumped to 76 million; 5·3 million higher-education students became 13·3 million.

School enrolments were growing twice as fast as population in the sixties. Primary enrolment grew six times faster in the poor countries than in the rich. Behind the figures lay a gigantic effort in building new schools, opening new colleges and universities, training new teachers and teachers of teachers. Education, which governments saw as one of the greatest contributors to development and national integration, took a massive proportion of budgets, often more than 20 per cent. For comparison, it took only 18 per cent in the USA and 14 per cent in Sweden in 1973. As a proportion of the total gross national product of developing countries, education spending rose from 2·4 per cent in 1960 to 3·2 per cent in 1970. But this still lagged behind the 5·4 per cent of the developed countries. The distribution of world spending on education in 1970 remained grossly uneven: the rich countries spent $149 billions, the poor spent only $12 billions. With more than half the world's pupils, they spent less than 8 per cent of the world's education budget.

Yet of all this effort, all this expense, much went to create social and economic misfits. And much was wasted. Sadly, the poorer a country is, the more it costs to produce one fully fledged graduate at any level. If a wealthy country puts ten pupils in at one end of the educational assembly line, it will get nine or ten finished products out at the other end. The poor country will get only four or five, wasting a great deal of resources on drop-outs and repeaters. In the Dominican Republic, where the official primary course lasts six years, it takes nine pupil years to produce a single successful completer. In the rural areas it takes twenty-seven pupil years. In rural Colombia, instead of the official five years to take one pupil through primary school, sixty-six pupil years of education are needed.

Supporting the educational effort is becoming an increasing burden for developing countries. In 1965 every one thousand working adults had to support only 336 pupils in school. By 1975 they were supporting 430, and the figure is expected to rise to 456 by 1985.

As a result, the great boom in education seems to be over, and countries will be hard pressed to maintain even their present levels. Already in the late sixties the growth in enrolments had started to slow down considerably. In 1960, two regional conferences on education in Africa and Asia set the tempting target of universal primary education by 1980. There is not the remotest chance of that occurring in any of the three continents. In the early seventies, the oil price rises and deepening debt took their toll of public spending programmes. By 1975 the growth in the proportion enrolled had more or less ground to a halt, with 62 per cent of primary age children enrolled, 35 per cent of secondary and 4·5 per cent in higher education (compare this with the developed countries' ratios of 94 per cent, 91 per cent and 16 per cent respectively).

Projecting current trends, UNESCO does not expect any significant progress in enrolment ratios by 1985. These will probably stick at roughly the same levels as in 1975 for all three continents: 78 per cent of primary age children in school in Latin America and 57 per cent of secondary; in Asia, 64 per cent primary and 35 per cent secondary; and in Africa 51 per cent primary and 31 per cent secondary.

The tragic result is that the number of Third World children who do not attend school at all will increase considerably over the next decade. UNESCO predicts that primary and secondary age children out of school will grow from 305 millions in 1975 to 405 millions in 1985.

Failures from the cradle

All this effort and sacrifice has not helped to alleviate poverty and has, if anything, increased inequality. The fact is that education, chief path to higher pay, is loaded against the poor in most developing countries. The poor have less access to it, and even when they have access they are more likely to fail academically.

Access is a matter of miles and of money. School enrolment, absenteeism and drop-out rates increase in direct relation to distance from school. Even if schools were evenly distributed according to population, the more sparsely settled rural areas would be at a disadvantage compared to towns. In the depths of the African bush you often meet little troops of children, shading their heads with dog-eared exercise books, jogging along dirt roads soon after dawn, an hour or more away from the nearest school.

But schools are not evenly distributed. Rural areas have fewer of them, and the ones they do have are likely to be poor in staff and facilities. Teachers, like all other professionals in the Third World, prefer to live in cities where all the benefits of what they consider to be civilization are found. The bush is a kind of exile which only the saintly or the unqualified will accept. Many rural schools have only one teacher and a single class taking in all age groups. In the poorest countries (with per capita incomes below $250 in 1972) only about a third of rural primary schools offer the full range of grades. Children wanting to complete their primary schooling would have a much further trek to school, a much greater deterrent to continuing. Cities are much better provided than rural areas, in all three continents. In Africa 79 per cent of urban primary schools offer all grades against only 54 per cent of rural schools; in Asia the proportions are 94 per cent and 66 per cent; the gap is widest in Latin America, where 88 per cent of urban schools are complete but only 34 per cent of rural schools. At secondary level things are much worse. Almost all secondary schools are located in large towns, so peasant pupils have to become boarders. For the few able to afford this, the physical separation from home reinforces the growing spiritual alienation which the curriculum produces in the rural pupil. It is the first step towards leaving the village altogether.

As a result of this gross underprovision, the average adult in a rural area has much less education than his urban counterpart. In Kenya, in 1969, 80 per cent of rural adults over twenty-five had had no schooling, against only 47 per cent of city dwellers. In Colombia in 1973, 38 per cent of rural residents above twenty had no schooling, but only 14 per cent of townees. In India, 79 per cent of rural over-twenty-fives never attended school, compared with 47 per cent of urban adults. The discrepancy in educational provision is made even worse by migration: almost every village boy who gets even a full primary education will hot foot it to the nearest metropolis, leaving his village to rot in its ignorance.

But the squatter areas of the big cities are not a great deal better off. Schools are scarcer and of lower quality than in the official cities, so the slum child has a smaller chance of getting into school. In Lusaka, the Zambian capital, only one child in 385 in the shanty town of Matero got a primary school place at first attempt — but one in six did in the more established area of Kapwepwe.

Having got into school, the children of the poor are much more likely to leave it prematurely. In Guatemala only 4 per cent of rural children who start primary school complete it successfully, against 50 per cent of urban children. In four Latin American countries studied by UNESCO, half of urban pupils ran the whole course against only one in five rural children.

Wastage from drop-outs is a chronic ailment of education in poor countries: it is the concrete expression of the educational handicaps of the poor. Schooling is rarely compulsory — the funds do not reach to that. As children get older, more and more drop out of school, as a bored middle-class western student might drop out of university. For every hundred pupils in developing countries who entered grade one primary in 1967, only seventy-one reached grade two and sixty-three grade three. By grade four only fifty-four were left.

In some countries the casualty rate is higher than that in Britain's Grand National steeplechase, where every jump brings more horses crashing down. Of one hundred pupils who entered grade one in Colombia in 1962, thirty-six dropped out before grade two. The fence before grade three brought down another twenty-two. Eight fell at the grade four leap, another five shied before grade five's water jump and four retired at the grade six hedge. Only twenty-four of the original hundred ran the full course, and many had taken some jumps twice by repeating a class. The attrition in rural areas is appalling. In Colombia, where only one in seven rural schools offer grades four and five, only 3 per cent of rural pupils are left by grade five against 44 per cent of urban pupils. Of one hundred rural entrants to grade one, only fifty-one reach grade two, fourteen grade three, seven grade four and three or four reach grade five.

The couple of years that drop-outs have served on school benches are wasted years of servitude. They will rarely have picked anything up that will be of the remotest use to them in their working or domestic lives. They may not even have learned to speak the foreign language in which education is so often given, let alone become literate. If they have learned the crudest rudiments of reading and writing, few of them will have reached the stage where they can cope with the written materials of the real world, with newspapers, forms and books. And so without practice their skills will fade, and the semi-literate drop-out will lapse into total illiteracy.

There are many reasons why the poor fare so badly in the education race. Schools are further away from them, and they lack the social pull with headmasters in the struggle for scarce places. Parents are too poor to bear the direct and indirect costs of school. Few developing countries have yet abolished school fees, even at primary level, and fees can be prohibitive for the poor. The fees for secondary school in Uganda, for example, amount to 40 per cent of the minimum wage, and few workers on the land or in the informal sector earn even that. In Cameroon the fees amount to a quarter of the minimum wage, in the Philippines one eighth. And on top of that there are the textbooks, the pens, the paper, the uniforms, the shoes. A committee in Sri Lanka, inquiring into reasons for school non-attendance, often got the response from poor parents: 'How could we send our children to school in the rags they wear and expect them to sit with those who are better off?' The committee found that for every increase in the father's income of twenty rupees, the chance of school attendance rose by 1 to 3 per cent. Finally, as the child gets older, there are the costs of forgoing the child's labour power, which could supplement the family income. Poor families are surprisingly ready to make all these sacrifices to put at least one of their children through school. But if he does not show much promise, they will be much more ready to pull him out of school, thus nullifying everything they have already spent. The poorer the family, the greater the sacrifice involved in educating a child, and the more it is likely to be wasted.

The poor child's school performance is handicapped by his

parents' poverty. He will be more susceptible to disease and will lose more time through absence. When older relatives are ill, he may have to take time off to do their normal work.

These handicaps prevent many able children from lower socio-economic classes and rural areas from reaching their educational potential – a waste of human talent which has been called the 'internal brain drain' of developing countries. Development economists Sebastian Piñera and Marcelo Selowsky have calculated that this brain drain reduces the economic contribution of educational systems, and that reforms that equalized educational opportunity could increase the value of education's contribution to economic development by anything from 26 per cent to 145 per cent.

But the most tragic handicap of many poor and rural children may be that, on average, they are actually less intelligent than their wealthier classmates. In intelligence tests conducted in the Philippines children in poor families scored up to 10 percentage points less than those from better-off homes, and rural children 3 or 4 points less than urban ones. Large families – more common among the poor – dragged down the scores even further.

It is highly unlikely that the poor or rural child is genetically less intelligent than his rich or urban chum, though a few more generations of migration and of limited social mobility may eventually produce this effect. At present, it is clearly nurture, not nature, that curses the poor child, hereditary environment rather than pure heredity. We have seen the disastrous effect malnutrition can have on the developing brain. A child can be condemned to educational failure while still in his mother's womb, and his fate can be signed and sealed in his first two years of life. Education begins at home – in most countries the child will have six to eight years here before he first goes to school, and that is ample time for irreparable damage to be done.

Malnutrition is not always a death sentence for the intelligence. Stimulation can compensate for a lot of the harm it does. As a mother plays with her child, exercises its little muscles, gives it toys that teach it to perceive and manipulate the external world, nerve connections are quietly building up that will form the basis of later abilities. Laboratory studies have found that malnourished rats develop only 70 per cent of normal exploratory behaviour. Rats that are both malnourished and deprived of stimulation develop only 10 per cent. Among humans, a stimulating home background can make a difference of 10 or 20 per cent on intelligence test scores. One study in Jamaica found that undernourished children who came from a stimulating home background scored slightly better than well-fed children from a non-stimulating home. Stimulation can be even more important in developing intelligence than good nutrition. When the two disadvantages are combined, the result is disastrous. Undernourished children from drab homes scored 40 per cent less on IQ tests than well-fed children from stimulating homes.

And the child in a poor home is likely to be both under-nourished and understimulated. His home may be a dark, windowless hut containing a few sparse possessions. His mother, harassed by the demands of a numerous brood, will have little time to devote to developing each one. Children who are more closely spaced in age – as happens with poor families using no contraception – have been found to perform worse on intelligence tests than children who are more widely spaced. Most Third World children have no toys. When they are three or four, they start to make their own. But those typical western aids to intellectual development like coloured boxes and discs that you fit together are completely lacking.

Traditions of child rearing in some cultures can make up for this lack of equipment by encouraging parents to spend a lot of time playing with their children. In Bali – where nutrition is worse than the poor average for Indonesia – children are fussed from the cradle and taught to dance and act almost as soon as they can walk, ready for the roles they will play in dance drama. As a result, Balinese children and adults are more than usually bright, alert and lively. Yet in other cultures, as in much of Africa and Latin America, parents do not fuss children overmuch. The most intellectually deprived children I have met were the round-faced, woolly capped Indian children of the Andes. They seem to get little stimulation or even affection, and are subject to harsh discipline. As far as I could see, most of them do not make themselves toys – as soon as they are old enough, even at the age of four, they will be sent out to look after the livestock on the bleak pastures. Everywhere else in the world, children run up full of fun and curiosity if they see someone with a camera: the Quechua and Aymara children of the Andes stare quietly and anxiously and run away like frightened deer if you approach them.

With all these handicaps on the poor horses, it is hardly surprising if the stayers and winners in the educational stakes are predominantly the children of the privileged. The highest reaches of upper secondary and higher education are becoming the almost exclusive preserve of the children of the elite. For example, the child of a public official in Upper Volta is nine times more likely to get a place at secondary school than the child of a worker in the informal sector, and sixty times more likely than a farmer's child. In the Ivory Coast, an employee in the modern sector has a twenty-four times better chance of getting his son to secondary school than a peasant. The children of Kenya's professionals, civil servants or teachers are one thousand times more likely to get to university than farmers' children.

As time goes on, and unless radical reforms are undertaken, this situation is likely to get worse. In the early years of independence, the registers of schools, colleges and universities exploded, and the modern sector elite was small. In those days (still continuing for the least developed countries) it was much easier for an able farmer's son to climb the socio-economic ladder. But as educational expansion slows down and the modern sector fills the key posts that were vacant, the elite becomes increasingly self-recruiting, because of the immense advantages its children enjoy in playing the educational game.

Yet the system appears to work impartially, giving out passes or failures strictly according to ability. On the face of it, it is not obviously loaded against the poor. A few children of poor parents can and do make it all the way, creating an illusion of hope for all the rest. It is what economist Charles Elliott has dubbed a con-mech, or confidence mechanism, an elaborate fraud perpetrated on the poor. For if the educational system helps the elite to hand on its status and privileges to its children, it also keeps the poor in their place. It is another of those interlocking mechanisms that serve to turn the poor into a new caste from which escape is difficult. Because the poor have children who tend to fail in school, and as education holds the key to higher incomes, they are condemned to low pay and insecurity. The education system ensures that the children of the poor are also poor. And, with its superficial appearance of objective testing, it provides a perfect excuse for the perpetuation of gross inequalities.

Great expectations

It may seem inexplicable why the rural and urban poor are willing to make such sacrifices for their children to go through a gruelling exercise in disorientation, in which in any case most of them will fall by the wayside. But they do have their reasons.

In many local cultures, even before the development of the modern mandarin class, manual work had low status and was something to be avoided if at all possible. In India the two highest *varnas* or great caste divisions were the priestly Brahmins and the warrior *kshatriyas*. In China the literary bureaucracy was the pinnacle of ambition and finger nails were grown long as visual proof of idleness. In the empires of Africa the ruling families would have slaves to do all their work. And in Latin America the Iberians got the Indians and Africans to do all the hard labour.

Today a school certificate is seen as a one-way ticket out of the poverty and depression of rural life and the curse of manual labour. To invest in your son's schooling is like buying an expensive lottery ticket. Though his chances are slim if you are poor, he could just be one of the chosen few, and then all your worries would be over. Everyone knows at least someone who made it, and that encourages all the rest to try. In Africa the whole vast extended family of grandparents, uncles, cousins and nephews will all save up to put a child through secondary school, and a whole village might chip in to pay for a university education for one of its sons. This is not done out of charity: it is an investment which they hope will pay off. The lucky man is expected to land a nice government job and help his brothers, cousins and townsmen to get jobs as gardeners, drivers, cleaners. Or, if he makes it into the highest echelons, to pull strings and make sure the village gets favourable consideration for roads, electricity, piped water or anything else that's going. The value of education, seen from the consumer's point of view, lies precisely in its scarcity value. If everyone was successful, the winners could not gain so much. There are always more people willing to enter a lottery with a few big prizes, than one with a lot of small ones.

The reward, and the reason for all the pushing and perseverance, is the vast pay differential between the humble labourers and the higher brainworkers. In Britain, for example, the town hall department head may get only two or three times the pay of his dustman. In developing countries the gap may be ten or twenty to one. The differential originated in colonial days, when Europeans staffed the bureaucracies and had to be paid European salaries, and local parents had to be offered a worthwhile inducement to put their children through school to get enough junior clerks. At independence locals inherited the white men's jobs and expected to inherit their pay checks too.

Education, above all else, became the ladder to the upper reaches. The higher the level of education, the higher the average income. A man with primary education in Sri Lanka could expect, in 1969–70, to earn 1·6 times more than a man with none; a man with middle school education, 2·4 times more; a man with Ordinary level exams, 4·2 times more. Advanced level exams would earn him 6·4 times more and a degree 10·7 times more. Because of these pay differentials, private spending on education in the Third World is a good investment. The extra income earned, after tax, with a secondary education amounts to an interest rate of 18·5 per cent on its cost. The rate of return on higher education is a handsome 22 per cent per year of the investment. This is twice the rate of return in developed countries, where salary differentials are much lower.

The paper chase

In selecting for the desirable, better-paid posts, competence and intelligence are not measured by skill on the job, or performance in special tests related to the job. They are assessed solely and simply by the number of exams a man has endured and the marks he managed to scrabble together. Job applicants in West Bengal are expected to submit elaborate forms laying out in immense detail their performance in the Board of Secondary Education's exams, their marks in every subject, their grand total out of a thousand, and the division that puts them into. First division: 600 marks or more. Second division: 450 to 600. Third: 340 to 450.

This system of deep differentials based on exam-assessed schooling has lead to several symptoms of the pathology of education in the Third World (the West suffers them too, though in milder forms). When exams matter so terribly, rote learning is encouraged and creative, adaptable thinking is suppressed. Anyone who has taught in a developing country cannot help noticing the problems of bringing out students' self-confidence and ability to make independent judgements. The reason is often that the sheer weight of relatives' expectations of students puts an immense burden on them. They cannot afford to fail. They cannot take any risks. My own students in Nigeria told me that if they were to fail their exams they might as well be dead – they would never be able to show their face in their home village again. This explained their entrenched conservatism. They felt unhappy when I asked them for their viewpoint. I was there to tell them mine, which they would write down verbatim and learn by heart and rattle off again in the exams. I was sure to give good marks, they reasoned, to someone who wrote down my own opinions. Some of them told me that they consulted oracles in the hope of divining the exam questions in advance, or prayed that they would be revealed in dreams. In India nothing is allowed to stand in the way of success: invigilators have been murdered in the examination halls for trying to stop candidates cheating.

Because of the awesome import of these bits of paper, the whole structure of education at lower levels is geared to preparing pupils for the eventual paper-chase. Between 65 and 95 per cent of primary pupils will get no further education, yet the content of primary education in most countries is not to prepare them for life, but for secondary school. Only a tiny minority of secondary school pupils – between 0·3 and 11 per cent in one international survey – reach higher education, yet secondary schooling is largely a preparation for university and the leaving exams are basically university entrance tests. None of the earlier stages are self-sufficient, each is a preparation for the next, more academic phase, not a preparation for real life and work. So the majority leave having undergone a process of systematic alienation and disorientation, unfit for modern-sector work, equally unfit (and unwilling) to go back to a lowly place in their villages, and branded as failures to boot. Some 81 per cent of candidates failed Sri Lanka's Ordinary level maths exam in one recent year, and 86 per cent failed English. As the International Labour Office mission to that country remarked in its report: 'The whole system seems to be geared to producing either drop-outs or "O" level school leavers who aspire to holding clerical jobs.'

The excessive importance of exams contributes to another sad aspect of Third World education: the repeaters. Those who are most discouraged by the system drop out altogether. The more persistent repeat a year, in the hope of staggering on to the next hurdle in the race. Promotion is rarely automatic; usually it is based on mini-exams or teachers' assessments of school performance. The proportion of pupils repeating one class or another is extremely high, indicating that teachers' expectations are probably exaggerated, or that the type of education given just does not bring out the best in pupils. In Africa between 10 and 46 per cent of pupils repeat their first year in primary school, in Latin America between 18 and 35 per cent. The final year of primary school – when pupils will pass or fail their primary certificate – is the favourite for repetition. Between 20 and 54 per cent of African pupils repeat primary grade six. By the time they reach the final year only a minority of pupils will have passed up through the school without repeating one or two years. In the Congo, only one in eight pupils in grade six had been in school the regulation six years. One third had been there seven years, another third eight years, and one in five had spent nine or more years at school, having repeated at least three years. Nearly half of Colombia's 2·7 million pupils in 1968 were repeaters.

The lotus eaters: educated unemployment

The silvery oasis of high pay, shimmering beyond the sands of family sacrifice and anxiety, is not a mirage. It does exist, and some people stagger through and reach it. But there is not enough room at the cool water's edge for everyone who sets out on the journey.

The excessive pay differentials bring excessive floods of aspiring candidates, many of whom cannot hope to get the kind of job they aspire to even if they pass all their exams. It is precisely the same problem, with the same causes in inequality, as the superfluous armies of migrants invading the cities, drawn by the grotesque gaps in income between urban and rural areas. In colonial days the numbers going through secondary school were few, and most of them could realistically aspire to high rewards and clerical jobs at the end of it. After independence these expectations did not change. But education expanded faster than the number of jobs of the kind people believed an educated man was entitled to.

The result was an oversupply of qualified people with exaggerated hopes, and the curse of educated employment. More and more of those who fought their way over every fence and finished the course found there weren't enough glittering prizes to go round. Sometimes this was the fault of the planners: India, for example, for a long time provided more university places for engineers than the economy could absorb. Sums of that kind are hard to get right in any country. And as long as 'academic freedom' exists, students are liable to choose courses according to their expected earnings on graduation, rather than according to their country's manpower needs. But more frequently this oversupply was due to a refusal of the educated unemployed to lower their sights closer to solid earth. In a free market, when the supply of something exceeds the demand, the price drops. But the oversupply of educated people did not bring pay differentials down. These were kept high by trade-union activity and by politicians and bureaucrats fixing their own income levels to suit themselves.

Up to matriculation level, the more educated someone is, the more likely he is to be unemployed. In Sri Lanka the International Labour Office found that 25 per cent of uneducated men aged fifteen to twenty-four were out of work in 1969, against 39 per cent of men with six to ten years at school and 51 per cent of those with an Ordinary level exam pass. In all age groups, the possession of 'O' level seemed to bring with it three times as much risk of unemployment as lack of any schooling at all. The same pattern was found in a survey of the Indian state of Kerala in 1965: only 6 per cent of illiterates were unemployed, against one in three matriculates. But the risks diminished among graduates (13 per cent unemployed) and post-graduates (9 per cent). A little knowledge does seem to be a dangerous thing.

The educated unemployed are, more than anything else, victims of the excessive expectations which the system has engendered in them. They are, of course, free to take up labouring jobs, but they will not. In Sri Lanka, three quarters of people with 'O' level wanted white-collar employment, and less than one in five was willing to take any job that came up. Most of these people do not remain permanently unemployed. If they hold out long enough, eventually something more or less suitable does turn up and their place in the long queue is taken by the next generation of hopefuls. But the waiting period lengthens as employment rates rise. The Kerala survey found that matriculates spent an average of four and a half years on the unemployment register before getting a job.

I met one of these latter-day lotus eaters in Calcutta. Rattan Ram had been on the register of the employment exchange for two years, ever since he arrived from his native state of Bihar. A black-haired, brown-eyed twenty-two-year-old, he had the fatal sum of eleven years' schooling behind him: enough to raise his sights impossibly, but not enough to make him a desirable acquisition for an employer. To put it bluntly, people like him were two a penny. Why did he leave Bihar, I asked him. 'Here we have to wait a few years for a job. There we would never get one,' he replied. For 'job' read 'good job'. His father even owned some land. So why couldn't he work on it? 'I don't want that kind of work. Maybe I will go back if my father should die.' Rattan had no particular idea of the kind of work he wanted to do, provided it was white collar, well paid, and preferably public service. 'In public service it is very good,' he informed me, 'because you can keep your job no matter what happens.' He would definitely not accept a job paying less than 800 rupees a month (at that time £40 or $80), though in fact he had next to no chance of attaining that figure, which was twice the starting salary of a primary schoolteacher. This sum was what the economic jargon calls his 'refusal wage'. He would not take less because then he would be more hampered in his search for the ideal job in which he hopes to remain for the rest of his life. Meanwhile he spends his days roaming the streets of Calcutta from cinema to labour exchange and back to cinema again, living off the dwindling patience of an uncle who owns a small business, where Rattan helps out with minor office and household chores.

There is little hope of an early end to the waste of educated unemployment – unless, that is, radical policies cut deep into excess income differentials. In developed countries, few people would presume to an office job simply because they had passed through the secondary school sausage machine. Because everyone has a secondary education, it has no scarcity value at all. But demystification of exam passes depends partly on everyone getting a secondary education. The poor countries are a very long way from that goal.

Daffodils in the rainforest: the irrelevant curriculum

There is something very curious about the whole business of education, anywhere. It has suffered from irrelevance in most societies, past and present. It seems to take longer to readjust to changing reality, to have a greater cultural lag, than almost any other sphere except religion.

The Romans reared their children on Greek literature. Throughout the middle ages in Europe, monks and pages pored over ancient texts and futile Aristotelian syllogisms. Until the beginning of this century, education in industrial societies was dominated by the study of literary works from ancient agrarian civilizations: Israel, Greece, Rome. Even today education in most western countries is too academic in bias, teaches children very little about the real world of work and family they will have to cope with, and fails to produce the right mixture of skills that each country can employ.

The poor countries are not exempt from these problems, indeed they suffer them in more acute form than the West, although they can tolerate them less. The origin of the misfit between education and reality in the Third World has to be sought in colonial times. In the earliest periods of colonial contacts, and indeed later, education was dominated by the Christian Church. The Papal Bull of 1493 authorized Spain and Portugal to subjugate the world, but they were instructed 'to dispatch virtuous and godfearing men to instruct the natives and to imbue them with Christian faith and sound morals'. Missionaries pioneered western education in Asia and in Africa.

Far from respecting local traditions and cultures – however sophisticated – they did their best to stamp them out, convinced that they were the works of the devil or at best the products of benighted ignorance. Their purpose in setting up missionary schools was not to impart skills and knowledge that could be useful in the workshop and the fields, but to preach the faith, to teach the natives the colonial language, and teach them to read it so they could study the Bible. And to eradicate religions decried as idolatry and customs denounced as barbarous and evil. The *African Times* of 1 July 1880 proclaimed: 'The educated elite, more or less under the influence of Christian faith, are and will be indispensable as a vanguard of the great army of civilization that must be projected upon the ignorant barbarism of heathen Africa.' The essential function of missionary schools was to alienate their pupils from native society and culture, to make them scorn it and, indeed, to transform them into the brainwashed advance guard of the foreign culture who would go out and spread its influence among their own people.

Colonial administrators became interested in education much later. Their problem was that, as colonial governments and economies expanded, they needed more and more junior staff to help them run things, and it was expensive to import Europeans for such humble purposes. The Frenchman Albert Sarraut summed up the purpose of colonial education perfectly, as late as 1923: it was 'to train, from among the labouring masses, elites of collaborators who, as technical assistants, foremen, employees or clerks, will make up for the numerical insufficiency of Europeans and satisfy the growing demands of colonial agricultural, industrial and commercial enterprises'.

The products of this government-backed education had to be loyal and disciplined and literate in the colonial language, so they could do the administrative chores required of them. Education for the masses was neglected as unnecessary, and a native elite was created in the image of the Europeans to help dominate and exploit their countrymen. These new elites and their heirs later turned on the colonial masters and demanded independence. But they continued to teach their children in very much the same way as before.

The situation in Latin America was different. There the elite was European and naturally educated its children in its own culture. For the rural masses, the Indians, African slaves and poor whites, education could be dangerous. They were needed to work the fields of the big estates, and for that no education was required. Indeed the landowning class often opposed the spread of education to their labourers. But when it did come to the poor masses, it took little account of their Indian and

African heritages, but thrust Iberian culture down their throats in Iberian languages.

Political independence in Africa and Asia did not bring with it cultural independence. The style and content of education continued along largely European lines. Education was oriented to theory and distant facts, not to the practical life of the village. Even at university level, the humanities outweighed the sciences, and the balance of students seemed to bear little relation to the needs of countries. In 1977 UNESCO published some figures on university courses which make depressing reading. Brazil, Indonesia and the Ivory Coast, for example, had more law students than medics, as did Algeria, Morocco, Senegal and Colombia. Though all developing countries need desperately to increase their capacity for scientific research and development, so that they can be less dependent on western technology, students of natural sciences were outnumbered by social scientists in almost all developing countries – often heavily outnumbered. And agriculture, which employs two thirds of Third World populations and must be the foundation stone of development, almost everywhere had pathetically small contingents of students, outnumbered by engineers by anything from two to one to sixteen to one.

In the school, English and French literature dominated the classrooms of Africa and Asia and the gap between the curriculum and real experience was an abyss into which the pupil's confused mind fell headlong. I stayed in several African secondary schools in 1968. In all of them the pupils were alienated by sheer distance from their homes, made to wear shorts and shirt or frilly dress, and to live in a social structure – authoritarian teachers, discipline, dormitories – that was as different from the village set-up as it was possible to conceive. And they were taught, in a language they only partially understood, the writings of poets from a far clime. 'I wandered lonely as a cloud,' the children in one class chanted Wordsworth's verse mechanically. 'And then my heart with pleasure fills/And dances with the daffodils.' 'Sir, please what is a daffodil?' one bold boy asked. So the teacher drew one on the board, because none of his pupils had ever seen one.

When I was teaching French in a Nigerian university, some of my students were very intrigued by the ideas of the early Sartre. One of the brightest, a farmer's son, had been asked by his father what kind of things he was learning. He proceeded to expound the views of Sartre on the futility and absurdity of existence. His father began shouting 'Is this what we are all ruining ourselves to pay for?', and with a well-placed sandal kicked him out of the house. Quite right too, though it was me and the university he should have been kicking.

Things have improved in Nigeria since then. The curriculum is more relevant at all levels and many more local textbooks are being produced. But the problem persists in many countries. In the main bookshop in Ouagadougou, the set texts for the 1976 secondary school leaving exam are piled neatly on a shelf: Racine's *Andromaque*, Corneille's *Le Cid*. It is bad enough that French children must addle their brains with these stilted and constipated works, but to teach them to African children is positively criminal. On a near-by shelf is a prominent display of another tell-tale volume: *Practical Guide for Candidates in Administrative Exams*. Aspirants to Upper Volta's civil service, the pinnacle of all employment hopes, apparently find it useful. It contains problems on such relevant topics as France's trade patterns, and essay questions (with sample answers) on quotes from Pascal or other troubles peculiar to the European mind such as 'What is boredom? Where does it come from? How can we fight it?'

Adding insult to injury the teaching above the lowest primary levels is often in the language of the former colonial power. In his first years at school the child is plunged into a world of alien thoughts expressed in an alien tongue.

But the language problem is not an easy one to escape. The official language of most African countries is English, French or Portuguese. Many countries have dozens of mutually incomprehensible tribal languages, so even if one of the local tongues is adopted officially, it will still be a foreign language for many pupils.

Bahasa Indonesia, a new language based on bazaar Malay, is the language of instruction in Indonesia, though it is a foreign

326 The Lost People

language for most village people. Many local languages have not even been written down and systematized. Even the better-established ones cannot be used for school instruction until there are enough teachers speaking it. Textbooks have to be written, edited, printed and distributed – a costly business in a country with a market too small for commercial profitability. At higher levels, difficulties are compounded: science, maths, geography, present immense problems of vocabulary. Terms in local languages have to be invented, when equivalent concepts may not exist. In Yoruba, for example, it is hard to be precise about colours as the same word, *pupa*, is used for anything with a reddish tinge, including pink, orange and brown. Electricity has to be translated almost pidgin fashion as *ina mona mona*, the light that comes from lightning. A project to teach science in local languages in Sri Lanka had to start with the creation of a new vocabulary, often simply loaned from the English: prism became *prismaya*, siphon *siphonaya*. And how would you translate deoxyribonucleic acid or pi-meson into Tamil, Igbo or Quechua?

This diversity of local languages and shortage of local materials helps to explain how the old colonial powers still keep a hold on the minds of their former subjects. The textbooks market in most of the Third World is dominated by American, English, French and Spanish publishers. While Spain published 1,789 different titles in school texts in 1974, and the United Kingdom 1,306, Bangladesh published only five, Bolivia eleven and Ghana two. Only the countries with a large internal market and a well-established policy of local production escaped textbook colonialism. Nigeria published ninety-seven titles, Indonesia 476 and India 529. While Spain produced five textbook copies per student in 1972, Kenya printed only 0·42, Nigeria 0·08, and Ghana 0·01.

Not only the content, but even the style of teaching is copied from colonial models. Visiting a typical Third World school is like walking into a piece of history, like a western school of twenty years ago. While the West is moving onto more pupil-centred methods aimed at developing creativity, teaching in most developing countries still centres on the memorizing of often irrelevant information, in which the teacher's omniscience and authority is unquestioned.

Government services, in education and in health, should have tried to compensate for the considerable disadvantages of the poor. Instead, as in agriculture, housing and industry, the poor were discriminated against. Services were provided out of all proportion for people who were already privileged by the imbalances of the economy. The injustice of man compounded the injustice of nature.

Governments were right to believe that education is a keystone of development. But not the kind of education made up of academic irrelevances, alien concepts and sentiments, the kind that fills children's heads with dreams of the city and unfits them for their role in the village, the kind that brands the many as failures so the few can enjoy the excessive rewards of success. Education in the developing countries ought to be – and is becoming in some countries and pilot projects – a powerful instrument for community improvement. Villages desperately need education in its broadest sense, for all age groups, in or out of school. They need basic literacy, basic maths, of the kinds required in everyday life. They need practical knowledge about how to look after their nutrition and health, how to regulate their family size, what are their legal rights and how to obtain them, how to organize themselves into cooperatives and trade unions, and how to make their land or their workshop more productive.

They do not need an education system that helps to drain the life blood out of the village, but one that will revitalize it. They do not need an education system that perpetuates poverty and inequality, but one that will help end it.

Part Five

The Power Context

'There is always more misery among the lower classes than there is humanity in the higher.'

Victor Hugo, *Les Misérables*

Poverty and inequality in developing nations are often described as if they were almost a natural phenomenon. Or again as if they were the unintended outcome of unfortunate mistakes. Or as an inevitable, if regrettable and temporary, necessity on the runway towards economic take-off.

In reality, gross inequality is rarely an accident. It is more usually the result of deliberate and calculated attempts by the rich to increase their wealth, to widen the gap between themselves and the masses. Often this can be done only at the cost of greater absolute poverty.

The national poverty of the developing countries is not only the result of the inclemency of nature. The international economic order adds injustice to natural handicap. Through it, the western economies exploit the weakness of the poor countries to weaken them further, by mechanisms we shall examine in Chapter 18. The poverty of the poor and the riches of the rich within each country are no more of an accident. Development policies have been biased against the poor, the backward, the rural, and skewed in favour of the rich, the westernized and the urban, for a very simple reason. It is politics that determines the direction of development, and the privileged groups have infinitely more access to political power than the poor. In Chapter 19 we shall look at the reasons for this, and the prospects for change.

The overall result of these international and national processes is a world of pronounced inequalities, a world where both the capacity to create wealth and the incidence of unbelievable poverty have never been greater. Chapter 20 looks at the facts of poverty and inequality and summarizes the mechanisms by which both are generated.

Yet the poverty of poor people and poor nations is not an unmixed blessing for the rich who owe part of their wealth to exploiting the poor. The modern sector in the Third World is blocked in its expansion by the sheer poverty of the masses who have been neglected in its favour. The economic growth of the West is hamstrung by the lack of purchasing power in the massive potential market made up by the poor of the Third World. Chapter 21 examines these connections.

So the destinies of the overprivileged and underprivileged are linked. The extremes of wealth and poverty hamper each other. They prevent the full development of human potential, which will only be possible in a far more equal world.

18. Unto Every One That Hath: The Unfair World Economy*

'And the princes said . . . Let them live; but let them be hewers of wood and drawers of water unto all the congregation.'
JOSHUA

The tea-growing uplands of Sri Lanka have a beauty of their own. A thick green carpet of dense bushes clothes the rolling hills, as even as a close-cropped golf green. The neat white factories that dot it look like cottage tea cosies. The Tamil pluckers, with their dark pastel saris wrapped with sackcloth to protect them, pick two leaves and a bud, two leaves and a bud, and toss them dexterously into the baskets on their backs.

From closer quarters the idyll evaporates. I visited Sri Lanka in 1975, before the estates were nationalized and tea price rises finally brought some relief to the country. The suffering and poverty of the tea workers was typical of the tribulations imposed on the poor of the Third World by their countries' place in the international economic order. An order that condemns most of them to production of commodities at wildly fluctuating prices, while the price of the western machinery they need gradually climbs and climbs. An order that is plunging most non-oil developing countries into deeper and deeper debt.

The tea estate was an inhuman invention — a sort of total institution, to use sociologist Erving Goffman's term, like gaol or mental hospital, where people are born, raised, marry, multiply and die within perpetual sight of the crop on which their lives depend. The labourers live in 'lines' — barrack-like rows of single-room dwellings, many of them back to back — that have not altered since the British built them in the late nineteenth century. The British writer H. W. Cave no doubt expressed a common rationalization when he wrote around the turn of the century: 'Each compartment accommodates about

* Readers who do not like statistics may find this chapter heavy going, and may prefer to return to it at leisure.

four coolies, and it is obvious that they do not enjoy the luxury of much space ... But their ideals of comfort are not ours, and they are better pleased to live huddled together upon the mud floors of these tiny hovels, than to occupy superior apartments.'

The dwelling of Puryana Supaya, a thirty-seven-year-old Tamil living on the Langland estate, was typical of those I saw: a dark cell about ten feet square without windows, that had to serve as bedroom, kitchen and living room for Supaya, his wife and their three young children. It was in a row of about twenty similar dwellings back to back with another row. Supaya's cell was bare of all possessions except two cooking pots. At night the family slept on sacks on the cold cement floor. Supaya earned five rupees a day in 1975 – about 30p or $0.60. Men's work was hoeing, weeding, pruning the bushes, planting new ones, but it was irregular: Supaya had to queue up at the factory every morning to see if there was any work, and was lucky to get employment for more than four days in the week. His wife got more regular employment as a plucker, earning 3.76 rupees a day. Part of her earnings was made up of a bonus, paid if she plucked more than thirty-three pounds of leaves a day. For that reason the Tamil workers often prayed in their little Hindu temples for rain, because rain brings an extra flush of leaves to the bushes and makes plucking easier.

The Supayas were lucky if they averaged more than 200 rupees a month between them (at the time about £13 or $26). Their basic food rations, at subsidized government prices, cost around 150 rupees. This consisted of the bare essentials: eight pounds of rice per head, nine pounds of flour, half an ounce each of sugar, tea and dried fish, a couple of ounces of herbs to make sauce for the rice, and two tins of condensed milk. Sri Lanka's unique welfare-state approach made sure the poor got at least a survival minimum, and also provided free education and health. Deductions for a provident fund amounted to thirty-six rupees. That left just fourteen rupees, or three rupees per person per month (about 20p or $0.40), for everything else, including pulses, green vegetables, meat and fish, clothes, soap, cooking oil, kerosene, household utensils. The Supayas can afford nothing but food, though they never eat meat or fish. They even sell part of their ration, the sugar and tea, to get money for more flour and rice. I asked Supaya what they ate that day. He showed me a plain flat *chapati* bread: they had three of those each, and that was all.

The misery of people like Supaya was paying for the western housewife's cheap cup of tea. The price of tea fell and fell, even in nominal terms, from 1954 when it fetched 2.61 rupees a pound until 1969, when it reached a low of only 1.53 rupees per pound. It fell partly because of disunity among producing countries. Supplies grew more rapidly than demand. Uganda, Kenya and Malawi all started growing tea and there was no co-ordination among countries to plan their production so as to match supply with demand. Against the lack of organization among producer countries, purchases of tea were dominated world-wide by three multinational companies who controlled 60 per cent of the market. Before the Sri Lankans forbade the practice, the companies and their agents used to ship tea to the London auctions where prices were generally much lower than in Colombo. A government commission of inquiry claimed in 1975 that the purpose of this was to build up profits outside Sri Lanka and avoid taxation. They calculated that this practice cost the country 6·8 million rupees in 1967, or around 14 per cent of the trade deficit. While tea prices tumbled, the price of Sri Lanka's imports of food, oil, fertilizers, manufactures and machinery rose. In 1974 a given quantity of her exports could buy only 43 per cent of the imports they were worth in 1954.

Not surprisingly, Sri Lanka developed an endemic balance of payments problem. Even in the early sixties she used to run a surplus averaging some $36 million a year, but from 1966 until 1975 her balance of payments was in the red every year to an average tune of $60 million. And so Sri Lanka fell into increasing debt. By 1975 her foreign owings amounted to $1 billion, and the cost of paying back capital and interest on this sum was eating up 20 per cent of her export earnings each year.

The declining price of tea led to lower incomes throughout the country, so the amount people had left over to spend on manufactured goods fell, and the country started to de-industrialize. Employment in industry declined by one third between 1972 and 1976. As the labour force grew faster than jobs, unemployment climbed above the million mark, and one man in five was unemployed.

But at the same time, government revenue had been declining, and the government was forced to dismantle part of Sri Lanka's welfare state, cutting back the free food rations and food subsidies. The poor like Puryana Supaya were assailed from all directions. It was they, ultimately, who bore the burden of an unjust world economic system.

Riding the switchback: fluctuating commodity prices

To the developing countries the great world market place must often seem like a casino where all the wheels, dice and decks are rigged, loaded and marked so that the bankers of the West always win.

Lady luck reigns over their foreign exchange earnings. For example: in 1970 Tanzania earned 179 million shillings (about £13 million or $26 million) for her exports of sisal. For the next three years she was on a winning streak: the price of sisal went up and up and in 1974 she 'staked' 60 per cent less sisal than in 1970 – and cleaned up winnings of 464 million shillings, over two and a half times more. Then her luck changed and prices started a downward plunge. In 1976 she bet roughly the same quantity of sisal as in 1974, but earned only half as much from it.

Meanwhile the price of the chips the bankers were selling – the manufactures and machinery the Third World imports from the West – continued its steady climb. As Tanzania's President Julius Nyerere complained: why should Tanzania have to hand over twice as many bales of sisal this year as she did last, to buy the very same farm tractor? The same amount of hard labour, scarce land and capital had gone into a given quantity of product on both sides as had done the year before. Suddenly the Tanzanian sisal worker had to sweat twice as hard as before while the French, Japanese or British worker made no extra effort.

Not only does the Third World have to ride this vertiginous switchback of rising and falling prices, but for twenty years up to 1973 it was steadily sinking, while the West was riding higher and higher. The terms of trade were running against the poor countries, that is, they were having to export more and more to buy the same amount of manufactures.

To understand how this state of affairs came about, we have to go back to colonial days. Colonies have always been exploited as sources of primary products: metals, raw fibres, food. Spain milked Latin America of its gold and silver, and later much of the western hemisphere was transformed into one great plantation, producing sugar, cotton or tobacco for Europe. Later still the plantation system was introduced into Asia and then Africa. As their own supplies of metals and fuels began to fall short of demand, the industrialized countries began to plunder their colonies of natural resources.

So the function of colonies was to supply raw materials on the one hand – and on the other, to purchase the manufactured goods of the 'mother' country. Often this function was quite explicit. As the French politician Jules Ferry remarked in 1885: 'The foundation of a colony is the creation of a market.' Another Frenchman, Paul Leroy-Beaulieu, summed it up in 1874 when he wrote: 'The most useful function which colonies perform ... is to supply the mother country's trade with a ready-made market to get its industry going and maintain it, and to supply the inhabitants of the mother country – whether as industrialists, workers or consumers – with increased profits, wages or commodities.' Once the economic life of the colony had been forcibly harnessed to the needs of the colonial power, political control became an unnecessary expense: the system perpetuated itself. The ex-colonies still had their mines, their plantations and outgrowers, on which they depended to earn foreign exchange. They could not easily develop alternatives. They still had their sad little colonial transport systems, with all railways and major roads leading to the main port – a visible symbol that their economies' purpose was not to provide for its own needs, but to serve foreign ends. They still had the branches of the old colonial trading companies monopolizing their trade. The links of economic subjection had been forged to last.

In the present international division of labour, more than three quarters of the Third World's exports are primary products, and nearly two thirds of its imports are manufactured goods. Liberal economic theorists from Ricardo onwards accepted this as a natural and beneficial state of affairs, in which each nation specialized in those goods which it could produce more cheaply, so everyone benefited by lower prices. The truth is that the present division of labour originated not in this comparative advantage, but in conquest by force and rule by repression – or, with the non-colonies, in the premature imposition of free trade by gunboat diplomacy.

Primary products, with very few exceptions, are a bad business to be in if you want a steady livelihood, but most of the developing countries depend on just one, two or at most three commodities. Hence their balance of payments, and the foreign exchange they need to buy machinery for their fledgling industries, are completely at the mercy of the fickle commodity trade winds. In the mid-seventies, many countries still had all their eggs in a single basket. Two thirds of Chad's exports were cotton, two thirds of Chile's were copper. Wood made up 65 per cent of the Congo's exports, sugar four fifths of Cuba's, cocoa two thirds of Ghana's. Three quarters of Liberia's produce was iron ore, sugar nine tenths of Mauritius's, cotton and yarn three fifths of Egypt's. Tea accounted for three fifths of Sri Lanka's exports, copper for three fifths of Zaire's and nine tenths of Zambia's. Coffee was a major earner for many countries, amounting to 37 per cent of Haiti's exports, 43 per cent of Rwanda's, 48 per cent of Ethiopia's, 50 per cent of Colombia's, 61 per cent of Uganda's and 84 per cent of Burundi's.

By contrast, rich countries have diversified into many different branches of trade, each one of which provides an insurance policy against problems in any of the others. Rarely does a single type of product account for more than 15 per cent of exports. Only a few developing countries have succeeded in diversifying enough to make themselves less vulnerable to ups and downs. Among producers whose main exports are manufactures, Singapore, Korea, Brazil, Mexico and India have very diverse exports. There are even a few producers of agricultural goods who depend on a wider range of products, offering them some protection against sudden bankruptcy if the bottom falls out of the market in any one product. Among these are Morocco, Mozambique, Thailand and Tanzania.

The danger of depending on one or two primary products lies in the insane behaviour of their prices. Cocoa, for example, was 21·5 cents a pound in 1949, rose to 57·8 cents in 1954, fell to 27 cents in 1956. In 1958 up again to 44·3 cents, in 1965 right down to 17·2 cents. It zoomed to 45·7 cents in 1969, and plummeted to 25·8 cents in 1971. Since then, up, up and away, reaching 231 cents in July of 1977. Sugar rose from 8 cents a pound in 1970 to a dizzy peak of 47·5 cents in 1974, and by April 1977 was back where it started from at 10 cents a pound. At that price it simply did not pay to grow it any more. Coffee, which used to be 80 cents a pound way back in 1954, had dropped back to 45 cents a pound in 1971. From then on it rose and rose against all reason to 315 cents a pound in April 1977, and started falling again thereafter.

Fluctuations like these play havoc with planning and budgeting for developing countries. Unless a single country controls a major proportion of the supply of any particular commodity, or belongs to a strong cartel, it cannot predict with much accuracy, let alone control, the price of its major product. A sudden windfall can fuel inflation and encourage excessive import-buying, which will continue for a while even after prices have started falling. Loan instalments have to be repaid in slump years as well as boom years. Sudden price drops can threaten development plans. Zambia provides a cruel example of this: in 1977 the price of copper fell spectacularly, reaching its lowest price in real terms for twenty years. The price was so low that many mine companies were making a loss, and Zambia's mines were costing her more in foreign exchange for imports than they were earning in exports of copper. The balance of payments ran massive deficits year after year. Zambia could not repay her debts and new creditors would not lend to her. Half of government revenues had come from copper before 1975 – but by January 1978 the contribution was nil. The 1978 budget slashed back on all government spending, cutting capital expenditure – the seedbed of development – by almost a third in real terms. Food subsidies had to be cut, leading to price rises that lowered the nutrition standards of the poor. The IMF loaned Zambia some of the money she needed to hold off her clamouring creditors, but only on condition that she devalued and deflated her economy drastically. Zambia was being treated as if her troubles were due to some mental aberration of her own, whereas the madness of the international economic order was the real cause. The roulette had turned into Russian roulette, and the game had thrown up a loaded chamber.

The fluctuations of commodity prices seem more curious if you compare them with prices for manufactured goods. Demand for family cars can vary with the ups and downs of the trade cycle, in the same way as the demand for copper – so why don't car prices drop to £500 or $1,000 each in a depression and shoot up to £5,000 or $10,000 each in a boom? In liberal economic theory, the market price is supposed to reflect the relationship of supply and demand, and this does, in fact, explain some of the difference in behaviour between commodities and manufactures. Agricultural products – especially in the Third World, with its uncertain rainfall and epidemics of diseases and pests – are liable to vary considerably in their supply. On the other hand, the demand for foodstuffs remain fairly steady. When the sugar supply drops, for example, people need their two spoonfuls in a cup of coffee and scramble for available supplies, so the price goes up steeply. But if there is a surplus of sugar, people aren't going to start putting four spoonfuls per cup, so the price has to drop quite a way to make people buy up the surplus. Agricultural commodities produced only in the West and in countries like Australia and New Zealand, with more predictable climates, have a more even supply and hence tend to have a more even price.

Industrial raw materials such as minerals are more likely to vary in supply when the Third World is the main source, because political instability and problems of obtaining spare parts for mines are more likely to interfere with production. The demand for minerals tends to vary more than for food-stuffs, rising and falling with the western business cycle.

But the trade in commodities is not a simple matter of the balance between producers' supply and consumers' demand. A whole series of middlemen intervene between the two sides – and it is their curious behaviour that causes much of the fluctuation. Commodities are bought up by export merchants, who sell them to commodity dealers, who sell them to importers, who sell them to processors or the retail trade. In theory, dealers should keep prices steady by evening out supply and demand. When prices rise, they should sell from their stocks, to make a profit, and so bring prices down again. When prices fall, they should buy up supplies while they are cheap and hence hike the price up. But this rational model of behaviour bears little relation to the reality of speculation. Commodity dealers aggravate price instability. If the price of something is rising and they think it will go on rising, they buy up as much as they can get their hands on in the hope of selling it at a higher price later, and this buying activity pushes the price up even further – a self-fulfilling prophecy. Only when dealers feel a downturn is round the corner will they stop buying in as prices rise. A peak is reached: and after it, prices start to fall. And they fall rapidly, because merchants have garnered enough stocks to meet customers' needs for months ahead, and don't need to buy any more for a while. And when prices are falling, the speculators do not usually step in to buy up the bargain goods. Far from it: if they think the price will go on falling they sell everything they have got for fear of being stuck with a load of cheap goods, and their selling drags the price down lower still – another self-fulfilling prophecy. Everyone holds off buying as long as they can, if they think the price still has a way to drop. But then, at the bottom of the abyss, they start buying again with a vengeance. In other words, for most of the time speculators are doing the exact opposite of what most people do. They are buying more when prices rise, and buying less when they drop. Third World commodity prices would certainly rise and fall anyway as supply and demand changed. But it is the activities of hoarders and speculators that turn the hills and valleys into towering peaks and terrifying abysses.

Climbing the down escalator: declining terms of trade

Fluctuation in itself is bad enough. It does not encourage thrift or hard work. It fosters a casino mentality. But if, in the long run, the average value of a country's major export remained more or less steady, it could take the rough with the smooth. The second headache of Third World countries has been that the prices of their exports have tended to fall in real terms over a long period. Until the commodity boom of 1973–4, the amount of imports a given quantity of the exports could buy had been declining. Until recently it was commonly thought that this decline had been going on for a century, but detailed research by economic historian Paul Bairoch suggests that they rose by perhaps 50 per cent between 1870 and 1950. After 1953 they began to fall, so that by 1970, a standard amount of a non-oil developing country's exports could buy 11 per cent fewer imports than in 1953. Conversely, a standard amount of an industrialized country's exports could buy 11 per cent more. The rich had become better off at the direct expense of the poor. As Bairoch points out, it does not look like an accident that the deterioration happened as most developing countries were gaining their independence.

After 1973 the oil price rises altered the picture considerably. The major oil producers of the Organization of Petroleum Exporting Countries unilaterally pushed up their prices, and by 1975 their terms of trade were 227 per cent up on 1954–6. This brought the rich countries' terms of trade down, wiping out the 11 per cent gain and leaving them, in 1975, more or less where they had been twenty years earlier in terms of how much their exports could buy. The non-oil developing countries did not benefit from the commodity war victory of their oil-rich brethren. On the contrary, they lost out, so that by 1975 a given quantity of their exports could buy 21 per cent fewer imports than twenty years earlier: in the case of the poorest countries (average incomes below $200) 32 per cent less. The high cost of oil was added to the other injustices suffered by the majority of developing countries.

The terms of trade of many non-oil countries fell drastically between 1970 and 1975: India's worsened by 27 per cent, Peru's by 32 per cent, Sri Lanka's by 35 per cent. Overall, the share in world trade of the non-oil developing countries declined from 24 per cent in 1950 and 15 per cent in 1960 to 10 per cent in 1976.

The standard explanation for the declining terms of trade between 1953 and 1973 is that there is a general tendency for the supply of Third World primary commodities to grow faster than the demand. Too many new countries, looking out for new sources of foreign exchange, decided to start up production of this or that commodity, without taking into account the fact that others might do, and were doing, the same. Oversupply was therefore partly due to lack of organization and coordination among producers. On the other hand, demand declined for some commodities, especially rubber and fibres, because of the introduction of synthetic alternatives.

But it is not only governments that lack organization and coordination. Where cars, for example, are produced by a few giant manufacturers who can cut back or increase production to suit the market, agricultural commodities are often grown by a mass of small producers, each one aiming to make a profit yet taking little account of what his fellow producers intend to do. Smallholders do not adjust their production rationally to the behaviour of market prices. When the price goes up high, they increase their capacity in the hope of future gain. So little cocoa planters in the Ivory Coast will plant more trees, Brazilian farmers put in a few hundred more coffee bushes; inevitably, a few years later, there is overproduction and prices hit the floor. Optimism is easily corrected in the case of crops like sugar cane, bananas and pineapples, which produce a harvest within a year or two of planting. But a coffee bush takes five years to mature, a tea bush six years, an oil palm seven, rubber trees and coconut palms eight years and cocoa fifteen. Mistakes are hard to correct. The smallholder does not react to a price drop in the same way as to a rise: he will not rip up bushes that have taken so much loving care to mature, destroying an investment that took five years or more to start paying off. The longer the life of the tree, the less likely he is to destroy it, and he will want to sell whatever it produces even when the price is low. He cannot readily cut his supply to match market conditions, any more than his country can if it is poor. Both of them have to sell because they need the money. Sometimes the smallholder is cushioned from the market by a government marketing board. If the board's policies are judicious and far-sighted, they can help a lot. But none of them are clairvoyant, and if the market changes radically, there is a limit to a marketing board's powers. If the price drops drastically or over a long period, it may not have the funds to maintain the producer's income. If the price rises considerably, a board cannot withhold the higher price from producers for long, or they will cause political disturbances or start smuggling.

Western producers, whether governments, companies or workers, tend by contrast to be well organized at all levels. If demand for cars drops, for example, there is no question of cutting prices or workers' wages. The manufacturers, unlike commodity-producing countries and smallholders, fix their own prices because they also control marketing and distribution. Car workers are organized and militant; there is no chance of getting them to accept a wage cut. So if demand falls, the company lays men off and the national government picks up the bill in unemployment pay. Western farmers are equally well organized into pressure groups: their political muscle has won them high guaranteed prices and protective barriers against competing imports. This not only reduces western demand for several Third World agricultural products, but also generates surpluses which are dumped on the world market and depress prices there. When the disorganized poor commodity producers of the Third World, whether nations or individuals, encounter the organized and wealthy countries, companies and workers of the West in the market place, the result is: declining terms of trade.

It is wealth that helps western interests to be well organized: governments have large reserves, manufacturers can afford to hold stocks off the market to keep prices up, workers have strike funds, social security and unemployment pay. Conversely, Third World governments are poorly organized because they are poor. They often have to go on producing, even at low prices, because they have low reserves and need the money to stay solvent. They do not control the marketing of their produce: the dealers of London, New York and Tokyo do it for them. Except in the case of oil, and to some extent with tin, bauxite and phosphates, none of their commodity associations has succeeded in permanently and securely pushing up the price of its product, because there is always some pauper country who will break ranks and start selling again. For similar reasons small farmers cannot afford to stop producing, or build up stockpiles, if prices fall. They are poor enough to need whatever money they can get just to survive. I have met hawkers and farmers selling goods at a loss, because they needed money then and there to pay the taxman or the local Shylock, or just to go on living. Nor are they often politically organized; indeed, as most Third World countries are not democracies, they don't even have their votes to bargain with. And so, if they are enterprising enough to produce more, they earn less for the extra production. Third World farmers have increased their productivity in most crops, through improved seeds, more use of fertilizer, better husbandry. But often they have not reaped the benefit in higher incomes. Instead the West has expropriated it in lower prices. At the same time the West, and western workers, have kept a firm hold on the benefits of their own increased productivity. The message is clear: because the rich can organize more easily, they get richer; because the poor can not, they get poorer.

Private empires: the multinationals

But it is not only by the seemingly impersonal forces of the world market that the poor nations are bled. They are exploited directly by the great multinational corporations which dominate a growing proportion of the economic and social life of the Third World. [They are the gunboats and soldiers of the new economic style of imperialism.] The global giants can exert a powerful influence over crucial aspects of development, such as trade balances, the direction of industrial growth, the choice of technology, the rate at which natural resources are extracted, even the culture, values and aspirations of ordinary people. The total stock of western investment in the Third World in 1967 was worth $33 billions (£16·5 billions). By 1975 this had more than doubled to $68 billion, and in that year alone another $10 billion plus was invested. By far the largest investor in the Third World was the United States, whose stock totalled $29 billion in 1976. Next came Japan and Germany, with around $6 billion each, followed by the United Kingdom, with just over $5 billion. The largest proportion of these funds – some 35 per cent in 1972 – was invested in petroleum, with 30 per cent in manufacturing and 10 per cent in mining.

Not all regions were equally infiltrated by multinationals. Just over half of the total investment in 1972 was in Latin America, while Africa had 21 per cent and Asia 18 per cent. The individual countries with the heaviest totals of foreign investment were Brazil with $9 billion in 1976, Indonesia with $6·4 billion (1976) and Mexico with $4·7 billion (1975).

The great world companies offer considerable attractions to Third World nations who are prepared to tolerate their equally considerable drawbacks. The prime advantage is probably that they help the balance of payments with an immediate inflow of capital, and (or so it is hoped) improve it in the longer term by manufacturing locally what used to be imported, and perhaps doing some exporting too. (Although, in practice, many multinationals often import more in components than they export.) Multinationals help, too, with the rapid growth of an industrial sector along western lines, and that is what most developing countries want more than anything else. The globals bring with them a unique package deal which the poor countries could not easily assemble themselves: capital, technology, management expertise and access to a well-developed world-wide marketing network. They rarely employ more than a skeleton staff of expatriates at the highest levels, and train up large numbers of local people as clerks, accountants, junior managers and skilled workers.

But the multinationals are not philanthropic institutions and the bargain struck with them carries heavy costs. They can come to dominate the commanding heights of local industry, as their immense advantages of resources and knowhow give them a massive start on local firms. Affiliates of multinationals now command large sectors of industry in many countries. In 1957 they produced only 12 per cent of Latin America's exports, but by 1966 were turning out 41 per cent. In Brazil 70 per cent of the 1970 profits of the most dynamic sectors of the economy went to global corporations; multinationals controlled all tyre and car production and two thirds of the manufacture of machinery and appliances. By 1976, foreign investors controlled 33 per cent of Brazil's electrical machinery industry, 44 per cent of rubber, 51 per cent of chemicals, 55 per cent of non-electrical machinery, 61 per cent of iron and steel and 100 per cent of automobiles. The foreign-controlled share of Argentina's output rose from 18 per cent in 1955 to 31 per cent in 1972. In 1970, multinationals controlled 45 per cent of the assets of medium and large-scale firms in Mexico. But foreign control was substantial in other regions, too. In Nigeria, 70 per cent of the assets of manufacturing companies were foreign-owned in 1968. In Ghana, 50 per cent of 1974 manufacturing sales were accounted for by foreign-owned enterprises. In Turkey, 54 per cent of the electrical machinery industry, 56 per cent of paper, 59 per cent of rubber and 74 per cent of textiles were foreign-owned.

There are considerable dangers in handing over such a degree of local power to foreign bodies, whose purpose is to maximize profits for western owners and shareholders, not to promote the welfare of their host nations. By anticipations and delays in their currency dealings they can influence exchange rates to their own advantage. Except in countries sitting on scarce and valuable commodities, who have been able to obtain a measure of control, in most countries the rate of exploitation and exhaustion of natural resources, from metals to forests, is in the hands of foreigners. Multinationals choose their technology to suit their global purposes and generally prefer capital-intensive techniques: they are not concerned with the impact on local employment. They determine their wage structures regardless of the expectations their pay levels can raise in local firms and public service. They advertise and market their products without regard to their customers' real interests, inducing the poor to spend more on unnecessary items like Coca-Cola or powdered milk and so have less left over for essentials. They command a disproportionate share of what little savings are available locally – studies in Latin America have shown that perhaps four fifths of their finance is raised locally. Their marketing of western lifestyles exerts a destructive influence on local cultures.

An example of the excessive influence the transnationals can exert on local economies is the case of bananas, on which the livelihoods of several Central American and South American states depend. Bananas account for 28 per cent of the export earnings of Costa Rica and 45 per cent of her agricultural employment, they make up one fifth of Panama's exports and employ half her agricultural labour force, and they are of crucial importance to Ecuador, Honduras, Jamaica and the Windward Islands.

The world's trade in bananas is dominated by just three huge food multinationals: United Brands (with a 34 per cent market share in 1974), Standard Fruit (with 23 per cent) and Del Monte (10 per cent). As with many other commodities, the companies control the transport, packaging, shipment, storage and marketing of the fruit. As a result, the profits from bananas go largely into western pockets, while the producer countries get only a pittance. A study for the United Nations Conference on Trade and Development found that the exporting countries get only eleven and a half cents of each dollar the consumer spends on bananas. The exporter and shipper (usually the multinational) pockets thirty-eight cents. The ripener collects ninteen cents. The retailer, who does no more than carry the fruit on his shelves for a day or two, keeps thirty-two cents.

As with so many other commodities, the real price of bananas dropped by 30 to 60 per cent in the main consuming countries between 1950 and 1972. Three tons of bananas could buy a tractor in 1960. Ten years later, eleven tons were required. Although the producer countries' futures depended on banana prices, it was the food multinationals whose actions determined these. They owned large tracts of land and grew as many bananas as they saw fit – overproduction was one factor that kept prices low. And they controlled marketing and mark-ups.

In 1974 five of the main producer nations started to hit back, to try to recoup more of the banana dollar for themselves. They formed the Union of Banana Exporting Countries, and slapped an export tax on every case of bananas that left their ports. The multinationals did not take this lying down. One of them halted exports for a while and destroyed 145,000 cases of fruit, to try to force the tax to be cut or withdrawn. United Brands adopted another tactic. It paid a bribe of $1·25 million to Honduras's then minister of economy and commerce. As a sign of his gratitude, he promptly halved his country's proposed export tax from 50 cents a case to 25 cents. This transaction saved United Brands an estimated $6 to $7 million. The Honduran people lost a similar amount. But the deal, unlike many others, went wrong. News of the bribe leaked out, and the Honduras military regime of Oswaldo Lopez Arellano was toppled in a coup. On 3 February 1975, United Brands' chairman, Eli Black, leapt to his death from the forty-fourth floor of a New York skyscraper.

The last but not least drawback of the transnationals is that they make money and send it back home, for that, after all, is their *raison d'être*. Multinationals' declared profit levels are often higher in the Third World than in the West – their executives would argue that they have to be to justify the political risks. Profits of American companies between 1965 and 1968 averaged 17·5 per cent in less developed countries, against 7·9 per cent in developed countries. The usual defence of profit is that it is essential for new investment. But this rationale simply does not apply for multinationals in the Third World. They take out every year, in declared profits alone, three times what they put in. In the latter half of the sixties on official figures, they were extracting $3·4 billions a year more in income on past investments than they were putting in in new investment. Between 1971 and 1974 the drain averaged $7·5 billion a year. An increasing proportion of investment is, in any case, being financed out of locally generated profits: the share averaged around 40 per cent between 1970 and 1976.

Much of the multinationals' income comes from charges for intellectual property, which many developing countries argue should be the common inheritance of mankind. The multinationals keep a tight grip on their knowhow. One study of five countries (India, Turkey, Egypt, Pakistan and Trinidad) found that 89 per cent of all patents were owned by foreigners. In Chile the proportion of foreign-owned patents rose from 65 per cent in 1937 to 95 per cent in 1967. Another six-country study found that payments for royalties and related fees (patents, licences, trademarks, management and technical services) ate up 7·5 per cent of these countries' total export earnings.

Towards the end of the 1960s, payment for western technology was costing the Third World an estimated $1·5 billion a year in precious foreign exchange. This figure was predicted to rise six-fold by 1980. And the technology supplied was rarely offered without restrictive conditions attached: users were often required to purchase inputs such as raw materials and spares from the supplier, and forbidden to export any of the production.

The technological dependence of developing countries arises in part from the massive concentration of scientists and research in the West. In the early seventies the average developed country had 10·4 scientists and engineers engaged in research and development for every 10,000 people. Asia had 1·6, Latin America 1·15 and Africa a mere 0·35. With its under-developed higher education systems, biased towards the humanities, the Third World produces only a small number of highly skilled scientific personnel. The West, with its higher salary levels, drained off around 30,000 of these every year over the sixties. Between the early years of that decade and 1972, the United States acquired 90,000 Third World brains, the United Kingdom gained 84,000 and Canada 56,000. The United Nations Conference on Trade and Development has calculated that this human traffic – a reverse flow of technology – was worth a total of $51 billions to these three countries alone, some $4·6 billions more than the aid they gave to the Third World in the same period.

The real income of multinationals is almost certainly much higher than the official figures suggest. The huge global conglomerates are amoral beings. Their ethics are the minimum required for political survival. As the investigations of various United States agencies reveal, they are not above committing criminal acts if they think they can get away with it. By 1977, no less than 360 US companies had admitted to making 'questionable payments' in foreign countries – in other words, bribes. The ninety-five largest had paid out around $1 million each in the space of a few years.

One of the favourite tactics for sailing close to the wind is the dodge known as transfer pricing. Most affiliates of global corporations trade imports and exports with other parts of their parent company. It is easy for multinationals to over-charge their subsidiary for imports supplied to it, and under-pay it for its exports to the parent, hence siphoning off concealed profits. Few poor countries have the accounting expertise to police this kind of sleight of hand. Latin American studies indicate that multinationals may regularly overcharge their subsidiaries for inputs by anything between 16 per cent and 700 per cent, and pay them perhaps 40 per cent below the going price for their output. On the basis of similar data, the economist Constantine Vaitsos has calculated that US drug companies in Colombia, which declared profits of 6·7 per cent for tax purposes in one year, had a real rate of return of 79 per cent. Rubber companies were declaring profits of 16 per cent but earning 43 per cent. If these figures are representative, then the true level of repatriated income of multinationals in the early seventies may have ranged from $20 billions to $90 billions.

Resources for whose development?

The multinationals are key agents in another depredation which in the long term could jeopardize the future growth of much of the Third World, that is, the auction of its natural resources to the wasteful West. North American and Western Europe between them take something like two thirds of world imports of fossil fuels, three quarters of metal ores and iron and steel, and four fifths of non-ferrous metals and non-metals. In 1975 North America and Europe burned up just over half the world's total energy consumption. While Latin Americans used 813 kilograms of coal equivalent per head, Asians 545 kilos and Africans only 395 kilos, the people of the United States used up nearly 11,000 kilos each and Europeans over 4,000 each. These figures show clearly whose populations are the greatest threat to world resources.

While the less developed countries produced one third of world output of minerals in 1970, they consumed only 6 per cent. Four fifths of their production was exported to the West. And, except for North America and Oceania, western countries were becoming increasingly dependent on imports. In 1950, Western Europe imported 65 per cent of her consumption of nine key minerals – by 1970 she was importing 73 per cent. The share of imports in Japan's consumption rose from 17 per cent to 89 per cent over the same period, and Japan's multinationals were scouring the world, tying up supplies of minerals in long-term contracts.

For the Third World, the most obvious danger of this rate of consumption in the West is that of outright exhaustion. The United States Bureau of Mines has estimated that known reserves of silver, mercury and fluorspar may be exhausted in less than fifteen years; reserves of lead, tin and zinc within twenty years; of copper and tungsten before the end of the century; and of bauxite (for aluminium), sulphur, antimony and titanium early in the twenty-first century. Known reserves of fuel oil will not take us much beyond the end of this century.

In reality, complete exhaustion of most of these minerals is unlikely to be quite so imminent. As reserves of high-grade ores run down, prices rise and provide a stimulus to new exploration and the discovery of new reserves. They also make the exploitation of lower grades of ore a profitable venture. These have more impurities and cost more to mine and refine, but are much more abundant. This mechanism has kept up the world's stock of known resources so far. For most minerals, estimates of known reserves have not decreased with use, but increased as new deposits were discovered. However, it would be foolishly optimistic to assume that this process can be our fairy godmother forever. For several minerals – tungsten, tin, manganese – known reserves have decreased or increased only a little since the late forties.

If the real prices of key minerals do rise, those Third World countries lucky enough to be sitting on rich deposits will, of course, benefit. Those without will find the bar they have to leap into industrialization correspondingly raised. The stakes for entering the game will be upped, and quite a few players may no longer be able to opt in. The sudden oil price rise of 1973–5 was a harbinger of future problems, and was a serious setback to progress of industrialization in the non-oil-rich poor countries. Lower-grade ores of metal also demand more energy to exploit: so the deepening energy crisis will inevitably raise the price of other materials. Price rises for mineral resources also make recycling a much more economical proposal. But the bulk of material for recycling, including the precious past resources of much of the Third World, will be concentrated in the scrap-heaps of the West.

In the shorter run, the mineral-producing developing countries have other legitimate grievances against the mining multinationals. The companies have concentrated most of their processing facilities in the rich consumer countries, so the minerals that poor countries produce are largely exported in a raw or nearly raw state. In 1970 they processed only 29 per cent of minerals mined in their areas, and collected only 30 per cent of the final value they would have when processed to metal bar stage. The other 70 per cent was pocketed by western shippers and refiners, often the sister companies of the mining concerns.

Mining companies have neglected exploration in developing countries, as they have been afraid of nationalization, high levels of taxation or government interference. In recent years, 85 per cent of exploration expenditure has been invested in the rich countries. As a result, the developing countries, with 49 per cent of the world's land area, have only 38 per cent of the estimated mineral reserves, though there may be much more lying undiscovered and unexploited, because unexplored. So far the great mining multinationals have monopolized the capital, technology and expert manpower needed for exploration. If governments of developing countries wish to expand their reserves, they will have to do more of their own exploration, drawing on foreign aid to finance it and pooling manpower and knowhow with other countries.

Debtors' prison

The loaded dice of the world trade casino and the rising cost of industrialization have led to another chronic problem of developing countries, one that besets all casino habitués: debt.

Since 1950, most non-oil developing countries have tended to run deficits on their current account balance of payments. Part of this has been due to worsening terms of trade, part to high imports of capital goods which are considered essential for development. Until 1975 their balance of payments deficits just went on growing. They amounted to $15·6 billion in 1973. Then came the oil price hikes. In 1974 the deficits soared to $39·5 billions, reaching a high in 1975 of $52·8 billions. By mid-1977 they had subsided a little to $39 billions. By this point the industrial countries had recovered from the oil shock and were breaking more or less even, while the oil producers were running a massive surplus. How did the western countries pull it off? Almost all of them ran a current account surplus with the Third World more or less equal to their deficits with the oil producers.

The non-oil developing countries have covered their persistent deficits and managed to go on importing machinery for development, and essentials like food and fertilizer, by running up an increasing mountain of debt. Their outstanding debts more than trebled, from $54·6 billions in 1969 to $172 billions in 1976. Within this total, debt to private creditors – banks and exporters – at commercial rates of interest, rose twice as fast as debt to government and international agencies, on softer terms. Debts were being incurred to stave off immediate bankruptcy, but at the cost of mortgaging the future. Debt itself was becoming as big a burden on the balance of payments – or bigger – than the terms of trade problem. Debt service payments – that is, repayment of capital and interest – increased rapidly from $7·6 billion in 1969 to $25·6 billion in 1976. New debts were being run up to cover service payments on old debts, and the whole debt burden was inexorably rising. Several large non-oil countries had, by the seventies, run up debts so large that service payments were taking up more than 20 per cent of their export earnings – a very dangerous situation when export earnings are vulnerable to sudden changes in commodity prices. Over the period 1969–75, debt service payments averaged 27 per cent of export earnings for Egypt, 21 per cent for India, 20 per cent for Pakistan and Sri Lanka. Latin America was becoming a continent of debtors: Uruguay's service payments amounted to 29 per cent of exports, Mexico's to 23 per cent, Peru's to 21 per cent and Argentina's to 20 per cent. Every now and then many Third World countries reach the stage of acute debtor's disease. They have such problems paying back debts that private credit is drying up, exporters are unwilling to supply goods on credit, export insurance agencies will not insure exports to them, banks will not lend to them and even international development banks dare not lend any more. At such a point the debt crisis reaches deep into the political and social fabric of the victim country, cutting living standards of the poor, increasing inequality and strengthening the influence of right-wing groups.

The creditworthiness trap

Countries suffering from an acute attack of debtors' disease are forced to prove their 'creditworthiness' by swallowing bitter medicine – a cure for indebtedness that is often worse for the patient than the disease itself.

The International Monetary Fund has become the principal doctor and consultant in these cases: increasingly private bankers and official loan agencies are waiting for the IMF to give the patient a clean bill of health before they will lend him any more money. Sooner or later the acute debtor is bound to come hobbling along to the Fund asking for extra credit, holding out his tongue for the pill, though he knows it will produce the most appalling convulsions in his system.

The creditors and their conditions for lending further money are not the root problem in all this. They have no interest in bringing a country to its knees. Their responsibility is to see that the money they lend will be repaid. The real root of the problem is the fact that so much debt is run up in the first place, and for that, the whole international economic order is responsible.

The patient with acute debtors' disease has to take enough medicine to show that the disease will not recur as soon as he leaves hospital – in other words, that he will not start running up appalling balance of payments deficits which will make him likely to default even on these lifebelt loans. A country that wants more credit has to get its balance of payments into a healthy state.

Usually the International Monetary Fund insists on a quick and painful devaluation of the currency. This is intended to make imports more expensive and cut the import bill. But it has other effects. It fuels inflation. If the country is not self-sufficient in food – as many Third World countries are not – it

will push up food prices and hit the nutrition and labour productivity of the poorest.

Deflation at home is usually also part of the IMF prescrip-
tion, like a good hard purge or the application of a dozen
leeches. Deflation is intended to cut spending power in the
country so it can afford fewer imports. But, once again, there
are very unpleasant side effects. Interest rates may be raised,
which slows down investment. The government is expected to
slash its own spending heavily. This may involve cutting back
on important development projects, cutting food subsidies –
again, hitting the poor hardest – putting up transport and
petrol prices, and raising taxes.

The patient may also be encouraged to attract an inflow of
foreign capital, inviting the multinationals to set up shop. And
that brings with it a whole host of further requirements such
as relaxing controls over repatriation of profits, or clamping
down on troublesome trade unions.

Third World countries often impose such strictures on
themselves. It is the debt problem and the need to prove
creditworthiness that drives them to it. This is why committed
nationalists and socialists in the Third World paradoxically
open their doors to multinational private enterprise. Governments with plummeting commodity revenues are often forced
to cut back expenditures and raise taxes.

But self-medication is preferable to an IMF-administered
dose. The IMF's articles require it to disapprove of exchange
and import controls, because they prejudice (though only
slightly) the rest of the international economic community. Yet
these methods are often a less painful way of cutting a
balance of payments deficit, and import controls, in addition,
give protection to local industry.

Whether the creditworthiness package is self-imposed or
IMF-imposed the results are similar. Real incomes drop. Those
of the poorest groups are worst hit, so malnutrition and disease
increase automatically, with all their consequences for work
and education. Increased vulnerability of the poor will make
marginal smallholders even more likely to sell their holdings –

hence inequality on the land will increase. Home-based industry may be severely shaken by higher interest rates and the shrinking of the home market. Devaluation and higher interest rates are not entirely a bad thing: they make capital more expensive and therefore encourage business to change to more labour-intensive methods. But the value of this is wiped out if multinationals, with their highly capital-intensive methods, move into the breach left by bankrupt local entrepreneurs.

The creditworthiness trap tends to slow down reform aimed at reducing inequalities, hamstring important development programmes and strengthen the political influence of anti-reform groups. A socialist government will have difficulty accepting a creditworthiness package, which will go against all its principles; but delay will result in even more stringent requirements. If there is delay, debt and declining government revenues will force the government to introduce some elements of the package. The result, in the Third World, is usually rioting on the streets and paralysing strikes. If an election is forthcoming the government may lose it. If not, internal chaos will increase pressures for repression, suspension of human rights, and military intervention. Sometimes debt is caused by imprudent government spending to win votes or glory. More often it is caused by the defects in the international economic order. Debts are often rescheduled: after all, deferred payment is better than default. But the West is unwilling to accept fundamental reforms, so debtor countries are pushed into crises that strengthen internal mechanisms of inequality.

Reform of the international economic order is essential not only to transfer more resources to the Third World, but also to ease the way for internal reform. National and international inequalities are closely interrelated: social justice on a world level will help the cause of social justice inside the developing countries.

Giving with one hand: so-called aid

'It is more blessed to give than to receive.'
Acts 20:35

The word 'aid' means help. It implies a one-way traffic of assistance. It connotes charity. It makes the giver feel warm and self-righteous about his own generosity and is supposed to make the receiver feel grateful for it. The crowning irony of an international economic order that takes so much from the poor countries is that the small proportion the rich give back is labelled 'aid'. And they are giving back less now than ever before. Aid from western donors amounted to 0·52 per cent of their combined gross national products in 1962. As their wealth increased, one might have expected that aid might have increased more than correspondingly, as a richer man has more to spare over and above his basic needs. Instead, there was a steady decline in the proportion of GNP given as aid right down until 1973, when it reached the all-time low of 0·3 per cent, rising again slightly to 0·33 per cent in 1976, but dropping again to 0·31 per cent in 1977.

Perhaps the sense of colonial guilt was receding and there was greater resentment at the growing political rebelliousness of developing countries.

Most of the decline in aid was accounted for by the three countries which in the early sixties were the most generous donors. Britain's aid dropped steadily from 0·52 per cent of her GNP in 1962 to 0·38 per cent in 1977. The United States' fell from 0·56 per cent to 0·22 per cent. The value of British aid in 1975, at constant prices, was actually $10 million lower than in 1965, while that of the United States was worth $1,656 million less. France's official aid halved from 1·27 per cent of her GNP in 1962 to 0·63 per cent in 1977. Though this figure seems a high proportion, it is really a gross deception. Some 40 per cent of it went to France's colonies, dependencies and overseas departments and is no more aid than the Common Market's grants to its depressed regions. Nearly half of French aid went on technical cooperation. In France's case, this involves the dumping of raw French national service conscripts on their present and former colonies, mostly to indoctrinate their schoolchildren with the glories of French language and culture. Britain, too, classes development funds paid to her dependencies as 'aid'.

The fact that western aid did not decline even more was due to the rise of a new class of donor nation – small, relatively prosperous northern countries with enlightened electorates. Sweden, who was giving only 0·12 per cent of her GNP as aid in 1962, became the first country to pass the aid target of the United Nations Second Development Decade – 0·7 per cent of GNP. She gave 0·99 per cent in 1977, while the Netherlands gave 0·85 per cent and Norway gave 0·82 per cent. No other countries came up the target in 1977, though Denmark gave a creditable 0·61 per cent, Canada 0·51 per cent and Belgium 0·46 per cent.

The total aid given by western countries in 1977 amounted to $14·76 billion.

The communist countries' performance was even less creditable. At one point they seemed to be using aid to make a bid for Third World influence. In 1973, they were giving $1·1 billion to developing countries, but three years later this had halved to $0·5 billion, or one thirtieth of one per cent of their GNPs.

The oil producers, by contrast, became very significant donors in the seventies. In 1973 they gave $1·3 billion to the Third World. Three years later their aid total had risen to $5·2 billion. This amounted to a colossal 2·14 per cent of their combined gross national products, seven times the proportion the West was giving. Saudi Arabia, the United Arab Emirates and Quatar each gave about 5 per cent of their national incomes in aid. Iran, a populous country needing most of its funds for its own development, gave a higher proportion than any western country – 1·1 per cent of GNP. Even Nigeria, with a 1976 income of only $380 per head, outperformed the United States, Japan and Switzerland, giving 0·28 per cent of her GNP.

What, in theory, ought one to expect of good aid? As far as its sources and destinations go, it surely ought to conform to the old principle 'From each according to his ability, to each according to his need'. To pass as charitable, it ought to be given without self-interest or strings. As currently practised, 'aid' lives up to neither of these expectations.

There is no relationship between aid given and the ability to pay. The West's three most powerful economies came low on the list of generosity: the USA gave only 0·22 per cent of GNP in 1977, Germany 0·27 per cent and Japan 0·21 per cent. Switzerland, with the highest per capita income of any western country, gave only 0·19 per cent. Three of these countries, at the same time as they were pleading public penury, were pumping massive amounts of private funds into the Third World for the purpose of extracting an eventual profit. The United States could afford 0·82 per cent of her 1975 GNP for this, Germany 0·87 per cent of her 1976 income, while the Swiss invested 1·08 per cent in 1975 and 2·09 per cent in 1976.

Just how low a priority aid has in the minds of western governments and public can be seen from spending patterns in the United States. In 1975, she gave just over $4 billion in aid. This was barely ahead of the $3·7 billion Americans spent on brokerage charges and investment counselling in that same year, but behind the $4·3 billion blued on barbershop, beauty parlour and bath services. Twice as much went on non-durable toys and sport services as on aid, smoking burned up four times as much, and drinking swallowed six times as much.

The level of aid stems not from ability to pay, but from political attitudes with long historical and cultural pedigrees. The USA has a perennial tendency to insularity which has recently been reinforced as Third World countries reject her political and economic leadership. Switzerland's isolationist attitudes came to the fore in a referendum in June 1976, asking whether the country should contribute to the funds of the International Development Association, which lends to the poorest developing countries. 56 per cent voted against. A 1977 survey of British public opinion found that two thirds of respondents felt Britain was too poor to concern herself with aid, and less than half thought Britain should give aid.

Attitudes like these stem from chauvinistic ignorance of the extent of need in the Third World. Instead of blindly following public opinion, political leaders ought to attempt to change it. Ethnocentric education systems could help by teaching children about the problems of three quarters of the human race. By and large the function of educating public opinion, in all but a handful of western countries, is going by default. Significantly, the three countries with the best aid performance also spent most on education about development. In 1975 Sweden spent 15p (30 cts) per head, Norway and the Netherlands 10p each. By contrast, Germany spent 2p and Britain a mere 0·3p.

Aid is not going to those who need it most. In 1975 the largest amount of aid per head – $11·60 – went to the richest group of developing countries, those with per capita incomes of $1,000 or more. The least developed countries did next best, with $7·50 per head, but the other countries with average incomes below $200, which contained 46 per cent of the world's population, got least of any group, only $3·40 per head.

The distribution of aid corresponds not to need, but to client relationships, historical links, political reliability in the cold war. In this respect the otherwise generous Arabs are the worst offenders, giving overwhelmingly to other Arab or Moslem League countries. In 1975 Arab countries got 81 per cent of the aid given by the countries of OPEC – Egypt alone getting 42 per cent of the total. In 1976 aid was less partially distributed, but just five countries – Egypt, Pakistan, Syria, India and Jordan – got 70 per cent of OPEC aid.

The terms of aid are important too. Ideally, it should be made up of outright grants and not loans. It should be multilateral – that is, channelled through the United Nations agencies, the World Bank and the regional development banks, because they have the necessary impartiality and expertise for effective programmes in the real interests of the receivers. And aid should not be tied to the purchase of goods from the donor country, because that prevents the recipient from getting the best bargain for his money and reinforces his trade dependence on the donor.

The grant element in aid has been creeping up every year

and reached 89 per cent in 1977. Because of the loan element in past aid, repayment of past loans has been eating increasingly into aid transfers – they took up 22 per cent of total aid in 1975. Aid is still largely bilateral. In 1977 only 31 per cent was channelled through the multilateral agencies, though this was a great improvement on 1965, when they received only 6 per cent.

And the bulk of aid is still tied to purchase of goods from the donor country. Some 60 per cent of aid was tied in 1975, though this fell to 48 per cent in the following year. The worst in this respect were the United States, Britain and France, all with 60 per cent of their aid tied in 1976, though Belgium, Canada and the Netherlands were pretty bad offenders too. Tied aid is little better than a disguised subsidy to the donor country's exporters. In that, it is typical of aid as currently given: basically an instrument for the furtherance of national self-interest.

How much do we really owe the Third World?

It should be possible, in summary, to calculate how much the western-dominated world economic order extracts from developing countries, by methods which the Third World itself does not regard as legitimate. This is not the place, nor am I the person, to make such a calculation, but a rough order of magnitude can be outlined.

One: Paul Bairoch has estimated that declining terms of trade cost the Third World between $3·5 billion and $11 billion dollars in 1962, and anything from $5 billion up in 1970. Taking the lowest 1962 figure as average for the whole period of declining terms of trade between 1953 and 1973, one could estimate that the cost to the poor countries was anything from $70 billions up. Repayment of this at prevailing interest rates might cost $7 billion a year.

Two: the multinationals are now taking out at least $7 billion a year more than they are putting in, on official figures alone, and probably a good deal more via transfer payments.

Three: the brain drain is costing the Third World at least $5 billion a year.

Four: service payments on non-oil countries' debts, accumulated as a result of all the imbalances of the international economic order, averaged around $16 billions a year between 1971 and 1976.

Five: it might do to think about a figure for reparation: for the exactions of colonial regimes in taxes, rents, tributes, thefts and plunder, trading profits, raw materials bought at a fraction of their value. Plus the damages wreaked on life, property and industry by uninvited conquest and repression and enforced 'free trade'. Less, to be fair, an allowance for any genuinely productive investment such as railways, roads and irrigation systems. I shall not even attempt a guess at the total, which would probably be astronomical.

As a small taster recall the calculations made by the Chilean government of Salvador Allende when deciding on compensation for nationalizing the copper multinationals. The Chileans estimated that the companies had made excess profits of $774 millions and that far from having a right to any compensation, the companies actually owed Chile $378 millions.

Leaving aside the question of reparations, the total cost of the inequities in the prevailing economic order appears to be at least $35 billions a year, on the most conservative estimates. This figure is, of course, only the crudest of guesses, but it gives some idea of the order of aid necessary simply to restore the balance, let alone really qualify for the name of aid. This is two and a half times the amount given by the western nations in 1977, or about 0·75 per cent of their GNP. Paul Bairoch has calculated – arguing from needs rather than entitlements – that western countries should be giving 2 per cent of their national incomes as aid, if Third World countries are to be helped to achieve more rapid rates of growth.

The benefit to the poor of the Third World, even taking the 'entitlement' of an annual extra $22 billions in aid from the West, would be far greater than the cost to the West. If it were concentrated on the poorer countries (with per capita incomes below $520 in 1976) it would add up to 7 per cent of their national product. This could double their real, growth-producing investment. If devoted entirely to the poorest countries (1976, incomes below $265) it would amount to 19 per cent of their GNP and could completely revolutionize the prospects for 1,210 million people.

To prevent the drain of funds continuing in the future, it will be necessary to correct some of the inequities and iniquities of the international economic order, along the lines that Third World countries have themselves suggested throughout the north–south dialogue.

The new common fund for commodities, acting in the interests of producers, will help to counteract fluctuations in prices. To keep prices from deteriorating in the long run, co-ordination among developing countries is needed to restrict the supply. More commodity cartels like OPEC are needed. But developing countries can never prosper as long as primary commodities are their chief meal ticket. They have to diversify, and each one of them should aim at maximum feasible self-sufficiency in food. The development of industry is a more difficult problem. As the West looks set to become more protectionist, the best bet seems to be to develop regional markets, with each country in a region specializing in certain products.

With reforms like these, debt would become a less pressing problem. In the meantime, the International Monetary Fund ought to become more tolerant of exchange and import controls, and more considerate of the welfare of the poor in the spending cuts they urge on debtor governments. With a strengthened balance of payments, developing countries would be less at the mercy of multinationals, more able to dictate their own terms instead of competing with each other as to who can offer the most concessions.

19. Something is Rotten in the State: The Politics of Poverty

'Your pocket will decide.' *Ghanaian bribe request*

The cancer of corruption

When I lived in western Nigeria I had a steward called Sunday. He was an Efik tribesman from the Eastern Region. A lithe, energetic young man, he ruptured himself playing football one afternoon and developed a hernia like a balloon. He had to go to hospital for an operation, which cost, officially, £9 ($18) or the best part of a month's wages. But the real price was £18. The extra £9 went in bribes to the nurses, of the Yoruba tribe, who had intimated that things might not go too well for Sunday if he didn't pay up. But if he did, he would get extra special treatment and double the amount of penicillin (because more must equal better). The nurses were already getting government salaries to do the work: now they were expecting to be paid again, by the public who had already paid in taxes and fees, as if public service was their own private business.

Corruption was there, invisible, in all dealings between public and officials. Even the law was administered according to ability to pay. I once travelled in a mammy wagon – a lorry converted for transporting people – the back of which the greedy owner had loaded with at least twenty tons of yams, leaving about three feet for twelve passengers to crush together in. The load was way beyond the legal limits and sure enough the first policemen we passed stopped us. Their job was to enforce the law, but they suggested that the offence might be overlooked in exchange for a consideration: they would exempt us from the law, as if the law were nothing more than their private whim. The driver duly handed over his £1 and drove on. A few miles down the bush road, the back axle broke and we had to spend the night on the roof, with leopards howling in the distance.

No one guards the guards themselves in a country riddled

with corruption. If you wanted a driving licence – the pass to a lucrative chauffeur's job – you had to pay the examiner £10, Sunday told me. If you did, you would pass, however bad you were. If you didn't, no amount of skill would save you from failure. If you wanted a good watch, cut price, then you had to go to Lagos, where customs officers sold stuff they had confiscated. They were employed to prevent smuggling, yet some of them were the biggest smugglers in the country.

And if you wanted a job, in a land where good jobs were hard to come by, then naturally you had to pay for it. At the university where I taught, all new lecturers would pass first through the guest house before being allocated a house. The chief cook had a nice little side line: he would recommend people as stewards, provided they paid him two weeks' wages if they were taken on. One of Nigeria's innumerable corruption inquiries found that the town clerk of Igbo, who had paid £400 ($800) to get his own job, extracted £100 from anyone wanting a clerking job in the town hall, unless they happened to be a member of his family, in which case they got the job free. In the same town three town councillors promised the same official tailoring contract worth £17 to three separate tailors, for £3 each. Honest corruption is where the bribee delivers the goods he has been bribed for. This was dishonest corruption.

Corruption is a cancer at the heart of most Third World states. It eats away at the foundations of trust between people and their rulers. It exemplifies the two key weaknesses of the developing state: the unholy marriage of political and economic power, whereby money buys influence, and power attracts money; and the 'softness' of the state, to use economist Gunnar Myrdal's term – its inability to apply and enforce its own laws and regulations, so that reform – even if it is legislated – rarely gets put into effect.

Corruption riddles every part of the public edifice like a bad infestation of woodworm. Along the coast from Nigeria, an official commission of inquiry into bribery and corruption in Ghana, reporting in 1975, found such practices were rife in no less than fifty-four government departments: 'The list is a roll call of practically every department of state, office, corporation and institution in the country.' The commission went on to enumerate 162 separate activities where corruption was practised. A sampler: staff appointments, promotion, transfers; clearance of goods from customs; grading of cocoa; issue of labour cards to the unemployed; allocation of market stalls; leakage of exam questions to students; privileges for prisoners; the sale of files on criminal investigations to the criminals being investigated. Nothing was sacred and secure against graft: mortuary attendants were even demanding payment to release dead bodies to relatives. And priests were extracting 'gifts' in exchange for burying non-churchgoers in consecrated ground.

The most common method used by Ghanaian officials would be to confuse and fluster members of the public with the complex procedures of bureaucratic red tape, or subject them to intolerable delays – and then suggest that a bribe might produce a quick solution or preferential treatment (this is known as 'speed money'). The bribe is rarely solicited openly. Instead, suggestive phrases are used which have developed into a whole language of fraud, from the relatively direct: 'loosen your hand', 'bring out a feed for me', 'let your pocket decide', 'let something talk'; to the ambiguous: 'are you strong?', 'go behind the truck', 'stretch my neck', 'see me in the dark', 'let me laugh'; to the positively bizarre: 'clean Nana's sandals', 'utter a hornbill cry', or 'let your armpit collect water'.

Widespread corruption, the committee concluded (and their conclusions are valid for all developing countries with the problem), created a climate of moral degeneration and made a mockery of government. It was a symptom of government incompetence, and in itself further undermined government's ability to rule. Corruption was rarely uncovered – often those responsible for eradicating it themselves became corrupt. Even if they did not, evidence was hard to come by: if the bribe-giver had actually received the service he paid for, he was a satisfied customer and so kept his mouth shut. If he was a victim of 'corruption with cheating added' he could not prove it, as there are no written contracts for corrupt deals.

Corruption does not only weaken government and undermine social discipline at all levels. It is, in addition, another of the mechanisms by which inequalities are created and increased. Corruption is the use of public office for private gain. Some commentators say it is caused by low salaries in the public sector and could be cured by increasing them. But in most countries public-sector jobs are already overpaid in relation to the average income. If you pay people more, it is quite possible that they will simply develop even more inflated expectations and charge more for bribes. Corruption increases differentials: it gives a free, unseen pay rise to people already earning many times the poor man's income. The corrupt, who have been dubbed the kleptocracy by political scientist Stanislaw Andrewski, are using their political power to extract an economic surplus.

And the higher the office, the bigger are the stakes to be won. Ghana's Nkrumah was said to have salted away £4 million ($8 million). Trujillo, Dominican president for two decades, accumulated $400 million. The Venezuelan *caudillo* Marcos Perez Jimenez had only 105,000 bolivars to his name when he took over the helm of state in 1948. When he left, in 1958, he had amassed a fortune of 80 million bolivars. His public trial found he had taken commissions on big government contracts for viaducts, planes, tanks, launches. Another of his tricks was to force people to sell supplies to the government at inflated prices and give him the excess over the normal price. By similar means the Nicaraguan dictator Somoza accumulated enough wealth from the thirties to buy half the land and industry in the country. He turned political power into economic power, which made his political power even stronger.

From the user's point of view, corruption means that money talks. Import licences, government contracts, jobs, educational success are given out not according to rational principles such as need, ability or place in the queue, but according to who can pay most. The rich can buy themselves further advantages over the poor. And, as we shall see, they can buy themselves exemption from laws designed to redistribute some of their surplus wealth and income to the poor. Corruption diverts social reform. It can also pervert and hamstring development. It can undermine the entire economy of a state, make a mockery of rational planning, and lead to substandard civil engineering that costs more in lives than it shaves off in materials.

From corruption to clampdown: India's Watergate

India has suffered from all these malignancies in advanced form. There is an invisible tumour in the Indian economy known as black money. This is income that has not been declared so as to avoid tax, or income from illegal activities such as selling goods on the black market. Black money is hidden away in unofficial account books kept in locked drawers. Physically, it may be stored in gold and jewels: one household raided by the Bombay police had kitchen pots and pans made of gold concealed under nickel plating. Black money multiplies like mould on stale bread, because if it is used in trade and business any profits automatically become black money. So more and more of the official economy can be eaten up by this unofficial economy over which the government has no control. In 1971 the Direct Taxes Enquiry Committee estimated that, in 1961, black money amounted to 5 per cent of the national income. In 1968–9, the Indian state may have lost taxes on $2,000 million (£1,000 million) of income.

India is riddled with corruption from the lowest levels up to the highest. Tourists to the Taj Mahal may have noticed that the attendants have turned face to the wall the notice saying that on no account should they be tipped, and actually order humbler-looking Indian visitors to leave gratuities. Owners of food ration shops keep the ration cards of dead or removed people and go on getting their allocation so they can sell it on the black market. Adulteration of everything from milk and drugs to fertilizer is common: every now and then a quiet massacre will take place as dozens of people die from adulterated liquor or poisonous pills sold as cure-alls. As Morarji

Desai told me before he became prime minister: 'In India we do not have Watergate, we have floodgate.'

India's endemic corruption led directly to political chaos in 1974 and 1975, culminating in Mrs Gandhi's two-year dictatorship. The case is worth quoting at length as it interweaves several of the characteristic problems of the politics of poor nations, from restive students to rioting mobs and repression.

What became known as the 'agitation' started in Mahatma Gandhi's home state of Gujarat, in January 1974, when the hostel bills in one of Ahmedabad's engineering colleges were suddenly raised by 50 per cent. The students' protest degenerated into a riot and they set fire to their rooms and laboratories. It is no accident that they were engineering students, as this field had one of the highest rates of graduate unemployment. The protests spread to other colleges and an organizing committee was formed. The students tried to see beyond their immediate sectional interests. They decided, somewhat simplistically, that the root cause of their higher mess bills was general inflation, fostered by corrupt politicians. The rumour they picked up to prove this was that Gujarat's portly, balding chief minister, Chimanbhai Patel, had been asked by Congress Party's High Command in Delhi to collect 2·5 million rupees (about £140,000 or $280,000) towards the cost of crucial state election campaigns in Uttar Pradesh. He was said to have collected this money from the edible-oil manufacturers of the state, in return for permission to sell oil freely outside the state. Gujaratis are mostly vegetarians and use copious quantities of *vanaspati* for frying. At this time supplies of oil did become scarce and prices rose. The corruption allegation was the simplest explanation. Chimanbhai denied it when I met him: but he freely conceded that Congress High Command might have collected the money directly in similar ways.

The students burned effigies of Chimanbhai. They held mock trials of politicians. They ceremonially buried a time capsule of corruption, as Mrs Gandhi had buried a capsule of official Indian history. And they used Gandhi's old methods of civil disobedience, hijacking buses, surrounding politicians in the street, staging sit-down strikes that paralysed the traffic and general strikes that paralysed entire cities. Under the cover of this chaos, the urban mobs ran amok, as they always seem ready to, rioting away the frustrations of poverty in a frenzy of arson, looting and communal attacks on Moslems. The police responded with characteristic hysteria, suppressing hostile crowds with *lathi* (truncheon) charges and volleys of rifle fire, not over the heads of demonstrators, but into their bodies. More than a hundred people were killed in police firings before order was restored. One Indian judge complained that there were more police firings now than under the British. Another called the police 'the largest organized gang of lawless elements in the country'.

Chimanbhai finally resigned on 9 February 1974, pushed by Mrs Gandhi who had never liked him, and president's rule was imposed. Only three days after the trouble in Gujarat ended, the state of Bihar exploded.

Although it has a major part of India's mineral wealth in coal, iron ore, uranium and bauxite, and two of the largest steel works in Asia, Bihar is India's poorest state in terms of per capita income. The profit from its wealth has gone into the pockets of a small class of large landowners, capitalists and politicians.

In Bihar government has often been run as if it were a private family business. In 1970 the Aiyar commission reported on charges of corruption against six former ministers who had held office between 1946 and 1967. Former chief minister Krishna Ballabh Sahay was found to have granted mining leases to his own son, in preference to more qualified competitors, and to have exempted him from ten years' rent. He encouraged the state to take over the near-bankrupt car firm of a friend. He protected the black market activities of other friends by getting criminal proceedings withdrawn.

The former Bihar irrigation minister Mahesh Prasad Sinha evolved a watertight system for milking the state. First he appointed two henchmen of his, over the heads of their betters, to the key posts of chief engineer and chief administrator of the river valley projects – these aimed to control the floods of the wandering tributaries of the Ganges and improve irrigation, and hence were crucial to the prosperity and even lives of Biharis. With the help of his stooges, Sinha awarded contracts to favoured firms by manipulating the tender requirements to suit them. He also authorized overpayment of contractors. So key contracts were awarded on the basis of corruption rather than competence, and strict standards were not enforced. The protective barriers of the river valley projects have collapsed under floods, making millions homeless and ruining their crops and fields.

To protest against continuing abuses of this kind, students started the same kind of disruptive protests as in Gujarat, but this time the confrontation was more intense. The students were joined by J. P. Narayan and his Gandhian followers and by opposition political parties. They were demanding the resignation of the government, which they said had forfeited its mandate through corruption. On the other side, Mrs Gandhi was determined not to give in, because the chief minister Abdul Ghafoor was one of her protégés, and in any case it looked as if similar tactics might be applied on a national level. This was, in fact, what started to happen.

One of the chief targets of corruption allegations was India's railway minister, L. N. Mishra, who also happened to be the political boss of Bihar. In his career as a businessman and politician Mishra had been accused of taking land belonging to outcastes and tribals; conniving at substandard work on dam projects; bribing MPs to cross the floor so as to topple state governments that looked like investigating him; suppressing investigations of the black market sale of *ghee* (clarified butter) and rice smuggling from Nepal; selling the use of railway wagons under his personal control; and granting import licences to traders who did not use them, but sold them to other people. Before a general investigation could be held, Mishra met his end in a bomb explosion on 2 January 1975 as he was inaugurating a new railway line at Samastipur, Bihar.

A thorough and totally impartial inquiry into central and state corruption could perhaps have defused the anti-corruption agitation. But Mrs Gandhi herself was in a weak position to order an inquiry, as her own son Sanjay was the target for accusations of nepotism. In 1970, when he was only twenty-two, Sanjay had been awarded a coveted licence to produce a people's car for India. All he had to offer against the competition of established engineering firms was a home-made car and the experience of an unfinished apprenticeship with Rolls-Royce in Britain. Apart from a total of just twenty cars cobbled together by hand-made methods, the factory produced little other than mounting losses.

Mrs Gandhi's response to the anti-corruption agitation was not reform, nor an inquiry into corruption, but the imposition of the so-called emergency, democratic India's first taste of dictatorship.

Corruption has its traditional antecedents in the Third World. The indigenous empires had their bureaucrats and tax farmers to collect tribute and taxes, and not all of this would find its way to the treasury. In Africa, chiefs would receive customary gifts for allocating land rights or settling disputes – a personal reward for a personal service. And petty kings and emperors made their living from extracting protection money from traders passing through.

Then the Europeans came along with their endemic hypocrisy. For them, the state was supposed to aim at the general welfare, by impartial, rational means, with everyone equal before the law. Even their own practice violated the theory: employees of the East India company enriched themselves by all means licit or otherwise. Modern-style corruption is largely a European invention: it is nothing more than the reality of individual or group greed masquerading under the façade of rationality. At independence, the new states did not take naturally to bureaucratic impartiality. Personal, face-to-face, hand-to-hand methods were more in the local tradition than long-winded procedures, especially as the majority of people were illiterate.

Loyalty to family, village or tribe came before loyalty to this strange new entity, the modern state. And the get-rich-quick mentality spread as people jockeyed for status, in the social vacuum created by independence, in the only universally acknowledged manner: material ostentation. India's black money commission lamented the 'marked tendency towards putting greater premiums on material values, and a growing craze for getting rich quick by all means, fair or foul'.

These factors explain the greater *propensity* to corruption in the Third World. The *opportunity* is provided by the poverty of the economy and the complexity of bureaucratic regulation. The government controls so many precious scarce resources, from jobs and houses to contracts and licences. These things are all officially free or have a fixed price, but demand for them far exceeds supply so they can easily command a premium or black market price.

Corruption can contribute to mass poverty, as well as to elite wealth. If a businessman is willing to pay a bribe, he sees it in the nature of an investment which will pay off a profit like any other, helping him to evade taxes, charge excessive prices to the public or the state, or use less materials than the law stipulates. By whatever channel, the extra profit that justifies the 'investment' of a bribe is milked from the masses. Either the state loses revenue that could be spent on development – or the public pay more for their goods. The bribe only appears to come from the businessman's pocket: in reality it is extorted from the public at large.

And wherever power-holders and policy-makers become rich through corruption, the policies they make are less likely to threaten wealth or alleviate poverty. Bureaucrats who own large tracts of urban housing land will advise their ministers against urban land reform. Politicians who run factories or own estates will not vote in favour of more preferential treatment for small businesses (who may compete) or land reform. And, when politics comes to be considered as a path to wealth as well as power, it tends to attract fewer idealists and more opportunists, whose presence speeds up the degeneration process.

The plutocrats: the power of money

Through corruption, political power is used to win economic power. But the converse process is just as common, whereby economic power is used to gain political power. Using all their resources, the wealthy can win political office for themselves or their favoured candidates. They can influence the direction of development policy and put obstacles in the way of any reforms directed against their privilege. Through these converging processes the political and economic elites of the poor countries tend to grow together and fuse. Political and economic inequalities interlock and frustrate the adoption of policies aimed at reducing inequality.

It is not surprising that the privileged try to influence the political system. In the perpetual struggle for survival and advantage that goes on in most developing countries, the state is a focal institution. It controls access to credit, licences and even raw materials. It decides on import tariffs, many prices, and contracts. It is the prime fount of business opportunity in almost all countries. In addition, it passes laws that regulate the balance of wealth and income between social groups: income taxes, indirect taxes, regulations on minimum wages, urban and rural rents and tenancy conditions, and, most explosive of all, laws on the distribution of land and the rights of trade unions. It has, in theory, the power to impose its decisions on any of these matters on the whole society by the use of its control over the police and army, the largest concentrations of force in any country (though in practice, as we shall see, its power to regulate the rich is often limited). With so much at stake, the privileged do not stand idly by and let due democratic process take its course. The bigger the gap between them and the masses, the fewer their scruples in fighting to preserve or increase it.

Large-scale modern industry, big farmers and the modern sector of cities have managed to corner most of the investment and advantage so far, because they have used their superior organization and influence to push things their own way, and away from the small craftsman, workshop owner or subsistence farmer. And they have often succeeded in frustrating genuine reform and redistribution by using their political muscle, either to prevent reform being legislated or, failing that, to prevent it being implemented.

The local power of the big man is immense in the Third World. He has money to buy votes, to bribe politicians, administrators and police, to pay for lawyers. He has social pull and can influence the careers of civil servants. He has economic power over many people through ownership of land, houses, businesses. He uses all of these resources to move things his own way.

He can usually get candidates elected who are to his taste. Votes are a marketable commodity in many developing countries, and poor men's votes are easy to buy in all three continents, either by straight payment, or promise of jobs and other material benefits. Stories of the purchase of votes for around five rupees or two days' wages are commonplace in India. Political scientist F. G. Bailey, in a study of elections in Orissa, found that candidates paid people for their votes on the pretext of their becoming 'agents'. Men were quite ready to sell their votes, he found, because they were poor and needed the money. They felt that the government was distant and free elections were little more than an empty formality that could have no effect on local events. Selling the vote seemed a legitimate business transaction, a way of putting the apparently useless to good use. Although the ballot was secret, the vote sellers usually honoured their side of the bargain.

Where purchase fails, electoral fraud and intimidation can be resorted to. Democracy's roots in the Third World are so tenuous that these practices are widespread. Faked or stolen ballot forms are given out so friends can vote more than once. Dead people vote mysteriously and the living are impersonated. Known supporters of political opponents may be physically prevented from voting. Pakistan's 1977 elections were a veritable jamboree of fraudulent practices, and the ensuing protests over rigging led to military rule. In the 1965 Western State elections in Nigeria the parties dug ditches round polling stations to keep non-supporters away. In India a similar practice is known as 'booth capture' – hired thugs simply take over the polling station and let only supporters or friendly impersonators through. All these practices take money, so the side with the richest supporters has a considerable advantage.

But neither vote purchase nor fraud may be necessary where the rich man simply uses his economic pull over a locality to make people vote the way he wants. The local political boss or *cacique* is a familiar figure in all poor countries (as well as some rich ones). In Asia he may be the biggest landlord or the head of a caste, in Africa the village chief, the transport contractor or cash crop buyer, in Latin America the big estate owner or the lawyer on whom smallholders depend for their constant litigation against one another.

In Colombia, for example, entire villages or parishes will vote as the *cacique* directs, almost to a man. In one polling district all the campaign flags will be red for the Liberals – and at the boundary give way to a uniform blue for Conservatives. There are even urban *caciques* – store owners on whom the poor depend for food supplies and consumer credit, or landlords on whom they rely for a roof over their heads. Politicians who have been elected by the votes drummed together by the *caciques* dare not legislate reforms that go against their interest. For this reason the social policies of Colombia's two main parties are almost indistinguishable in their conservatism. Indeed the joke has it that the only difference between them is that the Conservatives go to the nine o'clock mass and the Liberals to the ten o'clock.

Elections cost money and where there is stiff political competition the privileged can win considerable influence over party policy in exchange for campaign contributions. In India the Congress Party had a smooth ride for two decades after independence, first because it fought for freedom, then largely because it was in government and controlled local jobs, credit, the provision of water, electricity, schools and so on: if both sides were making promises, Congress was more likely to be able to deliver the goods. But in 1969 political competition intensified when Mrs Gandhi split the Congress party into two warring factions. For the 1971 elections more had to be spent on vote-buying, beanfeasts, payments to local bosses, jeeps for candidates and lorries to herd voters to the booths. In 1969, company donations to political parties had been made illegal, but big business was the only possible source of the immense funds needed. Mrs Gandhi's Congress campaigned on a programme of sweeping social reform, but its debts to what Indians call the 'moneybags' meant that it could not carry out its programme. Apart from nationalizing the banks and abolishing the Rajah's privy purses, no fundamental changes in the distribution of wealth or income were undertaken. 'n 1977 the hold of Congress was finally broken: all the money in the world could not save it from defeat after the excess of the sterilization drive.

Despite all these stratagems, reform legislation and even governments sincerely committed to across-the-board reforms sometimes do win through. The privileged then fall back on their local pull, over administrators, judges and police, to prevent reform being enacted, in other words, to evade and even defy the law. The law as generally practised throughout the world is a weapon that the rich can easily handle but the poor can hardly lift. To provide work for lawyers, laws are invariably framed in tortuous jargon copied from hoary British statutes or the Code Napoléon. They are intended to be inaccessible to the common herd, so that anyone who wants access to the law must go through the legal profession.

In almost all developing countries, the institutions of the law prevent equality before the law. The cost of becoming a lawyer ensures that the legal profession, from advocates and solicitors to judges, is largely staffed by members of elite families. Juries are usually selected from among property owners. Even if the poor can get access to the law, decisions are more likely to go in favour of the rich. But access is difficult. The cost of going to law weighs far more heavily on the poor man than the rich, whether in lawyers' fees, the cost of documents, or the cost in money and time lost in travelling to court. The poor man is less likely to be able to get bail guarantees or pay fines, more likely to be remanded in custody before trial and imprisoned after it.

Legal form is one of the principal obstacles to the poor obtaining justice in the Third World.

The battle over the law is well illustrated by the fight of peasants in north-east Brazil to abolish the infamous 'yoke' of compulsory free labour (see page 107). The yoke was already illegal and had been for decades. Landlords were simply ignoring the law, and with impunity, because local police and administrators were choosing not to enforce it. No one did anything about this situation until the Peasant Leagues attempted to alter it in the late 1950s. The leagues, headed by lawyer Francisco Julião, encouraged peasants to refuse the yoke service. When this happened, landlords often resorted to violence — one peasant was threatened by the landlords' *capangas* or thugs, his crops were trampled and his animals killed. He went to law, but here the landlords had other weapons. The parish priest in this case told his parishioners not to give evidence, they complied, and the peasant was evicted. Landlords would intimidate witnesses, force plaintiffs to withdraw their cases. Judges, clerks of the court, surveyors were bribed to rule in the landlords' favour or to pull the wool over the peasants' eyes, confuse them about procedures, tempt them into legal errors that would lose them the case. As Julião has pointed out, it is easy to apply a legal principle against the unprotected, but difficult to use it in their defence. But the privileged do not only ignore reform laws: they frequently break the most basic laws against violence. Landlord violence against the poor is widespread in Asia and Latin America — witness the harassment of Colombian peasants or the intimidation of labourers in India, described in Part Two. The landlord's thug is a familiar institution: there are always enough poor people around willing to let themselves be used against their fellows in this way. The pay is better than for labouring, and it is better to administer violence than be on the receiving end of it.

The local police frequently ignore landlord violence and lawbreaking. They are only likely to intervene if the poor defend themselves or retaliate. Police are usually on the side of the privileged. The local commander will probably mix socially with the local elite – he may be living in their pockets. In any case, his training will have taught him certain stereotypes. Crime, to the typical policeman, is essentially the violation of property rights by the propertyless, not the assertion of excessive or illegal property rights by the propertied. A police presence is usually enough to quieten the poor; but if they resist, then public order itself, the very authority of the state, is challenged and troops may be sent in. This kind of disorder, repeated on a national scale, can often lead to military intervention.

But things need not come to this pass. For the execution of government policy depends on local administrators and they, too, are often in the pockets and at the dinner tables of the rich. They may themselves own land and other property. It is easy for them to delay implementation of radical reform, or to turn a blind eye to evasions. Except where there are vigilant and vigorous local MPs independent of local vested interests, there is no independent check to see how local bureaucrats are carrying out central directives. The local prefect or district officer is himself the eyes and ears of the government. He reports only favourable information up the line to his superiors. Failures or wide defiance of regulations – whether these have occurred with his knowledge or not – will only reflect badly on him. They may cost him his job. So naturally he keeps quiet about them. These little local conspiracies of rich people and government employees are among the most serious obstacles to reform in the Third World. Central governments may not even be aware that their policies are not being carried out.

Bonded labour in India has been outlawed since the 1947 constitution. Official surveys by state governments – each of them eager to prove their own social progress – have often implied that it no longer existed. But it continued to thrive, because labourers were poor, they needed loans for consumption and only private moneylenders would provide these. The only security the landless could offer was their labour. The institution, though illegal, was made inevitable by poverty and the lack of official sources for consumption credits.

In the mid-seventies the number of debt slaves was estimated at half a million. And so, under the emergency, Mrs Gandhi found it necessary to outlaw bonded labour yet again. The Bonded Labour System Abolition Act (surely one of the few acts outlawing what was already illegal) encouraged the setting-up of local vigilance committees to take an active role in stamping out bonded labour, and placed a positive duty on district magistrates to investigate the extent of the practice in their areas and to get rid of it. These provisions were intended to get round the perennial problem of non-application of the law at local level.

Naturally enough, they themselves were not applied either. An International Labour Organization mission to India in 1977 found no evidence of the activities or even the existence of vigilance committees, and reported that few district magistrates had launched investigations. After all, if bonded labour was widespread in their area, that would show they had not enforced the constitution. So they treated each case individually, as it came to their attention. And few cases did, because the moneylenders would not admit the practice and forced their bonded labourers to keep their mouths shut too. The labourers were so poor and needed credit at least in part because other legislation had been ignored. India's land reform laws, which should have given land to the poor, were honoured mainly in the breach – large holdings were simply split up among family members down to the smallest brat in the cradle. Practically every state had minimum wage regulations, but they were a dead letter. The ILO mission found that the average wages being paid were only half the legal minimum in most places.

So the state in most poor countries is weak or 'soft'. It is not fully in control of its own machinery. The brain cannot be sure that the hand is doing its bidding, and has not evolved ways of finding out (for that you need a vigilant press, free of the control of government or vested interests, and that is conspicuously absent in most of the Third World). There is administrative inefficiency, procedures are lax, line discipline is weak. Even dictatorships suffer from this failing. But in most countries it is not simply general bumbling incompetence (though there is an element of that, due to lack of education). The structure does not turn out a set of completely random errors. The errors form a pattern and the incompetence is biased incompetence. The system fails consistently to the advantage of the rich.

The state, in other words, is not uniformly soft. It would be more accurate to describe it as a soft-centred state with an extremely hard exterior: soft to the privileged, hard to the poor, a sort of dictatorship of the elite over the poor masses, while the rich are left to get away, often literally, with murder.

By the various mechanisms described above, the rich are able to control the very apparatus of the state, the machinery of administration, of law and law enforcement at local level. Until that hold is loosed, it will always prove extremely difficult to pass or to enforce laws of the kind that are essential to eradicate poverty and reduce inequality. Measures to combat the insidious political pull of privilege are hard to frame and execute. Clearly the poor need to be organized into peasant leagues, trade unions and cooperatives, so they can press for their rights. The legal system needs to be reformed to give the poor equal access – perhaps through the creation of 'barefoot lawyers' or people's tribunes. Line discipline in the bureaucracy could be tightened up, for example, by the creation of local ombudsmen. Alternatively, a single political party with mass membership can oversee the performance of local administrators. But all these measures can be fought by the rich, using the old methods. They will find ways of perverting any reform as long as the source of their political power – their economic power – remains intact. Similarly the poor are likely to remain weak, politically, as long as they are so economically weak.

Economic reform is difficult without political reform, and political reform difficult without economic reform. The two must go forward hand in hand, in the same way that political and economic privilege have done.

*Ploughshares into swords: the external instability of
developing countries*

If politics have helped to keep poor people poor, they have also
helped to keep the poor nations in poverty.

The typical Third World government is often unstable, much
more liable to wars and civil strife than industrialized nations.
That instability slows up development, eats up funds for
swords that should be spent on ploughshares. Political instability accentuates poverty, and poverty fuels instability, leading sooner or later to dictatorship and repression. The
deprivation of liberty is added to all the other deprivations of
the poor countries.

External instability is yet another of the many curses that
the colonial powers left behind when they pulled out. The
Europeans drew the boundaries between their possessions for-
tuitously, at some outpost where rival garrisons happened to
meet – or boldly sketching arbitrary lines through uncharted
blank spaces on the map. They carved straight through the
ancient territories of kingdoms and tribes, and then sliced up
their own bits, for convenience, into administrative units, with
the same cavalier attitude to established ties.

The Spanish and Portuguese divided up Latin America between them, roughly following a line fixed by a pope who had
never set foot on the continent. At independence the new
Spanish-speaking states emerged according to the boundaries
of the old vice-royalties, or the power bases of the military
caudillos who fought for independence. The new frontiers had
no deep-rooted legitimacy, and were soon challenged in a
series of costly and futile wars. Between 1865 and 1870
Paraguay was decimated in the war of the triple alliance,
against Uruguay, Argentina and Brazil. Bolivia lost the nitrate-
rich Atacama desert, and with it her outlet to the sea, in the
Pacific War of 1879, in which she was allied with Peru against
Chile. As the centenary of this war neared there was talk of a
return match. Bolivia lost more territory in the Chaco war with
Paraguay (1935–7). In 1941 Ecuador and Peru came to blows
over large tracts of Amazon forest. Argentina and Chile have an

ancient dispute over the windswept wastes and islands of Pata-
gonia. None of these old wounds have really healed.

In Asia and especially in Africa (which was carved up before
it had been properly explored) the pieces of territory vacated
by the imperial powers were even more arbitrary. Yet the indigenous groups who took them over clung to their boundaries
as if they were sacred, and armed themselves to the teeth to
defend them. This seems curious, but the explanation is that
the ruling elites who took over power for the most part came
out of the European educated class and did not belong to the
traditional power groups. The sole source of their new power,
wealth and status was the new artificial state. If the states had
reformed into their original ethnic or political components,
power might have reverted to the traditional rulers. But the
attachment to lines on the map has not prevented states from
laying loud claim to the territory of other states. In recent
years territorial claims and disputes have been intensified by
the world-wide search for oil and other resources, the possibility of getting minerals from the sea bed, and the struggle
for dwindling fishery stocks.

In Africa, Somalia invaded the Ogaden desert of Ethiopia, to
reclaim territory conquered in the nineteenth century. Somalia
maintains similar claims against parts of Kenya and Djibouti,
where there are significant groups of Somali descent. A latent
conflict simmers between Upper Volta and Mali over the precise boundaries of local government districts in colonial French
West Africa. Algeria was embroiled against Morocco and
Mauretania over the fate of the former Spanish Sahara.

In Asia the colonial carve-up of Borneo created a permanent
bone of contention between Indonesia, Malaysia and the
Philippines. The first two nearly went to war over it in the
early 1960s. The boundaries of Indochina, criss-crossed by hill
tribes, are disputed. But south Asia has suffered most from
frontier conflicts. India went to war with China in 1962 over
the McMahon line frontier between the two, which China
claimed was forced upon a weak Tibet by the western powers.
The territory involved in the dispute is so remote and sparsely
populated that China was able to build a military road across

the Indian-claimed area of Aksai Chin without the Indians even noticing it. India and Pakistan warred in 1965 over Kashmir, a state of largely Moslem people whose ruler signed them over, without consulting them, to largely Hindu India. Afghanistan and Pakistan are at perpetual loggerheads over the divided Pathan region.

The West bequeathed even the Middle East conflict to the Third World. It was the British, while ruling Palestine under a mandate from the League of Nations, who decided, regardless of the views of the local population, that here was a suitable place to create a 'national home' for a Jewish people who had been hounded into Zionism by European persecution.

As a result of all these latent and blatant troubles, the world has not been at peace for a single day since the Second World War ended. According to Hungarian war analyst Professor Istvan Kende, between 1945 and 1976 there were no less than 133 wars involving eighty states. On an average day twelve wars were being fought, and practically every one of them was in the Third World.

And so the Third World spends a great deal of its limited funds on armaments, in senseless arms races which bring huge profits to western suppliers. The Stockholm International Peace Research Institute estimates that the global arms trade was worth around $10 billions a year in the late seventies. Three quarters of the weapons go to the Third World, and nearly two thirds of the payment goes back to the West. In 1976 the world spent $334,000 million on war, armies and weapons, more than seventeen times what it spent on aid.

The Third World itself burned up $51 billion in military expenditure in the same year. The average developing country spent some 4 per cent of its gross national product. That is no more than the average western country, but the poor nations can ill afford it. This 4 per cent is part of their small economic surplus, and if it were invested in development, it could have a marked effect.

Twelve out of the thirteen countries spending more than 10 per cent of their gross national products on defence in 1975 were developing countries. Military spending in poor countries was often far higher than spending on key development sectors. In 1973, for example, India spent twice as much on arms and armies as on education, and four times as much as on health. Iran spent $73 per head on defence, but only $29 on education and $9 on health.

In individual countries the situation was much more serious. Some of the Middle Eastern countries' development efforts are crippled by military expenditure. The Institute of Strategic Studies in London calculates that Egypt spent 23 per cent of her gross national product on the military budget in 1975. The 1976 budget amounted to $6·1 billions, two fifths of all government spending. Iraq spent 18·7 per cent of her GNP, Syria 15·1 per cent and Jordan 12·2 per cent. Iran, a traditional adversary of Iraq, spent 17·4 per cent of her GNP. Turkey, whose sparring partner over Cyprus and the Aegean is Greece, spent 9 per cent, Pakistan 7·2 per cent and South Korea (divided from the north by the great powers) spent 5·1 per cent and had one in twelve of her men aged eighteen to forty-five in the army.

So the external instability of developing countries helped to keep them poor, causing them to spend on armaments what they could have invested in development. But external instability is closely related to internal instability. It has led to the excessive growth of armies, enhanced their national prestige and importance and hence the likelihood of military coups. And aggressive nationalism has since time immemorial always been a standard ploy for ruling groups wishing to divert attention from conflicts at home. Armies are equally useful for suppressing dissent at home as waging war abroad. The internal instability of poor nations makes them even more prone to external conflicts: poverty and strife at home may help to turn border disputes into outright wars.

Coups and classes: the internal instability of poor countries

'A society divided between a large impoverished mass and a small favoured elite results either in oligarchy (dictatorial rule of the small upper stratum) or in tyranny (popular based dictatorship).

SEYMOUR MARTIN LIPSET

'Another coup in Dahomey.' This is the kind of news that has appeared so many times before that it merits only a down-page filler paragraph on an inside page with a one-line, twelve-point headline. Instability in Third World governments is taken for granted. It is part of the media stereotype, along with famines and disasters. And with some justification. Political scientist Professor S. E. Finer calculates that between 1962 and 1975 there were no less than 104 coups, all but a handful of them in the Third World. Dahomey (now Benin) had six coups between 1958 and 1973, Bolivia had six, Sudan five. In 1975, one quarter of all the sovereign states in the United Nations were ruled by governments that had won power by way of a coup.

Internal instability, like external instability, contributes to the poverty of the Third World. It undermines the confidence of foreign investors and inclines those at home to stash away their funds in Swiss bank accounts rather than invest in industry or agriculture. As one ruling group follows another, development policy is subjected to fits and starts and sudden turnabouts, and key development personnel are liable to have their heads roll in mid-project.

Political stability is a precious treasure which citizens of the handful of cossetted democracies in the West take too easily for granted. Almost every western nation has had its era of revolution or civil war. It can be argued that those nations free of them for the past century or so – and they are an even smaller bunch – owe at least part of their stability to colonialism and neo-colonialism. As that great colonizer Cecil Rhodes pointed out, the colonies provided new lands for settling the surplus labour force, and new markets for selling surplus goods. Without these outlets, unemployment would have been higher, incomes lower and class conflict more bitter, and revolution or fascism would have been the result. 'If you want to avoid civil war, you must become imperialists,' said Rhodes. Significantly, the major industrial nations who were latecomers in the scramble for colonies – Germany, Japan and Italy – were the ones that succumbed to fascism and militarism.

The Third World has had no external pork barrel to dip into to keep its unruly masses happy: on the contrary, its own pork barrel has been depleted to render that service to the West.

Stable democratic government demands other requirements, most of which take several generations to build. It needs legitimacy: that is, the state must command the general consent of its citizens to its rule. Otherwise, it must govern by coercion. If it is to avoid palace intrigues over succession, it needs a set of criteria for the transfer of power from one group of rulers to the next, accepted by all major claimants to power. It thrives – as Aristotle, on the evidence of the Greek city states, was the first to notice – on a large, participating middle class acting as a buffer between the rich and the poor. Few states in the Third World meet any of these requirements.

The modern state, in the Third World, was an alien implant with little legitimacy. In many states, independence from the colonial powers was won by subversion, armed rebellion or massive civil unrest, rather than by agreement with the backing of popular referenda. It is difficult for any state or government born out of violence to have strong legitimacy, freeing it from the need to continue ruling by force. The people of the new states such as India or Nigeria were united by patriotism against the British, but it was a reactive patriotism, a temporary unity directed against a common enemy. Once the enemy was removed, internal division came to the fore.

And the new states had to contend with deep-rooted popular attitudes towards government which had been developed during colonial times. Colonial taxes, levies, forced labour, forced cultivation of cash crops, extortionate rents, all these demands of government were unjust, evil impositions which only a fool would willingly or fully comply with. Almost as a natural human reflex, the colonialized peoples developed the ability to comply as little as possible with government orders, without actually getting themselves gaoled or assaulted by a punitive expedition. They learned to conceal, to dissimulate, to lie and cheat officials, to withhold from Caesar what Caesar wrongly claimed was his, while the more courageous resorted to open and sometimes violent defiance. In the colonial situation these minor and major forms of rebellion were heroic and laudable. Unfortunately, habits and attitudes that have been socialized into a new generation as children are slow to die away, and these negative attitudes have persisted into independence. Violence became an accepted method for airing grievances.

In India, for example, Mahatma Gandhi called a general tax strike in Bardoli in 1921, and in 1930 led a ceremonial procession to the sea to pan salt in defiance of British salt taxes. He gave an aura of patriotism to tax evasion, which was to become no less widespread under an Indian government than it had been under the British. And he pioneered the use of civil disobedience to create total chaos. His methods were turned in 1974 and 1975 against a democratically elected Indian government. Where there are shortcomings in the new governments themselves – corruption, favouritism of all brands, ostentatious wealth among the ruling elite – the negative attitudes to government are reinforced. And so loyalty tends to be given not to the state, but to the primary group: the extended family, the village, the tribe. The state is seen simply as a means to advance the interests of these groups, if necessary at the expense of all the rest.

In most Third World countries there is no stable consensus about the means for transferring power. Outgroups rarely hesitate to seize power by violence if the prevailing order does not serve their interests. A single successful coup lasting more than a couple of years can permanently undermine agreement on succession rules. Dictatorships and coup governments have no accepted rules of succession even for themselves. Many derive a temporary stability from a single powerful personality and his charismatic influence: when he goes, chaos breaks out. Military coup governments are even more unstable than the regimes they supplant. They rule only by the right of might, which can be turned against them by the very next group of colonels that decides it can run things better. S. E. Finer has calculated that half of all military regimes last for less than two years. Three out of five are over within five years. He who arrives by the sword is likely to depart by it.

Some coup governments try to evolve into democratic regimes, by winning retrospective approval at the ballot box. Others gradually prepare their people for a return to democracy. But even where democracy is part of the tradition, it is rarely stable in countries that have also known periods of dictatorship. Most Latin American countries have had spells of classical parliamentary government in the past, and in many of them it has alternated almost like clockwork with the rule of the military *caudillo*.

In many countries of Asia and Africa, not only the form of government but even the territorial integrity of the state has been threatened by tribes and other groups demanding a state of their own. The Kurds, split between Iran, Turkey, Syria and Iraq, have been demanding their own state for the best part of the century. Indonesia has been threatened by rebellions in the South Moluccas, Sumatra and West Irian. The Pathans of Pakistan, the Mizos and Nagas of India, the Karens and Shans of Burma, the Montagnards of Vietnam, the Moslems of southern Philippines, have all at one time or another taken up arms to try to win a state that corresponded to their own ideas of what constituted a nation. The partition of India was the result of Moslems' desire for their own state, and of itself led to further problems: Kashmir's persistent claim for autonomy from India, the rebellion in East Pakistan that led to the creation of Bangladesh.

Africa has been torn by secessionist rebellions: Katanga in the Congo, Biafra in Nigeria, Arabs in Negro-dominated Chad, Negroes in Arab-dominated Sudan, Eritreans in Ethiopia.

Palestinian refugees have led to problems in Jordan, Iraq and Lebanon, but in general the much more homogeneous populations of Arab and Latin American states have been far less troubled by separatism. In Africa and Asia, poverty makes cohesive groups with a strong group consciousness even more prone to separatism. If their group is sitting on a source of wealth, as were the Katangese (copper) and the Biafrans (oil), they may resent sharing it with a larger, poorer group. If they are not, they may blame their poverty on mismanagement by the dominant group and see secession as their road to Shangri-La.

The processes of rapid economic change and urbanization are, in themselves, a cause of political instability.

Men and women embedded in the complex web of social obligations and values of traditional rural society are less attracted to extremist or ethnic political movements. Development is transforming the countries of the Third World into what political scientists term mass societies: societies whose members have no roots, no strong social ties, no investment in the stability of the social system.

Increasing landlessness and unemployment is creating a growing class of men without property, without even a stable source of income, and therefore with no interest in supporting the status quo. Urbanization breaks more bonds, disintegrating the extended family, weakening traditions, stable beliefs and values. People become more susceptible to the appeal of millenarian, nationalistic, ethnic or extremist movements. Similar conditions in western countries earlier this century contributed to the emergence of fascism and communism: in Germany economic recession and the ruin of small businessmen and artisans by large-scale enterprise helped the Nazis win votes and power. Tsarist Russia saw an extremely rapid growth of industry and cities – and the uprooted rural migrants turned new proletariat became the rank and file of the revolution.

A new source of political instability and conflict is gaining increasing prominence in the Third World: social polarization and poverty. The absence of a sizable middle class is a danger for stable democracy. Where states are polarized into a rich elite and a mass of poor people, the poor have nothing to lose from rebellion, while the rich have too much to lose from reform. There is no middle way: he who is not for reform is against it. For any meaningful change to occur, one side must lose what the other side gains.

As we shall see in the next chapter, poverty and inequality have both been deepening in the majority of Third World countries. Static, perennial poverty is often tolerated stoically. Increasing poverty and inequality have spelled political trouble throughout history. In the Third World today they have become more explosive than ever, because they have been accompanied by what has been called the revolution of rising expectations. This has been generated by government rhetoric and the growth of the affluent but small modern sector, to which everyone feels called but few are admitted. The whole of the Third World is tense with expectations that have risen way beyond the limits of possibility.

Governments of all shades, democratic and otherwise, have made grandiose promises of progress and equality of opportunity, to win votes or love, or sometimes to spur people to greater efforts. These pledges have been relayed into the remotest bush villages by transistor radios and party activists. Yet few non-oil governments have been able to live up to the expectations they have created. Funds have been short, while power politics have frequently frustrated reform. The masses compare the slogans with the reality and note the discrepancy. They quietly record the consistent breaking of electoral and coup promises. The longer the accepted channels fail to deliver the goods, the greater direct action seems appealing.

The urban areas are the real powder kegs. The potential for chaos lies simmering beneath the surface, a diffuse tension created by deprivation, injustice, even simple hunger. (Low blood sugar, or hypoglycaemia, common among people who do not eat much, can increase tension and irritability in breaking point.) It can erupt at any moment, sometimes in revolution or demonstration, but more often in acts of disorganized lawlessness. I once saw a thief snatch a watch from a stall in Ibadan market, Nigeria. The owner cried out, and hundreds of men started after the thief in a sudden stampede. He was cornered, beaten and stoned almost to death. It was a frightening outburst of collective anger. The law is a façade, more brittle in most developing countries than in a black American ghetto on a hot summer's night.

Most of the civil strife is undirected. Only two non-elite groups present any kind of organized challenge: trade unions (whether of workers or of peasants) and students. Except in Latin America, and a few isolated countries like Sri Lanka, trade unions are small. Usually only the urban workers -- an already privileged group -- are organized and when this is the case their strikes for higher pay may do nothing to help the cause of the real rural and urban poor. They cannot, in most of the lower-income Third World countries, be considered as a vanguard in the fight for social justice.

Students are a greater threat, not just because of their demonstrations, but because they can, when they manage to look beyond their own egotistical horizons, give expression, theoretical perspective and organizational abilities to the frustrations of the masses. They are an explosive force throughout Latin America, in South-East Asia and the Middle East, though less so in the poorer countries of southern Asia and black Africa. Their high propensity to demonstrate stems from the immense strain many of them are under, pressurized on the one hand by families who have made sacrifices for them and demand success, on the other by the knowledge that they face the possibility of unemployment when they graduate. Resentment against government can arise from educational fees and mess bills, to exam pass rates and the state of the labour market. The most dangerous situation occurs when the students also infect the educated unemployed, most of whom have a lower level of education and are surprisingly inactive as a group.

In Africa and most of Asia, there is little sign of students, educated unemployed or workers becoming an organized vanguard of revolution or even significant reform. Where groups of them have formed revolutionary parties, they have usually found themselves an isolated skirmishing party with no army behind them.

Because for all their frustrated expectations and potential lawlessness, the poor of Africa and Asia show few signs of developing anything like class-consciousness. The rural majority of the population is hardly organized at all, and in any case does not often divide into two neat classes with opposing interests. In rural Asia there is a continuum from landless labourer, through micro-smallholder who is part landowner, part labourer, to self-sufficient smallholders and large landowners, and even though the middle-income class is small, the poor do not see themselves as a cohesive group. In most of sub-Saharan Africa the rural majority still have access to some land.

Even in the urban areas the non-elite are divided among themselves. The working class are a relatively privileged group compared to the marginal urban poor. Many of the latter are self-employed, with no clear-cut oppressor to rebel against. The informally employed work in small enterprises on close terms with the owner, who is often just as oppressed and discriminated against as they are. On the housing front, residents range from owner occupiers of self-built, rent-free shanties, through lodgers with relatives, and owners of one or two properties, to the big landlords and speculators. Where class oppositions are obvious — as between labouring and land-owning castes in India — other social ties often slice through them. The average man is far more conscious of caste, tribe, language, religion, village, faction or family than he is of class.

This explains why the poor of Africa and Asia, by and large, have not sought collective solutions to their poverty either through the ballot box or the barrel of a gun, and why the prospects for radical reform or revolution are not bright in most countries. Most people do not think of changing the unequal system, but simply hope that they or their little group will end up on the right side of the tracks. They resort to individual solutions, use magic, juju, prayers, join irrational sects that promise the millennium tomorrow, latch onto powerful patrons who can throw small favours their way. Or they blame scapegoats for their troubles and attack communal enemies who may be just as much victims of the system as themselves.

All this means that internal instability in Africa and Asia is often aimless and chaotic, made up of the separate actions of many distinct groups fighting for contradictory purposes. In most countries there is no clear and united constituency for reform to oppose the better organized pressure groups of the privileged.

In Latin America the situation is much clearer. With a common language, religion and culture in each country, there are fewer divisions to confuse the central issues of privilege and poverty. Urban workers and students here have often forged links, while rural groups are organized into peasant syndicates in many countries. Because of the blatant exploitation of the *latifundia* system, landless labourers, tenants with labour obligations and smallholders who have to depend on labour for part of their income are more easily united in action against the landlords. In Peru, for example, all three types of peasant joined together in occupying the great estates.

Hence the potential for radical reform in Latin America is much stronger. But so, paradoxically, is the potential for embittered resistance by privileged groups. Because of this, the probability of successful reform or revolution is not much greater here than anywhere else. In most countries the privileged can still count on the support of the police and the armed forces, and that support is decisive.

Dictatorship and development

The poor people of poor nations lack what might be considered the most basic of human rights: the right to employment, to adequate shelter, to freedom from hunger and disease. They are also deprived of those more refined rights that are generally meant when western politicians talk about the subject: political freedoms and civil liberties.

The United Nations' International Declaration of Human Rights is an impressive list of ideals: it calls for freedom from torture (article six) and from arbitrary arrest (article ten); the right to a fair trial and the assumption of innocence until guilt is proved (article twelve); freedom of peaceful assembly and of association (article twenty-one); freedom of opinion and of expression (article twenty); and the right to participate in government through representatives freely chosen at free elections (article twenty-two). There are probably only two countries in the Third World -- Costa Rica and Barbados – which do not violate at least one of these rights to some degree.

To catalogue all the violations would be time-consuming. But take freedom from torture as an example – it is a good indicator of other rights, because the torture victim has almost always been arbitrarily arrested and held without trial, often for asserting his rights to freedom of expression or association. Amnesty International, in its world survey of the problem, lists evidence of torture from no less than fifty-seven Third World countries – twenty-two in Africa, twenty in Latin America, seven in Asia and eight in the Middle East. The absence of a country from the list, as the report points out, does not denote the absence of torture, merely the lack of solid evidence, and that is hard to come by. 'There are few states in Africa,' Amnesty comments, 'where torture has not been used over the past decade against internal political dissidents or suppressed racial and religious groups.' Or again: 'Costa Rica is the only country in Latin America from which Amnesty International has received no torture allegations in the past years.'

The general state of freedom in the world has been monitored by the New York based organization, Freedom House, each year since 1973. Their survey classifies nations according to the political rights and civil rights enjoyed. Despite its western-oriented definitions, it is relatively objective and no mere apologia for free enterprise.

Freedom House classes as free those democracies with freely elected leaders, competition between political parties, full freedom of expression and legal rights (category one), and also those countries where these rights exist, but on a less secure basis, threatened by inequality, illiteracy and widespread social violence (category two). Only twenty-one Third World nations out of 123 made it into the politically free group in Freedom House's 1978 survey. Only four countries came into category one: Costa Rica, Barbados, Venezuela and the

Bahamas (and only the first two were also rated top category for civil liberties).

In the centre of the spectrum came thirty-five partly free nations with varying degrees of limited democracy, *de facto* one-party states, and less than total dictatorships where other social groups were consulted. Most of these states would have varying numbers of political prisoners and degrees of censorship. Twenty-one of them came into the lowest category on the partly free band.

At the other end of the scale, outnumbering the free by more than three to one, came sixty-eight nations classed as politically unfree, ranging from capitalist Chile and Uganda to socialist countries like Kampuchea. Thirty-two of these countries were almost total despotisms, with self-appointed rulers taking little or no account of popular desires. Thirty-six were non-elected dictatorships, where rulers showed some response to popular feelings.

Repression was not quite so efficient on the civil liberties side: only eighteen Third World states came into the lowest category, where there was total control of expression reaching even to a pervasive atmosphere of fear in private conversation. There were twenty-seven nations in the next category up, where some dissent managed to creep through in private conversations, illegal demonstrations or underground literature.

Combining Freedom House's scores for political rights and civil liberties, you get a scale ranging from two for open democracies to fourteen for unmitigated tyrannies. The average score for western democracies is two and a half. The average for the Third World is around ten, corresponding to a dictatorship with a few limited elements of democracy, or a democracy with many of the characteristics of a dictatorship. Among the developing continents Africa appears to be the most despotic (average score 11·2) and Latin America the least (average 8·6).

If anything the Freedom House survey probably overestimates the extent of freedom in the Third World. India gets the high score of four – equal to Finland or Portugal – for its national performance, even though dozens of people are killed every year when police open fire on rioters – execution without even a summary trial. And at local level there may be un-official private dictatorships. It is of little consolation to the poor peasant that *habeas corpus* exists, if he cannot get a lawyer, or that he has the right, in theory, to form a trade union if landlords can gun him down without the police inter-vening. With politically free nations making up only one in six developing countries, one has to acknowledge that dictator-ship, of varying degrees of severity, is the dominant form of government in the Third World. Authoritarian regimes, whether of the left or the right, seem to be an almost in-evitable accompaniment of national poverty.

The word 'dictator' is of Latin origin. The Roman senate used to appoint dictators to assume all powers in times of ex-ternal or internal emergency and strife. The dictator was sup-posed to abdicate after six months, but as Rome's class conflicts and frontier wars became chronic, dictatorship was made permanent in the form of empire.

The typical Third World state is perpetually beset with in-ternal and external threats to its security. Riots are far more common than in the West, and if not controlled soon lead on to looting, arson and the total breakdown of civil order. Strikes are less common, but can be more disruptive. For ex-ample, India's survival as a nation depends on her ability to move food from surplus states to hungry states by rail: any interruption in the supply, and chaos would break loose in the cut-off areas. Hence the 1973 rail strike was stamped out with particular brutality.

The need for dictatorship varies in inverse proportion to the respect for government and law among citizens, and as we have seen that respect is often lacking – sometimes rightly so, sometimes wrongly – in the Third World. Add to these factors murderous communal clashes and armed rebellions, and it is difficult to see how a state threatened with such a range of dis-orders could survive as a functioning entity without some dic-tatorial powers. Western governments faced with similar threats soon respond in a similar manner. In Northern Ireland Catholics are liable to have their doors kicked in at midnight

by soldiers, with no search warrants, looking for IRA terror-
ists. In Italy and Germany the activities of Red Brigade and
Red Army lead to curtailed liberties for everyone.

On a deeper level, most of the manifestations of disorder
with which Third World nations are beset can be traced to
their roots in poverty and inequality. The tensions these create
may express themselves in false individual solutions such as
crime and rioting, in false group solutions like communal strife
and secession, or in more organized strikes, demonstrations
and rebellions. All these symptoms of discontent make authoritarian rule more probable.

The poorer a nation is, the more likely it is to suffer from
deprivation of political and civil rights. Comparing the Freedom House ratings of non-oil-rich nations with average incomes per capita for 1976, I found that the worst dictatorships (scoring thirteen or fourteen) had average incomes of
$245. Less repressive dictatorships and very limited demo-
cracies (scoring nine to twelve) had average incomes of $580.
The more open political systems, scoring eight or below,
had incomes of $760. The reasons for this link between
poverty and dictatorship lie in the effects of hunger, illiteracy
and unemployment. Generally, the poorer the country, the
smaller is the stabilizing middle class and the greater the
polarization between privileged and poor.

Inequality, too, is closely related to dictatorship. Generally
speaking, the more unequal the nation, the fewer liberties it
tends to possess. One way of measuring inequality is known as
the Gini coefficient: a value of zero represents perfect equality,
and of one, perfect inequality. In real life, countries range between 0·2 for the most equal nation to nearly 0·7 for the most
unequal. In a survey of income distribution in eighty-one
countries published by the World Bank, western democracies
averaged 0·38 and Third World countries 0·48, taking the most
comprehensive and recent figures for each country.

The open and limited Third World democracies, scoring
between two and eight on the Freedom scale, were slightly
more equal than average, with average Gini coefficients of 0·47.
The very restricted democracies, scoring nine and ten, had co-

efficients of 0·49. The dictatorships, scoring eleven and twelve, had coefficients of 0·52. The reason for this relationship is clear: the more unequal the society, the greater the resentment among the poor and the greater their rejection of the prevailing order. Hence increasing amounts of force are necessary to keep public order. Among the worst dictatorships, scoring thirteen and fourteen, the relationship appears to break down, for they are more egalitarian than the democracies, with average Gini coefficients of 0·43. The reason may be that many of these countries are socialist, operating the Leninist–Stalinist model of the state. In socialist countries dictatorship may be the cause of greater equality rather than the result. It may have arisen in previously extremely polarized societies, whether suffering under home-grown oppressors (like Cuba, Peru or Ethiopia) or, more frequently, foreign exploiters, or a combination of both (as in China, Vietnam, Guinea, Algeria, Indochina, South Yemen, Angola, Mozambique or Guinea-Bissau).

Dictatorship in the Third World often arises gradually as a civilian government takes more and more extreme powers to cope with civil strife. Even while calling itself a democracy, India was detaining political offenders without trial long before Mrs Gandhi's emergency, under the notorious Defence of India rules and the Maintenance of Internal Security Act. Colombia, though also, ostensibly, a democracy, has been under a near-permanent state of siege for most of this century.

More commonly dictatorship arises from a coup or military takeover. Part of the military's concept of its purpose and destiny is the preservation of national unity and order. When civil strife degenerates into near civil war, the military is given increasing powers and is increasingly likely to take all powers. As a centralized hierarchy with rigid discipline and good communications from Chief of Staff down to the ranks, it may be more able to execute its own policies than politicians and bureaucrats – but it rarely has personnel equipped to formulate social and economic policies. Usually the military do not intervene without some specific grievance of their own, such as resentment over pay and conditions, cuts in arms spending, foreign policy humiliations, threats to the status of the army as a whole or the position of key leaders. But occasions like these arise almost inevitably in developing countries. Authoritarian regimes, especially military ones, may be able to impose an artificial quiet on the country. Yet, because of the intensity of social polarization in poor countries, dictatorships are rarely impartial in the opposition between privilege and poverty. Some of them block reform aimed at reducing inequality, others push through a more radical reform than would have been possible under a regime of full civil liberties.

Unfortunately, reform-blocking dictatorships are more common than reform pushers. In polarized countries, the military hierarchy tends towards the right. Its officers usually stem from the same class as the landowners and urban privileged. European and American influence in their training, plus in many cases the experience of fighting left-wing guerillas, has made many top officers so fanatically anti-communist that anyone who favours a measure of redistribution is branded as a dangerous revolutionary. There have been left-wing army coups – Egypt, Peru, Libya, Ethiopia – but they are in a minority.

Moreover, the loss of the right to vote takes away what is often the poor's sole political weapon, poor and imperfect though it is. Possessing the vote – as we have seen – is no guarantee that a reform government will be elected, but it does mean that rulers have to make some concessions to the poor, even if it is only in bringing electricity and water and public construction jobs to the marginal constituencies. When the right to vote is taken away, the only pressures on rulers come from organized pressure groups: large capitalists and landowners, the military, the bureaucracy with its contingent of technocrats, foreign governments and the international financial establishment, and very occasionally (if they are lucky) trade unions and peasant organizations. Because they are so badly organized, the poor have less pull with a nonsocialist dictatorship than with a democracy, and must rely more than ever on the enlightenment of their rulers.

Sadly, the pressure for reform can itself lead to the emergence of authoritarian regimes, if government does not respond to it. In India demands for decisive action on corruption met with no response. Widespread civil disobedience followed, and the emergency was imposed. Timely investigation and reform could have defused the agitation more effectively. In Pakistan President Bhutto refused to replay the 1977 elections after fraud allegations. The ensuing riots led to military rule, with the execution of Bhutto.

The whole issue of dictatorship versus democracy in the Third World came into the limelight with Jimmy Carter's accession to the US presidency. America cut aid to several Latin American countries because of human rights violations, and Common Market donors began to think of making aid conditional on human rights performance, though, in practice, known violators of human rights such as Iran and South Korea were helped wherever cold war considerations outweighed moral ones. In this whole debate, human rights were generally taken to mean political rights and civil liberties.

As we have seen, the greatest threats to political rights and civil liberties in the Third World are poverty and inequality. Human rights, in other words, are impeded by strategies of unequal development and by the unjust international economic order. The best way for western governments to push for improved human rights is to help reduce poverty and inequality, by pressing for egalitarian development strategies and conceding reform in the world economic order.

In other words, the cause of political rights is best advanced by concentrating on economic rights. The major concern of aid donors should not be with what liberties are theoretically available under the constitution, but with the real welfare of the poor, who will never be able to enjoy any political rights until their economic situation is improved. In practical terms, this means that a distinction should be made between different kinds of authoritarian regimes on the basis of their record in helping the poor; between reform-blocking and reform-pushing dictatorships; between governments that violate their people's civil rights so as to frustrate their economic rights, and those who infringe civil rights but improve economic rights.

The genuinely reform-oriented regimes deserve all the aid they can get. If they can improve the lot of the poor and reduce inequality, civil strife will be reduced and political rights can be restored sooner. The anti-reform governments need more cautious treatment. It is desirable to cut military aid, which only helps regimes to meet reform demands with repression. It may also be advisable to reduce general budgetary aid which can be spent on repression or on massive prestige projects, and is unlikely to be used to help the poor. For this type of regime, the total amount of aid should probably not be reduced, but more closely tied to projects and programmes that will specifically improve the economic situation of the poor. And since the debt problem everywhere strengthens the hand of anti-reform groups, the prospects for peaceful reform can be improved by changes in the international economic order.

Freedom stands little chance in a world of such pronounced inequalities and it is useless to press for political and civil rights without pressing for the kind of equality that makes them meaningful. If prosperity does not spread more rapidly to wider groups, and if the absolute poverty of the poorest is not alleviated or eradicated, dictatorship of the right or of the left will continue to be the dominant form of government in the Third World.

20. Princes and Paupers:
Poverty and Inequality

'A growth process that benefits only the wealthiest minority and maintains or even increases the disparities between and within countries is not development. It is exploitation.'

The Cocoyoc Declaration

There are many ways of defining poverty, but all point to the same conclusion. In this age of Martian landings and grand tours to the outer planets, somewhere between one and one and a half billion people on our home planet earth are living in a state of absolute and abject poverty. As mankind reaches out for the stars, one man in three is unable to live his human life with dignity and free of want, unable in fact to be fully human. These are the forgotten people, underfed, underemployed, illiterate, ill-housed and in ill-health. The poor who should have been the focus of development, but whom the process of unequal development has passed by, or rolled over and crushed.

Estimates of the extent of poverty in the Third World show considerable agreement, whatever the particular measure that is used. In 1976 the International Labour Office, in figures prepared for the World Employment Conference, calculated that some 1,210 million people – two thirds of the population of non-communist developing countries – were 'seriously poor'. They drew the poverty line at the equivalent of $500 per head in western Europe. Because of lower local costs of living this amounted to $180 in Latin America, $115 in Africa and $100 in Asia. Of this total, some 700 million people, or 40 per cent of the population, were destitute – that is, receiving less than half the poverty-line income. In the decade from 1963, the ILO estimated that the number of seriously poor had increased by 119 millions, while the number of destitutes had increased by 43 millions.

A somewhat cruder set of estimates from World Bank

economist Montek Ahluwalia tie in well with these figures. In a sample of 1969 incomes from forty-four developing countries, he found that 48 per cent were very poor (with incomes below $75 – £37) and 31 per cent were extremely poor (incomes below $50). The proportion of very poor was lowest in Latin America (17 per cent), but 44 per cent of Africans and no less than 57 per cent of Asians were below the poverty line.

The ILO's figure of 700 million or 40 per cent destitute coincides, remarkably, almost exactly with two other measures of deprivation. The ILO also calculated that in 1975 40 per cent of the workforce of non-communist developing countries were unemployed or underemployed: no doubt the very same 40 per cent. And probably, for the most part, the same people as the 750 million who, in 1970, were illiterate.

Two thirds seriously poor, two fifths destitute: it is not an impressive record for two decades of going for growth. These are the people who are gaining least, and often actually losing out, as their countries develop. This immense army of the submerged, legions of the damned in this life, are the bottom layer in the great international pyramid. They are the very crux of the development issue, for if development is to mean anything, it must mean the eradication of this great mass of suffering.

The concept of poverty is not easy to define, as it comes in two models: absolute poverty, and relative poverty. When we talk of absolute poverty, we are implying a level of income that imposes real physical suffering on people in hunger, disease and the massacre of innocent children.

Hunger is the painful focus of absolute poverty. Disease goes hand in hand with it. Both bring physical discomfort and, worse, prevent children and adults from reaching their full physical and mental potential. Those who cannot afford to eat enough to provide protection against disease and productive labour invariably suffer in other ways: their housing and sanitation will probably be bad enough to contribute to disease, their education inadequate to obtain employment paying enough to feed them. All aspects of absolute poverty work together in denying the victims a fully, or sometimes even minimally, human existence.

Absolute poverty is on the increase, both in total numbers and in the proportion of the population affected. Two thirds of the absolutely poor live in Asia. Recent surveys from the continent paint an alarming, even horrifying picture. In many countries the proportion under the poverty line has increased and the real incomes of the poorest groups have declined.

* In Pakistan, in 1966–7, 64 per cent of the population were below a poverty income that would have bought them enough food to meet 95 per cent of their calorie needs. Five years later the proportion had risen to 74 per cent.

* In the Punjab, India's prosperous wheat-bowl, the proportion below the poverty line rose from 18 per cent to 23 per cent in the decade of the sixties.

* In Bihar, India's poorest state, it rose from 41 per cent to 59 per cent in the sixties.

* In Bangladesh, the number of absolutely poor shot up, in the ten years from 1963, from 40 per cent to 61 per cent of the population. The real wage of Bangladeshi agricultural labourers declined steeply. In 1949 they could earn 2·36 taka a day, in 1975 only 1·28 taka (at constant 1963 prices).

* In Uttar Pradesh, the biggest state in India, the amount of food a labourer could buy with his wages declined in many villages. In Muzaffarnagar the ploughman's daily wage could buy 6·58 kilos of wheat in 1954–5, but only 3·12 kilos in 1967–8.

* Real agricultural wages in the Philippines dropped from 3·84 pesos a day in 1957 to 1·48 a day in 1974 (at constant 1965 prices).

Relative poverty can be almost as destructive as absolute poverty, in the sense that it can preoccupy or even obsess one's thoughts and divert him from the enjoyment of his life. The man who is not suffering physically may suffer mentally when he compares himself with people vastly better off than he, and he can see no good reason for the discrepancy. Relative deprivation depends very much on expectations. An untouchable in India may not feel deprived in comparison to a Brahmin, if the caste system has brainwashed him into believing that the differences are natural and just. But expectations are high in the Third World today and the rhetoric of equality is universal. Elites compare their countries with the West, and feel deprived. Poor men compare themselves with the elites, and feel deprived. Poverty, in the egalitarian mood of the twentieth century, brings with it the worm of envy, as an inevitable reaction to unjust inequalities. Relative poverty, in most of the Third World, often means shame, too: shame that your house has a thatched roof while your neighbour has tin, shame that your children go barefoot to school, shame that your daughter's dowry or wedding feast is so pitiably small.

Relative poverty, in other words, is the mental suffering that derives from inequality. Pronounced inequalities make the burden of poverty that much harder to bear. Indeed in many cases one man's excess wealth may be the direct cause of another man's destitution.

Inequality, like poverty, is on the increase both internationally and nationally.

The distribution of the world's income is more unequal than even the most grotesquely unjust of national distributions. In 1976 the industrialized countries made up only 24 per cent of the world's population, but raked in 78 per cent of the income. The developing countries – 76 per cent of the people – got only 22 per cent of the income. The average income in the industrialized countries was $6,110 per person, eleven times that of the developing countries ($542). At the bottom of the heap, the poorest 43 per cent of the world's population got only 3·6 per cent of the world's income, giving them an average income one thirty-eighth of that of the top 24 per cent.

The absolute gap between rich and poor countries is widening. Between 1974 and 1975, for example, the average *increase* in income per capita in the richest countries – $480 – exceeded the average *total* income per head in the developing countries, or $416, and was four times greater than the poorest countries' increase.* (See Map 4, pages 460–61.)

---

* These figures, based on World Bank figures, have to be treated with some caution. They are obtained by converting national income figures

Between 1950 and 1975, economist David Morawetz has calculated, the absolute gap between the average incomes per person in western countries and those in developing countries, in constant 1974 dollars, grew from \$2,218 to \$4,863. Over the same period, the relative gap hardly changed at all. The average developing-country income remained at around 7 per cent of the average western income. While oil-boosted Middle Eastern incomes closed their relative gap with the West considerably, and China and eastern Asia recorded modest advances, incomes in Latin America, southern Asia and Africa represented a smaller percentage of western incomes in 1975 than in 1950. If the average growth rates of the fifteen years to 1975 continue, Morawetz calculates, some oil-rich and rapidly industrializing countries like Singapore, Hongkong, Korea and Taiwan could hope to close the absolute gap within the next seventy-five years. For the rest, it would take centuries, and for the poorest several millennia: even fast-growing Brazil would take 362 years, Turkey would need 675, Malawi 1,920, Malaysia 2,293 and Mauretania 3,223 years.

---

into US dollars at prevailing exchange rates, and do not really give an accurate picture of comparative purchasing power or welfare. Because goods and services are not freely traded throughout the world, price levels between countries vary considerably – in 1970 general price levels in India were only 30 per cent of those in the USA, for example, so a dollar would go very much further there. Prices in most Third World countries are lower than those in the West. What this means is that the relative income figures quoted here tend to exaggerate the inequality between rich and poor.

In 1968 the United Nations initiated its International Comparison Project to try to compare national incomes on the basis of real purchasing power for sixteen countries at different income levels. The initial results showed that, whereas India's per capita income in 1970 seemed to be only 2 per cent of the US level, its purchasing power was equivalent to 7 per cent. In nominal terms, the average per capita income of developed market economies was more than 13 times higher than that of developing countries in 1970. The ICP studies showed that, when price differences were allowed for, it was only about eight and a half times higher. But the gap remains a very wide one, and until the ICP allows comparative tables of real per capita incomes to be published each year for all countries, we have to use the imperfect World Bank ones.

Even between different groups of Third World countries, considerable inequalities have emerged and are increasing, as we shall see in the next chapter.

The quality of life

These income inequalities are shocking enough, but the figures convey little of the real meaning of inequality in everyday terms. For a feeling of this we have to look at some of the more concrete manifestations.

For example, compare a typical poor country like Indonesia with a rich one like Canada, around 1970. A newborn Canadian could expect to live seventy-three years, the newborn Indonesian only forty-eight. The Indonesian child had a one in three chance of going to school – the Canadian no chance of avoiding it. The average adult Canadian had eight or nine years of schooling, the average Indonesian eight months. The Canadian ate ninety-eight grams of protein per day, most of that meat. The Indonesian got only forty-three grams, almost all vegetable. Some 35,000 Indonesians had to share one doctor, against only 670 Canadians. All Canadians had access to clean water, but only one Indonesian in sixteen. These are inequalities not just of material possessions, but in lives, in minds, in flesh and blood, in wellbeing and confidence in the world.

An attempt to summarize the human content of international inequalities has been made by the Overseas Development Council of the United States. The council's staff tried to get over the problems of measuring relative wealth and poverty by average gross national product per person. This crude measure says nothing about the gross inequalities that exist within nations, and to accept it as a yardstick of progress is to assume that the growth of total material wealth is the goal of development, regardless of how unequally it is distributed. So the council developed what they called a physical quality of life index (PQLI). They gave each country a score from one (for the worst performer) to a hundred (for the best) in three fields: life expectancy, infant mortality and literacy. The PQLI index figure for each country was arrived at by taking an average of its scores on these three measures. The index provides a good judgement of the reach of health and educational systems and of the nutritional status of the people (which, in itself, reflects the state of employment, wages, landholding and so on). Since a nation can attain a high average score only if wide sections of the population have high literacy and good health, the index also gives an indication of how far the benefits of development have reached the majority.

The maximum score of one hundred was achieved by only one country in the world, Sweden. The higher-income countries as a whole scored an average of ninety-five.

Generally, the richer the country, the higher its score. The forty-nine poorest countries (with average incomes in 1974 of $152) scored an average on the PQLI of only thirty-nine. The thirty-nine lower middle-income countries (average income $338) rated fifty-nine, while the thirty-five upper-middle-income countries scored sixty-seven. Several individual countries, however, managed to score much higher than might have been expected. Despite her low income of $130 per head in 1974, Sri Lanka achieved the astonishing score of eighty-three, because of her high literacy and life expectancy and low infant mortality, reflecting her free education and health services and subsidized food rations. Among the lower-middle-income countries, Cuba scored best with 86. The index reveals the value of egalitarian development strategies oriented towards the welfare of the poor. Brazil, which has pursued a highly unequal strategy of growth, scored only fifty-eight though it had a per capita income of $920.

But even this kind of refined measure cannot convey the true quality of life, as a subjective experience. It cannot answer the question many people ask: how satisfied are the general run of Third World citizens with their lot? Are they happy in spite of their poverty? It must have occurred to many romantically inclined western travellers that the barefoot African peasant in his mud hut, with mango and bananas outside his door, year-round warmth and close community life, may be more contented than the isolated westerner commuting in traffic jams between television and convenience foods at home, and stressful, alienating routine at work. The peasant may indeed have been happy, once, but the revolution of rising expectations seems to have injected a large worm of discontent into the bud.

Fortunately we now have a little more evidence than just impression and intuition. Between 1974 and 1976, Gallup International conducted the first ever world-wide survey of public opinion in sixty nations, funded by the Charles F. Kettering Foundation. The results, running to eighteen thick volumes, suggest that the majority of people in developing countries are much less contented with almost every aspect of their lives than people in the rich countries. To measure satisfaction levels, interviewees were asked to place themselves on a 'mountain card' made up of eleven steps, the bottom one representing 'the worst possible life you can imagine', and the top one, the best. Asked if they were satisfied with their standard of living, less than 30 per cent of Europeans and Americans rated themselves on the bottom six steps, against 33 per cent of Latin Americans, 73 per cent of sub-Saharan Africans and 82 per cent of Indians. Third Worlders turned out to be far more dissatisfied with their personal health, their housing, even their family life (though Latin Americans were a good deal more satisfied than the rest). Two thirds of westerners and of Latin Americans rated themselves in the top three categories for family happiness, but less than one in five Africans and less than one in eight Indians did so.

As might have been expected, Third World residents were more often materially deprived. Small minorities of westerners said there had been times in the last year when they did not have enough money to buy food or clothing. Between two thirds and four fifths of Africans and Indians had experienced this. Crime appeared to be worse in the Third World than even in the USA: 40 per cent of Americans could think of places within twenty minutes of their home where they would be afraid to walk. Between 47 and 57 per cent of Third Worlders could.

Generally, people in developing countries tended to worry a

lot more than in industrialized countries, especially over finances. And they emerged as less happy overall. Those considering themselves very happy outnumbered the 'not too happy' by seven to one in Scandinavia, five to one in Britain and four to one in the USA. In Latin America the two groups were more or less equal, but the not-too-happies outnumbered the happies by five to three in Africa and by ten to one in India.

These results totally confound the nostalgic view that the people of poor countries may be more contented than the rich. Their discontent is related to the day-to-day frustrations of absolute poverty: lack of sufficient food, frequent ill health, shortage of funds for adequate clothing and shelter. But it is surely related, also, to their relative poverty when they compare their own situation with that of the overprivileged of their country, and with the expectations that politicians, the media and their own eyes have awakened in them.

The two nations

But inequalities are just as glaring inside most Third World countries. The majority are composed, just as much as Disraeli's Britain, of two nations: the privileged and the people. Those who benefit from economic growth, and those who do not. The guests at the feast, and the beggars who get only crumbs or are left gaping at the door. The two nations, in the Third World, are not so much the capitalists and the workers, nor even the landlords versus the landless. Those divisions exist too, but they are complicated by several others. The clearest dichotomy is between the winners and the losers in the development game.

The winners are all those with a foot in the door of the modern, westernized sector, state or private. Government employees, down to all but the humblest level, with their excessive salaries, their unshakeable security, their perks. The owners, managers and the salaried employees of modern-style enterprises, national or multinational. The fat city cats: owners of urban property cashing in on the goldmine produced by the rural exodus, businessmen, export and import merchants. On the land, there are the big landowners and, at a lower level, those with enough land to produce a sizable surplus for sale. Both groups have benefited disproportionately from state infrastructure, new roads, credit, extension work. Then there is a new class of rural privileged – some of them previously underprivileged – that is, the beneficiaries of limited development projects and of token land reform schemes. These people, like the big farmers, attract far more than their fair share of government and international resources.

Then there are the losers, the rural and urban sub- and lumpenproletariat, a motley collection of unfortunates whose very diversity prevents them from organizing and cooperating to change the system they are suffering under. The greater part of them live on the land. There are the *minifundistas*, owners of holdings so small that they cannot feed their families and have to rely on outside work. Dryland farmers can be in this boat even with quite large landholdings, because their land is so unproductive. Both groups are poor to the extent that they depend on the labour market for a large part of their income. The landless labourers, who depend on it entirely, are even more exposed. Outside agriculture, the losers are the workers in moribund traditional industries, the self-employed or insecurely employed of the urban informal sector, and the unemployed.

The degree of inequality inside most Third World countries is much more pronounced than in a typical industrialized country. In previous chapters, we have seen some of its concrete forms, in food, housing, water, education and so on. In income terms it is just as striking. World Bank economist Montek Ahluwalia calculates that in the typical developing country, the richest 20 per cent of the people corner 53 per cent of the personal income, while the poorest 40 per cent get only 12 per cent of the income. In western countries this bottom two fifths gets 16 per cent of total income. In socialist countries which, though still unequal, represent the highest degree of equality yet attained, their share is around 25 per cent.

A graphic way of looking at inequality is to measure how

much richer the average member of the top 20 per cent is than his counterpart in the bottom 40 per cent. Once again, the socialist countries are the most egalitarian: in Czechoslovakia the average income of the top 20 is only 2·25 times that of the bottom 40, in Hungary 2·79 times (all data are for various years between 1957 and 1971). Several developed western nations have achieved levels approaching these. Japan's top 20 receive 3·86 times the bottom 40, and the heartland of private enterprise, the United States, has an egalitarian ratio of 3·96. In the United Kingdom the discrepancy is 4·14 times, in Sweden 6·28, in Germany 6·86. France has an extremely unequal distribution: the richest get 11·3 times the poorest.

Only a few developing countries show egalitarian distributions. The poorest 40 per cent get 17 per cent or more of total income in Sri Lanka, Thailand, Pakistan, Korea and – the most egalitarian of all – Taiwan, where the top 20 get only 3·93 times the income of the bottom 40. Taiwan and Korea have both grown extremely fast. In Taiwan the income of the poorest 40 per cent grew nearly three times faster than that of the top 20.

In the typical developing country, the richest 20 per cent have average incomes nine times higher than the poorest 40 per cent. Many of the countries where alleged 'economic miracles' of rapid growth are going on are characterized by a high degree of inequality. In Kenya the richest earned 13·6 times the poorest, in Brazil 12·3 times. In Brazil the income gap widened in the sixties, as the richest group's average incomes grew by 8·4 per cent a year and the poorest's by only 5·2 per cent.

For most countries following the model of unequal development, economic growth has brought with it a widening of disparities. Indeed, the first stages of economic growth seem to lead to a rapid decline in their share of total income and an equally rapid rise in the share of the richest. Figures for fifty-six countries collected by International Labour Office economist Felix Paukert show that the income share of the poorest 40 per cent, which stands at 17 per cent of total income for countries with average incomes below $100, declines to only 12·4 per cent in countries between $300 and $500. Only when the country rises above $500 does their share start to rise again – but it never seems to regain the share it enjoyed before development really got going. At the same time the share of the richest 20 per cent – just over half, for countries under $100 – jumps to 58 per cent for countries between $200 and $300, declining slowly as the country gets wealthier. Every group except the richest gets a smaller share in the first stage of growth, the second richest 20 per cent starts to recover its share in the second phase, the middle 20 per cent in the third phase, the second poorest 20 per cent in the fourth phase, while the poorest 20 per cent do not recover their original share at all.

Paukert's figures are admittedly crude and not strictly comparable. But the pattern they reveal is convincing and rings true. Some countries, like Korea and Taiwan, have spread the benefits of growth widely. But economic growth of the prevalent model is like a dark tunnel in which equity and justice disappear, to re-emerge again only after a long and painful passage. The establishment of the modern sector at first lines the pockets of only a small elite group – the richest 20 per cent – and deals a blow to all the rest of society. But slowly this modern sector expands as more and more people are drawn into it as clerks, manual workers, subcontractors. As the expansion proceeds, the benefits of growth trickle down to wider groups. This has been the traditional justification for the going for growth strategy, but it is now clear that the trickle can be a very slow drip, and the lowest 40 per cent can be flung into a prolonged period of increasing relative and sometimes absolute poverty which may well last longer than is politically and morally acceptable.

If the share of the poorest in the total national income declines faster than the total is growing, then the poor can get poorer at the same time as the country as a whole seems to be getting richer. For example, in West Malaysia, the average household was 14 per cent better off in 1970 than in 1957. In reality, of course, there are no average households. In fact only the top 40 per cent saw any real improvement in their incomes, while the real incomes of all the rest declined. Incomes of the bottom 20 per cent declined by one third. Over the same period in the Philippines the real incomes of most groups rose, but for the poorest fifth they fell by 11 per cent.

Some analysts say this is an inevitable part of the growth process, like growing pains. Some even claim that it is desirable, because inequality provides the winners in the game with enough surplus for investment, whereas, if the kitty were divided up more equally, more would be spent on consumption, and investment would suffer as a result. This theory is morally and objectively untenable. To say that inequality and its attendant injustices are necessary for growth is to say that moral degeneration is a justifiable means towards the end of multiplying material wealth. That is to stand human values on their head. And, in practice, the rich of the Third World do not often behave like the puritanical capitalists of Western Europe: they are more inclined to salt their funds away in numbered Swiss bank accounts (abolishing this practice would do a lot to further the cause of justice in the Third World), or to squander them on ostentatious consumer goods imported from the West, from Mercedes to Martini. The rich elites of developing countries have a high propensity to import. Their spending does not generate so many local jobs as the spending of the poor on essentials which can be produced locally from local materials. Where it does give a stimulus to local industry, gross income inequality creates the wrong kind of industry, serving the wants of the rich rather than the needs of the poor, capital-intensive rather than job-creating.

The fact is, as the experience of Taiwan and Korea show clearly, that rapid growth can be achieved with greater equality, that the two are in no way incompatible. Indeed, in the rural sphere where both these countries are dominated by an egalitarian mass of smallholders, they are a standing proof that greater equality can produce much more rapid growth in food production.

It is not 'growth' as such, but the model of growth pursued by most Third World countries that has increased inequalities.

In almost every sector inappropriate western patterns have been followed, allowing for only small quantities of high-standard investment to be made. These have all been channelled to the modern and urban sector and the budding capitalist farmer, in other words to the already privileged, discriminating against the underprivileged. And the strengthened and favouritized modern sector has proceeded to kill off the non-modern sector through competition.

The mechanisms of impoverishment

Nature herself is unequal and generates poverty. This piece of land is low enough to be permanently irrigated, that piece is dry and dependent on erratic rainfall. This area has fertile alluvial soil, that one has heavily leached laterite. This country is sitting on a fortune in oil, that one has nothing but the labour power of her people to sell. Accidents hit some and miss others – the storm flattens this man's house and leaves that one's standing, the leaf hopper ruins this family's crop and spares the next family's. Traditional systems of alms, patronage or mutual support partly evened out nature's unevenhandedness. But today they are in an advanced state of decay all over the world.

Society today works to accentuate, rather than lessen, the inequalities of nature, and poverty and inequality are everywhere on the increase. I would like here to make an excursion into theory, at the risk of boring some readers, but in the hope of offering a systematic way of looking at the emergence of poverty and inequality. One can distinguish four modes of impoverishment – geographical, where the main factor is a natural or ecological process; social, where pauperization develops out of the agreed ground-rules of the society; economic, where it results from the forces of the marketplace; and political, where it is imposed by the use of state power. Some of these modes have two or three variants. In many situations, indeed, they are all at work together, and to cope with one while ignoring the others may lead to oversimplified solutions.

Geographical pauperization can come from totally natural processes such as long-term changes in the global weather machine resulting in declining rainfall – as in the Sahel where the equatorial rainbelts appear to have shifted south – or by short-term natural disasters such as droughts, earthquakes or typhoons. At present man's technological capacity does not extend to preventing these things from happening, though it can help to protect people against disaster with safer houses, more drought-resistant crops, more irrigation and better organization of relief. Ultimately, though, one has to admit that there are some areas of the world that are so naturally unproductive that only migration could guarantee their inhabitants a life above survival level.

More commonly, geographical pauperization results from the interaction of population and technology with sensitive ecosystems. One could call this the 'ecological' variant, and it is found in the kind of land degradation at work in desertification and deforestation. At its root is the stark fact that the land cannot sustain its present population (let alone any future increase) given the technology currently being used. The answer is first to limit population growth, and/or to relieve some of the pressure by migration to less pressurized areas. And to introduce technology that can sustain the population at reasonable income levels without damage to the land – for example, ploughs, fertilizers, mixed agriculture and wet rice cultivation in Africa, or tree plantations, bio-gas and solar energy for fuel. All the other forms of pauperization automatically involve increased inequality between social strata. The geographical mode need not, though it will do so in an unequal system. In an egalitarian social system like the traditional African village, everyone sinks with the ship together. But it does usually produce pronounced inequalities between different regions of the same country. These inequalities could be corrected by pouring in more investment into geographically less favoured areas, or alternatively, by encouraging migration, so as to spread the population evenly according to the carrying capacity of the land.

Social pauperization emerges from the interaction of ecological factors – geography, technology, population – with the basic rules of the social system. It usually brings increased inequality in its wake. Wherever ownership of land is private and individual, inequality is bound to emerge even without population pressure. One farmer has a pest invasion that destroys his crop one year. He borrows from another farmer, and the debt repayment reduces his margins and makes him even more vulnerable. As soon as disaster strikes the same man twice, he is liable to become landless while his creditor has double the amount of land. Population growth speeds up this process tremendously: land is subdivided until it shrinks below subsistence level, and families are forced onto the labour market, where wages get worse as the labour supply shoots ahead of demand. This is, of course, a highly simplified schema, but it is essentially what is happening in most of Asia. The answer here is once again to cut population growth and to improve technology so that smaller plots can support a family. In addition, the offending parts of the social system have to be modified, by limiting private property rights in land and redistributing land to the landless – but not in individual private plots, or the same process will simply start again, but in cooperatively owned or at least cooperatively worked estates. And plentiful cheap state credit for consumption purposes has to be provided.

The third mode of impoverishment is economic. Its first form, the pauperization of unequal exchange, occurs whenever two unequal parties meet in the marketplace to buy and sell with each other. As commercialization is spreading everywhere to replace subsistence economies (where very little market exchange takes place), this form is on the increase in all continents.

No market in the world is a perfectly free market, for which you need an equal exchange between equal parties. Even where two children are swapping conkers for marbles, the stronger one will get a better deal if he wants to. Take the cobblers of Agra (see page 198): they were forced to sell their shoes cheaply because they needed the money there and then, and there were many of them competing against each other. The merchants could delay buying, colluded with each other, and controlled the network of marketing and supplies. The outcome of any bargaining process is determined by the bargaining power of the participants: the strongest, the richest, the best informed, the best organized, usually win the contest hands down. The prices on a market of unequal exchange do not truly reflect supply and demand, but are distorted by relative market muscle.

This process is extremely widespread, and much worsened by population increase. It happens in the labour market, where there are too many workers chasing too few jobs and many landlords or employers may have thugs to keep wages down and prevent workers from organizing. It happens in the private credit market where the sheer pressure of numbers seeking loans from a limited number of individuals pushes interest rates up. It happens in the world commodity market where Third World countries' poverty forces them to produce and sell even when prices are low, and in the market for machinery and manufactures, where western countries, companies and workers can set their own prices, thanks to better organization and staying power. It happens in the land market, urban and rural, as more and more people compete for the same limited space. This pushes rents up and increases landlords' incomes – sometimes, in cities, spectacularly – and, by the same token, reduces the incomes of tenants.

There is an element of the straightforward play of market forces even in processes that look like clear exploitation: the abysmal wages of landless rural labourers in Asia are to a great extent the result of excess labour supply due to population growth. In this kind of situation it is not enough to organize the workers – as this might result in a smaller, well-paid permanent workforce with a mass of totally unemployed. The supply of and demand for labour have to be changed before things can improve: population growth has to be cut back, and more jobs created through labour-intensive agriculture and industry.

But where unequal market muscle is involved, the answer to this process is to body-build the weaker parties, by organizing them and backing them with resources and expertise. This means creating poor producers' and consumers' cooperatives. In many situations it may mean reducing their dependence on the labour market by giving them land of their own.

The second form of economic pauperization is caused by unequal competition between people on the same side of the market exchange: for example, between small rice growers with primitive technology and large-scale mechanized producers, or between home spinners and huge mills. The large-scale producer can sell his goods more cheaply than the small man, at prices that depress the latter's income lower and lower, until they sink below survival level. At that point the small man can no longer continue as an independent producer, and must work as a labourer for all or part of his income.

There are, of course, always inequalities of skill or productivity between producers on the same level. But gross disparities in productivity are generally the result of other factors, such as access to capital, credit, government services, markets. The straight answer to unequal competition is to even up access to capital and government services for all levels of producer. In the agricultural sector, and in the poorest countries, where there is hardly any large industry, there is still time for this approach. But in the urban sector of most Third World countries, the process has already gone too far: even with equal access to credit the small man cannot possibly compete on the same market terms as the large, and he will still be eaten alive. Those small producers who are in viable sectors need more than equal opportunity: they need favoured treatment. They need to get cheaper credit and more government help than the big men, and they need protected markets – as, for example, by reserving whole sectors of industry exclusively for small-scale enterprise.

Political pauperization, the fourth mode, involves the use of state power by certain social groups to generate and perpetuate gross inequalities and keep the poor at survival level.

Its first variant is the kind of forcible expropriation, enslavement and repression that followed the Iberian conquest of Latin America, and which is now happening to varying degrees in certain countries and localities of Asia and Africa. In this process, the elite seizes the apparatus of the state – at national or at local level – and uses its overwhelming violence to back up expropriation, and repress the rebellion of the poor against the injustices of the rich. Sometimes – as in many Latin American countries – this process goes on at national level and the only answer to it is political action, from election campaigns to revolution. The more extreme the repression, the more extreme the resistance has to be.

Sometimes the rich have made the local apparatus of the state their private plaything: here the answer must lie in tightening up central control over local government, stamping out the corruption that gives the rich much of their political muscle and organizing the poor to demand and defend their rights in every way from trade-union action to political activity.

The other forms of political impoverishment do not necessarily involve the use of state violence. They are more insidious and more widespread, and they can persist sometimes even under socialist and communist regimes. The second form is gross discrimination in government investment and support in favour of privileged social groups, especially in favour of the modern, privileged and urban sectors against the rural, informal and poor sectors. This need not involve the use of violence (except against occasional riots) because it is rationalized and given a spurious legitimacy by all kinds of specious arguments such as the need to 'modernize' or 'boost production'. But the money for urban privilege has to come from somewhere, and it is usually extracted willy-nilly from the rural areas.

The third form of political impoverishment involves the self-elevation of the group who man the state – as politicians or bureaucrats – into a 'new class', a new privileged elite, of the kind Yugoslav philosopher Milovan Djilas saw emerging in communist states. The personnel of the state vote or decree themselves fat salary cheques and perks, which are financed by everyone else through general taxation.

This form is worth examining a little more closely, as it is not so obvious as the others, and is likely to persist even when the others have been eliminated. It occurs in all developing countries to some extent, but it is more muted in a country like India, where civil servants get relatively modest salaries, and more pronounced in Africa, where blacks walked straight into whites' shoes and inherited their salary cheques too. It is at its clearest in the least developed countries, such as Upper Volta.

Here there are only two significant groups of people: farmers, and government employees. As there is so little industry, government is financed by aid (intended for the benefit of all), by a poll tax of about $3 per head on every person over fourteen, and by indirect duties and customs levies borne by the mass of the people.

The *minimum* pay for a government labourer or clerk when I visited Upper Volta was ten times the average income of the farmer whose taxes were paying for it. The national accounts show that the 5 per cent of the population engaged in 'services', that is, mostly public service, account for 40 per cent of the gross national product. The uncritical reader might think this showed that the service workers made a much greater contribution to creating the national wealth than the farmer. In reality, all it means is that government employees are grotesquely overpaid, at the direct expense of the farmers. They are a new mandarin class, exploiting the poor just as surely as if they were employing them in factories.

True, they build roads, schools, wells, provide health services and so on. But the bulk of these services still reach only a small and largely urban minority, a major proportion of whom are in public service. So the poor farmers are paying for public servants to enjoy inflated salaries and to allocate government services to themselves and their own families.

None of this involves conscious exploitation. Salary levels were inherited from the French. Tiny unrepresentative trade unions force pay rises out of the government that it can ill afford – the former civilian government was toppled in 1967 when it tried to prune urban salaries.

The answer to bias in government support for social groups,

and self-overpayment of government, must lie once again in the organization of the poor, especially the rural poor, into pressure groups, trade unions and political parties.

These, to summarize, are the principal mechanisms by which the poor get poor: natural impoverishment, and ecological impoverishment; social impoverishment; the impoverishment of unequal exchange and of unequal competition; and the impoverishment of state repression, state bias and state privilege. Most of these have their international counterparts by which poor nations get poor: social impoverishment corresponds to the growing burden of debt; unequal exchange to the unfair terms of trade; unequal competition to the destructive effect of the most efficient producers on the industries of those countries that are not protected against them. Political impoverishment is thankfully getting weaker, but was widespread when the United States used to intervene to defend reactionary governments and multinational investments, and still occurs in the bias of aid flows, and the overpayment of international bureaucrats and consultants.

Once the poor get poor, they tend to stay that way by the kind of circular mechanisms outlined in earlier parts of this book. The poor man has no capital, human or physical, to improve his lot. He is malnourished and therefore diseased, and so his labour is less productive – but he cannot make it more productive as he lacks money to invest in improving his land or his tools. Therefore he stays poor, and because he is poor, is less able to organize with others of his kind to improve their lot. And, if he finds himself in a situation of competition with the rich, he will probably get even poorer. Nations stay poor, strangely enough, by exactly the same process writ large. And the children of the poor also stay poor, because the environment of poverty is hereditary. Like their parents, the children of the poor are malnourished and unhealthy. Therefore they fail at school (if indeed they ever attend it), lose out in the employment race and remain in poverty.

Poverty is self-perpetuating, and inequality is self-reinforcing. Competition between social groups is like running several

Monopoly games at once so that the tokens you have won on one game can be used to enable you to win the other games more easily. As long as you are in a competitive situation, that kind of advantage can go on for ever unless someone comes along and knocks the board over.

21. The Limits to Unequal Growth

Growth has long been worshipped as the saviour of west and east, north and south. Economic growth, the quantitative multiplication of material wealth, has been pursued at the expense of moral development. It has been used as a front to increase privilege at the expense of the poor, and as a diversion from social reform.

All this does not mean that growth, at least in the Third World, is not necessary. Economic growth of a more balanced and equitable kind is as essential as social justice, if absolute poverty is to be eliminated.

The world seems to have arrived at a crucial turning point in its history of economic growth. At this point, the destinies of rich and poor nations are linked together as never before, and the futures of both are tied, curiously, to the fate of the poorest billion and a half. So far, growth has been achieved either at their direct expense, or at least by totally ignoring them. But we have now reached the stage where further sustained growth by developing countries and (if they insist on it) by developed countries may be impossible unless the poor are uplifted. Growth to date has been at the cost of social justice. Future growth in the medium term may depend on the achievement of social justice.

Whiz-kids and basket cases

The record of economic growth in the Third World has been impressive, and more rapid than that of the industrialized countries at similar stages in their growth. Economic historian Paul Bairoch has calculated that per capita income in western societies grew at around 1 per cent a year while they were industrializing. In the fifties, per capita income in the developing countries grew at 2·8 per cent a year, speeding up to 3·2 per cent a year in the sixties. Incomes in developed countries, with their much slower population growth, grew even faster over these two decades. In the seventies, the pace of growth in the Third World began to overtake that in the West, clobbered by oil price rises and trade stagnation. Western growth rates in per capita GNP slowed to 1·9 per cent a year between 1970 and 1975, while those in developing countries continued at 3 per cent, growing even in the crisis years of 1974 and 1975 when western incomes actually declined.

But the economic growth in the Third World has been very uneven, the bulk of it concentrated in a few favoured regions: Latin America, the oil-rich Middle East and eastern Asia.

Once again the parable of the talents seemed to be at work, giving to those who had already. The richer the country, the faster it tended to grow, and the correlation is very striking. Countries with average 1975 incomes per head of between $1,000 and $2,000 had seen those incomes grow at an (unweighted) average of 4·4 per cent a year since 1960. The lower the income band, the slower the growth: for countries between $500 and $1,000, incomes grew at 2·9 per cent a year. They grew at only 1·54 per cent for those in the $160 to $250 band, and clocked up an abysmal 0·66 per cent a year in the poorest countries with incomes of $150 or below. Six out of seventeen of this poorest group registered negative growth rates between 1960 and 1975.

Unequal growth has lead to a stringing out of the development field. Leading the pack are a group of whiz-kids obviously destined to become industrial states in the not too distant future: in South-East Asia, Singapore, Hongkong, South Korea and Taiwan; in Latin America, Brazil, Argentina and Mexico. The oil producers are using their temporary wealth to build industries that will guarantee a more permanent income: these include Algeria, Libya, Iran, Iraq, the Arabian peninsula, Venezuela and perhaps Nigeria. Among countries that are neither particularly resource rich nor, at present, very far advanced in industrialization, Malaysia, Kenya and the Ivory Coast look well set to make up the subsequent wave of new industrial states.

This broad stringing-out of the field has left at the starting gates a collection of hamstrung, skin-and-bone horses. There are twenty-nine of these 'least developed countries' as the United Nations officially designates them, with a total population of 245 million in 1975. Some hard-nosed economists have termed them basket cases and invented the idea of *triage*, or sorting out, by which those nations whose poverty appears to be insoluble should have all aid withdrawn, to stop prolonging the inevitable agony.

In reality, the problems that beset these so-called LLDCs are only an aggravated form of the ailments that all developing countries suffer from in some degree. Agriculture produces little or no surplus, therefore there are no savings to invest in improving agriculture or developing industry, and few government revenues to spend on roads, schools, health and other things that would boost productivity. Education is undeveloped, so these countries lack trained personnel: in 1970 Upper Volta had only 120 higher-education students, and none of them were in technical disciplines. Hence there are no engineers, no budding managers, next to no skilled workers.

The LLDCs have little or none of the infrastructure needed for industry: tarred roads in Upper Volta stop on the outskirts of the few large towns. Fifteen of the twenty-nine have the additional problem that they are landlocked: all their imports have to come hundreds or thousands of miles overland and so cost much more: at Gao, in the interior of Mali, cement costs nearly three times as much as in Dakar, on the coast.

Because industry is so poorly developed, agricultural products are exported in a raw state and other countries appropriate the profits – and employment – that processing can bring. As everyone is so poor, they save less than other developing countries and so have less to invest. As the banking system is so rudimentary – when I visited Upper Volta it had only three or four bank branches in the whole country outside the capital – what savings there are tend to waste away in gold ornaments or excess livestock. The least developed countries are trapped in a vicious circle of poverty just as hard to escape as the one in which poor people find themselves. Outside aid, far from being wasted, is the only way this circle can be broken into.

The much publicized advances of the whiz-kids will not alter the fundamental problems of underdevelopment. Looking towards the year 2000, the growth race will have left behind major areas of the world and major sections of society even in the most rapidly progressing countries. The problem of absolute poverty will dominate in south Asia, Indonesia, Haiti, Bolivia and most of sub-Saharan Africa, and however well the small modern sectors of these nations do it will not make much difference. As an example, take India, which was already in 1976 the thirteenth largest economic power in the world. India has the third biggest urban population in the world, she has more trained scientists than most European countries, her immense industrial capacity covers a wide range of products and she is now becoming a large exporter both of manufactures and of machinery. Yet her per capita income in 1976 was only $150, one of the poorest in the world. Outside the cities and a few privileged states, the poverty of 80 per cent who live in India's villages is so massive in its inertia that it has scarcely been budged by the bustling expansion of the modern sector.

And acute poverty is likely to persist for a long time in the poorest 20 to 40 per cent of most of the new industrial states, unless the unequal growth strategies outlined in this book are not altered. The entire spectrum of economic and human problems of development will remain, but they will become regional and class problems. Major rural areas will continue to suffer from them, as will the rural and urban sub-proletariat in more prosperous regions. The problem areas may gradually shrink in size, and the excluded groups in numbers, but it may take a century to absorb them, and their descendants will become the social misfits and unemployables of the twenty-second century.

Take the example of Brazil, whose former president, Emilio Medici, aptly remarked that the country was doing well but its inhabitants were not. Brazil's 1976 gross national product of $126 billions makes her the tenth biggest economic power in the world, and her 1976 per capita income of $1,140 had grown at 6·2 per cent a year for the previous decade. Brazil is rapidly becoming one of the world's major car, steel and shipbuilding nations. But her so-called economic miracle is geographically confined to the south, and socially confined, even there, to those with regular employment in the modern sector. It excludes the 40 or 50 per cent of city populations who work in the informal sector of hawkers and traders. It excludes 30 per cent of the rural workforce who are landless labourers. It excludes the 30 per cent of the national population who live in the states of the north-east. Overall, perhaps half the people of Brazil still suffer from acute poverty, over-crowding, disease, malnutrition, unemployment and official neglect, all the more demoralizing and disgraceful because of the prosperity of the middle class. While their nation is developing fast, they remain underdeveloped.

The economic costs of injustice

Unequal growth, national and international, has left behind the poor. And it is now beginning to pay the penalties of that omission. Its very inequality imposes limits on the pace of its development. The modern sector of the developing nations is slowed in its expansion precisely by the poverty of the groups it has neglected. The industrialized nations are braked in their growth precisely by the poverty of the developing countries whom they refuse to help adequately.

One of the principal obstacles to the growth of industry in the Third World is the deficient demand for industrial products. In the very smallest countries, the market will never be adequate for a full range of industry. But a market of four to eight million people is quite adequate for industrialization, as the cases of the Scandinavian countries, Switzerland and Austria show. In most developing countries, demand is deficient not so much because there are not enough people – but because they are so poor.

The poverty of the masses will increasingly impose limits on the growth of industry in the Third World. The import-substituting industries which first developed catered basically for the wants of the privileged classes, previously supplied by imports. The setting-up of these industries, and of the modern state, broadened the privileged class with urban wage and salary earners: but once the demand of these groups is satisfied, demand must grow more slowly. It can only grow as fast, in fact, as the productivity of the rural and urban poor. The discrimination against these groups, therefore, sets limits to the growth of the modern sector.

Seeing these limitations to internal demand, the industrializing nations of the Third World have looked to the wealthy markets of the West, hoping to carry on the impetus of import substitution into export-led growth. Countries with very poor home markets even hope to start their industrialization with export-led growth.

But export-led growth is also self-limiting, as the cheap clothing makers of Hongkong and Taiwan and the cheap steel makers of Brazil and South Korea are finding out as protectionist hedges sprout up around western countries. Protectionism may be deplorable, but it seems inevitable. The basic reason is that the western market is expanding much more slowly than in the past. It may not yet be fully saturated, but the exponential growth of the past is flattening out, for a variety of reasons.

One of these may be that the capacity of individuals and societies to absorb material goods is not infinite. Though it runs contrary to western consumerist materialism to admit it, there may be an upper limit to human material needs. Once you've got your TV, your fridge, your music centre, your car, you may not need all that much more. There are, of course, remaining pockets of poverty, but possession of the basic consumer durables has now reached very high proportions. Supplying a market for replacements or improvements is a much less buoyant business all round than feeding a market rapidly expanding from a low start. The western market is stagnating in other ways too: population growth has slowed right down and in some countries has started to decline. And the new technology of micro-electronics allows products to be made with far fewer components than before.

Western jobs would not grow very fast anyway in this market. Improvements in 'productivity' are threatening them further. Technological advances are improving productivity in manufacturing by around 4 per cent a year in the average western economy. This means that output must rise by that amount simply to prevent unemployment from rising. Productivity, moreover, is poised on the brink of even more rapid 'progress' through the new technology of micro-processors. These miniaturized monitoring and control devices, mini-computers mounted on tiny silicon chips, are so cheap they can be installed in every machine. Until now the progress of auto-mation has been slowed by the need for human workers to per-form highly complex operations, and to adjust and correct machinery. The new robot machines can do all that for them-selves.

It is true that some processes are working in the opposite direction, slowing the increase in productivity, but it is doubt-ful whether these will offset the effect of micro-processors. The increasing cost of fossil fuels makes the running of machinery more expensive and inclines manufacturers to choose more labour-intensive methods. But technology is quickly adapting by developing machinery which uses less energy. The increasing power of western trade unions has secured a high level of job security, making dismissal difficult or costly. As a result, employers are being forced to hoard more labour than they need. But this tendency, too, is counter-balanced as employers take on fewer young people.

Western growth is also limited by factors, which may be short-term or may last longer, connected with the complex interrelationships of trade balances, exchange rates and in-flation. One of these factors has been the dampening effect of the oil price rises. These brought unheard-of wealth to coun-tries which, unfortunately for the world economy, had popula-tions so small that they could not possibly spend it all on im-ports from other countries. So these countries ran large balance of payments surpluses, while other countries ran cor-responding deficits. Many western countries were afraid that, if they boosted growth in their economies beyond a modest level, imports would increase and their balances of payments deteriorate further. Others, like Germany and Japan, themselves running large surpluses, were afraid to grow too fast because of the dangers of inflation.

The Third World poses another threat to western employment. It is not only Third World governments but multinationals too who are fostering the strategy of export-led growth. Third World nations in the middle stages of development offer unbeatable attractions: wages are low, unions weak or banned, fringe benefits minute, social security costs minimal. The lack of skills is becoming less of a problem as the new technology of production allows many processes to be de-skilled. Third World workers can be trained to use the most modern and productive methods very quickly indeed. So now the Third World is beginning to export to the West not only those labour-intensive goods that everyone agrees they are best suited for, but more and more sophisticated products, from consumer electricals and electronics to steel and ships. As well as exporting more to the West, the Third World now produces for itself an increasing proportion of the things that the West used to export.

The usual response to worries of this kind, which legitimately preoccupy western trade unionists, is to say that the West can move out of these areas where the Third World leaders are most competitive, into more and more high-technology products and services. This kind of statement is based more on faith than on fact. The problem is that no such activities have yet emerged that could possibly employ people on the same scale as the older products. The move into high technology has, of course, begun and already it is creating immense social problems: it demands a more skilled workforce. Disadvantaged groups with poor educational backgrounds are likely to become, indeed are already becoming, an unemployable sub-proletariat, getting kicks and supplementary incomes from deviancy. Ironically, in France, Britain and the United States a significant part of this new sub-class is made up of Third Worlders and their descendants imported by western nations as unskilled labour in rosier days.

The only way the West could absorb the challenge of Third World industrialization would be to export more machinery and capital goods and expertise. But the slower growth of internal markets in the developing countries – due to the poverty of the majority – will limit the prospects for this. So western and Third World industries are competing with each other for a restricted market, made up of the whole of the West plus the elites of the Third World. Whenever market demand slows down, this competition becomes a zero-sum game, in which the winners can win only if the losers lose. This is why, unless the Third World market itself grows much faster, western protectionism against the Third World is bound to intensify. Protectionism may be blind and stupid: but as long as affected workers have the vote, and affected trade unions the right to strike, it is unavoidable.

There is an alternative to protectionism and trade wars between north and south. All along there is an enormous potential market lying dormant, not because it is approaching saturation like the West, but because it is so desperately poor that if it does earn an extra penny, it goes on food. That market is the one and a half billion poor of the world, half of whom are destitute. Poor people who desperately need, but cannot afford, the basics of life: tin roofs, windows, concrete floors, more clothes, more shoes, water filters, fertilizer, better tools and simple machines, bicycles, cheap carts, radios. Poor barefoot businessmen who could use pocket calculators, cash registers, better lathes and presses. People whose productivity would be greatly improved by all these things, so they would earn more still and be able to buy more consumer goods and durables.

This sleeping giant of a market could double in size the present non-communist world market. If its purchasing power could be increased, it would contain enough demand to allow all the factories of the Third World to run at full capacity and all the unemployment of the West to be absorbed by industries supplying the machinery needed, for a long time to come. This could not go on indefinitely, but it would get the world out of its economic doldrums and provide industrialized countries with several decades of grace in which to find longer-term solutions.

Yet the elites of most of the developing countries are reluctant or unable to carry out the radical social reforms and redistribution of government spending that are needed to increase the purchasing power of the poor. Nor are the western industrial nations willing to accept the scale of changes in the international economic order that are needed to increase the purchasing power of the Third World.

The reluctance of both sides to act on the scale required has led World Bank President Robert McNamara to put forward the idea of an international bargain or linkage: the West would agree to more aid, if Third World elites would agree to more redistribution. The idea has not proved overpopular. The present reality is more like a linkage of non-reform. The West uses the Third World's inequalities and human rights abuses as an excuse to resist the demands for a new international economic order. The Third World will not listen to the West telling it how it ought to reform itself, as long as the West will not accept reform. The kettle and the pot are calling each other black and could go on doing so for all eternity as an excuse for not cleaning themselves up.

Each side has an interest and a duty to act unconditionally to help the poorest. The West must increase the flow of real resources to the Third World to expand the world market, so western economies will not be so perilously dependent on each other's hiccups. There is an excellent precedent for such action. At the end of the Second World War the United States realized that Europe could not continue to buy American goods unless her economy was rebuilt, so the Marshall Plan was launched. Between 1945 and 1951, it pumped some $4 billion a year into Western Europe, and 90 per cent of that was in outright grants. In 1949, this aid amounted to 2 per cent of the gross national product of the USA – nine times the proportion now given as aid to the developing countries. What is now needed is a second Marshall Plan, directed, like the first 'against hunger, poverty, desperation and chaos'. Such aid can, where necessary with anti-reform governments, be automatically linked to internal reform in the Third World by tying it to specific projects designed to help the urban and especially the rural poor – as, for example, is done with many of the World Bank's projects.

In this way, aid donors and agencies can act as a sort of external pressure group for the poor of the Third World, helping governments to overcome the powerful constituency of the rich. Reform of the international economic order so as to alleviate the debt problem would also remove one of the strongest cards in the hand of anti-reform groups inside each country.

We have seen some of the internal changes required in earlier chapters. To single out the key problems for each continent, in Africa the chief block to more rapid development is probably the low level of education and of agricultural technology. In Asia, it is overpopulation working on a competitive social system that automatically generates landlessness and acute poverty. In Latin America the principal obstacle appears to be the political power structure which puts its weight behind grotesque inequalities. Blanket solutions, such as the call for revolution, may be realistic in one region or country and not in another. But some political way has to be found in all three continents to transfer productive assets – land and capital – to the poor, and to channel government spending away from the shiny new prestige imitation western sector, ending the discrimination against everything that is non-western, indigenous and poor.

If these changes are not made voluntarily, it is utopian to suggest they will be pushed through by violence, because as we have seen the poor are also weak, and that is half the problem. In some countries the poor or people dedicated to their interests may succeed in taking power. In others, possibly the majority, increasingly strident demands for justice may be met by repression, which can be very long-lived if it is efficient enough.

The choice before the West, and before the leaders of developing countries, is clear. On the one hand social justice, radical, meaningful reform without delays or token measures. On the other, a world of revolutions and fascist dictatorships and stagnant economies, perpetual wars and civil wars becoming proxy conflicts between the super powers, and world peace under constant threat. A world, in other words, very much like the one we live in at present.

Bibliographical Note: Sources and Recommended Reading

Chapter 1: The Cruel Sun

The best summaries of the geographical handicaps of the developing countries are David Grigg, *The Harsh Lands*, Macmillan, 1970, which concentrates on agricultural factors, and Andrew Kamarck, *The Tropics and Economic Development*, Johns Hopkins, Baltimore, 1976, which also covers nutrition, health and other factors. The data in this chapter are also based on Arthur Strahler, *Physical Geography*, third edition, Wiley, New York, 1969, and *The University Atlas*, thirteenth edition, George Philip, 1969. Data on the effects of heat and disease on labour productivity are from C. E. A. Winslow, *The Cost of Sickness and the Price of Health*, WHO, Geneva, 1973. On disasters, the summary of events for 1975–6 is gleaned from disasters recorded in *Keesing's Contemporary Archives*. The findings of the University of Bradford study are reported in Ben Wisner et al., 'Poverty and Disaster', *New Society*, 9 September 1976.

Chapter 2: Winner Takes All

Pre-colonial societies: For Africa, see R. Oliver and J. D. Fage, *A Short History of Africa*, Penguin Books, 1966, and Michael Crowder, *The Story of Nigeria*, third edition, Faber, 1973. An entertaining view of one such market empire in Uganda is found in John Hanning Speke, *Journal of the Discovery of the Source of the Nile*, Dent, 1906. On the early empires of the Americas, see Victor von Hagen, *The Ancient Sun Kingdoms of the Americas*, Panther, 1967, and for the Incas see William Prescott, *The Conquest of Peru*, Dent, 1908; Louis Baudin, *L'Empire Socialiste des Incas*, Paris, 1928; and Garcilaso de la Vega, *Comentarios Reales de los Inca*, Biblioteca Peruana, Lima, 1973. On Asia generally, see Karl Wittfogel, *Oriental Despotism*, Yale, 1957. For India, Romila Thapar, *A History of India*, Vol. 1, Penguin Books, 1966, and Romila Thapar, *The Past and Prejudice*, National Book Trust, New Delhi, 1975, which contains a critique of Wittfogel's ideas as applied to India. The analysis of China's arrested development is based on Mark Elvin, *The Pattern of the Chinese Past*, Eyre Methuen, 1973.

440 *Biographical Note*

The Rise of the West: On early medieval technology, see Lynn White, *Medieval Technology and Social Change*, Oxford University Press, 1962, and for the nature of the European city, see Lewis Mumford, *The City in History*, Penguin Books, 1966. A valuable analysis of the emergence of western experimental and mathematical science is given in Joseph Needham, *Mathematics and Science in China and the West, Science and Society*, Vol. 20, pp. 320–43, 1956. For the development of industrial civilization in Britain, see for example Peter Mathias, *The First Industrial Nation*, Methuen, 1969. The role of mercantilism and slavery in the accumulation of capital in the West is discussed in Eric Williams, *Capitalism and Slavery*, André Deutsch, 1964. For the emergence of Europe's military and exploratory capacities, Carlo Cipolla, *European Culture and Overseas Expansion*, Penguin Books, 1970, and J. H. Parry, *The Age of Reconnaissance*, Weidenfeld and Nicolson, 1963.

Colonialism and neo-colonialism: The racial and agricultural transplantations of empire are outlined in Fernand Braudel, *Capitalism and Material Life*, Weidenfeld and Nicolson, 1973, and C. H. Darlington, *The Evolution of Man and Society*, Allen and Unwin, 1969. For Spanish imperialism, see Prescott, op. cit.; Bernal Diaz, *The Conquest of New Spain*, Penguin Books, 1963; and Bartolomé de las Casas, *The Tears of the Indians*, Oriole Chapbooks, New York, 1972. For the Dutch East Indies, D. G. E. Hall, *A History of South East Asia*, third edition, Macmillan, 1968. A good history of British imperialism is John Bowle, *The Imperial Achievement*, Secker and Warburg, 1974. The motives and profits of empire are usefully analysed in D. K. Fieldhouse, *Economics and Empire 1830–1914*, Weidenfeld and Nicolson, 1973, while Michael Barratt Brown, *The Economics of Imperialism*, Penguin Books, 1974, is a good summary.

Chapter 3: The Westernization of the World

On the racialism and/or culture-ism characteristic of European colonial rule, see V. G. Kiernan, *The Lords of Human Kind*, Penguin Books, 1972, and Philip Mason, *Patterns of Dominance*, Oxford University Press, 1970. For the impact of the West on China and Japan, see John K. Fairbank et al., *East Asia*, Allen and Unwin, 1973. The psychology of colonialism is discussed in two books by Frantz Fanon, *Black Skins, White Masks*, MacGibbon and Kee, 1968, and *The Wretched of the Earth*, Penguin Books, 1967. Insights into the mentality of the westernized elites of developing countries are provided by Nirad Chaudhuri, *The Continent of Circe*, Jaico Publishing House, Bombay, 1966, and E. A. Ayandele, *The Educated Elite in the Nigerian Society*, Ibadan University Press, 1974. For cultural imperialism, see Jeremy Tunstall, *The Media are American*, Constable, 1977, Chapter 6 of R. J. Barnet and R. E. Muller, *Global Reach*, Simon and Schuster, New York, 1974, and the devastating attack on western tourism in the Third World, Jacques Bugnicourt, 'A New Colonialism', *Development Forum*, July–August 1977; also Daniel Boorstin, *The Image*, Weidenfeld and Nicolson, 1962. Material on the breakdown of parental authority and the extended family is provided in William J. Goode, *World Revolution and Family Patterns*, Free Press, New York, 1970.

Chapter 4: Eco-Catastrophe in Africa

An excellent overall survey of all types of tropical agriculture, including shifting cultivation, fallow systems and pastoral nomadism, is Hans Ruthenberg, *Farming Systems in the Tropics*, second edition, Clarendon Press, 1976. Africa's special agricultural problems are covered in René Dumont, *Types of Rural Economy*, Methuen, 1957, and in his *L'Afrique noire est mal partie*, Éditions du Seuil, Paris, 1972. On African systems of land tenure and European efforts to change them, see Melville Herskovits, *The Human Factor in Changing Africa*, Alfred Knopf, New York, 1958; David Apter, *Ghana in Transition*, Atheneum, New York, 1966; and Eric Jacoby, *Man and Land*, André Deutsch, 1971. See also John C. de Wilde et al., *Experiences with Agricultural Development in Tropical Africa*, Johns Hopkins, Baltimore, 1967.

Chapter 5: Polarization in Asia

The classic statement on agricultural involution as applied to paddy is Clifford Geertz, *Agricultural Involution*, University of California Press, Los Angeles, 1968. The decline of Java's traditional harvesting system and the job-destroying effects of the sickle and rice mills is documented in Ingrid Palmer, *The New Rice in Indonesia*, UN Research Institute for Social Development, Geneva, 1976. Data on land availability in Asia are from *Land Reform*, Sector Policy Paper, World Bank, Washington, 1975, and *Review and Analysis of Agrarian Reform*, FAO, Rome, 1979. On landlessness, see A. R. Khan et al., *Poverty and Landlessness in Rural Asia*, ILO, Geneva, 1977. Interest rates quoted are taken from *Agricultural Credit*, Sector Policy Paper, World Bank, Washington, 1975, and B. H. Farmer, ed., *Green Revolution?*, Macmillan, 1977. Additional material on debt and bonded labour is found in David Selbourne, *An Eye to India*, Penguin Books, 1977. The treatment of the caste and *jajmani* system is based on Louis Dumont, *Homo Hierarchicus*, Weidenfeld and Nicolson, 1970. The account of the Green Revolution is based on Lester Brown, *Seeds of Change*, and the series from the UN Research Institute for Social Development, Ingrid Palmer, op. cit.; Ingrid Palmer, *Science and Agricultural Production*, Geneva, 1972; Ingrid Palmer, *Food and the New Agricultural Technology*, Geneva, 1972; *The Social and Economic Implications of Large Scale Introduction of New Varieties of Foodgrain*, Geneva, 1974; Ingrid Palmer, *The New Rice in the Philippines*, Geneva, 1975; N. D. Abdul Hameed, *The Rice Revolution in Sri Lanka*, Geneva, 1977.

Some of the effects of mechanization on employment and inequality are given in B. H. Farmer, op. cit., for India and Sri Lanka, and in John P. McInerney and Graham Donaldson, *The Consequences of Farm Tractors in Pakistan*, World Bank Staff Working Paper No. 210, Washington, 1975. Examples of agrarian unrest in India are given in H. P. Sharma, 'The Green Revolution in India', in Kathleen Gough and H. P. Sharma, eds., *Imperialism and Revolution in South Asia*, Monthly Review Press, New York, 1973, and in Maria Mies, 'The Shahada Movement', *Journal of Peasant Studies*, Vol. 3, No. 4, p. 472.

Chapter 6: Land or Death in Latin America

On the historical origins of agrarian relations in Latin America, and on the present situation, see the essays by Andrew Pearse and Solon Barraclough in Rodolfo Stavenhagen, ed., *Agrarian Problems and Peasant Movements in Latin America*, Anchor Books, New York, 1970, and any general history such as E. Bradford Burns, *Latin America*, Prentice Hall, New Jersey, 1972, from which the edict of Isabel is quoted. On the obstacles to change in the *latifundio* and the *minifundio* see Andrew Pearse's essay, op. cit. More evidence of modern versus traditional dualism in Mexico can be found in Montague Yudelman et al., *Technological Change in Agriculture and Employment*, Development Centre, OECD, Paris, 1971, and of an earlier dualism – pre-Columbian and Spanish – in Oscar Lewis, *Life in a Mexican Village*, University of Illinois Press, 1963. On the mechanics of repression in rural areas, Francisco Julião, *Cambão –*

The Yoke, Penguin Books, 1972, is a good case study. Data on Puno province are from *Analisis Regional* (unpublished), Southern Regional Office, National Planning Institute, Peru. On guerilla movements, see Richard Gott, *Rural Guerrillas in Latin America*, revised edition, Penguin Books, 1973. On peasant movements generally, see Rodolfo Stavenhagen, op. cit., which contains a good essay by Ernesto Feder on counter-reform. Richard Bourne, *Assault on the Amazon*, Gollancz, London, 1978, describes Brazil's colonization programme. Treatment of Colombia's INCORA is based on research in the institute's files.

Chapter 7: The Shrinking Earth

The best summary of the ecological threats to agriculture is Erik Eckholm, *Losing Ground*, Norton, New York, 1976. Overall land loss figures are from Mostafa Tolba, *The State of the Environment 1977*, UN Environment Programme, Nairobi, 1977. Material on desertification is from the papers of the UN Conference on Desertification, August–September 1977 (A/CONF/74/1–8) and the special issues of *World Health* (July 1977), *Ceres* (March–April 1977) and *UNESCO Courier* (July 1977). Figures on deforestation from *The State of Food and Agriculture 1977*, FAO, Rome, 1978, and from World Bank, *Forestry*, Sector Policy Paper, Washington, 1978.

Chapter 8: Exodus

Data on rural–urban migration are quoted in the background paper for the 1976 Habitat United Nations Conference on Human Settlements, *Global Review of Human Settlements* (A/CONF/70/A1). International flows of migration for work are assessed in J. H. Lasserre-Bigorry, *General Survey of Present-Day International Migration for Employment*, General Conditions of Work Series No. 34, ILO, Geneva, 1975. Data on rural/urban income differentials are from Paul Bairoch, *Urban Unemployment in Developing Countries*, ILO, Geneva, 1973. Other rural/urban differences taken from the World Bank Sector Policy Papers *Education*; *Health*; and *Village Water Supply* (Washington, 1974, 1975 and 1976). On the general topic of urban bias, see Michael Lipton, *Why Poor People Stay Poor*, Temple Smith, London, 1977. Nyerere's quote on the dangers of cities exploiting the countryside is from the Arusha declaration, reprinted in Julius Nyerere, *Ujamaa*, Oxford University Press, Dar-es-Salaam, 1968.

. General readings on Third World urbanization will be found in Aidan Southall, *Urban Anthropology*, Oxford University Press, 1973, and in Gerald Breese, ed., *The City in Newly Developing Countries*, Prentice Hall International, New Jersey, 1972. On the causes of migration see Michael P. Todaro, *Internal Migration in Developing Countries*, ILO, Geneva, 1976, and Lorene Y. L. Yap, *Internal Migration in Less Developed Countries: A Survey of the Literature*, World Bank Staff Working Paper No. 215, Washington, 1975.

Chapter 9: The Promised Land

Generally, see works quoted under Exodus, *Global Review of Human Settlements*, op. cit., Breese, op. cit., Southall, op. cit. Data on the growth of cities and squatter settlements, along with some illustrative material on squatter settlements, are from UN Department of Economic and Social Affairs, *World Housing Survey 1974*, New York, 1976, and from the World Bank Sector Policy Papers, *Housing* and *Urban Transport* (both Washington, 1975). See also Orville F. Grimes, Jr, *Housing for Low Income Urban Families*, Johns Hopkins, Baltimore, 1976. On the *gamines* of Bogotá, see Jose Gutierrez, *Gamin*, Libros McGraw-Hill, Mexico, 1972. For Calcutta, see Geoffrey Moorhouse, *Calcutta*, Weidenfeld and Nicolson, 1971, and Harold Lubell, *Calcutta*, ILO, Geneva, 1974. On Abidjan, see Heather Joshi, *Abidjan*, ILO, Geneva, 1976. For an account of the demolition of slums in Delhi under Mrs Gandhi's emergency, see David Selbourne, *An Eye to India*, Penguin Books, 1977, and Shah Commission of Inquiry, *Interim Report II*, Government of India, April 1978.

Chapter 10: Workless of the World

The definitions and estimates of unemployment and underemployment are from *Employment, Growth and Basic Needs*, ILO, Geneva, 1976, and data on urban unemployment from Paul Bairoch, *Urban Unemployment in Developing Countries*, ILO, Geneva, 1973, and from *Yearbook of Labour Statistics, 1977*, ILO, Geneva, 1977. Predictions of the growth of the labour force are from *Labour Force Estimates and Projections 1950–2000*, ILO, Geneva, 1977. On the history of pre-colonial and colonial development of industry in Asia see Vol. 2 of Gunnar Myrdal, *Asian Drama*, Penguin Books, 1968. Marx's contemporary writings on the impact of British colonialism on India's industry are quoted in Shlomo Avineri, ed., *Karl Marx on Colonialism and Modernization*, Doubleday, New York, 1968.

For the situation in Latin America, see E. Bradford Burns, *Latin America*, Prentice Hall, New Jersey, 1972, and on the reasons why industry failed to develop here despite independence since the early nineteenth century, see André Gunder Frank, *Lumpenbourgeoisie, Lumpendevelopment*, Monthly Review Press, New York, 1972, and Frank's *Capitalism and Underdevelopment in Latin America*, revised edition, Monthly Review Press, New York, 1969. On growth of Third World industry since 1900 see Paul Bairoch, *The Economic Development of the Third World since 1900*, Methuen, 1975, and for development since 1950, UN Industrial Development Organization, *Industrial Development Survey*, UN, New York, 1974. For the dysfunctions of large-scale industry, see Keith Marsden, 'Progressive Technologies for Developing Countries', *International Labour Review*, Vol. 101, No. 5, May 1970. Data on under-use of capacity can be found in J. Mouly and E. Costa, *Employment Policies in Developing Countries*, Allen and Unwin, 1975, and in Helen Hughes et al., *Capital Utilization in Manufacturing in Developing Countries*, World Bank Staff Working Paper No. 242, Washington, 1976, which also analyses the causes of this phenomenon. The Tanzanian material is from S. M. Wangwe, 'Factors Influencing Capacity Utilization in Tanzanian Manufacturing', *International Labour Review*, Vol. 115, No. 1, January–February 1977.

Chapter 11: The Barefoot Businessman

Data on the continued importance of rural traditional industry is from World Bank, *Rural Enterprise*, Sector Policy Paper, Washington, 1978. An excellent general review of small-scale and traditional industries, their problems and what can be done to help them, is Eugene Staley and Richard Morse, *Modern Small Industry for Developing Countries*, McGraw-Hill, New York, 1965. Discussion of the concept of the informal sector and how it applies in Kenya can be found in *Employment, Incomes and Equality in Kenya*, ILO, Geneva, 1972. More data for individual cities can be found in Heather Joshi et al., *Abidjan*; Kalman Schaefer, *São Paulo*; and S. V. Sethuraman, *Jakarta*; all ILO, Geneva, 1976. Data on Lima is from Yves Sabolo, *Les Tertiaires*, ILO, Geneva, 1974. Survey of informal sector entrepreneurs is reported in S. V. Sethuraman, 'The Urban Informal Sector in Africa', *International Labour Review*, Vol. 116, No. 3, November–December 1977.

Chapter 14: The Sorcerer's Apprentice

A good introduction to the concepts and problems of population growth is Quentin H. Stanford, ed., *The World's Population*, Oxford University Press, 1972. Comprehensive and compendious general surveys of the dimensions and causes are the papers of the World Population Conference in Bucharest, 1974, collected in UN Department of Economic and Social Affairs, *The Population Debate* (two vols.), Population Studies No. 57, United Nations, New York, 1975, UN Department of Economic and Social Affairs, *The Determinants and Consequences of Population Growth*, Vol. 1, United Nations, New York, 1973. See also UN Department of Economic and Social Affairs Population Division, *Selected World Demographic Indicators 1950–2000*, UN, New York, 1975, and UN Department of Economic and Social Affairs, *Levels and Trends of Fertility throughout the World 1950–1970*, UN, New York, 1971. An excellent thesis on why poor rural families want large families is put forward in Mahood Mamdani, *The Myth of Population Control*, Monthly Review Press, New York, 1972. The international survey of Asian attitudes to children is reported in Free Arnold et al., *The Value of Children*, Vol. 1, East West Population Institute, Honolulu, 1975. A summary of survey findings on ideal family size may be found in Helen Ware, *Ideal Family Size*, World Fertility Survey Occasional Papers No. 13, October 1974. Government attitudes to population growth are surveyed in *Population and Family Planning Programmes, A Factbook*, Population Council, New York, 1976. On religious attitudes, see readings in Stanley Johnson, ed., *The Population Problem*, David and Charles, London, 1973, which includes the encyclical *Humanae Vitae*. On abortion, see the special issue of *People*, Vol. 5, No. 2, 1978, and Jean van der Tak, *Abortion, Fertility and Changing Legislation*, Lexington Books, Massachusetts, 1974. For a study illustrating the upward spiral see Monica Das Gupta, 'Economics, Fertility and the Green Revolution', *Populi*, Vol. 3, No. 1, and on the downward spiral and the impact of population on economic growth, see *Population and Labour*, ILO, Geneva, 1973. Assessments of the outlook for world population are, for example, Thomas Frejka, *The Future of Population Growth*, Wiley, New York, 1973, and UN Department of Economic and Social Affairs, *World Population Prospects as Assessed in 1973*, UN, New York, 1977. Useful appraisals of current trends are Lester Brown, *World Population Trends: Signs of Hope, Signs of Stress*, World Watch Institute, Washington

1976; *World Fertility 1976*, Population Reports J, No.12, 1976; and World Bank, *World Development Report*, Washington, 1978.

Chapter 15: Man is What He Eats

The Food and Agriculture Organization's annual report, *The State of Food and Agriculture*, provides ongoing figures on food production and consumption. More comprehensive surveys are the FAO's *Fourth World Food Survey*, FAO, Rome, 1978; the background paper for the World Food Conference in Rome, 1974: *Assessment of the World Food Situation, Present and Future*, E/CONF/65/3; and the mid-term review for the second UN Development Decade, in *The State of Food and Agriculture 1975*, FAO, Rome, 1976. Other valuable overviews are given by the special issues of *World Development*, May–July 1977, and of *Scientific American*, September 1976. See also Shlomo Reutlinger and Marcelo Selowsky, *Malnutrition and Poverty*, World Bank Staff Occasional Papers No. 23, Washington, 1976.

An excellent summary of the main nutritional problems, their extent and causes is G. H. Beaton and J. M. Bengoa, eds., *Nutrition in Preventive Medicine*, WHO, Geneva, 1976. Alan Berg et al., eds., *Nutrition, National Development and Planning*, contains useful essays on the effects of malnutrition on growth and brain development. Both these books also draw the important links between malnutrition and disease. On the impact of cultural practices on malnutrition, see Leonard Mata, 'Not Just the Lack of Food', in the special nutrition issue of *World Health*, May 1977. More useful material in other special issues, of *People*, Vol. 3, No. 1, 1976; and *UNICEF News* issues 85 and 86, 1975. Mike Muller, *The Baby Killer*, third edition, War on Want, 1977, describes the practices of multinationals in marketing canned and powdered milk in the Third World. For Franz Rosa's estimate of the contraceptive value of breastfeeding, see *People*, Vol. 3, No. 1, 1976. The food resources pre-empted by western meat consumption are detailed in Frances Moore Lappé, *Diet for a Small Planet*, revised edition, Ballantine Books, New York, 1975. Grain used as feed is quoted in FAO *Fourth World Food Survey*, op. cit. For the food consumption of pets, see Robie Fears, 'Pet Foods and Human Nutrition', *New Scientist*, 18 March 1976. A résumé of surveys on the relation between income level and other factors, and food consumption is given in *The State of Food and Agriculture 1974*, FAO, Rome, 1975, and in the *Fourth World Food Survey*, op. cit.

Chapter 16: Death Control

Life expectancies and disease patterns in developing and developed countries are taken from World Bank, *Health*, Sector Policy Paper, Washington, 1975, which is an excellent survey of the problems and possible solutions. Estimates of the incidence of various diseases are from several sources, including World Health Organization press releases and Andrew Kamarck, *The Tropics and Economic Development*. Figures on infant mortality are quoted from Population Reference Bureau, *1977 World Population Data Sheet*, Washington, 1977. The Nigerian *abiku* tradition is cited in Una MacClean, *Magical Medicine*, Allen Lane, 1971. Data on the effect of disease on productivity and income can be found in World Bank, *Health*, op. cit., Kamarck, op. cit., C. E. A. Winslow, *The Cost of Sickness and the Price of Health*, WHO, Geneva, 1973. Food losses due to roundworms are estimated in L. Latham et al., *The Nutritional and Economic Implications of Ascaris Infection in Kenya*, World Bank Staff Working Paper No. 271, Washington, 1977, and productivity losses due to anaemia are reported in S. S. Basta and A. Churchil, *Iron Deficiency Anemia and the Productivity of Adult Males in Indonesia*, World Bank Staff Working Paper No. 175, Washington, 1974. Study of water-boiling in Peru is from B. Paul, ed., *Health, Culture and Community*, Russell Sage Foundation, New York, 1955. Statistics on water supply and excreta disposal are from WHO, *World Health Statistics Report*, Vol. 29, No. 10, 1976, and estimates of the potential reduction in various diseases through clean water supply are given in *Assignment Children* No. 34, April–June 1976. See also Robert J. Saunders and Jeremy J. Warford, *Village Water Supply*, Johns Hopkins, Baltimore, 1976. The Orissa experience with concrete loos is reported in T. M. Fraser, 'Socio-Cultural Parameters in Directed Change', *Human Organization*, Spring 1963.

Figures on the provision of doctors nationally are from World Health Organization, *World Health Statistics 1973–76*, Vol. 3, Geneva, 1977, and on national expenditure on health from World Bank, *Health*, op. cit., which also contains data on the cost of training doctors and their distribution between cities and rural areas. An excellent summary of the rate and causes of doctor migration may be found in A. Mejia and H. Pizurki, 'World Migration of Health Manpower', *WHO Chronicle* 30, 1976. *New Scientist* has published a number of articles on drugs in the Third World, including E. Anderson, 'Medicines to Match the Market',

27 January 1977; Mike Muller, 'Drug Companies and the Third World', 29 April 1976; and Mike Muller, 'Selling Health – or Buying Favour', 3 February 1977. On multinational drug companies and their pricing policies, see the special issue of *New Internationalist*, April 1977; M. Silverman and P. R. Lee, *Pills, Profits and Politics*, University of California, 1974; and R. J. Barnet and R. E. Muller, *Global Reach*, Simon and Schuster, New York, 1974.

Chapter 17: The Alienation Machine

For figures on literacy, see *UNESCO Statistical Yearbook 1972*, UNESCO, Paris, and *Statistics of Educational Attainment and Illiteracy 1945–74*, UNESCO Statistical Reports and Studies No. 22, Paris, 1977. For figures on present and projected enrolment ratios and numbers in and out of school, see UN Department of Social and Economic Affairs, *The Population Debate*, Vol. 1, UN, New York, 1975. Extensive data on educational wastage, drop-outs and repeaters is given in M. A. Brimer and L. Pauli, *Wastage in Education – a World Problem*, UNESCO, Paris, 1971, and in UNESCO Office of Statistics, *A Statistical Study of Wastage at School*, UNESCO, Paris, 1972. On differences in school provision between urban and rural areas, see World Bank, *Education*, Sector Working Paper, Washington, 1974, while rural/urban differences in schooling are given in UNESCO, *Statistics of Educational Attainment ... op. cit.*

A good source on the educational disadvantages of the poor and advantages of the rich is Charles Elliott, *Patterns of Poverty in the Third World*, Praeger, New York, 1975. The economic costs of this kind of injustice are estimated in Sebastian Piñera and Marcelo Selowsky, *The Economic Cost of the Internal Brain Drain*, World Bank Staff Working Paper No. 243, Washington, 1976. Intelligence scores related to social class can be found in A. R. Omran and C. C. Standley, *Family Formation Patterns and Health*, WHO, Geneva, 1978, and in Joe Wray, 'Population Pressure on Families', in US National Academy of Sciences, *Rapid Population Growth*, Vol 2, Johns Hopkins, Baltimore, 1971.

Income differentials to be expected from more education in Sri Lanka are from *Matching Employment Opportunities and Expectations*, Technical Papers, ILO, Geneva, 1971. Private rates of return are given in Mark Blaug, *Education and the Employment Problem in Developing Countries*, ILO, Geneva, 1973. Both of these are good references on the problem of educated unemployment.

Educational continuation figures from primary to secondary and secondary to higher are from Elliott, op. cit.

On colonial education in Asia, see Chapter 31 of Gunnar Myrdal, *Asian Drama*, Vol. 3, Penguin Books, 1968. On West Africa, see Michael Crowder, *West Africa under Colonial Rule*, Hutchinson, 1968, from which the quotes from the *African Times* and Albert Sarraut are taken. Figures on student subjects are from UNESCO *Statistical Yearbook 1976*, UNESCO, Paris, 1977. The problem of education in local languages is discussed with case studies in *Prospects*, Vol. 6, No. 3, 1976. Textbook production figures are from UNESCO *Statistical Yearbook 1975*.

Chapter 18: Unto Every One That Hath

On the specific case of Sri Lanka, see *Report of the Commission of Inquiry on Agency Houses*, Sessional Paper No. XII, Government of Sri Lanka, 1974, and United Kingdom Department of Trade and Industry, *Sri Lanka Tea Estates*, HMSO, 1975. Janice Jiggins, 'Dismantling Welfarism in Sri Lanka', *Overseas Development Institute Review*, No. 2, 1976, shows how balance of payments constraints have lead to the progressive whittling away of food subsidies. On the economic function of colonies, see Michael Barratt Brown, *The Economics of Imperialism*, Penguin Books, 1974, and D. K. Fieldhouse, *Economics and Empire 1830–1914*, Weidenfeld and Nicolson, 1973, from which the two French quotes here are taken. Data on degree of dependence on commodities are from UN Conference on Trade and Development, *Handbook of International Trade and Development, 1976*, UN, New York, 1976. Figures on share of world trade, and terms of trade, are from the handbook and from UNCTAD, *Supplement 1977, Handbook of International Trade and Development*, UN, New York, 1978. On commodity price movements, see *International Financial Statistics*, monthly, IMF, Washington. For the historical changes in the pattern and terms of trade, see Paul Bairoch, *The Economic Development of the Third World Since 1900*, Methuen, 1975. For a general discussion of the commodity problem as well as an analysis of the behaviour of speculators, see J. F. Rowe, *Primary Commodities in International Trade*, Cambridge University Press, 1965, and Kathryn Morton and Peter Tulloch, *Trade and Developing Countries*, Croom Helm, 1977.

The best overviews on the multinationals are R. J. Barnet and R. E. Muller, *Global Reach*, Simon and Schuster, New York, 1974, and the two UN surveys: *Multinational Corporations in World*

Development, UN, New York, 1973, and its sequel, Commission on Transnational Corporations, *Transnational Corporations in World Development: A Re-examination*, E/C/10/38, UN, New York, 1978. These studies contain the data on profit levels, distribution of investment, transfer pricing, ownership of knowhow, foreign control of national industries which I have quoted. See also Hugo Radice, ed., *International Firms and Modern Imperialism*, Penguin Books, 1975. More figures on the cost of technology transfer and and the cost of the brain drain are given in UN Development Programme, *Less Expensive and More Appropriate Technology*, Development Issue Paper No. 11, UNDP, New York, 1976, while the case of bananas is examined in *The Latin American Banana Crisis*, Development Issue Paper No. 1, UNDP, New York, 1977.

On resources for development, see US National Academy of Sciences, *Resources and Man*, W. H. Freeman, San Francisco, 1969; Dennis Meadows et al., *The Limits to Growth*, Earth Island, 1972; Philip Connelly and Robert Perlman, *The Politics of Scarcity*, Oxford University Press, 1975; and for recent estimates of reserves, Rex Bosson and Bension Varon, *The Mining Industry and the Developing Countries*, Oxford University Press, 1977. For figures on debt and aid, see *Development Cooperation 1977*, OECD, Paris, 1977, and earlier issues of this annual publication. Also World Bank, *Annual Report 1977*, Washington, 1977 (and earlier years) and World Bank, *World Debt Tables*, Washington, 1977. On the impact of lending conditions of the International Monetary Fund, see Cheryl Payer, *The Debt Trap*, Penguin Books, 1974.

Chapter 19: Something is Rotten in the State

For the concept of the soft state, see Gunnar Myrdal, *The Challenge of World Poverty*, Allen Lane, 1970. On corruption, see Chapter 20 of Gunnar Myrdal, *Asian Drama*, Vol. II, Penguin Books, 1968, and James Nye, 'Corruption and Political Development', *American Political Science Review*, June 1961. On India, see the reports of the Sanantham Committee, Government of India, 1964; the *Direct Taxes Enquiry Committee*, Government of India, New Delhi, 1971; and the report of the Aiyar Commission, Government of Bihar, Patna. The Ghanaian material is from *Final Report of the Commission of Enquiry into Bribery and Corruption*, Government of Ghana, Accra, 1975. The precise influence of the rich on legislation and administration is, in the nature of things, hard to pin down. On Colombia, see J. P. Bernard et al., *Guide to the Political Parties of Latin*

America, Penguin Books, 1973, and A. E. Harvey, ed., *Internal Colonialism and Structural Change in Colombia*, Praeger, New York, 1970. For India, at national level, see Kuldip Nayar, *India: the Critical Years*, Weidenfeld and Nicolson, 1971, and at local level, F. G. Bailey, *Politics and Social Change in Orissa*, University of California, 1963, and Henry Orenstein, *Conflict and Cohesion in an India Village*, Princeton University Press, 1965. For the influence of the rich on law, see Francisco Julião, *Cambão — The Yoke*, Penguin Books, 1972, and Mohammed Ahmed Abu Rannat, *Study of Equality in the Administration of Justice*, United Nations, New York, 1972.

On external instability, see the summary of Asia's frontier problems in Gunnar Myrdal, *Asian Drama*, Vol. 1, Penguin Books, 1968. Data on military spending are taken from Institute of Strategic Studies, *The Military Balance 1976*, ISS, 1977, and from Frank Barnaby, 'Arms and the Third World', *New Scientist*, 7 April 1977. See also Stockholm International Peace Research Institute, *The Arms Trade with the Third World*, Penguin Books, 1975. A survey of secessionist movements can be found in *Freedom at Issue*, January 1978 issue, Freedom House, New York, while the problem of tribalism in Africa is discussed in P. C. Lloyd, *Africa in Social Change*, revised edition, Penguin Books, 1972. On the relationship between economic development and democracy, see S. M. Lipser, *Political Man*, Heinemann, 1963.

For dictatorship and human rights, see Amnesty International, *Report on Torture*, Duckworth, 1975, and *Amnesty International Report 1977*, Amnesty International, 1977. For the causation and characteristics of military coups, see S. E. Finer, *The Man on Horseback*, Pall Mall Press, 1962; and S. E. Finer, 'The Mind of the Military', *New Society*, 7 August 1975, for figures on numbers of coups. The Freedom House survey of the state of civil and political rights is summaried in *Freedom at Issue*, op. cit. The relation between the degree of 'freedom' and poverty and inequality is based on my own calculations, with data on income levels taken from *World Bank Atlas 1977*, Washington, 1977, and the most comprehensive and recent figures on inequality for each country from Shail Jain, *Size Distribution of Income*, World Bank, Washington, 1975.

Chapter 20: Princes and Paupers

The ILO estimates of world poverty are to be found in *Employment, Growth and Basic Needs*, ILO, Geneva, 1976, while the Ahluwalia figures are quoted in Hollis Chenery et al., *Redistribution with Growth*, Oxford University Press, 1974. Data on increasing poverty in Asia are from A. R. Khan et al., *Poverty and Landlessness in Rural Asia*, ILO, Geneva, 1977. The international distribution of income is calculated from figures given in *Development Cooperation 1977*, page 38, OECD, Paris, 1977. Increasing income gap is based on *World Bank Atlas* for 1976 and 1977, and data from David Morawetz, *Twenty-Five Years of Economic Development 1950 to 1975*, World Bank, Washington, 1977. The comparison of Canada and Indonesia is based on page 57 of *Development Cooperation 1975*, OECD, Paris, 1975. The method of calculation and the results of the physical quality of life index (PQLI) can be found in John Sewell et al., *The United States and World Development Agenda 1977*, Praeger, New York, 1977. The results of the international Gallup poll are reported in Gallup International Research Institute, *Human Needs and Satisfactions, A Global Survey*, Summary volume, Charles F. Kettering Foundation, Dayton, Ohio, 1977.

For income distribution inside developing countries, see Shail Jain, *Size Distribution of Income*, World Bank, Washington, 1975, and Chenery et al., op. cit., pages 8–9, from which the relationship between the top 20 per cent and the bottom 40 per cent is calculated. See also Felix Paukert, 'Income Distribution at Different Levels of Development', *International Labour Review*, Vol. 108, Nos. 2–3 August–September 1973. Data on the impoverishment of the poorest sections in Malaysia and Philippines is from A. R. Khan et al., op cit.

Chapter 21: The Limits to Unequal Growth

Growth rates for different income groups of countries are calculated from page 6 of *World Bank Atlas 1977*, Washington, 1977. Overviews of the problems of the least developed countries may be found in Chapter 8 of UN Industrial Development Organization, *Industrial Development Survey*, UN, New York, 1974, and in Chapter 3 of *Development Cooperation 1975*, OECD, Paris, 1975. See also Fred Hirsch, *The Social Limits of Growth*, Routledge, 1978.

For a general survey of progressive development programmes in all the spheres covered by this book, the reader should consult Paul Harrison, *The Third World Tomorrow*. Penguin Books, 1980.

Disasters

⎯⎯⎯ Seismic belts

• Major earthquakes

- - - → Tropical cyclone paths

Map 1. The disastrous climate

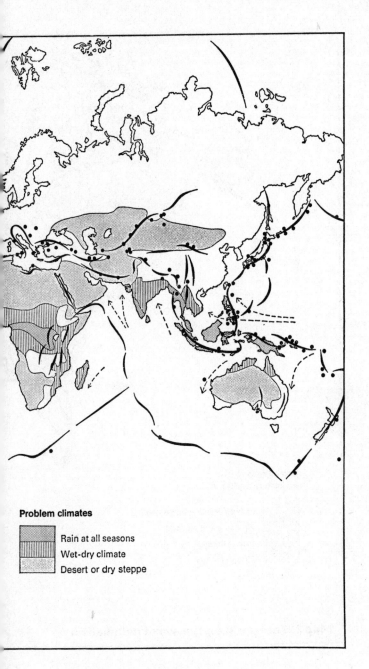

Problem climates

Rain at all seasons

Wet-dry climate

Desert or dry steppe

AZTECS
1519

INCAS
1525

**Dominant form of
agriculture c.1500:**

 Fishing, hunting and gathering
Nomadic and pastoral
Hoe culture
Plough culture

Map 2. The world on the eve of colonialism

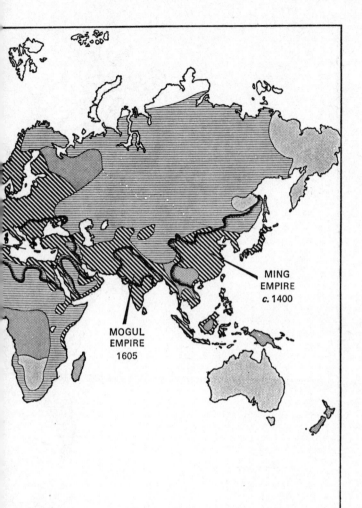

MING
EMPIRE
c. 1400

MOGUL
EMPIRE
1605

OTTOMAN
EMPIRE
1683

major non-European empire and date of borders marked

Map 3. The Colonial Past

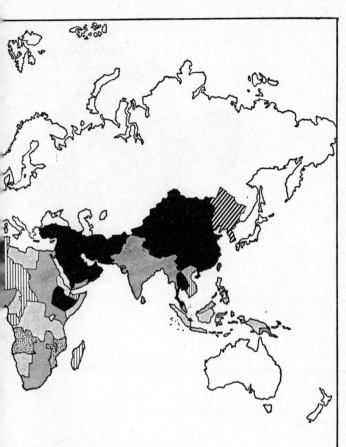

Present day Third world: former rulers

Spanish
Portuguese
British
French
Other European
Japanese
Areas never colonized

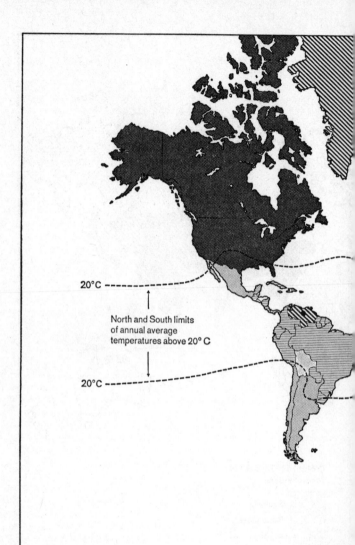

20°C ‑ ‑ ‑ ‑ ‑ ‑ ‑ ‑ ‑ ‑ ‑ ‑ ‑ ‑ ‑ ‑

North and South limits
of annual average
temperatures above 20° C

20°C ‑ ‑ ‑ ‑ ‑ ‑ ‑ ‑ ‑ ‑ ‑ ‑ ‑ ‑ ‑ ‑

● Oil wealth

Map 4. Rich temperate world, poor hot world.

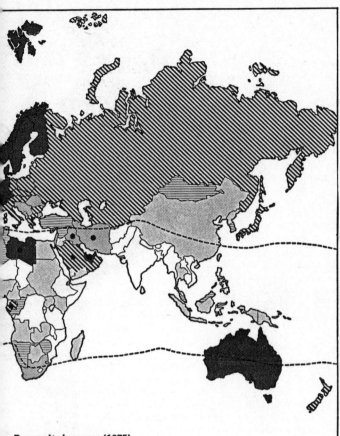

Per capita incomes (1975)

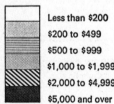

	Less than $200
	$200 to $499
	$500 to $999
	$1,000 to $1,999
	$2,000 to $4,999
	$5,000 and over

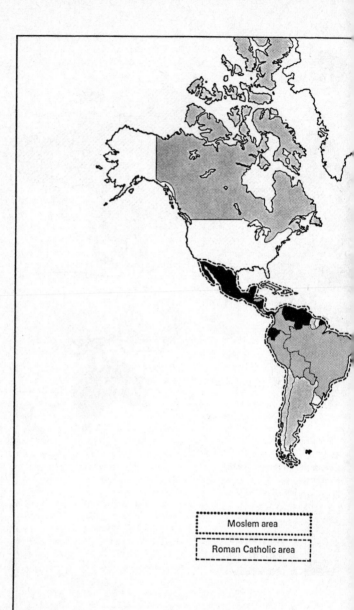

Moslem area

Roman Catholic area

Map 5. Population growth and the religious factor

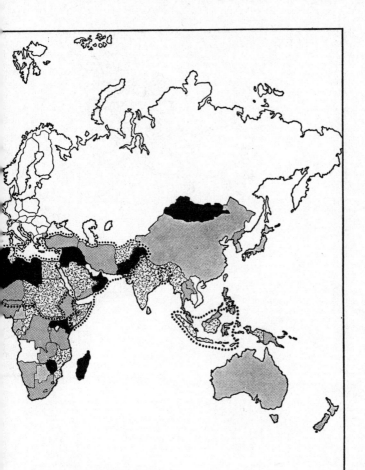

Annual growth rates (1970-75)

Less than 1.0%
1.0% to less than 2.0%
2.0% to less than 2.5%
2.5% to less than 3.0%
3.0% and over

limit of invasion of locust

limits of tsetse fly (Africa)

Map 6. Pests and diseases

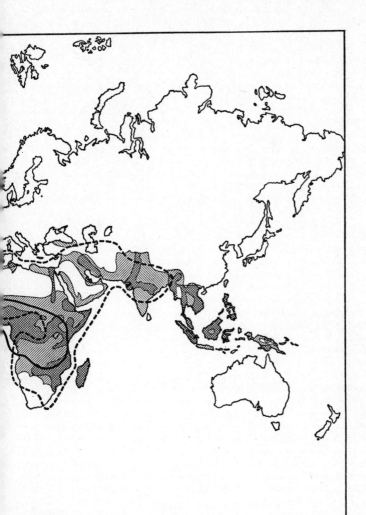

 area subject to malaria transmission (1975)

areas with endemic hookworm

areas with malaria and hookworm

Index